Hans Urs von Balthasar's
Theological Aesthetics

Hans Urs von Balthasar's
Theological Aesthetics

A MODEL FOR POST-CRITICAL BIBLICAL INTERPRETATION

W. T. Dickens

UNIVERSITY OF NOTRE DAME PRESS

Notre Dame, Indiana

Library of Congress Cataloging-in-Publication Data
Dickens, W. T. (William Thomas), 1957–
    Hans Urs von Balthasar's theological aesthetics : a model for
post-critical biblical interpretation / W. T. Dickens.
        p.   cm.
    Includes bibliographical references (p.   ) and index.
    ISBN 0-268-03063-4
    ISBN 0-268-03064-2 (pbk.)
        1. Bible—Hermeneutics.   2. Balthasar, Hans Urs von, 1905–
Herrlichkeit. 3. Aesthetics—Religious aspects—Catholic Church.
4. Catholic Church—Doctrines.   5. Theology, Doctrinal.   I. Title.
BS476 .D53 2003
                          230'.2'092—dc21
                          2003013588

for my mother

&

in memory of my father

CONTENTS

ACKNOWLEDGMENTS

I have had the great fortune to learn from outstanding teachers. Marcus Borg and Bardwell Smith nurtured my interest in the interpretation of religious texts during my undergraduate years at Carleton College. While I was at Yale, Brevard Childs, perhaps the best classroom instructor I ever had, provided a first demonstration of biblical exegesis that seeks to serve the Church while remaining attuned to the lessons of historical criticism. Rowan Greer, a particularly striking example of the benefits of a learned clergy, was an early, encouraging guide through the thickets of ancient biblical interpretation. Readers of this book's fourth chapter will recognize my reliance on David Kelsey's keen analytical mind, though I am equally grateful to him for the hours he spent with me in directed reading courses. George Lindbeck has been unfailingly kind and supportive, both while I was at Yale and since. Of the many things I have learned from him, I would highlight his insistence on setting oneself the goal of reading critically, yet charitably. Along with Professors Greer, Kelsey, and Lindbeck, Cyril O'Regan, Nicholas Wolterstorff, Paul Molnar, and Edward Oakes all read and commented on the manuscript. Their suggestions measurably improved it.

For the editorial staff at the University of Notre Dame Press and especially its director, Barbara Hanrahan, I have nothing but praise and gratitude. It is a privilege to work with such fine people. And I could not have completed the final stages of bringing the manuscript to press without the generous support of the benefactors of the Cornell Catholic Community.

My wife, Joyce Schuld, deserves special thanks, not simply because of her remarkable intellect and rhetorical skills, but also because, through more than a dozen years of marriage, her devotion, compassion, and steadfastness have been to me a shield and a buckler.

I gratefully dedicate this book to my parents, whose patient work as my teachers—and as so much else—I hope to honor with this effort.

Hans Urs von Balthasar's
Theological Aesthetics

INTRODUCTION

The purpose of this book is twofold. Its immediate goal is to explore Hans Urs von Balthasar's doctrine of scripture in his seven-volume *The Glory of the Lord: A Theological Aesthetics,* the first panel of his fifteen-volume theological triptych. Given Balthasar's conviction that theology must be authorized by the Word of God, as it is manifest in scripture faithfully interpreted in the Church, it is surprising how little attention has been paid to this theme. Although a handful of articles has been written on the topic,[1] no monograph has been devoted to it to date. Typically, both his view and his uses of scripture are simply ignored by theologians and biblical scholars alike.[2] This is in spite of the fact that his more avowedly exegetical works are replete with scriptural references.

When Balthasar's doctrine of scripture does draw attention, it is usually not described in laudatory terms. Joseph Fitzmyer, S.J., has complained that Balthasar's view of the Bible as the body of the Logos is precisely what Balthasar denies it to be, namely an "arbitrary piece of allegorizing."[3] Fitzmyer goes on to say, "This is a good example of the scholarly *Schwärmerei* [enthusiasm] to which those who advocate a

I

spiritual exegesis of Scripture are led. It is not 'exegesis' at all; it is *eise-gesis.*"[4] Others have echoed Fitzmyer's worries about Balthasar's seem-ing insouciance with respect to the findings of historical criticism. John O'Donnell, S.J., complains that Balthasar "at times persists in scrip-tural interpretations which have no exegetical support, brushing aside current opinions with a few polemical remarks about modern biblical methods of interpretation."[5] Stephen Happel describes Balthasar's use of scripture as "a conflation of biblical texts rather than a critical sift-ing of the warrants for faith."[6] And Louis Dupré argues that Balthasar's treatment of the New Testament (in distinction from that of the Old) evidences little of the openness to philosophical systems of thought that Dupré maintains the New Testament itself calls for.[7] Not everyone is critical, of course. Christoph Schönborn, O.P., speaks of Balthasar's "incomparable *reverence for the Word of God*" and of scripture being "the center and medium of his theology."[8] And John Riches believes that Balthasar's work may help to contribute to "the present revival of in-terest in the enterprise of biblical theology."[9] But Schönborn and Riches represent a small minority. Although Edward Oakes may be overstating the case when he asserts that the impact of Balthasar's theology in the twenty-first century and beyond will turn, in large measure, on how his approach to scripture is evaluated,[10] it is obvious that there remains much work to be done on this question.

A second, more important, aim of this book is to examine the ex-tent to which Balthasar's approaches to scripture in the *Theological Aes-thetics,* while remaining conversant with historical criticism, are com-patible with certain aspects of pre-modern approaches that helped to nourish the capacity, once widespread among Christians, to understand themselves and their world in terms of the images, stories, and concep-tual patterns of the Bible. I hope to show that given certain modifications that are fully consistent with his own aims, Balthasar's views and uses of scripture in the *Theological Aesthetics* generally abide by several impor-tant conventions characteristic of pre-modern exegesis without aban-doning contemporary theology's responsibility to learn from historical critics. Although I have some reservations about Balthasar's theologi-cal hermeneutics, exegesis, and understandings of the unity and the au-thority of scripture, I believe that his work nevertheless has much to offer Christians concerned to articulate how the Bible can function authoritatively without denying the fruitfulness and importance of historical-critical methods. His work at least partially reflects a growing consensus among Christian theologians that pre-modern resources can be appropriated in a post-modern context without neglecting the insights of modernity's hermeneutics of suspicion. As such, it constitutes a model for ecclesially fruitful post-critical biblical interpretation.[11]

The perspective from which I undertake to fulfill these two purposes should be outlined. Questions concerning the status and authority of scripture and what constitutes its appropriate interpretation have exercised Christian theologians since the Church's beginnings. With the Reformation, these questions, among others, became divisive. The scope of the canon, the material sufficiency of scripture, the proper relation of scripture and tradition, the role of the magisterium, the aims and methods of interpretation—all of these, to one degree or another, were controverted. And so it remained until the middle decades of the twentieth century, by which time there was a fairly substantial degree of convergence between Catholics and Protestants on these issues. Without wishing to minimize the differences that still exist, Avery Dulles, S.J., argues that the great chasm once dividing the Western churches has largely disappeared. There is now, he believes, at least a widespread rapprochement, if not consensus, on most of the problematic controversies that fall under the rubric of the doctrine of scripture.[12]

This development, as welcome as it certainly is, may be less significant than it first appears because of a diminishing familiarity with, and use of, the Bible among Protestants and Catholics. One observer, James D. Smart, has decried the "strange silence of the Bible in the Church" characteristic of Protestant congregations since the early 1960s.[13] He cites in support of this the widening appeal among clergy and laity of topical sermons at the expense of expository preaching, the diminished length of sermons, and the virtual disappearance of Sunday and midweek Bible study groups. Another Protestant observer, James Barr, echoes Smart's description and adds that this situation is associated, less with an articulate and well-organized movement rejecting the centrality of the Bible in the Church's thought and practice, than with a vague sense of suspicion about its pertinence and uncertainty about its import.[14] But he disagrees with Smart that this silence is in fact so strange. He wonders whether the years from 1920 to 1960, when neo-orthodoxy was in its ascendancy and acceptance of the Bible's authority seemed once again natural (despite the onslaught of biblical criticism) represented, not so much a return to normalcy, as an interruption in an ineluctable decline in the status of the scriptures.[15]

A third Protestant, George A. Lindbeck, in contrast to Barr, shares Smart's concerns about the diminished role played by the Bible in the lives of most Christians in the West. But he agrees with both that this silence has deep historical roots, reaching back at least to the Enlightenment, if not to the confessional wars in Europe that preceded it. On Lindbeck's view, current members of North Atlantic societies are both less familiar with the Bible than their forebears and less able to use its stories, images, and conceptual patterns to understand themselves and their world. This state of affairs represents a twofold change from what has obtained during the bulk of Western Christian history. First, he contends that traditionally Christian lands have witnessed a dramatic and pervasive loss of biblical literacy in the last half century.[16] Well-educated secularists of the late 1940s were better acquainted with the Bible than are most contemporary students from church-going families. Literature professors and political scientists today report that their students often miss the biblical allusions in the texts they seek to interpret. And the biblical knowledge of those now studying for the ministry or priesthood is neither as comprehensive nor as detailed as that of seminarians of a few decades ago. One could add to these examples of Lindbeck's with little difficulty.[17] The point they are intended to illustrate is that most of us simply do not know our Bible as well as our parents and grandparents did.

The second aspect of the change Lindbeck describes concerns, not our lack of familiarity with the Bible, but the pronounced atrophy of the power of imagination to see ourselves and our world through scriptural lenses. This capacity was sustained by (indeed, aspects of it are coterminous with) an approach to scripture that has largely fallen out of favor in the modern age.[18] When examining this approach, we need to be aware that it is not a method of interpretation in the modern sense, that is, one having clearly stated and genre-encompassing criteria of evidence, intelligibility, and appropriateness. Indeed, to speak of something as singular as a method of pre-modern exegesis would be to ignore its irreducible diversity.[19] We ought to qualify our remarks nearly every step of the way when speaking of something so complex as the history of Christian biblical interpretation. And yet, with that note of caution in mind, we can still identify several features common to procedures for interpreting the Bible in the pre-modern era.

First, the biblical narratives were held to mean what they say. To our ears, that tends to sound like a remark about the reliability of the narratives as factual reports. While it is true that prior to the seventeenth century most Christians simply assumed the coherence of literal sense and historical reference, the conviction to which I wish to draw attention is different. Hans Frei described it as the realistic quality of biblical narratives.[20] One of the features of such stories is that their structure, that is, the way they render their characters and depict the deeds, words, circumstances, and events in which the characters' identities are constituted, are integral to their meaning. Unlike stories that illustrate general truths, or evoke particular responses, the narrative shape of the biblical stories is indispensable to their meaning.[21] A literal reading of these texts, that is, one in which the descriptions of the actions, sayings, and incidents are predicated of the actor whose identity is rendered in and through them, served as the dominant means of interpretation during most of the pre-modern era. Although ways of reading the narratives developed (like allegory, tropology, and anagogy) that did not highlight this realistic quality of the texts, as a literal reading did, none of these displaced the primacy of the literal sense in the central Gospel stories. The multivocity of these stories, and of the rest of the New Testament and the Old Testament, was bounded by this hermeneutical consensus.

Second, the various biblical narratives were read as forming a cumulative story, depicting the creative and redemptive dealings of the triune God with creation, that embraces each of its constitutive episodes as well as the Bible's non-narrative elements. For Christians, the story's climax, in light of which all of its parts from beginning to end were understood, is the incarnation, death, and resurrection of Jesus Christ. Thus the non-narrative elements in the Old and New Testaments were seen to derive their significance in relation to the Bible's christological centerpiece, the stories of Jesus.[22] One clear consequence of this approach is that the Old Testament was regarded as an indispensable part of the canon of Christian scriptures with its own authoritative theological voice. Another is that the Bible was regarded as self-glossing.

Interpreters sought the meaning of obscure passages by reading them in light of those that were more fully understood.

Third, proper explication of the Bible involved using it, by means of the Holy Spirit, for practical and intellectual religious instruction within an ecclesial setting. Some form of typology (or, as it is also called, figuration) is the primary hermeneutical device by which these applications of the text were effected.[23] As Frei made plain, far from denigrating a literal reading of the texts, typology was seen as its natural correlate, a kind of extension of the literal reading of individual texts enabling one to range them and the story of one's own life under an overarching narrative frame.[24] Further, this religious use of the text was viewed less as a creative act on the part of the interpreter than as one of mimesis, simply comprehending, through the ministrations of the Holy Spirit, the way things really are.[25]

In sum, then, throughout most of Christian history up through the Reformation the Bible was read as a christologically centered, canonically unified narrative that rendered the identities of a faithful, triune God and God's faithless people (through whom creation is to be redeemed and consummated) and shaped, primarily through typological applications, the individual and corporate identities of its interpreters.[26]

When read according to what I shall refer to as the classic pattern of literal-figurative interpretation, the text provided the dominant discourse in terms of which actions, thoughts, and affective states were constituted, described, and assessed. Non-biblical concepts, images, events, and stories were conceptually recast into a biblical idiom whose ruled use was determined, in large measure, by the trinitarian and christological dogmas. To switch the image, when the classic hermeneutics guided biblical interpretation, Christians lived within the imaginative and linguistic world of the Bible, drawing within its horizons, and thereby modifying, such non-biblical elements of their cultural heritage as were needed faithfully to meet the exigencies of time and place. It is this capacity, which Lindbeck calls biblical imagination, that is largely absent in contemporary North Atlantic societies.

Two aspects of this now largely lost skill need to be stressed. First, no extra-biblical scheme of meaning was seen as providing the key to interpreting the Bible. No redescriptions, either in storied form, as for example the Niceno-Constantinopolitan creed, or in a more abstract form, like the Chalcedonian definition, were seen as supplanting the biblical text. They were at most road maps directing one's travels in the biblically inscribed world, or, perhaps, signposts marking out the boundaries within which ecclesially apt biblical interpretations could be carried out. They did not serve as substitutes for the literal-figural interpretive enterprise. This point is best illustrated with reference to the Gospel narratives, although on Hans Frei's reading of the history of interpretation, it applies "by a kind of gradually attenuating extension" to the rest of the New Testament and of the Old Testament as well.[27] If no reductive readings of the Gospel narratives are tolerated, then the stories about Jesus are understood to be about him and not something else, say a christological doctrine, a fact of sacred or secular history, or a graced form of life. The reality Jesus embodies may well be discussed in any of these terms provided that one acknowledges that these descriptions are derivative of, and therefore always secondary to, a literal reading:[28]

> The relationship between Jesus in his story and what he says, does, and undergoes is a deeply intimate one: his identity is not illustrated but constituted by these things. He is not a logical substance unchangeably posited behind his qualities and deeds, as it were accidentally related to them. No, he is what he does and undergoes; he is the Kingdom he proclaims, the self-enacted parable of God which he speaks; he is himself as the crucified and resurrected Jesus. His titles may be substitutable and dispensable for identifying him. Messiah to some, he is Son of Man to others, Logos for others yet. But his passion and resurrection are not substitutable. He is the subject of his personal predicates and his doings and sufferings, and holds them together, essentially, rather than they him; he is the subject to whom descriptions are ascribed.[29]

A second aspect of this now atrophied biblical imagination concerns the multivocity of the biblical texts. For example, as Frei indicated, since this broad consensus regarding the priority of the literal sense (or reading) over other, non-literal readings was restricted to hermeneutics, the meaning of the stories about Jesus was subject to continual emendation as interpreters sought to grapple with changing circumstances and ways of thinking.[30] Jaroslav Pelikan demonstrates that

Jesus has meant very different things to Christians (and non-Christians) throughout Western history.[31] On the classic hermeneutical model, a range of possible meanings opens up before the interpreter (bounded, to be sure, by the rule of faith, which was later crystallized in the trinitarian and christological dogmas) by which the ascended Lord is believed able to conform his followers to his image.[32] Accordingly, during most of the pre-modern era, Jesus Christ as risen and present to his Church was understood to elude all efforts to capture him in fixed and unchanging definitions. It was widely recognized, if not always practiced, that Jesus' "present meaning—what he says to believers through Scripture, worship, etc.—continues to be 'new every morning.'"[33]

As the classic hermeneutics went into eclipse, it was replaced by interpretive strategies that fastened upon the Bible less as a guide to life and thought (with changing applications and therefore changing meanings) and more as an object of study (with a univocal meaning best discerned by experts).[34] When read in this fashion, the broad hermeneutical consensus regarding the priority of the Bible's literal sense collapses, or—to the extent that the modern period has remained fixated on the literal sense as the *sensus originalis*—the definition of the literal sense in whose terms the consensus continues to be articulated is drastically changed.[35] In our day, the biblical narratives no longer tend to mean what they say, but find their meaning in reference to some putative realm above, below, behind, or in front of the text.[36] A doctrinal proposition, perhaps, or maybe a mode of thought and behavior, or even an historically reconstructed fact or setting will replace Jesus as what the Gospel narratives are really about. When that happens, the Bible tends to serve as the occasion for reflections that carry readers farther and farther from the biblical text, and rob them (not to mention their audience or conversation partners) of the opportunity to nourish their biblical imagination through a sustained conversation with the text in light of personal and communal concerns. This practice, in some of its forms at least, may also undermine traditional Christian proclamation about the necessary connection between salvation and the actual person of Jesus. If, for instance, the story of Jesus is salvific to the degree that it evokes the appropriate response to the disclosure of the transcendent mode of being it mediates, then the story could conceivably continue to trigger this response regardless of whether the mode of being had ever been instantiated in an actual, historical individual.

Clearly, this sort of subordination of the text to personal interpretation need not happen. More often than not, however, the requisite interpretive restraint to prevent this occurring is set aside in an attempt to reconceptualize biblical categories in terms congenial to (and often stipulated by) a given philosophical system. Reconceptualizations per se are not just permissible, they are required if we are, in Frei's words, to avoid "enthroning verbal repetition as the highest form of understanding."[37] The challenge, of course, is to treat such conceptual redescriptions, not as encapsulating the entirety of the text's meaning(s), but as heuristic devices to help oneself and others to perceive what, on this occasion, God may be using the text to do. Otherwise one puts at risk one's capacity imaginatively to inscribe oneself and one's world within the story of God's dealings with creation that Christians traditionally have found told in the Bible.

Two words of qualification are in order. First, it is not as though all modern exegetes simply transpose the elements of the biblical world into a secular key, while all pre-moderns did the reverse. Both ages provide examples of both processes.[38] Nevertheless, it is clear that not only have most modern biblical interpreters been enthralled by the notion of the text having a single, fixed meaning, but they have also very often sought to translate this into an idiom whose terms are set by a non-biblical frame of reference.[39] Second, to go back to the image of living within the biblical world, pre-modern Christians lived in other worlds besides the biblical one, just as we do. Lindbeck expresses this well in the following: "In most periods of Christendom, the poorly catechized masses lived also in a world of hobgoblins, fairies, necromancy, and superstition; in the educated classes, everyone, not least devout Christians, had their imagination shaped by the pagan classics of the Greeks and Romans, to a degree we tend to forget."[40] But, as Lindbeck goes on to say, the dominant worldview, and the one in whose terms most of the other elements were understood (at least when those worlds came into conflict), was thoroughly biblical. Though we, too, live in multiple worlds (or in a single world that is described through a host of idioms drawn from often conflicting traditions), there appears at present to be no single, overarching discourse, either within the Church or without, to replace what the Bible once provided.

The foregoing summary of pre-modern exegetical approaches, especially the assertion regarding the centrality of typology, seems, on the face of it at least, to be called into question by the dubiousness with which Henri de Lubac regarded such claims. Given his virtually unrivaled familiarity with patristic and medieval exegesis, his concerns need to be taken seriously. Before doing so, we should note that there are readily discernible areas of agreement between him and Frei et al. De Lubac agreed that the current preoccupation with establishing by means of a "scientific method" a single, unchanging biblical meaning marks a significant departure from pre-modern practices.[41] Without wishing to deny the importance of "arriving at a better historical knowledge," he maintained that treating the Bible *merely* as an historical document, rather than as also the Word of God received in faith, ignores ancient and medieval convictions about the very purpose of the text.[42] The scriptures are intended for the "spiritual 'edification' of both the Church as a whole and of each one of us."[43] He also endorsed the notion that the Bible offers the faithful an unfathomable abundance of senses. "Scripture is like the world: 'undecipherable in its fullness and in the multiplicity of its meanings'."[44] The interpretive task for the Church in its earthly pilgrimage is therefore unending: "the mystery of the spiritual understanding . . . is a direction that is indicated rather than a landmark that is ever attained."[45] And de Lubac argued that the multivocity of the scriptural Word is grounded in the "primordial unity that it possesses in the [incarnate] Word."[46] What he called the "doctrine" or "principle" of the fourfold senses (as distinct from its sometimes incoherent historical applications) depends on their being united by a common reference to Christ.[47] He is the center around which both Testaments, "bearing witness to the Lord in the same measure," are oriented.[48]

Notwithstanding the extent and significance of such agreement, there still remains the seeming dispute over the importance accorded typology by pre-modern exegetes. On the more narrow issue of the prevalence of the terminology, de Lubac made the convincing contention, in response to an article by Jean Daniélou, that the term itself is "neither scriptural nor truly traditional."[49] But, as de Lubac conceded, typology has received "good press" in the last half century,[50] a fact that compelled him to examine its usefulness for describing what he, in fidelity to scripture and tradition, called allegory. He readily acknowledged that the term is subject to some "inconveniences."[51] For one thing, it is used equivocally. It can designate either the spiritual senses in general or, more narrowly, one of the senses in contrast to two others (tropology and anagogy).[52] Or it can designate the method by which the "vital connection" is drawn between a type and its antitype.[53] Moreover, as a method it has been abused, yielding "childish" and "quite artificial" pairings of things "that are too widely disparate."[54] However well intended, such interpretations cannot be called " 'pious' in the true sense of the word."[55] He realized that, since the Reformation, Christians on both sides of that divide have increasingly tended to view all allegorical interpretations in light of such abuses. "Today," he lamented in 1947, "it almost inevitably evokes a lack of realism contrary to the Faith combined with a disdain for historical science that is shocking to our minds."[56]

On de Lubac's view, much of the current unease with the term results from the failure to distinguish "Hellenistic," "pagan," or "Philonic" allegory from "Christian" or "Pauline" allegory. True, this failure is not restricted to the modern era: "Christian writers never succeeded in any rigorous way in reserving 'allegory' for its Pauline significance alone."[57] De Lubac nevertheless insisted that the occasional deformation of allegory at the hands of some Christians (usually, but not always, Platonists) must not blind us to the essential role it played in the ancient and medieval Church.

To what features of both did de Lubac wish to draw attention in distinguishing between them? On his view, only of Hellenistic allegory is it accurate to say, in the words of Hans Frei, that it involves "the attachment of a temporally free-floating meaning pattern to any temporal occasion whatever, without any intrinsic connection between sensuous time-bound picture and the meaning represented by it."[58] Hellenistic allegory, which de Lubac also called "figurative literal" or "metaphorical" interpretation,[59] denies "the literal meaning in order to escape from an awkward dogma."[60] Philo's allegories sometimes took this form, treating the scriptural narratives as presenting "a kind of spiritual history of the soul."[61] In our day we find this in psychologizing interpretations of the Exodus, wilderness wanderings, and entry into the Promised Land as symbols for the internal dynamics of personal growth. The defining characteristic of such "pagan" or "Philonic" allegory is its virtually complete dismissal of the persons, events, and injunctions of the biblical texts as quaint, if not disconcerting, images of truths that are more straightforwardly, or less embarrassingly, articulated by other means.

Genuinely Christian allegory, by contrast, acknowledges the literal or historical sense of the biblical text while investing it with, or adding to it, a new meaning. According to de Lubac, who cites dozens of ancient and medieval sources, pre-modern Christianity was virtually unanimous in its contention that this is how Paul treated the stories of Hagar and Sarah in his famous allegory in Gal 4.24. For instance, Hilary of Poitiers said in his commentary on the Psalms, "The Apostle teaches us that, while respecting historical truth, we should recognize in it the prefigurement of spiritual teaching and works."[62] Or again, Augustine asserted that when Paul saw in Abraham's two sons an allegory of the two covenants, he did not thereby impugn what we might now call the historicity of either Abraham or his sons. By the same token, in affirming an allegorical meaning to the raising of Lazarus, Augustine had no intention of denying that Lazarus was actually brought back to life.[63] It will be useful to quote de Lubac at some length in order to clarify the point:

> When St. Paul and all the Christians following him distinguish the letter from the spirit, or the history from the mystery that it contains, or the figure from its fulfillment or even darkness from truth, they are not inspired by the Platonic distinction between opinion and true knowledge in order to contrast, as Anthistene or Zeno did, a κατὰ ἀλήθειαν exegesis to a κατὰ δόξαν one. It is true that the latter distinction . . . "directed an entire exegetical trend among the commentaries on Homer." But the bounds of reality are overstepped if it is added that "this distinction between an apparent meaning, which does not surpass the ordinary reader, and a deep meaning to which only the learned have access is the precise definition of allegory in whatever milieu it is used." Neither St. Paul . . . or even the author of the Epistle to the Hebrews, in spite of the element of 'Platonism' that can be found there . . . says anything that is really similar. Two meanings that make one, or of which the first, very real in itself, must step aside for the other from the moment

that the creative transfiguring Event takes place, are not at all the same as two meanings that exclude each other in the way that appearance and reality or 'illusion' and truth do.[64]

From the first century until the modern era, then, "Christian allegory" is a "spiritual understanding" that sees in the literal sense of the biblical texts *sacramenta Christi et Ecclesia*. The newness of meaning that is tagged "allegorical" is seen in the light brought by Christ. His coming transfigures, or fulfills, the literal sense without denying or diminishing its historical, literal realism, that is, its character as a unique person, event, or injunction. Having thus clarified the term, de Lubac granted that when allegory is so understood and practiced, "it means essentially what Fr. Daniélou and others call 'typology'."[65]

This difference between Frei et al. and de Lubac over the primacy of typology in the ancient and medieval Church therefore appears to be one of terminology rather than substance. Regrettably, both sides contributed to the confusion by failing to be as precise or as consistent as one might hope. When Frei contrasted typological interpretations to allegorical ones in terms of the distinction between "chronological" and temporally "free-floating" patterns of meaning, he obscured the fact (of which he was well aware) that typological interpretations do not depend on a careful reconstruction of the historical links between the type and anti-type, but on an appeal to an eternal divine action and plan embracing them both. For this reason, Erich Auerbach, Frei's source for understanding both the method and pre-modern prominence of figural or typological interpretation, said that figuration is not an exercise in discerning the "rational, continuous, earthly connections between things. . . . It can be established only if both occurrences are vertically linked to Divine Providence, which alone is able to devise such a plan of history and supply the key to its understanding."[66] Indeed, "[t]he horizontal, that is the temporal and causal, connection of occurrences is dissolved" in typological interpretations without, it should be noted, thereby denying the historical or realistic quality of each element so conjoined.[67] There is nothing even remotely resembling a "historical necessity" or "causal connection" between Isaac and Christ when the former is regarded as a type fulfilled by the latter. Yet doing so involves allowing the type and its fulfillment "to retain the characteristics of concrete historical reality."[68] Citing Auerbach, Frei noted that one of the risks attendant to typological interpretations is having the type's original or prefigural meaning get crushed beneath the weight of its new meaning as a prefigurement.[69] (De Lubac, recall, spoke of the sometimes irresistible temptations posed by a Hellenistic form of allegory that do just that.) When figuration is done well, however, an "event taken as a figure preserves its literal and historical meaning. It remains an event, does not become a mere sign."[70]

For his part, de Lubac should be faulted for seeming so readily to accept, indeed to promote, images of the relations between the Old and New Testaments that suggest an all too "Hellenistic" treatment of the former. "Christ," he said, "*kills* the shadows and images in terms of their literal meaning."[71] " 'He transforms the shadowy world of figurative expressions into truth;' 'he puts an end to the literal and ascribes a pre-eminence to a new, spiritual understanding.' "[72] Such remarks were doubtless prompted by the laudable and entirely appropriate desire to convey the radical newness of Christ and to indicate the abrupt change of register he effects on the Old Testament. But that intention does not excuse the supersessionist implications of de Lubac's rhetorical excesses. We are no longer speaking solely of hermeneutics. Remarks about the "effacement of the Old Testament in its literal dimension" are backed by claims that "the Church took the place of Israel. . . . She is Abraham's posterity, the only one in possession of his heritage. . . . The Church takes the place of the Synagogue . . . which has become blind and sterile, [and] is merely her librarian."[73] "Such explanations," to quote one of de Lubac's jibes, "condemn themselves."[74]

The problems I have identified on either side of this debate should not prevent us realizing that both parties nevertheless want to affirm many of the same things. They agree on the pre-modern prominence among Christian exegetes of figural interpretations (if I may temporarily choose that as a mutually acceptable term) that while comprehending in faith the connection between type and anti-type do not disregard the sheer contingency and irreducible individuality of historical persons, events, or injunctions. And they agree that such comprehension does not rest on the application of various scientific methods in hopes thereby of providing an indubitable basis for Christian claims about the unity of the Bible and the uniqueness of Christ. Figuration must therefore be sharply distinguished from the postwar biblical theology movement's attempts, which failed spectacularly, to discern in the features of the Hebrew language a unique Hebrew capacity to grasp the revelation of a God who acts in history. Granted, de Lubac would likely balk at the suggestion that the literal sense assumed the importance in pre-modern exegesis that Frei and others have ascribed to it. But that, too, is likely a disagreement over terminology rather than substance. Frei did not want to deny the importance of the spiritual senses. His concern accurately to distinguish acceptable and unacceptable forms of figuration would be pointless otherwise. By speaking of the priority of the literal sense, Frei sought, among other things, to convey the pre-modern view that for figuration to be truly pious, for it to respect the realistic quality of the faith (to use two of de Lubac's phrases), it must be anchored in ways I have already described in the realistic, historical individuality of the type. "The Spirit," as de Lubac put it, "is not separated from the letter. . . . The letter is good and necessary, because it leads to the spirit."[75] Frei articulated this concern, as we have seen, in reference to his desire to preserve the uniqueness of Jesus Christ as he is described in the Gospel narratives. But the same christological case can be made with reference to the Old Testament. If, for example, the prophets are regarded as having intentionally veiled their visions of the Christ-event in order to accommodate the weaknesses of their audiences, then the incarnation of God in Christ loses its radical newness, its absolutely gratuitous *un*predictability. Although de Lubac did not, so far as I am aware, criticize pre-modern exegetes for having interpreted the prophetic utterances in this way, it can be reasonably inferred from his repeated emphasis of Christ's newness that he would have found such criticisms warranted. In other words, given de Lubac's insistence that what distinguishes Christian allegory from midrash—which he asserted, quoting Beryl Smalley, gives new meanings through "a progressive addition" to the past—is that the Old Testament texts are interpreted in light of the event of Jesus Christ, which is not "a simple moment in a series," but an "eternal instant" and the "unique *kairos*," there seems to be little ground for him to complain about Frei's formulation.[76]

To simultaneously conclude this comparison and to recall the earlier argument about the modern atrophy of biblical fluency and imagination, de Lubac repeatedly deplored the fact that Christian allegory has lost its savor among the faithful. When we can no longer hear the rich base tones of the trinitarian melodies the scriptures sing, figuration is bound to sound tinny and discordant. He knew we cannot simply return to an earlier era's ideas and practices. He showed nothing but contempt for those "archaizers" who would be "cool toward the scientific knowledge and the mental habits of our own time" while hoping to retrieve "the mental habits of times gone by. . . . [They] belong to neither the present nor the past. They lose the one without finding the other."[77] Rather, his magisterial work on ancient and medieval exegesis was intended, at least in part, to revive interest in a pattern of reading the text that, when "set to rights," but not replaced by historical criticism, can continue to be of great service to the Church.[78] His views in this regard, then, comport well with those of Frei and Lindbeck.

Although the observations of Smart, Barr, Lindbeck, Frei—and now de Lubac—that we have lost our biblical fluency and imagination have a *prima facie* plausibility about them, two features of North Atlantic culture would seem to support a rather different assessment. One is the continued strength of the fundamentalist movement in the United States. Even to a casual observer, fundamentalists would seem to embody precisely the sort of biblically saturated worldview that our authors, to one degree or another, think is on the wane. But while few would doubt the biblical fluency of most fundamentalists, the vigor of their biblical imagination may be open to question. The declining popularity of expository sermons among Protestants has not been restricted to the so-called mainline denominations. Today's more popular televangelists move rapidly from text to text citing passages to illustrate the (sometimes political, often moral, occasionally more nearly theological) point they wish to make. To be sure, it is still possible to hear a careful retelling of a biblical story, or a nuanced exegesis of part of an epistle, but this is rare. The far more common practice among fundamentalists is to treat the Bible as an inerrant source of divinely inspired doctrines or as an inspired report of events in nature and history. But this is to trade on the same presuppositions about how the Bible means as do most moderns. On the fundamentalist reading, the narratives about Jesus make explicative sense by referring either to a doctrine that they illustrate in storied form, or to natural and/or historical occurrences. This confusion of explicative sense and ostensive reference has characterized most biblical interpretation for the better part of three centuries. As we have seen, owing to its concern to identify a single, determinate meaning, one of the effects of this mode of exegesis is to hamper the development of the imaginative skills necessary to construe oneself and one's world biblically. To read the Bible as the source for a set of fundamental facts of salvation risks turning it into a mere container of information. While admittedly important, these facts by themselves and considered as such cannot nourish the imagination, and, over time, likely become ossified and lifeless. The letter alone, as Luther often said, is dead and death dealing.

There is another group within North Atlantic culture whose presence would seem to raise doubts about the demise of biblical literacy and imagination. The status of the Bible for those in the Roman Catholic Church during the last half century appears at first glance to be utterly different from what these Protestant commentators have described. Roger Aubert noted in the mid-1950s that among western European Catholics there was a palpable resurgence in interest in, and exposure to, the Bible. This was evident at the popular level, as well as among academics.[79] Robert Murray, S.J., observes that in keeping with its aim to cultivate a deeper understanding of the scriptures, the Second Vatican Council's Dogmatic Constitution on Divine Revelation, *Dei Verbum,* enjoins scholarly biblical studies, the use of the Bible in the training and spiritual formation of the clergy, and daily devotional reading among the laity. He believes that although there has been considerable progress since the Council on the first two fronts, on the third "the brief hints in the text have been totally transcended through the amazing growth of lay groups meeting for prayer or study."[80] Sandra Schneiders notes with satisfaction that after nearly four centuries of "famine," the post-conciliar Church has finally "come . . . upon the promised land of sacred scripture."[81] She cites in support of this claim an "unprecedented interest in conferences and summer sessions on the Bible, in articles and books of *haute vulgarisation* that provide a reliable but readable entrée to the biblical texts, and in the use of scripture for personal meditation."[82] Denis Farkasfalvy describes an "explosion of biblical culture" among Catholics since the end of the Second World War.[83] He argues that the decrees of the Second Vatican Council institutionalized and further extended the biblical renewal that was one of the aims of *la nouvelle théologie.* After the Council, modern translations from the Hebrew and Greek were made available; the liturgy was modified to include biblical readings in the vernacular; the number of readings was increased from two to three, with one of these being from an Old Testament text; and selections from the Psalms began to be read between the readings.[84] As a result of these changes, priests and laity alike have been exposed to large segments of the Bible that had not been regularly used in the Catholic Church in centuries.

But the question must be asked, as Murray, Schneiders, and Farkasfalvy have done, whether these changes bore the fruit that one might have hoped they would. Has the Catholic Church been able, on the basis of its renewed enthusiasm for the Bible, to offer contemporary Catholics a religiously satisfying version of the Gospel? Have most Catholics been able to assimilate all or even very much of the new biblical material, to integrate it into their thought and experience? Or, to turn it around, have Catholics been able to understand their experience in terms of the images, stories, and conceptual patterns of the Bible? Is their view of the world shaped by its narrative rhythms and turns of phrase to any greater extent than that of contemporary Protestants?

All three observers readily acknowledge that such is not the case. Murray suspects that the reasons for this are manifold. In part they have to do with the tragic loss to the Church of those clergy who retired from ministry in the 1960s and 1970s. He maintains that many of these men were among those best able to explain the Council's encouragement of a less propositional view of revelation and laments as immoral the decision to bar them, once retired, from any teaching.[85] He also believes that the sheer size of some Catholic churches, while permitting large numbers to attend Mass, "often hinder[s] an effective liturgy of the Word."[86] Schneiders believes the blame ought to be attributed, in large measure, to the patriarchy she finds both in the composition and subsequent uses of the biblical texts. For feminists, both men and women, an ideological critique of the Bible that presents it as a text written by and for men raises the question of its revelatory character with particular urgency. In response, an increasing number have set the Bible aside as bearing a content simply too degrading and culturally hamstrung to be of religious value.[87] For his part, Farkasfalvy is inclined to lay the blame more squarely upon the slow disintegration of the cooperation among patristic, liturgical, and biblical scholars to renew the Church's theology that characterized Catholic thought from the interwar period up through the Council. He is especially critical of the burgeoning influence of the historical-critical methods of biblical interpretation and the positivist assumptions and secular aims he believes undergird them.[88] Despite their differences, all three agree that among Catholics the Bible simply no longer functions in the lives of the faithful as it once did to provide the interpretive lenses through which they view and understand reality.

Whatever may be the causes of this evidently widespread decline in biblical fluency and biblically informed imaginative power, it would seem inevitably to dampen the enthusiasm of those cheered by the recent rapprochement on the doctrine of scripture between Catholics and Protestants. Just when it might have appeared that these two groups of Christians were beginning to overcome some of their differences concerning the status and role of the Bible, it looks as though this development might not have much of an impact on either the Church or the wider culture. If the foregoing description of the contemporary scene is correct, at least on balance, then Catholics and Protestants must ask: What can be done to revive both biblical literacy and a biblically informed imagination?

Before I suggest an answer to that question, let me first distinguish between a concern to restore these skills among Christians and to do so among all members of Western societies generally. As Constantinian Christendom collapses, it no longer seems possible to ensure that all citizens of what were once predominantly Christian countries receive a thorough grounding in the Bible. This may not, however, be an altogether disheartening turn of events. Naturally, one hears such sentiments from non-Christians who are wary of the consequences of past alliances between priests and princes. But Christians, too, have echoed these remarks by welcoming the opportunity, presented by the failure of Christian attempts to provide Western culture with "ideological coherence, foundation, and stability," for Christians to recover an intratextually based communal self-description.[89] Likewise, there are many Christians who believe that the dethroning of a Christian biblical discourse from its former preeminence is salutary because it helps Christians resist the temptation to see the Christian perspective as flawless and complete.[90] Conversations with non-Christians that proceed without a shared idiom are necessarily fragmentary, piecemeal, and provisional; but they are not, for all that, a waste of time.[91] The lessons such encounters teach are analogous to some of those provided by a literal-figurative interpretive approach: all readings must remain open to renewal and revision. No smug interpretative complacency can be tolerated because the Gospel itself is not at home in this fallen world. Just as it impels the faithful to remain restlessly critical of any political status quo, so too does it urge them to remain attentive to the Spirit's unpredictable counsel by returning to the text in order to revisit seemingly settled questions.

Although providing the West with a biblically based, culturally unifying interpretive matrix seems no longer to be Christianity's vocation, it is certainly not unwarranted to hope and work for the restoration among Christians of biblical fluency and the abilities requisite to imagine oneself and one's world in biblical categories. If the withering of Constantinian Christendom casts doubts upon the viability of the first aim, it appears to make pursuing the second all the more pressing. The reason for alarm is twofold. It lies both in the impasse to which so many of the conversations among theological professionals have come and in the difficulty ordinary Christians have agreeing upon what is essential to the faith. These two, although distinguishable, are related. The arguments among theologians are but an instance, in a small population, of the more widespread inability to discern what is authentically Christian. As George Lindbeck has observed, if both of these conditions obtain, then the legitimacy of ecclesial authority is imperiled.[92] When ordinary Christians do not share a sense of what lies at the heart of the Gospel, and professional theologians and exegetes regularly speak past each other, the decisions of ecclesiastical leaders will likely appear arbitrary. Although troubling in the most stable of times, such illegitimacy could be disastrous during the upheavals brought on as Christianity breaks loose from its Constantinian moorings.

Over the centuries, fruitful dialogue among theologians and the vigor of a continually revised communal sense of what is essential to Christian proclamation and action were enabled and sustained by the literal-figurative interpretive approach to the Bible. With the breakdown of this pattern of reading and the consequent disintegration of a shared, biblically informed idiom, it has become increasingly difficult to discern a common assessment of what is integral to the faith and what is ancillary. It may be possible, of course, to achieve some minimal consensus about what it means to be Christian without such a common linguistic stock. If so, then conversations among Christians would tend to be no less ad hoc and fragmentary than those among Christians and non-Christians. And, again, that may have its lessons to teach. But when confronted with the dramatic changes the post-Constantinian Church is likely to undergo, it would seem beneficial to have a materially fuller, less formal agreement than that which a more piecemeal and disjointed conversation is apt to yield.[93] The Church would seem to need a weightier sheet anchor with which to weather the approaching storms.

This concern to revive a strong *sensus fidelium* among theological experts and nonexperts alike that is based upon a widely shared biblical idiom and a common construal of the Bible brings us back to the original question: How might the retrieval, at least within the Church, of a biblically literate imagination be brought about? A return to a pre-critical mode of exegesis offers little promise of success—if only because the fruits of historical criticism have been so liberally distributed throughout the Church by way of countless critical commentaries. So we cannot stuff the historical-critical genie back into its bottle, even if we were unwise enough to want to do so. Perhaps one step toward encouraging the development of the diverse skills necessary to see oneself and one's world through biblical spectacles would be to offer the Church interpretations of scripture that are fully conversant with historical criticism, yet adhere to the principles of the classic hermeneutics that I have outlined. Naturally, putting forward such readings cannot be all that is done to encourage the development of such skills. We do learn by example, but not solely by example. Nevertheless, reading and hearing good, close interpretations that construe the Bible primarily as the storied depiction of the identities of the triune God and God's people—rather than as, say, a treasury of sacred doctrine, or a more or less jumbled account of historical and natural facts, or a storehouse of symbols expressing religious experience—can be a significant part of acquiring the capacities to do such exegesis. So it may be that post-critical readings of scripture as the Word of God can help to revitalize the skills Christians need to reach a more substantive and widely held sense of what is essential to Christianity.

The hope with which this book is written is that Hans Urs von Balthasar might be a fruitful stimulus of such readings. Although he used language different from mine, he thought that to provide and foster the sorts of biblical interpretations I have characterized as the classic approach was one of the perennial tasks of Christian theology. To that end, he sought in his seven-volume *The Glory of the Lord: A Theological Aesthetics* to articulate a biblically authorized theology that focused upon the Bible as the mediation, not just of God's truth and goodness, but also of God's glory. As I indicated at the outset, my immediate aim in taking up this project is to examine Balthasar's doctrine of scripture in the *Theological Aesthetics*. This involves describing how Balthasar tried to take up this task and evaluating the degree of his success in accomplishing it. This book's second purpose, which I also indicated above, is to make the case that Balthasar's views and uses of scripture in the *Theological Aesthetics* generally abide by the principles of the pre-modern hermeneutics that I have described without shirking contemporary theology's responsibility to take seriously the fruits of historical criticism. As such, they have the necessary features to stimulate a historical-critical chastening of literal-figurative readings of the Bible that could nurture the *sensus fidelium*.

Since the successful fulfillment of both aims rests on the cogency of my analysis and critique, let me indicate in general terms what lies ahead. I begin with an overview of Balthasar's theological aesthetics that regards it as an attempt, in part, to rectify what he saw as the nearly universal tendency among theologians and biblical scholars in the modern era to forsake the natural and historical forms of revelation presented in scripture in favor of the transcendent mysteries to which they are held to point or be transparent. After indicating some of the costs of that approach, I summarize the principal objective and subjective analogies Balthasar contended exist between God's glory and earthly beauty. In the second chapter, I elucidate the principal hermeneutical implications of these analogies and begin to assess the degree to which he abided by them in his own exegesis. In the course of that discussion, I also describe his view of the proper roles and limitations of historical criticism and examine some of the ways he used historical-critical findings in his exegesis. In the third chapter, I summarize Balthasar's view of the relations of the Old and New Testaments by describing his two-fold justification for construing the Bible as having a christologically focused (yet ultimately trinitarian) theocentricity. I also identify some of the principal strengths and weaknesses of his uses of the Old Testament in the process of defending that view. The fourth chapter explicates and assesses both Balthasar's views of scriptural authority in the Church and the ways in which scripture actually functions authoritatively in the *Theological Aesthetics*. In the final chapter, I complete the assessment of the consistency with which Balthasar followed his own hermeneutical guidelines and the analysis of his uses of historical criticism. I conclude the chapter by examining the usefulness of redescribing his exegetical practices in terms of a theory of performance interpretation and a theory of authorial-discourse interpretation.

Although in what follows I have largely confined my citations of Balthasar's work to the *Theological Aesthetics*, on occasion I cite materials that fall outside of the *Theological Aesthetics*, either when he explicitly referred his reader to them or when the claims made therein help to clarify those advanced in the *Theological Aesthetics*. I concentrate on Balthasar's *Theological Aesthetics* principally because its final two volumes provide the nearest thing to an extended example of scriptural exegesis in his entire theological corpus. There are virtually no excurses in Balthasar's work, as one finds, for example, in Karl Barth's *Church Dogmatics*, where Balthasar might have interrupted the flow of his argument to present a more or less carefully developed exegetical case for the theological proposal just advanced. To find Balthasar engaging the Bible with the sort of sustained directness and vigor that makes a detailed analysis possible and fruitful, one must look to the concluding volumes of the *Theological Aesthetics*. In the following analysis, then, the *Theological Aesthetics* constitutes a case study of manageable size and sufficient complexity to provide a firm basis for my conclusions. Moreover, what I identify regarding the hermeneutical guidelines that derive from Balthasar's theological aesthetics, the degree of consistency with which he followed them when exegeting the Bible, the complexities of his views and uses of historical criticism, and the limitations and merits of his conceptions of scriptural authority also holds true—though with an important exception—for his *Theo-Drama* and

Theo-Logic. Given a concern to avoid an unnecessary multiplication of examples, it seems best to examine these issues as they present themselves in their most concentrated form. This is consistent with my primary aim, namely, to determine to what extent Balthasar's views and uses of scripture in the *Theological Aesthetics* provides a model for postcritical biblical interpretation that may help counteract the current disintegration of the *sensus fidelium*.

I

THEOLOGICAL AESTHETICS

A Methodological and Historical Orientation

This chapter provides an overview of Hans Urs von Balthasar's theological aesthetics and explains the sensibilities and skills he believed one must possess in order to avoid misreading the biblical mediation of God's self-revelation in nature and history. In the first section, I describe his criticisms of modern theology for having failed, by and large, to appreciate the analogies between beauty and revelation. Unless one's scriptural interpretation be disciplined by a theological aesthetics, he argued, the natural and historical forms of revelation presented in scripture inevitably pale in significance next to the transcendent mysteries to which they purportedly point or are transparent. I begin the second section by arguing that Balthasar's concern to interpret revelation and its scriptural mediation with the aid of categories drawn from aesthetics is both compatible with Kierkegaard's critique of the aesthetic form of life and relies on the ancient and medieval conviction that God's work as creator is not contradicted, but perfected in God's work as redeemer. Lest Balthasar's advocacy of a theological aesthetics be misunderstood to undermine the ontological difference between creation and God—indeed, their ever greater dissimilarity—I go on to explain the importance for him of an analogical method that resists the temptation of a theology of identity while avoiding the self-contradictory trap of a strict dialectics. In the third section, I analyze the main objective and subjective analogies Balthasar drew between our perception of beautiful forms and the faithful's perception of God's self-revelation and indicate their principal hermeneutical correlates. In the course of the discussion, I identify four instances in which Balthasar's criticisms of modern theology, or his proposed solution to its problems, are compatible with the hermeneutical guidelines followed by most pre-modern biblical interpreters.

THE AILMENTS OF MODERN THEOLOGY

Balthasar was deeply concerned about what he saw as the "fatal cleavage" between theology and spirituality in contemporary Christianity. He addressed the topic explicitly on at least five occasions,[1] and the theme echoes in the background of a host of articles and books, as well as throughout his theological triptych. As Balthasar understood the problem, the work of dogmatic theology has become largely irrelevant to the practical, pastoral needs of the Church, while spirituality has become preoccupied with descriptions of faith's psychological dynamics at the expense of contemplative reflections upon the central, objective mysteries of divine revelation. In order better to understand Balthasar's proposal for reconciling theology and spirituality, we need briefly to examine his view of the chief failings of both.

Balthasar was convinced that this mutually debilitating separation of theology and spirituality is a result of the gradual vitiation of the concept of beauty that began in the later Middle Ages. Beauty was transformed from a transcendental determination of Being itself to what is merely decorative and evanescent. Balthasar believed that the cultural losses of this transformation have been enormous. Given my aim to elucidate his doctrine of scripture, the losses of greatest interest are those that bear on what he took to be one of theology's main responsibilities, namely, interpreting the Bible as authoritative for Christian life and thought.

The following is, in effect, a tripartite typology. Typologies of this sort are inevitably dubious, especially when, as in this case, their creator tends to see his own work falling within the *via media* where he believes all right thinking persons belong. Two points, therefore, should be stressed at the outset. First, this typology sheds more light on Balthasar's position than on those against which he polemicized. This should be borne in mind especially when I briefly address some of Balthasar's reservations about transcendental Thomism. When criticizing various theological methods, he usually took issue with what he believed were problematic tendencies and predilections, rather than explicit proposals ardently defended. Second, by speaking of the two approaches he attacked as extrinsicist and immanentist, I am adopting solely for the sake of convenience a set of shorthand descriptions that have been used in Catholic theology since the days of Loisy and Blondel. Although this has the advantage of following Balthasar's own practices, I recognize the inadequacies of these terms for other purposes, not least because they are laden with decades of polemical baggage.

As is widely recognized, the neoscholasticism that dominated official Roman Catholic theology well into the middle of the twentieth century was abstract, rationalistic, and dull.[2] After the promulgation by Pope Leo XIII of *Æterni Patris* in 1879, those holding positions in Rome's theological schools who were reluctant to embrace the scholastic revival were replaced with, as it turned out, far less able minds. By general consensus, they showed none of the inventiveness or synthetic power of a Liberatore or a Kleutgen. The textbooks they produced, which introduced more than a generation of Catholic clerics to the philosophy and theology of Thomas Aquinas, did little more than pass on what had been received. Balthasar voiced considerable personal distaste for this approach.[3] He saw it as the child, paradoxically, of profound fear and arrogance. From his perspective, by refusing to accept the Holy Spirit's ever new interpretation of the Son's witness to the Father and of the Father's to the Son, this approach sought shelter in the seeming security of the dead letter of scripture and tradition. To be a living appropriation of the mysteries of the divine-human encounter, theology requires, on Balthasar's view, a Pauline spirit of freedom and audacity. Such is the deftness and flexibility demanded by the Holy Spirit.

> In no case should the opinion arise that the Holy Spirit has said
> everything essential in the previous history of the Church, so that
> one has nothing more of importance to expect from him in the fu-
> ture. The entire work of the theologian would then be limited to re-
> peating what has already been said, where possible in the tone of
> the old governess who drums into the deaf children what they have
> forgotten time and again.[4]

At its worst, when no longer immersed in the wellsprings of divine revelation, neoscholasticism degenerated into a mind-numbing pettifog-
gery.[5] It began not, as Balthasar would have desired, with a reverent
and obedient meditation upon the self-manifestation of trinitarian love
as it is mediated by the Bible, but with faith's revealed first principles. It
then proceeded deductively through naturally known minor premises
to theologically firm conclusions. In this way, the legitimate noetic dimensions of Christian faith were exaggerated. Faith came to be seen
primarily as an assent to propositions held to be true on the authority
of the revealing God as mediated by the Catholic Church—which itself
was held to be a sign of the credibility of faith. To put the point polemi-
cally, in the hands of the neoscholastic theologians, Christian faith
became a belief *about* Jesus Christ instead of a belief *in* him.[6] This speculative "conclusion theology," based as it was on a knife-edged distinction between nature and grace, found itself increasingly cut off from
the workaday world of those in the pews.[7]

This virtually complete inability of neoscholastic theology to help
nourish and guide Christian prayer and service—its greatest flaw, on
Balthasar's view—overshadowed the gains in conceptual clarity it certainly won for the Catholic Church. It is not the neoscholastic passion
for making distinctions that Balthasar found troubling. He did not wish
anyone to suppose that a vague or slippery enthusiasm would advance
the cause of faith. As in any rational exercise, theology must define its
terms and establish its scope. But in so doing, Balthasar maintained that
theologians have to remember what the neoscholastics generally did
not: theology's object outstrips every domesticating definition and within
its conceptual boundaries lies, by grace, one who is unbounded.[8] The
problem with neoscholasticism lay rather in its nearly exclusive focus
upon revelation as a source of propositions to be believed and the cor-

relative understanding of theology's principle task to be drawing out the logical implications of these beliefs, to the virtual exclusion of other responsibilities. Operating within such constraints, it proved, for the most part, unable to sustain a life of prayer and service. Whether this is the result of the neoscholastics having themselves abandoned a "kneeling" theology in favor of one composed at deskside, as Balthasar asserted, is difficult to judge.[9] What is clear, however, is that Balthasar was not alone in his disdain for neoscholasticism. The birth, during the inter-war Catholic renewal in Europe, of *la nouvelle théologie, ressourcement,* the liturgical movement, and transcendental Thomism can all be traced, to one degree or another, to a dissatisfaction with the divorce between theory and practice characteristic of neoscholasticism.

Given the atrophy of neoscholasticism and the development of these alternatives to it, as well as the growth of political and liberation theologies since the end of the Second World War, does its style of theology still pose problems for contemporary Catholics? Is an arid propositionalism any longer much of a danger for the Church? Balthasar believed emphatically that it is. In our day, this pattern of doing theology takes the form of integralism or fundamentalism.

Since the conclusion of the Second Vatican Council, some of those who resist the reforms it authorized have looked upon Balthasar as one of their own.[10] His positions on ecclesial authority and the ordination of women are often cited as evidence of his theological conservatism.[11] It is true that Balthasar voiced deep misgivings about what he took to be hasty attempts to update the faith, and he asserted flatly that the tragedy of the Council lay in its settling for *aggiornamento* when its real intent was reform.[12] Nevertheless, he set himself firmly against those who would advocate an integralist agenda. Distinguishing it from his own attempts to strengthen the core of the Catholic Church through an "integration (into catholicity)," he said, "Integralism is the debilitating, mechanical attempt to hold together a disparate collection of individual truths and traditions; integration, in contrast, is the spontaneous art of aiming always at the Whole through the fragments of truth discussed and lived."[13] In chapter 4, which deals with the unity of scripture, I shall examine the sort of theological integration Balthasar espoused. For now, I want only to point out that whatever others may think about his work, plainly Balthasar saw himself as battling on his right flank against those who would diminish the freedom of the Spirit and neglect faith's volitional and affective dimensions.[14]

Notwithstanding Balthasar's concerns about those whom he regarded as undermining from the right his view of how theology should be properly conceived and conducted, it must be acknowledged that his efforts to strengthen his left flank were unstinting. Despite the depth of his contempt for a "mere 'fundamentalism' of facts of salvation strung together 'to be believed',"[15] he is far better known for his sometimes savage criticisms of transcendental Thomism, especially as it was elaborated by Karl Rahner.[16] He believed the central weakness of this theological method to be a latent subjectivism. By setting up in this way the discussion of Balthasar's views of spirituality in its mutually debilitating isolation from theology, I am making a connection that he himself did not make between two of the more frequent targets of his polemics. The link is nevertheless warranted because of their shared preoccupation with the believing subject—with its affective states, spiritual dynamism, (graced) potencies, innermost yearnings, and deepest personal or social needs.

From Balthasar's point of view, the spirituality of baroque Catholicism, as exemplified by Teresa of Ávila and John of the Cross, already showed signs of the turn toward the subject. True, Christian theology has always concerned itself with how the salvation wrought in and through Jesus Christ comes to animate the life of believing communities. One thinks, for example, of the rich heritage of reflection on the structure and interrelations of the theological virtues, to say nothing of other "fruits of the Spirit." In the Spanish writers, however, there is a subtle shifting of perspective, a transposition into a new key. As questions concerning the nature of God began increasingly to fall within the purview of the scholastically trained theological specialist, these mystics came to describe their experiences from within an ever more subjective frame of reference. The saints of the ancient and medieval world, so Balthasar held, were generally better able to understand their encounters with God as part of an ecclesial vocation whose task was "to serve a fuller understanding of the content of revelation, to orchestrate its great themes."[17] That is to say, the logic of believing more often than not found its proper center in, and remained subordinate to, the logic of belief. In the modern era, the emphasis has been reversed. Mystics "are required to describe the way in which they experienced God, and the accent is always on experience rather than on God."[18] When popularized by today's spiritual writers, this fascination with experiencing God can become an introverted, "unctuous, platitudinous piety," a sentimentalism devoid of dogmatic content.[19]

When compared to such works, the theological erudition and spiritual insight of Karl Rahner is of an utterly different order. And Balthasar recognized it as such. But if neoscholastics and integralists both understand revelation primarily as propositional or noetic, then Rahner's approach and that of the modern spiritualism just described share a view of revelation as, principally, what fulfills the needs of the graced subject. We find in Rahner and the new spiritualism a preoccupation with what Balthasar called the subjective evidence of belief, that is, with the structures and dynamics of human knowledge and action in their graced openness to divine revelation. In view of the extrinsicism from which transcendental Thomists and contemporary spiritual writers have sought to distance themselves, such an interest is eminently reasonable. Given the Christian conviction that God has poured out the Holy Spirit into believers' hearts in order to bring God's creation to perfection, it seems only natural for theologians to examine God's covenant partner so as better to view the mysteries of grace there unfolding. Such an approach has the further theological advantage of addressing itself to the concrete spiritual and existential situation of the believing Christian. In the best tradition of patristic theology, it seeks to illumine anew the divine mysteries from the inside out, rather than deducing conclusions from them. When done well, as Balthasar believed it had been by Rahner, this theological method can help to enrich the faithful's devotion to God and sustain a life of self-forgetting love for others. Balthasar, therefore, thought it should remain an important part of conceptual panoply Christian theologians use to interpret the catholic fullness of revelation.[20]

Balthasar worried, however, that Rahner's concern to demonstrate the affinities between the most deeply felt human aspirations and God's act in Jesus Christ threatens to turn those same aspirations into the fundamental criterion of the value and intelligibility of revelation. When that happens, of course, we are well down the road to modernism. Clearly Rahner was no modernist, as Balthasar knew, but in the hands of incautious or inept epigones, the extraordinary nuance and subtlety of his formulations can be lost in the zeal to open Christianity to the world in the name of grace's ultimate triumph. Balthasar, too, wished to open the Catholic Church to the world, to "raze its bastions" as he put it in the title of a pre-conciliar book,[21] but he worried that the anthropological fascination of the transcendental Thomists risks dissolving everything Christian into a faceless religiosity. Having highlighted, by means of the "supernatural existential," humanity's graced orientation to, and capacity for, divine self-revelation, Rahner had to surmount two obstacles: explaining the relevance of a concrete history of salvation; and the necessity of an explicit, sacramental Church.[22] On Balthasar's view, at least, Rahner sometimes (and his followers more frequently) failed to do so adequately. Within any theological method addressing itself primarily to the task of elucidating the subjective conditions of belief, Balthasar was persuaded, lies the danger of allowing, even if unwittingly, the needs and hopes of the believing subject to set the parameters within which one assesses the credibility of Christian proclamation and service.

Inasmuch as political and liberation theologies arose, in part, out of a frustration with the evident shortcomings of a subject-centered approach, Balthasar believed they represent welcome advances. By stressing at once the corporate dimensions and active character of the life of faith, specifically the Christian responsibility to help alleviate social and economic injustice, they are actually closer to what Balthasar called the true spiritual center of everything biblical: "where the issue is never the solitary self but the We of people, community and Church."[23] But on his view, at least, there are nevertheless serious risks attendant to these more communitarian procedures. They have to do with the perennial temptation to identify God's promised, earthly sovereignty with an existing political order or with a utopian vision. He worried that these theologies, however well-intended, risk establishing a particular view of what constitutes a just society as the criterion for judging Christian belief and obedience. What is at issue is not the threat of measuring and appreciating objective revelation and the means of grace by the degree to which they satisfy the individual's spiritual longings, as it is in transcendental Thomism. Rather, it is a question of treating what God does in history primarily as what fulfills our most pressing social needs.

Balthasar would have us ask whether there is not a common conviction uniting these two, seemingly contradictory theological options. In both, he believed, human capacities and incapacities, be they personal or communal, threaten to become the touchstone by which to measure divine revelation. Naturally, we are speaking here more of inclinations than explicit proposals. Yet Balthasar remained worried that a legitimate pastoral concern could, by a series of perhaps imperceptible steps, be transformed into a means of assessing what God has done, and is doing, to fulfill creation. He wondered whether the "whole orientation" of the transcendental school and political and liberation theologies "is not constantly threatened by a secret and, occasionally, even by an open bondage to philosophy which makes the internal standard for the striving spirit, even where it is conceived only as 'emptiness' or 'void', as *cor inquietum, potentia oboedientialis,* and so on, nevertheless to be somehow the measure of revelation itself."[24] He believed that these diverse theological approaches were but two more instances of the centuries-old program of advocating Christianity in terms of basically anthropological criteria.[25] This abiding preoccupation with the recipient of grace—with our yearnings, strivings, potencies, and needs— at the expense of an awestruck openness to God's saving inventiveness, is what Balthasar thought problematic. In both, as well as in the work of modern spiritual writers, Balthasar saw an unwarranted narrowing of grace's scope to what improves, enriches, or sustains our personal and public lives: "God's love converts, transforms or hardens men's hearts; but that is its effect, not its essence; and it would be a strange lover who wanted to measure how much he was loved in return, by the change, good or bad, wrought in him."[26]

Balthasar's polemics against threats on his left and right were neither particularly innovative nor insightful. It has become something of a commonplace to bemoan the Scylla of extrinsicism and the Charybdis of immanentism while seeking to ply a course in between.[27] What makes Balthasar's analysis of the problem interesting, and of significance for a book arguing that his doctrine of scripture echoes certain pre-modern themes, is his assertion that despite their obvious differences, the right and the left share a common frame of reference whose historical foundations are buried deep within the later Middle Ages. The great divorce between theology and spirituality, which itself can be traced to the same period, parallels, and quite probably was, a symptom of the gradual isolation and eventual disparagement of the concept of beauty.[28] Generally speaking, theologians of the ancient and medieval worlds saw beauty in its relation to the other transcendental attributes of Being more clearly than contemporary theologians. In our age, when beauty has been largely eliminated from the theological lexicon, theologians tend to favor one or the other of the remaining transcendentals in their analogous application to God's self-manifestation. I have already discussed some of the consequences of these developments for Christian life and thought. While neoscholastic, integralist, and fundamentalist theologians can be faulted for considering revelation primarily under the aspect of its truth, modern spirituality, transcendental Thomism, and political and liberation theologies are guilty of construing revelation principally under the rubric of the good. Balthasar was convinced that neither, alone, could hope to do justice to the fullness of the triune divine life as it is revealed in Jesus Christ and his Church.

Balthasar believed that extensive damage had been done to Christian reflection and practice by this withering of beauty. My purpose here is to focus on his analysis of two ways of "reading" revelation as presented by scripture—the extrinsicist as well as the immanentist programs just discussed—that he thought share a fundamental flaw. They are allied in ignoring the fruitfulness for Christian biblical interpretation of using, with all due caution and qualification, categories drawn from the field of aesthetics.

In their concern to demonstrate the veracity of the Catholic Church's teachings (and to discredit Protestant positions) neoscholastic theologians generally regarded the Bible as a source for proof texts. Individual verses, or even parts of verses, were plucked from the text without regard to their literary or historical context in order to buttress a given thesis. The impact of such a procedure on the narrative portions of scripture was especially deleterious. Events of salvation history were treated as signs pointing beyond themselves to divine mysteries that were to be believed. The acts of God on behalf of God's covenant partner—the divinely conferred leadership of the judges and kings, the prophetic call to repentance and fidelity, even the stories about Jesus Christ—were understood as indicators, credible in and of themselves, of the deeper, invisible mysteries of the faith. On this construal, what Jesus did and said and suffered are revelatory to the degree that they signify what stands more clearly expressed in the articles of faith. These episodes, as well as the rest of the Bible generally, were but the forms from which a rationalistic science of faith abstracted the dogmatic material to be used in the service of instruction and polemics. Balthasar applauded this approach for stressing the credibility of the historical witness and for noticing the way in which this credibility is supported by the inter-relation of the various elements of that witness.[29] Nevertheless, the het-eronomous relation faith bears to the historical, divine self-revelation mediated by scripture characteristic of neoscholasticism is manifest. The believer remains related to the object of faith externally, as some-thing to be assented to on the divine authority that is vouchsafed to the Catholic Church.[30]

The path followed by those described as immanentist has, on Bal-thasar's view, obvious advantages over this extrinsicist model of bibli-cal interpretation. Owing to the graced orientation of the subject to God, the unique, positive history of salvation is integrated into the dynamics of the believer's spiritual life. At its limits, of course, this can debouch into the modernist heresy: treating scripture and tradition as nothing but historically conditioned expressions of a logically prior encounter between the redeeming God and the redeemed soul, expressions which remain valid only insofar as they accord with that encounter. Balthasar was convinced that this extreme view remained less an overt threat to Catholic theology than to a Protestantism whose scriptural interpreta-tion was by and large governed by Bultmannian presuppositions. He saw in Bultmann's work a corrosive skepticism toward all biblical forms, which left behind an unseen God, veiled by myth, who is always on the verge of "turning into the subject that does the believing, thus vanish-ing within it."[31] If Jeffrey Ames Kay is correct, part of Balthasar's aim in writing the *Theological Aesthetics* was to steer Catholics away from just such hermeneutical reductionism.[32] Balthasar worried that in the transcendental school and in political and liberation theologies there is at least a covert tendency, owing to a passion for elucidating the sub-jective foundation of faith (understood personally or socially), to treat the historical forms of revelation as mere catalysts for a spiritual pro-cess that contained, implicitly at least, the entire substance of faith. The signs presented by the historical, positive forms of revelation's scrip-tural witness do not so much point beyond themselves to invisible mys-teries, as the neoscholastics maintained, as appear virtually transparent to them.[33]

Despite their differences, these two approaches share a serious her-meneutical shortcoming. In both instances the biblically mediated forms of revelation are, if not superfluous, at least dispensable. Once one has believed the mysteries to which they point or are transparent, they be-come secondary. The sign pales beside the luminosity of the signified.[34]

Balthasar contended that this common failing is the result of con-sidering revelation solely from the perspective of the true or the good. He thought it crucial to unite the best features of these two readings (i.e., the credibility of revelation's objective forms and the fulfillment of the believer's deepest personal or social yearnings). But that can hap-pen, he maintained, only by adopting a conceptual framework that rejects the debilitating parallelism of sign and ostensive referent on which both trade. To do so requires an appeal to a science of aesthetics in which what is beautiful is understood to comprise two moments that are indissolubly linked: *species* (form) and *lumen* (splendor). Baltha-sar found this notion of beauty first mooted in the work of Plotinus and given definitive expression by Thomas Aquinas and, especially, by Bonaventure.[35] On this view, the genuinely beautiful, as distinct from what is merely pretty or kitsch, cannot be analyzed into its constituent elements without destroying it. Indeed, to speak of the constituent ele-ments as such is already to risk identifying the "constituents" as pri-mary, as the terms by means of which to understand their union. The logical relation is exactly the other way around. Naturally, it is pos-sible to speak of form and splendor in isolation from each other, but this must be done provisionally, recognizing that such remarks will remain tentative. To go behind the form to view the light radiating from within it in isolation is to step into oblivion. The beautiful, radi-ant form is a "primal phenomenon."[36] When we see the beautiful form as such,

> if we really behold it, it is not as a detached form, rather in its unity with the depths that make their appearance in it. We are 'enrap-tured' by our contemplation of these depths and are 'transported' to them. But, so long as we are dealing with the beautiful, this never happens in such a way that we leave the (horizontal) form behind us in order to plunge (vertically) into the naked depths.[37]

This sheds light on why Balthasar was critical of the extrinsicist and immanentist interpretations of the biblically mediated forms of revelation. By ignoring the lessons that reflection upon our encounter with beautiful forms can teach, they unwittingly split apart the primal phenomenon of scripture's witness to salvation history and give precedence to what they take to be its essential core (be that understood as the true or the good). To use the categories of aesthetics, this favors the *lumen* over the *species* and assumes that the former can be somehow laid hold of in isolation from the latter. In terms more closely resembling the analyses provided by Hans Frei, George Lindbeck, and Henri de Lubac that I discussed in the introduction, these two misreadings fail to abide by the pre-modern hermeneutical convention of giving priority to the literal sense.[38] In particular, the biblical narratives are understood, not to mean what they say (by rendering the identities of their central characters), but to illustrate in storied form what can be redescribed more succinctly and persuasively otherwise. This is to take the scriptures as a mere starting point for theological reflection, which then thrives in an atmosphere virtually devoid of sustained, careful exegesis. And why should it not? If one assumes that the text can be better understood and believed when recast in another idiom, it is at best unnecessary, and at worst an impediment, to a faithful apprehension of the gospel.

Balthasar decisively rejected this assumption. He (along with Frei, Lindbeck, and de Lubac) maintained, by contrast, that the Bible ought to provide theologians, not just with a launching pad from which to get their work off the ground, but also with the fuel to sustain them in flight. Christian theology, Balthasar contended, does not simply start from the concrete, the historical, the sensual; it abides in them, seeing (by grace) the luminous depths of the triune divine life not behind, or in front of, but within them.[39] On his view, Bonaventure's work constitutes an enduring model of such an approach. The fact that Francis received his stigmata in the midst of an ecstatic encounter of love with God confirms for Bonaventure that such encounters are "not a flight out of the world that leaves it behind, but rather the opening of the world for God."[40] "For [Bonaventure], knowledge of God—even when this is 'negative'— is tied to the form of the world, which can be interpreted by man only with intellect and senses."[41] It therefore remains an ongoing theological obligation to resist the temptation to turn away from the phenomenal, from what is perceived, in a misguided effort to grasp the divine light.

To make such a claim raises the question of the role of historical-critical methods in biblical interpretation with an inescapable urgency. However, before turning in the next and subsequent chapters to Balthasar's views on that topic, we need first to examine in greater detail his proposed solution to the dualism of sign and referent that plagues the theology with which he was familiar: a theological aesthetics.

THEOLOGICAL AESTHETICS

To those persuaded by Søren Kierkegaard's polemics against an aesthetic existence, a "theological aesthetics" sounds like an oxymoron. After all, theology is supposed to be a serious business. Does the religious stage of life not represent a definitive rejection of all that animates the aesthete? Did Balthasar wish to cultivate interest in a form of life so episodic, driven as it is to seek satisfaction in the ephemeral? To evince a passion for beauty usually bespeaks a failure to grapple with life's deeper dimensions. It can suggest a bourgeois preoccupation with the latest shifts in fashion, a concern for appearances, prestige, and pleasure at the expense of an active and enduring commitment to other people or to causes other than one's own. On this reading of Kierkegaard, a passion for beauty is frivolous, self-indulgent, and sad; it remains a hindrance to the earnestness required of the ethical or religious life. On the face of it, then, Balthasar's advocacy of a theological aesthetics seems puzzling and ill conceived.

Balthasar was convinced, however, that the real target of Kierkegaard's attacks have been widely misunderstood.[42] Balthasar's rhetorical strategy, therefore, was to redirect his readers' Kierkegaardian antipathy for the beautiful toward a conception of beauty, ushered in with modernity, that Balthasar, too, wished to repudiate. He contended that Kierkegaard's contempt for the aesthetic stage of life is best understood when set within the context of the development of the modern science of aesthetics as an independent philosophical discipline. The notion of beauty on which such a science depends helps to provide aesthetes with their intellectual underpinnings. The bohemian behavior of characters like Kierkegaard's Johannes the Seducer, "whose whole life was motivated by enjoyment"[43] is given cover and credibility by a centuries-long process that Balthasar called the aestheticization of the beautiful.[44] For what follows, it is important to have some sense of that process in order to grasp the gravamen of Balthasar's criticisms of those biblical interpreters whose aesthetic sensibilities are, at best, vestigial.

Classical and Christian antiquity were allied in the conviction—Balthasar called it an intuition[45]—that transitory experiences of the unity, truth, goodness, and beauty of the cosmos are comprehensible only in reference to a transcendent order of Being that is absolutely one, true, good, and beautiful. A moment of intellectual communion among friends, a fair verdict, an act of kindness, or a brightly colored bird were each held to offer a glimpse of Being *qua* Being. They were brief encounters with what is ultimately real, with the gods, with the divine, with God—with what was believed to transcend the world of division, injustice, brutality, and ugliness. Significantly, such experiences were not limited to life's more obviously salutary side. Life as a whole was celebrated, without buffing out its blemishes. Thus, despite a legacy of occasionally grisly literature that might suggest otherwise, one finds widespread in the ancient world a perspective on human existence that is fundamentally affirmative.[46]

This capacity for viewing life in its wholeness is grounded in the belief that experiences of this sort involve, not just one, but all the determinations of Being. The four transcendentals, so to speak, dance together; a manifestation of one is a manifestation of them all. The ancients saw themselves, then, as experiencing, not different parts of Being, but its entirety considered under different modalities. Notwithstanding significant differences in the degree to which the transcendentals were integrated and anchored in a timeless substrate; the way in which Being's self-manifestations were experienced; and, most importantly, how the relation of Being itself to the divine sphere was conceived, the basic view of beauty in its dynamic interdependence with the one, the true, and the good as a transcendental determination of (theophanic) Being prevailed in the West until the later Middle Ages.

On Balthasar's view, this ancient and medieval perspective is enunciated with striking clarity by Thomas Aquinas, who, when "at his most competent," designated *esse,* that which for him is neither God nor yet the sum of individual worldly *entia* nor (what finally suggests itself) a conceptual abstraction *(conceptus entis)* but the first *created* reality proceeding from God, by participating in which all beings really are, something 'abundant, simple, non-subsisting', 'universal', 'flowing', participating in an infinite manner and thence in itself infinite, lending form inexhaustibly, which however is distinguished from God by the fact that God subsists in himself, while Being only subsists in finite beings. This Being . . . *is creaturely reality in so far as it is seen and conceived as the all-embracing manifestation of God.* It is therefore a *theophanic* Being, in the classical but also in a thoroughly Pauline sense (Rom 1.18–21; Acts 17.22–29), to which unity, truth, goodness and beauty do not belong as properties possessed at its own disposal—how could they, since this Being does not subsist as such? . . . [I]n so far as they adhere to it, *[esse]* refers to the primordial ground of Being which replicates itself in it like an image: *ipsum esse est similitudo divinae bonitatis.*[47]

By thus conceiving of Being in its dependence on God as subsisting in the luxuriant plenitude of finite forms, Thomas preserved both the concreteness of Being and the ontological distinction between God and creation.

It was Balthasar's contention that when either one or both of these is threatened (that is to say, when Thomas's conception of the *actus essendi* is ignored or misconstrued), beauty loses its rightful place in metaphysical discourse, and the cosmos is rendered unsuitable as a medium for God's self-manifestation.[48] When that happens, a wide range of capacities is impaired, chief among which, given our present concern with hermeneutics, is the ability correctly to read the biblical mediation of divine revelation.

But, of course, that is precisely what would come to pass. Both of these assertions and the delicate balance between them were undermined in the centuries that followed. The first fell victim to Duns Scotus, who, while seeking to defend divine transcendence, defined Being as the comprehensive concept of reason, thereby evacuating it of determinate content and suspending it above both the finite forms of reality and their transcendent ground.[49] The second was lost to sight in Eckhart's identification of Being and God. Though rooted in what Balthasar believed was a genuinely Christian experience of God, Eckhart's appropriation of the pious language of Christian antiquity made it appear that in and through the emergence of Being, God was coming to be.[50] Over time, both of these ideas, despite the faithfulness of their authors, would prove disastrous for theological aesthetics.

Naturally, the earlier view was not overturned at a stroke. Balthasar saw it retaining significant influence over aspects of European philosophy and literature well into the baroque. Even Kant, whose contribution in aesthetics, as in so much else, was immense, did not, by transforming the definition of transcendentality, extirpate entirely the older view of beauty. Indeed, it was to attain a brilliant recrudescence in the poetry and natural philosophy of Goethe, the mercurial genius whose work provided Balthasar with a crucial alternative to Kant's transcendental point of departure.[51]

The decisive feature of Goethe's thought that places him within the trajectory of what Balthasar (and others, of course) called "the great tradition" of a transcendental aesthetics is his morphology. He conceived of form in its indivisible connection to the transcendent splendor radiating from within it. Nature's " 'graven form' displays from within itself the infinitely mysterious Idea, which idea—being the one and only—always, however, remains the divine *beyond* all appearing phenomena."[52] One cannot hope adequately to understand a form without reference to this larger whole of which it is a part. On Goethe's view, although it is possible to acquire a firm grasp of the finite contexts within which to locate a given form (e.g., its species, genus, and family), doing so does not capture the infinite depths of Being of which it is an embodiment. Throughout his life, therefore, Goethe remained unalterably opposed to Newtonian mechanism. However useful it may be to represent the color, shape, or even behavior of a given existent with numerical values, such an approach leaves unanswered, or perhaps unasked, the question of its being, its sheer givenness. Goethe fought tirelessly against any such tyranny of the quantitative. "His aim," according to Balthasar, "was to combine the cool precision of scientific research with a constant awareness of the totality apparent only to the eye of reverence, the poetic-religious eye, the ancient sense for the cosmos."[53] The goal of scientific precision is only partly achieved so long as this qualitative dimension is left out. A numerically exact description must be supplemented with an aesthetic sense for the relation of parts and wholes in order to understand a given form as it really is: "Only by using such integration can so-called scientific exactitude really be anything like exact."[54]

It would appear that Goethe lost his battle with Newton, for, save but few exceptions, members of the societies bordering the North Atlantic (and, increasingly, of those along the Pacific rim) no longer possess the sensorium for beautiful forms. We are like Rilke's panther, numbed into an aesthetic torpor " 'from endlessly counting the bars' " of the materialist cage we have built for ourselves.[55] We have almost entirely lost the ability to perceive natural, artistic, and personal forms as radiating the beauty of Being's depths. Instead, we pry apart the primal phenomenon of beauty in order to analyze its constituent elements. As Balthasar put it, we have "become accustomed to read things by starting from the bottom and working our way up, rather than by working from the whole to the parts. Our multi-faceted glance is, indeed, suited to the fragmentary and the quantitative: we are the world's and the soul's analysts and no longer have a vision for wholeness."[56] The ancient and medieval view of beauty as the indivisible unity of *species* and *lumen* has largely been pushed aside in favor of the meaning given it in popular culture, namely, what is ornamental and fleeting.

As I indicated earlier, Balthasar maintained that this eviscerated conception of beauty, as well as the aesthetic existence that it helped legitimate, are the real objects of Kierkegaard's critique. How else, he contended, should one understand the argument developed in the second volume of *Either/Or* that the beautiful retains its validity for Christianity provided it be integrated within a life characterized by ethical commitment and religious devotion?[57] Even though theologians— practically without exception, on Balthasar's view—have missed this more positive notion of beauty in Kierkegaard, they are not wrong to have sought to banish the form of beauty he criticized.[58] That is so, not simply because of the form of life with which it is associated, but also because of the subjectivism or formalism of an aesthetics derived from a purely finite definition of beauty. Still, this virtually complete purging of aesthetics from theology has had considerable costs. I have already noted the two principal ways in which Balthasar saw it affecting biblical interpretation, though he believed the effects to be much more wide-spread. The elimination of aesthetics from theology has meant,

> broadly, the expulsion of contemplation from the act of faith, the exclusion of 'seeing' from 'hearing', the removal of the *inchoatio visionis* from the *fides,* and the relegation of the Christian to the old age which is passing away, while all elements of *doxa* and the *theologoumena* related to it are placed in the new age which is accessible only in hope.[59]

To this list, Balthasar added the increasing historicization of theology—in all its subdisciplines. He argued that in an effort to secure a place for itself in the academy, theology has adopted the procedures and tools of the historical sciences. By so doing, it has vastly increased its knowledge of the *historia* or *littera.* It has not, however, stimulated a corresponding enrichment of the understanding of revelation's content among the faithful. And, what is worse, theology has, by implication at least, unwittingly conceded to G. E. Lessing the definition of its central dogmas as accidental truths of history.[60]

Balthasar was persuaded that those theologies of the ancient and medieval worlds that remain positively influential did not sustain such losses because of two fundamental and interrelated affirmations. Since both lie at the heart of a theological aesthetics, it is to them that he wished to recall contemporary theology.

He argued, first, that the best theologies of the past share a doctrine of creation that attributes "creation's aesthetic values *eminenter* to the creating principle itself."[61] This is to be distinguished from the view of beauty as a transcendental attribute of Being itself. That was not abandoned, of course, but, remembering Thomas's formulation, the transcendentals were held to inhere in Being itself insofar as it was seen to refer to the ground of Being, namely, God. For Bonaventure, too,

> the world and man are intelligible in their being, and in their being what they are, only on the basis of the being, and the being of what he is, of God in himself—and indeed, on the basis of the being, and the being what it is, of the divine revelation in Jesus Christ. . . . [T]he created world expresses God because at the origin God expresses

himself and because, when he reveals himself outwardly, he wishes to make for himself a perfect self-expression in the God-man Jesus Christ: thus every worldly expression is a foreshadowing, an image, material directed to this end.[62]

Both theologians, Thomas and Bonaventure, reflect the pre-modern conviction that reality as such was conceived as one, true, good, and beautiful by participation in the transcendent fullness of God's unity, truth, goodness, and beauty. Creation, therefore, was seen as genuinely beautiful, but derivatively so. This was true even before the fall, though of course original sin was held to have distorted the capacity to perceive the likeness of the divine presence in the world. Accordingly, to appeal to another of Thomas's formulations, the sentence 'God is beautiful' means to the faithful, not just that God is the cause of beauty in creation, but that what one might call beauty "pre-exists in God in a higher way."[63] That is to say, from the perspective of how the word "beauty" is used to signify a creature (its *modum significandi*), it applies secondarily, i.e., metaphorically, to God and primarily to creatures. When considered from the perspective of what the word actually signifies (its *significatum*), however, "beauty" is literally true of God. Indeed, to the eyes of faith, beauty is more accurately applied to God than to anyone or anything else because its meaning preexists in God transcendentally and "flows" from God to creation. And this is despite the fact, on Thomas's view, that the faithful use the transcendentals literally *of* God without understanding or being able to specify the "higher way" in which they preexist *in* God.[64]

Second, Balthasar argued that those patristic and medieval theologies of continuing importance affirmed a doctrine of redemption that ascribes "to God's highest work the eminent sum of all of creation's values, particularly as concerns the eschatological form of God's work."[65] There is a lot woven into this claim that I will only begin to tease out. Three different threads should be marked. First, the incarnation of Jesus Christ, who for Balthasar is the crowning fulfillment of the covenant between heaven and earth (and therewith Israel), is not the "the limitation (πέρας) of an infinite non-form (ἄπειρον), but the appearance of an infinitely determined super-form [*Über-Gestalt*]."[66] As such, he is "the very apex and archetype of beauty in the world,"[67] "the form of all forms and the measure of all measures."[68] Second, God is the "primal Maker of Images,"[69] not just as creator, but also, and especially, as redeemer. In concert with the older tradition, Balthasar spoke of God as the divine artist who wills to fashion forms of life that bear God's image, thus perfecting the work begun in Eden.[70] From the perspective of theological aesthetics, the faithful, through their graced contemplation of the form of revelation as it culminates in Jesus Christ, are enabled to lead a life that is cruciform. Third, if creation is the preliminary stage in God's self-giving, the abasement of Christ's death and descent into hell together stand as the radically unpredictable prolepsis of its eschatological fulfillment. Although Paul and John, by speaking of the *kenosis* of Christ or the opprobrium the disciples will endure, may seem to be disparaging the aesthetic, they are in fact saying quite the opposite: God's beauty is beheld in all its fullness on earth in the cross of Christ (as it is bathed in the light of the resurrection). There, preeminently, do the faithful witness the plenitude of God's self-emptying love.[71]

Balthasar's concern to bolster contemporary doctrines of creation, therefore, rested on the supposition that if theology sacrifices creation's aesthetic values, then it will no longer be able to hear through it an echo of the divine Word. Thus to undercut the doctrine of creation, as Balthasar believed most modern theologians have done, inevitably creates havoc in the doctrine of Christ's person and work.[72] It violates a principle Balthasar regarded as basic to any theology attempting to discern God's ways with the world: the work of God as creator is not contradicted, but perfected, in the work of God as redeemer.[73] Whenever theology is able to recognize the created order as having a relative legitimacy and integrity of its own, without thereby being hermetically sealed off from its supernatural fulfillment, then theology has taken a crucial first step toward reacquiring the ability to see the beauty of nature, art, and persons as analogous to the glory of God's self-revelation in Jesus Christ.[74]

It was both on account of the losses to theology when it proceeds without the aid of categories drawn from aesthetics, and on the basis of what he took to be the pre-modern consensus view of the doctrines of creation and of Christ, that Balthasar sought to redirect theology back to the once grand avenue of theological aesthetics. No "great and historically fruitful theology," Balthasar asserted, has ever been done without it.[75]

That said, he was not blind to the dangers of this ancient approach. The warning signs must be posted along this road "in bold print."[76] After all, the Old Testament ban on images was never fully revoked by the New Testament, nor did the early Christian period evince anything like the interest in images characteristic of the Constantinian Church, let alone the baroque.[77] So it is that Balthasar, the twentieth-century champion of theological aesthetics, was able sympathetically to summarize the concerns of the eighth-century iconoclast Constantine V and to hear in them a permanently valid warning to the Church.[78] By the same token, although he usually read Luther very critically—as though Luther's work leads inexorably to that of Bultmann—he was able to grant the wisdom of Luther's protest against those schemes of thought that blunt the sharp edges of the Word of God.[79]

On Balthasar's view, what remains of lasting value for the Church in the warnings sounded by both thinkers is their insight that revelation must set the criteria and norms for its own interpretation. More specifically, Jesus Christ is his own measure. As the " 'Unique One' . . . no universal and external measure suffices to measure him; essentially, he can be measured only by himself."[80] Balthasar warned theology not to embrace this-worldly definitions of beauty, even those compatible with a transcendental aesthetics, and not to use them without modification to understand what Jesus said, did, and underwent. By subjecting him to a strictly philosophical criterion—be that borrowed from the realm of logic, ethics, or aesthetics—one has reversed the logic of the gospel. The Bible bears witness, so Balthasar said, to a divine summons to leave everything and follow Jesus Christ. Therefore Jesus Christ becomes the point of reference by which Christians are to evaluate themselves and their world. To subject Jesus Christ to their own standards would be to close their ears to the divine judgment of sin. To put the point another way, as Balthasar also did, gliding without pause or interruption from the realm of Being to that of the divine violates their ontological difference. The structures of creation must not be imposed upon the creator, "because the living God is neither an 'existent' (subordinate to Being) nor 'Being' itself, as it manifests and reveals itself essentially in everything that makes its appearance in form."[81]

Recognizing the importance of this, Balthasar was at pains to distinguish his own theological aesthetics from an aesthetic theology. He defined the former as "the attempt to do aesthetics at the level and with the methods of theology" and the latter as any overt or covert attempt to "betray . . . and sell . . . out theological substance to the current viewpoints of an inner-worldly theory of beauty."[82] Accordingly, in the *Theological Aesthetics* Balthasar ruled out any *mutually* critical correlation of philosophical and theological categories. That is to say, philosophical uses of a given concept should not provide the last court of appeal by which to judge the intelligibility and coherence of a given theological use of the same concept.[83] "Even if nature has its own regular laws and reason its own evidential character, still these laws and evidential characters can never appear as a final authority over against grace and faith. Their autonomies remain relative and stand as such always at the disposal of the final authority which belongs to the divine revelation, and to its plans and directives."[84]

Although Balthasar's claim in this regard has implications that extend well beyond hermeneutics, it is compatible with the ancient and medieval consensus regarding the priority of the literal sense. One of the interpretive consequences of abiding by the rule that Jesus Christ is unique and therefore his own measure is ensuring that interpretations of the relevant Gospel narratives do not replace Jesus, whom the stories are about, with a list of predicates understood independently of the (admittedly complex) ways Jesus enacts them. For instance, Balthasar would insist (once again with Frei, Lindbeck, and de Lubac) that we should not try to grasp what the Gospel narratives mean by Jesus' obedient suffering service solely on the basis of what obedience, suffering, and service mean in the extra-canonical literature. Investigating such information is not, of course, utterly immaterial. But Balthasar grew worried when these investigations served more to set the terms by which the biblical uses of a given set of concepts ought properly to be understood, than to illumine the ways in which they may have been taken up and transformed in the service of rendering the unique identity of the God-man, Jesus Christ.

It seems clear, then, that Balthasar was aware of the dangers (hermeneutical or otherwise) inherent in pursuing a theological aesthetics. He expressly forbade the univocal transposition of philosophical concepts into the sphere of theology.[85] To that extent he was chastened by the more typically Protestant reservations. He granted these critics, and Constantine V as well, that because of sin, everything human falls under the judgment of God.

But Balthasar did not let the matter rest there. He went on to ask whether God's judgment inevitably involves condemnation and rejection. Might it rather be a question of God's graciously "taking up and transfiguring what is human?"[86] This is what a strict theology of dialectic refuses to abide. But a dialectical theology poses certain risks of its own that cannot be minimized in the fervor to fight against a theology that, even if unwittingly, presupposes an identity between nature and grace. Does dialectics, if pursued with the sort of rigorous consistency required to banish aesthetics from theology, not entail a view of fallen creation as a virtually independent and thoroughly evil power standing over against God, which must be annihilated in order for God's purposes to be realized? If so, then a thoroughgoing dialectical theology would seem to hold, oddly enough, that humanity is destroyed in the very act in which it is supposed to be redeemed. But the greater irony of dialectics, Balthasar observed, consists in this: when taken as methodologically superior to all other approaches, it smuggles in the notion of identity that it purportedly opposes:

> At just the point where dialectics sees itself as the absolute [theological method], we once more encounter absolute identifications. . . . First, God is identified (in all his aseity!) with his revelation. Then the creature is defined as the pure opposite to God and thus is identified with nothingness. And finally, when the creature is retrieved by God through revelation and brought back to God through a dynamic movement (which is an absolute, because divine, movement), creation is then equated with God himself, at least in its origin and goal.[87]

In view of this, Balthasar maintained that dialectics could be of service to Christian theology only if its pretensions to methodological self-sufficiency are rejected. It must be seen as offering, not a fully adequate way of doing theology, but a necessary corrective to any unguarded enthusiasm for divine immanence. In this more moderate, circumscribed form, theological dialectics is invaluable.

Balthasar thus barred theology from two paths. Neither a theology of strict identity, nor one of rigorous dialectic is up to the task of interpreting revelation or its scriptural mediation. The only way forward, he maintained, is to develop a theology of analogy. But that is not, in fact, so very bold a move. The Fourth Lateran Council asserted the primacy of such an approach in 1215.[88] Nor, at least initially, is Balthasar's proposal entirely clear, since there are quite different forms of theology claiming to be analogical. I do not mean by that to allude to the famous dispute over whether theology should follow the lead of Erich Przywara and adopt an analogy of Being (*analogia entis*), or reject it, along with Karl Barth, in the name of an analogy of faith (*analogia fides*). Part of the genius of Balthasar's book on Barth's theology lies in its having shown conclusively that such a choice is false, at least if we take seriously what Barth and Przywara hoped to achieve and to protect.[89] Nevertheless, the terms used by Przywara and Barth, or at least their popular equivalents, have taken on lives independent of the works in which they were elaborated with periphrastic caution. One still hears calls for an ascending analogy that might be used if not to replace, then to link up with, a corresponding descending one.[90]

So if the choice were put before theology in such terms, what would Balthasar have it do? On this question he stood with both Przywara and Barth (despite their seeming differences), at least insofar as they believed that an analogy of faith at once embraces and makes room for a vigorous analogy of Being.[91] That is to say, he believed that a synthesis between, broadly speaking, the world and Christianity is possible, provided it is conducted "from the far side of the Cross and the descent into hell in the 'new earth,' the redeemed creation."[92] He therefore opposed an analogy from below that gets off the ground by appeal to a concept of nature stripped of any divine raiment.[93] However useful may be the " 'servant concept' "[94] *natura pura* to preserve the freedom of God's decision to enter into a covenant with humanity and to bestow the grace of redemption, it must not be abstracted from this rhetorical locus and pressed into the service of a natural theology that ignores the *de facto* intermingling of the orders of nature and grace.[95] The concept's

legitimacy is exclusively tied to its function as a protector of the gratuitousness of grace—and the tautology points to the extent to which the
word grace has been abused in the modern era.

A genuinely *theological* aesthetics will eschew both a procedure
assuming a fundamental identity between God and creation and one assuming a fundamental contradiction between the two. In place of both,
Balthasar favored an analogical method that respects the ever greater
dissimilarity (*in tanta similitudine major dissimilitudo*) between God
and creation enunciated at the Fourth Lateran Council. Or, as he put it:
"The more correctly the analogies are drawn, the more definitively will
the distances yawn."[96] He therefore developed analogies between the
perception of beautiful forms and the encounter with the forms of God's
self-revelation, while remaining keenly sensitive to the ways in which
the two are different.

Analogies between Revelation and Beauty

In what follows I examine the most important analogies for understanding Balthasar's hermeneutics that he developed between the structures
governing beautiful forms and our perception of them, on the one hand,
and God's self-revelation and the faithful's perception of it, on the other.
One corresponds to the objective dimension of perception; the other to
the subjective dimension. Either one, when taken in complete isolation
from the other, will distort our understanding of what is involved in perceiving creaturely or divine beauty. On Balthasar's view, therefore, both
aspects need to be given their due when pursuing a theological aesthetics. One must elucidate the conditions for the possibility of perception
in the object perceived as well as in the perceiving subject. Both are central to how aesthetics can nourish the Church's ability to interpret God's
self-revelation in nature and history. Naturally, since each condition has
a relative independence in relation to the other, they can be discussed
serially. That is the procedure I will follow, but as I do so, there is an
inevitable, if minimal, shading back and forth between them.

The foregoing discussion of (i) beauty as founded on the indissoluble
unity of form and splendor and (ii) the pre-modern view of the cosmos as
radiant with Being's light has anticipated some of what Balthasar had to

say about the objective side of this polarity. We saw that on his view, any created form bears witness to, or better, is suffused with, the light of Being. But to confine ourselves to this relatively high degree of abstraction obscures the fact that the different ways in which Balthasar used the terms form and splendor are distinguishable. He used the former to refer to inanimate objects, be they human artifacts or not, to plants, to animals, and to persons. Similarly, in his lexicon splendor had a range of meaning extending from the light of Being itself to the mysterious spontaneity of matter as it takes on particular forms; the life principle of plants; the soul of animals; and the free, rational spirit of persons.[97] So the bipolar schema of form and splendor to which Balthasar appealed when developing analogies between revelation and the beautiful is itself analogically structured. The analogical use of the terms form and splendor clears the ground for an additional, if qualitatively different, analogous application of this schema to God's self-revelation.[98]

Although Balthasar adverted with some frequency to the analogy of natural objects, like a flower, when speaking about the similarities (and, occasionally, the differences) between our perception of their beautiful, expressive forms and the perception of the form of God's self-revelation by the faithful, he gave much greater consideration to the analogy of a person's form of life. This was due, in part, to the greater freedom of spirit in humans and to what Balthasar sometimes called a deeper or richer interiority of persons as compared to other created forms.[99] It was also due, not surprisingly, to the fact that for Christians, God's self-revelation culminates in the God-man, Jesus Christ. In him, God uses created Being to fashion an image, an expression, an exegesis of Godself.[100] Believers and unbelievers alike are confronted with a concrete, historical subject who is a divine Person. Human relationships, therefore, provide the best analogy, the clearest natural echo of the faithful's relations with God in Jesus Christ.[101]

In ways analogous to those in which Being is said to be expressed in the abundance of created forms,[102] each of us, on Balthasar's view, expresses a mysterious and ultimately elusive inner depth in our words, gestures, and actions. Plainly, the means of such expressions are limited by the laws of biology, social conventions, our language's grammar, as well as by our family and psychological histories, the kind and extent of our education, and whatever talents we may possess. As embodied and historically situated, we are not utterly free in choosing the means of our self-expression. Still, the more powerful or creative our personality, the more we can express ourselves within the media governed by these constraints. A "unique and as such inaccessible interiority . . . reveals its richness precisely by the wealth and unpredictability of its manifestations."[103]

To those concerned to avoid the dualism of mind and body that has bedeviled theological anthropology at least since Origen's day, this notion of people having an "inaccessible interiority" has an unwelcome ring of familiarity about it.[104] It seems to suggest that our bodies are little more than instruments our spirits use as means of self-expression. My true self remains somehow behind or within my body, rather than being inextricably bound up with it. I am but a ghost lurking within a kind of biological machine, to borrow Gilbert Ryle's memorable phrase.[105] Since this view of persons can lead to enormous problems, both in ethics and hermeneutics, such a charge ought not be taken lightly. It would have greater merit, however, were it not for Balthasar's repeated insistence that form and splendor must not be severed in an attempt to find the real locus of beauty in disembodied light. While it is true both that form and splendor are not simply identified and that the two "mediate themselves to each other through each other in the primacy of the content,"[106] we cannot forget that this content is available to experience only in and through a particular form. Accordingly, Balthasar was able to contend without contradiction that through our bodies each of us is genuinely in the world, leaving our imprint indelibly upon it. He had no patience for the Cartesian problem of explaining how an originally private, spiritual, or rational being might manage to break out of itself in order to enter the "so-called 'exterior world.' "[107] It would appear, then, that advocates of other versions of this anthropology, which Hans Frei called self-differentiation in self-manifestation,[108] by trading on the modern view of form as divorced from its interior light, are less able than Balthasar was to respond to the charge of dualism.

Given Balthasar's view of the self, two things follow that bear on his hermeneutics. First, although a variety of identifiable factors may have shaped an individual's self-expression, the self-expression itself cannot be reduced to such factors. That is to say, the form of a person's life has an integrity, a wholeness about it that resists any corrosive or reductionist analysis. To know someone and to describe her unique identity, we must take the whole of her form of life seriously. In what particular and unique ways has she constituted herself in and through the laws governing such self-constitution? Balthasar made no attempt to skirt the issue of determinism; he took it as a guiding principle that a form is "determined by many antecedent factors." But at the same time, he insisted just as strongly on the principle that a form, when seen as it should be, is ultimately cohesive.[109] A person, like any other expressive form, is a "primal phenomenon. Whoever . . . cannot accept it, but rather seeks to 'break it up' critically into supposedly prior components . . . with the pretence of 'wanting to get behind it' genetically . . . falls into the void."[110] We do not come to know another person simply by virtue of establishing the genesis of her particular form of life. Nor can we deduce an individual's unique personality on the basis of such information. A person, just like any other expressive form, is more and other than the mere sum of her constituent elements.

The reason Balthasar gave for this assertion—which is, after all, something of a commonplace in aesthetics—concerns a feature characteristic of all human interaction: a paradoxical dynamic of revelation and concealment. This represents a second implication of his view of the self that bears on his hermeneutics. "All human relationships," he said, "are characterized by elements of self-revelation within a context of mystery."[111] This should come as no surprise, since all of us have been lied to. But Balthasar's point is not about the duplicity of the unscrupulous. Rather, he wished to indicate that in the closest of personal relations—his favorite example was the love of husband and wife—where the whole self is given to the beloved in and with one's utterances and actions, "what is manifested in a given manifestation is always, at the same time, the non-manifest."[112] This manifest non-manifest can be thought of as the mystery of Being itself. The question of why there is something rather than nothing impresses itself upon us in our encounters with any created form. More narrowly, with respect to persons, the depths that are simultaneously revealed and concealed may be thought of as the mystery of self-bestowing love. How can we squander ourselves in love for another without losing ourselves in the process?

However one might conceive of this paradoxical revealed concealment, it was Balthasar's contention that this dynamic interaction between form and splendor is what makes a form infinitely attractive, beguiling, enrapturing—in a word, beautiful. So beauty is always dynamic, but the dynamism presents itself to us solely within particular structures.[113] The locus of beauty lies in this tension between ground and manifestation. It lies, that is to say, both in the objective necessity with which a given form integrates and unites its parts, as well as in the proportion of the form as a whole to the depths of reality manifest in it. The interior rightness of a form *and* its participation in the depths of reality without thereby exhausting these depths give a form its integrity and desirability. This is what exalts a beautiful form beyond what satisfies utilitarian self-interest and makes it worthy of being loved for what it is in and of itself. It is also what lends a form its persuasiveness, its capacity to elicit assent, understanding, and ethical commitment. Balthasar spoke of this quality of expressive forms as constituting their objective evidence. It is the evidential power radiating from the form itself, showing itself, as it illuminates the perceiver, to be of the object itself and not a projection of the perceiving subject's own interiority.[114]

Having touched upon these two aspects of his anthropology, I can now indicate two of the *objective* analogies Balthasar wished to draw between beautiful forms and revelation. The first is his contention that the concrete forms of God's self-revelation in nature and history, culminating in Jesus Christ, have an irreproachable integrity that resists reductive analysis. These forms cannot, at least to the eyes of the believer, be explained by explaining them away.[115] With respect to the person and work of Jesus Christ, this meant, for Balthasar, that he cannot be adequately understood simply on the basis of a thoroughgoing analysis of the theological, philosophical, sociological, economic, and political forces that conditioned first-century Palestine. Such inquiry ought not to be irrelevant to one who wants to understand him,[116] but, in and of itself, it does not yield an individuating identity description. According to Balthasar, these methods might tell us that Jesus is best understood as a free-spirited wandering cynic,[117] or a Jewish peasant advocating political and economic egalitarianism,[118] or a charismatic sage,[119] or a prophet possessed of an apocalyptic eschatology,[120] but they do not tell us who he is in his irreducible uniqueness. That requires being able to see the unique integrity of his form of life: what he said, did, and underwent as portrayed, from various perspectives, in the New Testament.[121]

There is an obvious hermeneutical correlate to this claim about the form of Jesus Christ. Balthasar contended that the scriptural mediation of the Christ-form (*Christusgestalt*) has an analogous integrity that likewise resists all attempts to dissolve it into its literary components (be they understood as authorial strands, redactional layers, literary genres, the remains of earlier oral traditions, or linguistic structures). Naturally, Balthasar recognized that there is a polyphony of theological voices and perspectives in the Bible. But he maintained that the various biblical authors were each ringing changes on a common christological theme. This was especially clear to him in the New Testament, which, he believed, evidenced no fundamental disagreements among its authors:

> Each Gospel points to the others. Paul presupposes them, and the Acts of the Apostles is their continuation. When Ephesians goes further than Colossians it is simply by developing elements already present in germ, just as Colossians presupposes the letters to the Romans, Galatians and Corinthians. Paul's polemic against the (misused) Law is only an echo of Jesus' rebuking the Pharisees; but in calling the Law holy and good in itself he is continuing the Sermon on the Mount. And James is contradicting neither of them when—thinking in a different conceptual framework—he calls for a faith which gives evidence in works.[122]

Balthasar's point can easily be misunderstood. When speaking of the lack of basic disagreement among the authors, he did not mean to obscure the presence of real tensions within the New Testament (to say nothing of the Old or the relations between the two). But he deemed these tensions appropriate in light of the mysterious fullness of the figure whose identity the authors sought to render. In contrast, "those who try to smooth [such tensions] away—consider the idyllic Jesus of Renan or the pallid Jesus of Bultmann—render the figure unworthy of belief."[123]

Balthasar sometimes took this notion of the fundamental harmony and mutual interdependence of the New Testament (indeed, biblical) theologies to extremes. For example, appealing to the image of God as divine artist, Balthasar said: "The contour-lines [of the form of salvation history] have been drawn with such mastery that not the smallest detail can be altered. The weights have been poised in such a way that their balance extends to infinity, and they resist any displacement. God's art in the midst of history is irreproachable, and any criticism of his masterpiece immediately rebounds on the fault-finder."[124] Or again: "at no moment does contemplation detect a mistake in the construction and the proportions of the image, . . . if such a mistake is suspected, it will at once be shown to have been because of a defect in one's own vision."[125] Because Balthasar has been taken to task for such remarks,[126] I am inclined to make two brief observations.

First, since these are plainly polemical remarks, we ought to remember against what and whom Balthasar was fighting. His concern was to preserve the integrity of the biblical mediation of what he (and most Christians, traditionally) regarded as essential features of the form of salvation history. With respect to Jesus Christ, that means not severing the connection between the Jesus of history and the Christ of faith, or excising the Pauline *pro nobis* from an account of the crucifixion and resurrection, or leaving out the Spirit who interprets Jesus Christ by identifying the Father who sent him. It is not heavy-handed for a believer to insist that the elimination of any of these dimensions of the form of Christ (*Christusgestalt*) will render it incomprehensible.[127]

Second, in light of this, a literal interpretation of these passages does Balthasar an injustice. Since he never wished to advance a view of scripture as inerrant in every detail,[128] it seems wiser to suppose that from time to time his rhetoric simply outran his better judgment. Otherwise, there is a real danger of missing what is hermeneutically significant about such remarks. Balthasar insisted that the final or received form of the biblical text was authoritative. Although he went on to articulate this conviction with greater clarity in the second volume of *Theo-Drama*[129] than he had done in the *Theological Aesthetics*, Balthasar steadfastly maintained in the earlier work that it is wrong to countenance methods of interpretation founded on the supposition that a purportedly reconstructed *Urtext* offered a more faithful or theologically weighty interpretation of the gospel:[130] "Only the final result of the historical developments which lie behind a text—a history never to be adequately reconstructed—may be said to be inspired, not the bits and scraps which philological analysis thinks it can tear loose from the finished totality."[131] Setting aside for the moment the issue of inspiration, note that it is the stress on wholeness, once again, that sets the tone for his view of proper scriptural interpretation.

At that level of abstraction—prescinding from the questions of what exactly this emphasis on wholeness entails and of how consistently he practiced what he preached, topics addressed in the following and subsequent chapters—Balthasar's proposal is compatible with the descriptions of pre-modern approaches to the Bible provided by Hans Frei, George Lindbeck, and Henri de Lubac. As we saw in the introduction, the second characteristic of pre-modern interpretive practices they identified is that the Bible was typically construed as a christologically focused account of the creative and redemptive dealings of the triune God with God's people and the cosmos. The narrative portions of the Bible, both the Old and the New Testaments, provided the framework within which its non-narrative elements were to be properly understood. The Bible thus appeared to have the wholeness and integrity of an extraordinarily complex story whose various parts were used to interpret one another. By insisting that exegetes take the wholeness of the biblical mediation of God's self-revelation seriously, Balthasar can be read as having endorsed this ancient and medieval convention. True, his worries about the dangers of reductive analyses and his convictions about the fundamental harmony of the various biblical theologies seem exaggerated. But the basic point, which I will examine in more detail later, reflects a shared belief that biblical interpretation falters, when in an eagerness to discern the parts, it fails to consider the whole.

A second objective analogy between revelation and beauty suggests itself, which, like the first, has a more narrowly hermeneutical correlate. Earlier I mentioned Balthasar's contention that any expressive form is a simultaneous revelation and concealment of the depths of reality. The same, he said, holds true for the form of Jesus Christ. One of the ways he illustrated this claim was by exegeting the Markan messianic secret in terms of John's vision of Jesus Christ as the "working through in suffering of the contradiction of an infinite revealing love that immerses itself in a world of sin."[132] What is at issue, at least in part, is Luther's interpretation (and that of most Protestants) of the divine hiddenness in Jesus Christ. It seems only natural for Christians to suppose that in the crucifixion, the Word of God is rendered mute; it might well involve a wondrous exchange, or a rendering of satisfaction, or a paying of ransom, or a vicarious bearing of judgment against sin, but not, strictly speaking, with a revelation of divine glory. Setting aside the question of Balthasar's view of the atonement, it is important to note his insistence that Jesus Christ remains the supreme self-revelation of the triune God, up to and including "the very shattering of the image of eternal life on the Cross."[133] This is in keeping with the absolute centrality of the doctrine of revelation in Balthasar's *Theological Aesthetics*. To deny that the crucifixion is revelatory of God's glory would be, among other things, to fall victim to the dualism of form and splendor. It would be to see Jesus Christ as revealing the triune divine life alongside his humanity, rather than within it. And that would be both to flirt with Nestorianism and to risk implying that God is unable, or unwilling, to use the creation fashioned in the divine image as a form within which to manifest God's eternal glory.

Balthasar maintained, then, that divine self-revelation and conceal-ment must not be understood as utterly incompatible with each other. And neither should this dialectic be restricted to Jesus Christ's death on the cross. The faithful can already perceive it at work in the incarna-tion. In it is seen

> the most extreme manifestness within the deepest concealment. It is manifestness because here God is explained to man by no means other than himself—not primarily through words and instruction, but by his own Being and life. . . . But it is concealment because the translation of God's absolutely unique, absolute, and infinite Being into the ever more dissimilar, almost arbitrary and hopelessly rela-tivised reality of one individual man in the crowd from the outset appears to be an undertaking condemned to failure.[134]

That said, the paradox becomes most acute in the crucifixion; here, Balthasar cautioned, the temptation to resort to a negative theology by developing the notion of a completely abstract, formless God becomes nearly irresistible. But then the beautiful form of revelation in salvation history is destroyed and faith is turned into a naked, visionless grasping in the dark for what is absurd. The task of theology, and of all Chris-tians, according to Balthasar, is rather to follow the evangelist John in seeing the very formlessness of Jesus Christ on the cross as itself "a mode of his glory because a mode of his 'love to the end', to discover in his deformity the mystery of his super-form."[135] So the horror and scandal of the cross (together with the descent into hell) is luminous, on Balthasar's view, with the glory of God. Here, with supreme clarity, God reveals Godself as utterly self-sacrificing and boundless love and, therefore, as essentially incomprehensible.[136]

Before turning to the specifically hermeneutical correlate of this assertion, we need to remember Balthasar's conviction that just as with beautiful forms, the conditions for the possibility of perceiving the glory of God on the cross cannot be reduced to such as lie, even by grace, within the believing subject. The Christ-form's objective evidence of belief, the radiance of the triune life from within this form and the balance of its proportions, bears witness to believers of its credibility. As Balthasar said so often, these two features of the beauty of the Christ-form, that is, the uniqueness of the divine light and the unity of the form as reflected in the harmony with which the light integrates the form's diverse elements, belong indivisibly together.[137] But since I have just touched upon the luminance of the Christ-form, a word is in order about Balthasar's understanding of its internal harmony. I alluded to this harmony earlier when discussing his penchant for describing the form of revelation and its scriptural witness as perfect in every detail. As I said, it seems that one ought to be able to quibble with the extent of the harmony without undermining Balthasar's thesis. In any event, it is safe to say that he saw proportion, balance, and equilibrium nearly everywhere he looked in the Bible, though especially in the form of Christ:

> For instance: the relationship, in Jesus, between him and the Father; the distance of the man, the nearness and unity of the Son; the relationship between lord and servant, exaltation and humiliation: of exaltation in humiliation and humility in exaltation; the ever-new relationship between promise and fulfilment and, through it, of judgment and grace, rejection and election; the relationship between master and disciple, which is one of total redemptive representation by Christ through grace, and yet, also one of co-presence and of being taken into account with Christ in the redemption through grace.[138]

Balthasar maintained that each of these relationships, though often seeming *prima facie* irreconcilable, are demonstrably and objectively harmonized to the eyes of faith.

The hermeneutical correlate of Balthasar's assertion about the uniqueness and unity of the form of Christ when seen as the paradoxical revealed concealment of the incomprehensible Trinity can be stated simply. Just as there is a unique harmony among the assorted relationships constitutive of the form of Christ, there obtains a unique proportion between his form (and the form of salvation history, generally) and its scriptural mediation.[139] For this "true proportion [has been] instituted by God [*gottgesetzte Proportion*]" in order that the faithful may behold, through the medium of scripture, the forms of God's self-revelation.[140] To be more specific, the Holy Spirit guarantees this proportion through the guidance given the biblical authors "so that the likeness (*Nachbild*) which they drew up of the original image (*Ur-bild*) should correspond to the vision which God's Holy Spirit himself possesses of God's self-representation in the flesh."[141]

Two distinct hermeneutical implications of this view of inspiration should be mentioned. First, the proper interpretation of the biblical texts entails, among other things, attending both to the intention of the human authors and to the intention of the Holy Spirit under whose guidance they worked. Although Balthasar often spoke as though the two intentions were identical, on occasion he acknowledged that the meaning of a given biblical verse exceeds the conscious intent of its human author or redactor.[142] In order, therefore, to understand what, as he put it, is "*really* said, really presented to us, really meant" in the Bible, the interpreter has to discern what both its human and divine authors intended to say.[143]

Second, natural reason unaided by grace is blind to the proportion between the form of revelation and its biblical mediation because to see the validity of the scriptural reproduction of the form of God's self-revelation in history is already to see the *spiritus* in the *littera*: "How could we participate in this spiritual meaning other than by dying and rising along with Christ?"[144] So to a straightforward literary analysis, the Bible is a hodgepodge of documents, many of which are written in an almost embarrassingly crude style. It exhibits little of the integrity and none of the revelatory light Balthasar ascribed to it. Balthasar recognized this and appeared almost to welcome it. On this point he broke sharply with the, as it turned out, naïve hope of the postwar biblical theology movement that the historical-critical method would simply confirm faith's claims about salvation history. In Balthasar's hands, the lowliness of the scriptural form became evidence that it participates in the same dialectic of revelation and concealment as does Jesus Christ: "Scripture belongs to the Christ-form itself and is an expression of Christ's fulness and glory, even if, at the same time (because of the letter's 'servant-form', so stressed by Hamann) Scripture attests to and actually shows Christ's own humiliated form through *its* form of humiliation."[145]

Balthasar developed other analogies between revelation and beauty, but the foregoing are the two most important for understanding his hermeneutics. In the nature of the case, though, analogies are not drawn between identical phenomena. Although discussing the paradoxical beauty of Jesus Christ's crucifixion gave us a hint of some of the distinctions Balthasar wished to draw between a this-worldly aesthetics and an aesthetics that draws its proportions and measures from God's self-revelation, the most basic difference (considered from the perspective of the objective dimension of perception) between God's glory and earthly beauty still needs examination. This difference is fundamental for Balthasar, because all the other differences he stressed follow from it.

Recall that Balthasar believed persons manifest themselves in their words, gestures, and deeds. Because of the dialectic of revelation and concealment, a person is said to be fully present in such self-manifestations, but not exhaustively so. There remains a mysterious freedom or depth about persons that prevents us, or should prevent us, claiming to know another through and through. In ways analogous to all creaturely forms, a person's self-manifestation may thus be understood in terms of the categories of ground and appearance. As we have seen, Balthasar contended that there are certain similarities between the way this dynamic works itself out in the creaturely and divine spheres. Nevertheless, because Jesus Christ is the revelation of the depths of God's triune essence, the categories of ground and appearance cannot do full justice to what is presented to faith in him. The categories of a theological aesthetics are thus thoroughly trinitarian. To paraphrase Balthasar fairly closely, in the glorious form of Jesus Christ, faith sees one who sends and one who is sent, one who remains hidden and one who is fully disclosed, one who remains exalted and one who empties himself.[146] This duality, in itself, does not distinguish the form of Jesus Christ from creaturely forms; what sets it apart is the fact that this duality is seen by faith to be united by a third, personal reality within the divine nature.

> *This* is where God is an absolute mystery for us, precisely in his revelation. The absolute mystery does not lie in the fact that God becomes manifest to us in a manner analogous to the way worldly beings become manifest to us. Nor does it lie in the fact that he becomes manifest to us while retaining his freedom: ordinary persons can do this by 'bearing witness' to themselves, that is, by requiring trust and 'faith' from the other person. It lies in the fact that his self-revelation of Being and of nature presents itself as a relationship which, in itself, is (tri-)personal. This is what is absolutely incomprehensible to us, that in God relation-to-self and relation-to-other, eternal repose-in-self and eternal striving and loving can be identical.[147]

For Balthasar, therefore, this duality between Father and Son made manifest in and through the glorious form of Jesus Christ is neither resolved monistically, nor elevated into a principle of divine dualism. Instead, owing to the unity of nature and distinction of persons within the Trinity, it is seen as itself making manifest the love uniting the two, namely, the Holy Spirit.

The earlier discussion of beautiful forms as indissolubly united with Being's radiance anticipated some of what Balthasar wished to say about analogies within the objective dimension of the act of perception. The same can be said as we turn to examine perception's subjective dimension.

While recognizing the fact that there are irreducible differences among the various ways members of ancient and medieval cultures experienced themselves and their world, Balthasar maintained that wonderment in the face of Being's astounding variety was much more prevalent then than it is today. In addition to being the basic disposition requisite for philosophical reflection—for unless we are awestruck by the fact that there is something rather than nothing, we will never pursue the question why that is so—wonderment is the cast of mind without which beautiful forms cannot be seen for what they truly are. As already noted, Balthasar claimed that to see such forms we must let them disclose themselves in the fashion that befits them. The perceiving subject cannot conjure up the beautiful, the way Faust called forth Mephistopheles from that mysterious poodle. Beauty bestows itself graciously, suggesting to Balthasar that here the divine and natural χάρις may have a point of contact. At the risk of a certain, though now familiar, anthropomorphism, Balthasar said that beauty urges us to give up our desire to domesticate and master it. It asks us simply to enjoy it for what it is, rather than for what benefits it might provide. Beauty wants to be perceived as precious and endlessly fascinating, as worthy of love for its own sake.[148]

Corresponding to beauty's gracious self-bestowal is, on the subjective side, an analogous act of self-surrender on the part of the one who perceives it. Beauty's own disinterest (*Interesselosigkeit*), as Balthasar sometimes called it,[149] is met with an analogous subjective disinterest. The perception of beauty, he argued, entails an act of self-surrender. It is an act of steadfast contemplation that involves allowing ourselves to be enthralled by beautiful forms, to be enraptured by them and brought into their orbit. Who has not experienced this when transfixed by a setting sun, or held fast by the portrait of a noble old face? And who has not, almost against themselves, played the fool for beauty's sake? An avid musician blessed with perfect pitch, Balthasar often used musical metaphors to describe this mesmerizing effect of the beautiful: "when the interior space of a beautiful musical composition or painting opens itself to us and captivates us . . . the whole person . . . enters into a state of vibration and becomes responsive space, the 'sounding box' of the event of beauty occurring within him."[150] Although initially the beautiful may engage just one or two senses, soon the entire person resonates to its rhythms. In its presence, Balthasar maintained, we cannot be mere spectators; the disinterest required by beauty is of a wholly different sort. Rather than squeeze a beautiful form to fit our notions of beauty's proper limits and measures, Balthasar would have us allow the beautiful form to teach us how it should be perceived. This is perhaps most obviously the case in our interactions with other people. Most affirm that we ought not to allow our preconceptions to determine our judgments about another person, at least not if we hope to leave him room to be the unique and irreplaceable individual he is: "No I has the possibility or the right to master intellectually the Thou who encounters him in his own freedom, nor can he understand or deduce his attitude prior to their meeting. For love granted to me can only be 'understood' as a miracle; I can never account for it, either empirically or transcendentally—not even from knowledge of our common human 'nature'."[151]

None of this is to suggest that Balthasar believed the perception of beauty means simply to bask in Being's light without using all of our faculties to perceive what that light discloses. Balthasar was no naïve realist.[152] He understood that the subjective conditions for the perception of beauty help to shape what that perception involves. Although he did not, properly speaking, develop a transcendental deduction of such, he devoted nearly half of the first volume of the *Theological Aesthetics* to a thorough analysis of what the subject brings to the act of perception, both of beautiful forms and God's glory. He was quite critical, then, of a view of the experience of beauty that reduces it to an emotional effervescence or an enthusiasm without conceptual content:

> The young especially . . . find themselves in or transport themselves to a state of mind, an interior 'vibration', which transfigures nature, art, friendship and love in their sight, and which communicates the experience of the beautiful like a drug whose effect, as experience shows, quickly disappears. People who cling to this view of the subjective nature of taste's judgment have remained immature adolescents. By developing his soul according to the images of the objectively beautiful, the maturing person gradually learns to acquire the art of discrimination, that is, the art of perceiving what is beautiful in itself. In the process of their development, the subjective elements of perception (which doubtless, include state of mind and fantasy) more and more pass into the service of objective perception. Even in the case of a masterpiece, the mature observer of art can without difficulty give an objective and largely conceptual basis for his judgment.[153]

Ironically, the mature appreciation of beauty, to use his distinction, is actually more "childlike" than the immature. It is more trusting and less calculated. It wants primarily to enjoy the beautiful, to rest within its embrace. And it does so by tailoring its reflection to beauty's unique measurements. To discern the particular form, harmony, and radiance of beauty entails, for Balthasar, letting such objective structures govern reflection. It is, and will remain, genuinely objective reflection, provided it is carried on in conformity to the concrete, determinate content of the beautiful object.

It is clear that there are affinities between Balthasar's description of wonderment as entailing a disinterested act of self-surrender to beautiful forms in order to ensure an objective perception of such and the faithful's perception of God's self-revelation. But there are also significant differences. I will explore both in what follows, although I reserve my treatment of the hermeneutical correlates of the subjective analogies until I discuss the differences Balthasar saw between perceiving beauty and revelation.

Let me begin with a quotation that summarizes succinctly what Balthasar understood to be suggestive of faith in the perception of beautiful forms:

> The quality of 'being-in-itself' which belongs to the beautiful, the demand the beautiful itself makes to be allowed to be what it is, the demand, therefore, that we renounce our attempts to control and manipulate it, in order truly to be able to be happy by enjoying it: all of this is, in the natural realm, the foundation and foreshadowing of what in the realm of revelation and grace will be the attitude of faith.[154]

Three themes should be noted. The first is Balthasar's conviction that the faithful's perception of the form of revelation is correlative to, and conditioned by, the object perceived. Just as with the perception of created forms, primacy is given to the objective evidence. One must surrender oneself both to beauty and to God in order to perceive their respective luminous forms. Second, faith is somehow akin to vision. Although it is to be distinguished in terms of clarity (as Paul asserted) from the vision granted the *beati*, faith is not mere blind trust. Whatever the legitimate fiduciary dimension of faith may be, the faithful contemplation of the form of revelation involves actually *seeing* its proportions and radiance, on analogy to the way the perception of created forms does.[155] Third, perceiving the form of revelation requires that the faithful be drawn up into the divine life and allowed to enjoy its triune movements. This calls to mind the way Balthasar conceived of one's falling under the spell and entering happily into the interior space of beauty.[156]

When speaking of the relationship between faith and aesthetic contemplation, Balthasar was always careful to say that they stand at qualitatively different levels. It is not as though, he once observed, "one could, by means of rational inquiry and argument, recognize [Jesus] to be a (perfect? religious? inspired?) man and then, following the pointers provided by this rational knowledge, move to the conclusion that he is God's Son and himself God."[157] The contemplation of created forms and of those of revelation are not the same thing; one cannot simply identify the two and be done with the matter. Balthasar was nevertheless willing to use the same word, contemplation (θεωρία), to describe both phenomena, so long as it was clear that when he used it theologically, he did so bearing in mind the following three conditions: "incorporation into Christ through faith and sacraments; participation in the Holy Spirit, who introduces us to the fulness of truth; revelatory will of the heavenly Father, who through Word and Spirit already now, within the veil of faith, wants to grant us a share in his own triune truth."[158] These trinitarian conditions structure the remarks that follow.

First, with respect to the revelatory will of the Father, Balthasar held that the ever incomprehensible God nevertheless wants to be known and glorified in and through God's creation. It is therefore strictly on the basis of God's condescension that believers can apprehend (as distinct from comprehend) God's transcendence.[159] To that end, God employs what Balthasar called the "double vessel" of beautiful forms and interpersonal relations.[160] While the former provides an analogy for the perception of God's self-revelation, the latter points to the sheer graciousness of God's self-emptying love in Christ.[161] Putting to one side the question whether it is appropriate to regard the two as complementary instances of a self-squandering love analogous to God's own *kenosis* in Jesus Christ,[162] we can address Balthasar's conviction that because God has poured Godself into natural forms, above all the form of an individual human, the proper perception of such forms requires that believers resist the temptation to see such forms as a function of the fall, as something to be brushed aside by the spiritually discerning.

Based on the foregoing discussion of Balthasar's understanding of the doctrines of creation and redemption, it is now easier to understand why Balthasar insisted so passionately that theology, when properly practiced, does not just begin its reflection with historical forms, it also dwells and ought to thrive in them. But the anti-corporeal bias of Platonic aesthetics regularly reasserts itself and, appealing to the Pauline distinction between the spirit and the flesh, advances the thesis that theology ought to abstract from the scriptural mediation of revelation's historical forms in order to unveil the truths there shrouded. Doing so, however, ignores the fact that the "archetypal God-experience of the Bible is more than a material metaphor for the higher experience of God which pertains to 'pure faith', where 'pure' connotes 'purified from the sensory'."[163] The "primal lie" in both theology and spirituality, according to Balthasar, is the identification, witting or not, between the biblical view of flesh and the Platonic one of body.[164] To state the hermeneutical implications of this explicitly: Balthasar held that since God has revealed Godself in Jesus Christ as 'formed' trinitarianly, Christianity must not allow the apophatic approach to biblical interpretation to cut itself free from its moorings in the cataphatic tradition.[165] Doing so, he contended, offends both against the indissoluble relation of form and splendor in God's self-revelation and against the gratuitousness of God's love in that act of self-revelation.

A second condition Balthasar placed on the theological appropriation of the term contemplation concerns the faithful's incorporation into the body of Christ. This means that the faithful's contemplation of scripture partakes in the Church's vision of the revealed form of God. They do not stand before this form as isolated individuals, but as members of Christ's body sustained by his grace. Their perception of this form is fundamentally shaped by the history of the Church's own perception of it. It is likewise nurtured by the liturgical life of the Church, especially the sacraments. Here, Balthasar declared, the faithful are not only reminded of the importance of the corporeal, reminded of the need, that is, to rest within the sensual rather than somehow to transcend it, but they also participate in the death and resurrection of Jesus Christ. They are conformed to Christ, or as Balthasar often put it, Christ (through the ministrations of his Spirit) in-forms the believers by shaping them in his image.[166] These two aspects of being incorporated into Christ's body, the noetic and the existential, finally converge for Balthasar. He saw this expressed most clearly by Paul, in 2 Cor 3.18: "For Paul, this contemplation of the image of Christ is both theoretical and practical: it is the impressing of the form upon the memory and the understanding (γνῶσις) of the believers, so that it will determine all the more deeply their life, which must come to bear the form of Christ."[167] Balthasar held that since the Christian life ought to be cruciform, the contemplation that nourishes it ought to be too. Again, to state the hermeneutical implication of this explicitly: Balthasar believed that a cruciform contemplation is both enabled and sustained by a prolonged engagement with the Church's theological traditions and an active participation in its liturgical life. It is on the basis of such an understanding of what contemplation involves that Balthasar bemoaned the chasm that has separated theology and spirituality since the dawn of the modern era. How, he wanted to know, can a biblical interpretation that aims to be of service to the Church not be steeped in the mystery of love between the Church and her bridegroom?

Before turning to the third condition that Balthasar thought should govern the theological use of the term contemplation, let me indicate briefly that here, once again, Balthasar's convictions resemble those characteristic of the pre-modern approaches to scripture outlined in the introduction. One of the aspects of those approaches is the belief that proper interpretation of the Bible entailed using it, through the power of the Holy Spirit, for practical and intellectual religious instruction within an ecclesial setting. This is Balthasar's point in urging biblical exegetes to immerse themselves in the theological traditions of the Church and partake in its liturgies. The Bible, he believed, ought to shape one's sense of self and community. It ought to provide the conceptual tools and behavioral models with which the faithful seek to construct, and live within, a meaningful world. Otherwise it is just a more or less interesting collection of documents from the ancient Near East. According to Hans Frei, George Lindbeck, and Henri de Lubac's analyses of pre-modern hermeneutics, the primary interpretive device by which this fashioning of personal and communal identities was effected is some form of typology.[168] The subsequent chapters will explore the ways in which Balthasar made use of this ancient practice. Here I simply wish to point out this fourth example of the ways in which Balthasar's hermeneutical convictions resemble those of most pre-modern exegetes.

Finally, Balthasar believed that theologians could appropriate the term contemplation provided they remember that it is the role of the Holy Spirit to introduce the faithful into the fullness of truth. To stress one central feature of this, he contended that the interpreter of scripture must "enjoy an inspiration in accordance with the inspiration of his subject."[169] Since the scriptures were written under the guidance of the Holy Spirit, so, too, must their interpretation be so guided. Balthasar believed that all texts, or at least those that can credibly lay claim to being genuinely beautiful as he understood the term, can be said to be the result of inspiration. And the interpretation of such texts can also plausibly be described as inspired. But Balthasar maintained that the perception of the form of Jesus Christ is as unique as the form itself.[170] The hermeneutical correlate of this assertion is plain: interpreting the scriptural mediation of this form is also a unique undertaking. It is not necessary to rehearse Balthasar's understanding of the need to incorporate the analogy of Being into an analogy of faith in order to grasp his idea that the differences between the interpretation of scripture (when taken as such) and that of other literature are vastly greater than the similarities that do in fact exist. When he described biblical inspiration as being "integrated into the general forms of inspiration,"[171] he was not thereby endorsing the view that reading the Bible as authoritative for Christian life and thought is a species of a more general phenomena of hermeneutics patient of a philosophical description and analysis. Though there are analogies between both the production and interpretation of the Bible and other texts, they are not, according to Balthasar, finally determinative of the way the Holy Spirit uses scripture to achieve God's ends. Accordingly, theologians ought to use the conceptual tools of philosophical hermeneutics with the same caution and reserve characteristic of an appropriate borrowing from the science of aesthetics.

CONCLUSION

The foregoing has summarized in three steps Balthasar's diffuse and sprawling argument in favor of the use in theology, with certain qualifications, of the conceptual tools that a science of aesthetics provides. First, he contended that theology has suffered catastrophic losses as a result of it accepting, wittingly or not, modernity's aestheticization of the beautiful. Of paramount concern to him was the resulting habit of misreading scripture either as a sign pointing beyond itself to revealed truths, or as a more or less transparent symbol of what fulfills our deepest personal or social needs. Second, to recoup these losses Balthasar both pointed out their consequences and argued in favor of contemporary theologians adopting two ancient and medieval convictions: (i) beauty is an indissoluble unity of Being's light radiating from within created forms and, as such, must be seen in its perichoretic relation to the other transcendental determinations of theophanic Being; and (ii) creation's values are not destroyed, but surpassingly fulfilled, in the redemption wrought in the incarnation, death, and resurrection of Jesus Christ. Finally, he set forth a series of analogies between the perception of creation's beauty and of God's glorious self-revelation. For clarity's sake, I have analyzed the most significant of these analogies in terms of their objective and subjective dimensions and indicated their principal hermeneutical correlates.

The foregoing has also indicated four instances in which Balthasar's diagnosis of what ails modern theology and his proposed remedy to develop a theological aesthetics are compatible with Hans Frei, George Lindbeck, and Henri de Lubac's descriptions of pre-modern approaches to the Bible. When discussing two modern misreadings of scripture, when endorsing the qualified use of dialectics in theology, when urging biblical interpreters to take the wholeness of the Bible seriously, and when insisting that they participate in the life of the Church, Balthasar's points could plausibly be rephrased in terms resembling their own.

All agree on the importance for Christian theologians of resisting the Gnostic temptation to regard the scriptural mediation of God's self-revelation as an illustrative story or illuminating symbol that the spiritually discerning should dispense with once they have grasped its point. Christian theology cannot, without ignoring the hermeneutical implications of the incarnation, belittle the scriptural mediation of God's self-revelation by treating it as a mere husk surrounding a purely spiritual kernel. According to Balthasar, Frei, Lindbeck, and de Lubac, most pre-modern exegetes did not make this mistake.

They also agree on the importance for Christian theologians of allowing the meanings of the Bible's various concepts to be governed by the uses to which the biblical authors put them. In particular this means, to use Balthasar's terms, letting Christ be his own unique measure. Or, to use language closer to Frei's and Lindbeck's, it means letting the agent of a given biblical narrative control the meanings of the predicates ascribed to him or her, rather than letting the predicates define the identity of the agent. For his part, de Lubac enunciated this conviction in terms of the distinction he drew between "Hellenistic" and "Christian" allegory. As I demonstrated in the introduction, his chief complaint about post-Reformation criticisms of allegorical interpretation concerns their nearly universal failure to distinguish the way Paul used the term allegory and its synonyms from the way pagan and Jewish Platonists generally did. Christ's absolute uniqueness compelled Paul to transform an interpretive technique that was widespread among his contemporaries. With only relatively rare exceptions, most ancient and medieval Christian exegetes followed this Pauline pattern as they applied the method to other texts. So despite these differences in terminology, Balthasar, Frei, Lindbeck, and de Lubac are agreed that this hermeneutical convention was much more widely observed prior to the dawn of modernity than it is today.

These two areas of compatibility between Balthasar's hermeneutics and that of the pre-modern era both follow from endorsing the priority of the literal sense of scripture. A third area concerns the importance for Balthasar and the pre-moderns (for whom, again, Frei, Lindbeck, and de Lubac can be spokespersons) of construing the Bible as possessing a wholeness and integrity. Although Balthasar's protests against reductive analyses and his affirmations of the fundamental harmony of the Bible may be exaggerated, they rest on the belief that ecclesially apt interpretation requires that the Bible's various parts be seen in their complex relations to the whole. I will examine in the next and subsequent chapters the specific implications of this belief. For now we need only note that Balthasar shared with most pre-modern interpreters a view of the Bible as a canonically unified, christologically focused whole that mediates the natural and historical forms of God's self-revelation.

The fourth area of compatibility between Balthasar's hermeneutics and that of most pre-moderns has to do with the pre-modern conviction regarding the importance of interpreting the Bible within an ecclesial setting. Recall that Balthasar's criticisms of the mutually debilitating separation of theology and spirituality were prompted in large measure by his desire to counteract the resulting attenuation of theology's ability to be of service to those in the pews. He believed, as I indicated in my analysis of the subjective analogies between beauty and revelation, that theologians will properly exercise their obligation to interpret the Bible as authoritative for the Church's life and thought only as and when they allow themselves to be shaped noetically and existentially by immersing themselves in the traditions and liturgy of the Church.

2

THEOLOGICAL HERMENEUTICS

This chapter elaborates the hermeneutical implications of Hans Urs von Balthasar's theological aesthetics that have been adumbrated in the previous chapter. I begin by examining Balthasar's repeated insistence that biblical interpreters take seriously the wholeness of the forms of God's self-revelation. This will involve both an analysis of Balthasar's polemics against historical criticism and the beginnings of my assessment of the consistency with which he took his own advice when exegeting the Bible. I then examine the consequences of his conviction that biblical interpretation entails discerning the intent of the Bible's divine and human authors. Finally, I analyze his assertion that the proper interpretation of biblical texts inevitably involves an ecclesial mediation. Following a pattern established in the first chapter, I draw attention along the way to those places where Balthasar's views and uses of scripture reflect convictions, shared with the classic hermeneutics, that help to nurture biblical literacy and imagination.

The Wholeness of Forms

Balthasar's emphasis upon the wholeness of forms strikes the reader from the very first page of the introduction to the first volume of the *Theological Aesthetics*. We saw in the last chapter that he believed the form of God's self-revelation in creation and history, along with its biblical mediation, have an irreducible wholeness about them. There are five hermeneutical implications to this claim that need elaboration: the internal harmony of these forms, their intra-textuality, their uniqueness, the indissolubility of the forms and their luminous content, and the importance of the Bible's final or received form.

▮ Balthasar held, first, that once one reads the biblical mediation of God's self-revelation with the eyes of faith, one realizes that all the twists, turns, and, indeed, reversals of the story of God's dealings with creation find their resolution in the death and resurrection of Jesus Christ. What had seemed tragically fragmented and self-subverting appears from this perspective to bear an unassailable integrity. The form of salvation history when seen in light of the Christ-event has a necessary fittingness about it; it had to be just this way and no other.[1] On analogy to the way an art critic identifies the balance of elements constituting a painting's composition, or a drama critic points out the ways in which various plot lines in a play interact and find their resolution, the biblical exegete is to identify the diverse parts forming this whole and indicate the "reciprocity, mutual adjustment, and concordance" among them.[2]

Balthasar asserted that the proportions of the form of revelation seen by faith are conveyed by the biblical texts, even though the proportions of the Bible itself, as measured by the relative extent of attention paid a given theme, for instance, might not substantiate that theme's theological significance.[3] The best example of this is Balthasar's emphasis upon Jesus Christ's descent into hell.[4] Although the Bible appears to hint at it in some places,[5] the descent has nothing like the centrality at a literary level that it came to assume in the tradition or has in Balthasar's theology. For him, it is the climax of a unifying pattern of kenotic existence that he sees reflected, more or less clearly, everywhere in the Bible, from the creation accounts straight through to the Apocalypse. He went so far as to claim, as we have seen, that the texts themselves, in their literary poverty, participate in this divine self-abandonment. All of this recalls a point made in the first chapter of this book, namely, that Balthasar distinguished between the form of God's self-revelation and the form of its biblical mediation while nevertheless maintaining that God's own vision of the former is adequately rendered by the latter.

Balthasar repeatedly argued that a historical criticism that operates outside the arena of faith and with rationalist and historicist presuppositions is unable to see the internal harmony of the form of revelation in its biblical mediation. On this point, Balthasar was unyielding. He was also, it has to be said, not completely clear on it, since one can see things without believing them to be true. His point seems to be that believing Jesus is the Christ is at the same time to see him in his proper relation both to the horizontal movement of salvation history and to the vertical movement of God's *kenosis*. Faith, with its noetic as well as fiduciary components, enables one to see Jesus Christ as the climax of a "double and reciprocal *ekstasis*,"[6] a mutual going forth and meeting of God and humanity. And there is no seeing him thus apart from the light of God's grace, which shines forth from him. Balthasar's point accords with his definition of the objective evidence of a beautiful (or glorious) form. The glory of Jesus Christ consists both in the harmony of the relations seen (by faith) between him and the rest of salvation history, *and* in the radiance of the divine light shining from within him.[7] Naturally, only the faithful see Jesus as radiant with the triune divine light. Still, it does not seem unreasonable to contend that a non-believer can recognize the harmony of relations seen by a Christian without believing that Jesus is the Son of God. Just as a Christian can come to see the beauty of the *Bhagavad-Gita*'s theological synthesis of the ways of knowledge, action, and devotion without believing Krishna to be Lord of the cosmos, a Hindu can learn to appreciate the internal harmony of relations among the forms of salvation history as they coalesce around Jesus without accepting him as the Christ.

Balthasar's insistence that biblical exegetes interpret the Bible in light of what he regarded as its christologically focused internal harmony resembles one aspect of the classic hermeneutics outlined in the introduction. As Hans Frei, George Lindbeck, and Henri de Lubac argued, Christian biblical interpreters from antiquity until the dawn of the modern era generally read the Bible as forming a diverse but ultimately unified whole whose centerpiece is the life, death, and resurrection of Jesus Christ. It is important to note that those abiding by this hermeneutical convention need not (and in antiquity, at least, usually did not) construe this unifying christological focus primarily in terms of the *kenosis* of the second Person of the Trinity, as Balthasar did. We should also realize that although the classic hermeneutics construed the Bible as having the wholeness and integrity of a story, we have yet to put the question of just what sort of wholeness Balthasar ascribed to the Bible. Such provisos notwithstanding, his contention that the Bible should be read as a harmonious whole with Christ at its center is compatible with the classic approach.

▌ A second hermeneutical implication of Balthasar's emphasis on the wholeness of the biblical mediation of the form of God's self-revelation is his conviction that the Bible is self-glossing. Exegesis that wishes to be of service to the Church, he maintained, must listen for intra-textual melodies that resonate among the chapters, books, and Testaments of the Bible. It must read the Bible as a complex unity whose parts are in conversation with and interpreting one another. This is to favor synchronic over diachronic readings.[8] When addressing the fourth aspect of Balthasar's emphasis on wholeness, below, and in the fifth chapter's analysis of his exegesis of Eph 5.23 ff., I will examine some examples of his having done just that. And in the third chapter, on his understanding of the unity of scripture, I will explore in some detail the ways in which he believed the Johannine conviction regarding the unity of divine *kenosis* and glory helps believers see, not only the relation of the different theologies of the New Testament, but the relation of the Old and New Testaments as well. For now, though, the point to be stressed is that he believed that the Bible's credibility cannot be supported by reference to another text standing, as it were, behind or beneath it: "There is, in fact, no way of 'backing' or 'underpinning' the text of God's Word with another text, and giving it another background in the hope of making it more easy to read and more comprehensible. God's Word must interpret itself and wishes to do so."[9]

Balthasar therefore frequently denounced historical-critical readings of the Bible that seek, as he put it, "to steal up to the form from behind in the hope of enticing it to betray its mystery by exposing its development."[10] He asserted that the scientific exactitude of a historical criticism that occupies itself with establishing the seemingly bare facts of history can unearth countless interesting details, but it is unable to appreciate the wholeness of the form of revelation in its biblical mediation: "The figure which confronts us in Holy Scripture is more and more dissected in 'historical-critical' fashion until all that is left of what was once a living organism is a dead heap of flesh, blood and bones."[11] Echoing Goethe's contention that a quantitative analysis must be supplemented with an appreciation for the qualities of a given whole, Balthasar held that most historical critics do not have the necessary sensorium for the integrity of the forms they want to interpret. Instead, they chip away at the form in order better to understand the process of its creation. By focusing on the shards, they fail to see the pot they once held in their hands. The costs of relying exclusively on such "excavative" readings of the biblical literature are steep, however, since the unity of the whole is replaced with an assemblage of discreet pieces.[12] Indeed, on occasion Balthasar seems to have supposed that diachronic readings permanently impair the capacity of the faithful to read the Bible synchronically: "For we can be sure of one thing: we can never again recapture the living totality of form once it has been dissected and sawed into pieces."[13] As remarkable as it may sound, Balthasar found in Friedrich Nietzsche a most unlikely ally in his campaign against such "excavative" forms of historical inquiry. His fellow native of Basel decried the development of a purportedly "neutral" historiography that, under the influence of Hegel's dialectic of history, supposed it possible to explain events and movements in terms of their historical (or cultural, sociological, psychological, economic, etc.) antecedents. Lamenting that this "analytical and inartistic" approach inevitably "severed the roots of [one's] strength," Nietzsche noted that "[r]ecent theology seems to have entered into partnership with history out of pure innocence, and even now it almost refuses to see that, probably much against its will, it has thereby placed itself in the service of the Voltairean *écrasez*—destroy the infamous thing!"[14] Balthasar and Nietzsche are agreed, then, that contextualizing historical events, persons, or texts is not the same thing as understanding them.

The cogency of this feature of Balthasar's polemic against historical criticism is limited by anachronism and self-contradiction. As Edgar

Krentz noted in his introductory handbook, practitioners of diachronic approaches knew very well by the mid-1970s (i.e., a decade or so after Balthasar wrote the first volume of his *Theological Aesthetics*) that "[u]nderstanding is not etiology. It is valuable to know the source of an idea or movement; but it can lead to confusing 'ancestry with explanation.'"[15] Moreover, there have been quite dramatic changes in the discipline that began to make their impact at around the same time. With the development of rhetorical and structuralist methodologies, historical criticism now embraces both diachronic and synchronic approaches. In light of these changes within the discipline, it is no longer credible, if it ever was, to attack historical criticism on the grounds that it fails to appreciate the complex ways in which the Bible's parts interact with one another.

In addition, Balthasar's polemics against this aspect of historical criticism stands in considerable tension with two features of his work in the *Theological Aesthetics*. It is very difficult to square his polemical remarks with others in which he explicitly acknowledged the value of historical-critical inquiry. From time to time he granted that it can perform an invaluable service by helping to establish with greater clarity the meaning of the various parts of the Bible that theological exegesis will treat as in conversation with one another. Balthasar sounds this theme in his volume on the new covenant, consciously echoing the declarations of the Second Vatican Council: "The research into first the literary form, second the situation in which the text was produced, and third the pre-existing forms of thinking, speech and narration influenced by the contemporary world, is undoubtedly an indispensable means to acquire the correct understanding."[16] To be sure, Balthasar immediately went on to say that the judgment of the dogmatic theologian who appropriates historical-critical findings should be "influenced also by taking into consideration first the content and unity of the whole of Scripture, second the living tradition of the universal Church, and third the analogy of faith."[17] But in this and similar passages, he regarded historical criticism as an essential preparation for the subsequent work of the dogmatic theologian.[18]

Balthasar's polemics against diachronic readings also run afoul of his own aesthetic convictions. For instance, his comparison of a biblical interpreter's responsibilities to those of an art or drama critic depends on their sharing an appreciation for the interaction and relationships among the parts constituting a given whole. Indeed, recalling a point made in the first chapter, he contended that such analysis is necessary in order to transcend an immature appreciation of beautiful forms. That would seem to imply that diachronic readings enhance, rather than impair, the faithful's perception. Furthermore, his criticisms ignore what he called the double principle of all forms, namely, that they are indissoluble and that they are determined by a host of antecedent conditions.[19] The warrant for historical-critical investigations of the biblical texts could not be clearer. Granted, historical-critical readings are not sufficient, at least not from the perspective of theology's concern to hear the Bible as the Word of God. Tracing the genesis of a text (in all its text-, literary-, form-, tradition-, and redaction-critical complexities) does not replace reading it as bearing a diverse, though ultimately unified, witness to the creative and redemptive acts of the triune God.[20] In other words, diachronic readings should not supplant synchronic ones. But diachronic readings do have their value. As has been shown, Balthasar was on occasion willing to acknowledge that fact. And as we will see, he frequently put diachronic readings to use in his exegesis.

The best, and most obvious, way to interpret Balthasar's inconsistency with respect to diachronic readings is to argue that his polemics were addressed to those historical critics, like Rudolf Bultmann, who in his judgment wrongly supposed that their methods were sufficient to meet the needs of the Church. Still, it is regrettable that Balthasar so frequently allowed his disagreements with some historical critics to color his remarks about historical criticism in general. The problem with Balthasar's imprecision is that most of his readers are persuaded that he thought historical criticism incompatible with theological exegesis. Although some appear to welcome this, it does not comport with the general thrust of both Balthasar's views and uses of scripture.[21] Even more disturbing is the view of others that Balthasar's polemics are reason enough to dismiss his work as so hopelessly pre-critical as to be of little use in the twenty-first century.[22] By contrast, I argue that in spite of Balthasar's rhetorical excesses he can be read as having accepted, both in theory and in practice, the importance of historical criticism for theological exegesis without having abandoned a set of pre-modern hermeneutical conventions that helped to nourish the *sensus fidelium*.

In that connection, Balthasar's advocacy of synchronic readings is quite plainly compatible with the pre-modern hermeneutical convention of treating the entirety of the Bible as self-interpreting. When Augustine said that an obscure passage in scripture should be illumined with a clearer one, he described a practice widespread, not just in antiquity, but through the Reformation.[23] For Balthasar, as we have seen, reading the Bible as self-glossing was backed by two convictions. He believed that God wants God's Word to be so interpreted. And he believed that any aesthetic form, whether it be a text, a sculpture, a painting, or even a person, comprises parts whose relations help to constitute the form as such. Forms measure themselves in terms of their parts' interrelations and the parts' relations to the whole. Synchronic readings are, on Balthasar's view, an essential feature of taking seriously the wholeness of God's self-revelation in its biblical mediation. It is therefore all the more regrettable that he did not argue more forcefully and consistently that historical-critically generated diachronic readings can be a significant aid in that endeavor.

▌ A third implication for theological hermeneutics of Balthasar's emphasis on the wholeness of forms is his insistence upon the uniqueness of the form of revelation in its biblical mediation. Balthasar argued that historical critics are unable to perceive this, either. This blindness is especially apparent, he believed, in their treatments of the Gospel narratives.[24] The reductive analytical methods he thought characteristic of historical criticism simply cannot provide believers with an individuating identity description of Jesus Christ: "If it is true that the Word truly became 'flesh', man, world-history; if the Word nowhere encounters us nakedly but always in an envelopment of 'flesh'; then we shall have to grant that the uniqueness of the form cannot be ascertained 'scientifically'."[25]

Once again, Balthasar's polemic has lost a good deal of its punch in light of developments within the field itself. First, if all historical critics were to ply their trade according to the principles formulated by Ernst Troeltsch, in particular the principles of analogy (which rules out uniqueness) and of cause and effect (which rules out God's acts in history), then Balthasar's critique would have greater merit.[26] But its validity has been undermined by transformations in the presuppositions of historical criticism that were already under way when he was writing and that have grown increasingly clear over the course of the last three decades. The chief transformation in the method bearing on the issue of whether historical criticism can discern the uniqueness of the form of Jesus Christ is its break with a naïve historicism. Granted, some historical critics and theologians influenced by them do wish to continue operating underneath historicism's protective mantle. Van Harvey, so far as I am aware, has not amended the historicism of his book, *The Historian and the Believer.*[27] But the new hermeneuts like Gerhard Ebeling, Ernst Fuchs, and James M. Robinson all roundly rejected it.[28] They devoted their careers to demonstrating how historical-critical tools can serve the Church in its effort better to apprehend the uniqueness of the God-man.

The work of Norman Perrin provides an additional counterargument. Though indebted to the work of Bultmann's pupils (and critics), Perrin sought to combine their insights with the best of Joachim Jeremias's work, thereby establishing his own, independent position.[29] The principle methodological fruit of his labors is the now famous "criterion of dissimilarity." It assumes, as Perrin put it, that "if we are to seek that which is most characteristic of Jesus, it will be found not in the things which he shares with his contemporaries, but in the things wherein he differs from them."[30] Whatever difficulties there may be with the application of this criterion in the effort to determine Jesus' own words,[31] surely one of them is not that it fails to discern what is unique about him. Of course Balthasar could respond that the uniqueness of the form of Jesus Christ is not reducible to the purported uniqueness of what he taught. And in fairness to him, it should be acknowledged that historical critics have been very suspicious about the historical reliability of the early Church's redaction of Jesus' sayings. Yet Balthasar was willing to admit (as we shall see) that historical critics can shed fresh light on what they take to be the actual words of Jesus. So even if their list of the genuine teachings of Jesus should prove unacceptably meager, I would argue that what historical critics do accept can help to invigorate the perception of the uniqueness of the Christ-form by the faithful.

Redaction criticism also provides a counterexample because its practitioners look to explain why a particular Gospel editor handled the Jesus materials in just the way he did. They highlight the differences among the Gospel portraits of Jesus in order to discern the unique theological perspective of the editor whose work they are scrutinizing. It is possible to respond in Balthasar's defense that identifying the uniqueness of a Gospel's theological perspective is not the same as identifying the uniqueness of the Christ-form. Balthasar's complaint, then, would be with redaction criticism's apparent reductionism. It could appear that by identifying the theological perspective of a particular Gospel editor, one inevitably reduces that editor's Jesus to a kind of theological front man, a mere literary device to advance a theological program. But Balthasar did not voice such a criticism and, indeed, could have done so only at the price of contradicting his doctrine of biblical inspiration. He maintained that the Gospel editors worked under the guidance of the Holy Spirit who guarantees that their portrait of Jesus Christ does not distort God's own vision of the Christ-form. So although it might seem that redaction critics could help to identify only the uniqueness of a given Gospel editor's theological agenda, Balthasar's doctrine of inspiration warrants the view that a given Gospel editor's unique rendering of the Jesus materials accurately conveys the form of Jesus Christ. Even if that depiction is not entirely accurate historically, the Holy Spirit guarantees, so Balthasar said, that it nevertheless gives a reliable account of Jesus' unique identity. That does not mean, of course, that the redaction critic will be led by this method to see Jesus of Nazareth as the unique God-man. But that is a different matter. It is well to recall at this juncture Chrysostom's description of the differences between the ways unbelievers and believers regard baptism. Whereas the former see the same person enter and rise from the font, the faithful see the baptized as a new person, reborn in Christ. The same can be said of the differences between the way unbelievers and believers construe the biblical portraits of Jesus. Both can see him as unique. But only the faithful see him as the Christ, the unique fulfillment of salvation history. To confuse one sort of uniqueness with another, as Balthasar did when attacking historical critics on this matter, distorts the issues at stake as theologians try to come to terms with historical criticism.

So Balthasar's critique of historical criticism for being unable to discern the uniqueness of the Christ-form is misleading for three reasons. It does not take into account the ways in which historical critics have tried, with some degree of success, to free themselves from the historicism of Troeltsch's views. Nor does it adequately appreciate the ways in which historical critics can isolate, by using the criterion of dissimilarity, what is unique about the words (and deeds) of Jesus. And it fails to realize that redaction-critical findings may help the faithful more clearly recognize the unique identity of Jesus Christ. In short, Balthasar should be criticized for not having clearly acknowledged that historical critics can help the Church better appreciate the uniqueness of God's self-revelation and its biblical mediation.

Despite this shortcoming, Balthasar's insistence that biblical interpreters read the Bible as bearing a uniquely appropriate witness to the fulfillment of God's self-revelation is compatible with the pride of place given the literal sense in the classic hermeneutics. As I have shown, what likely prompted Balthasar's polemics against historical criticism in this regard was his fear that it would inevitably dissolve everything uniquely revelatory in the scriptures into a product of completely this-worldly forces. In concert with the classic approach, Balthasar believed that the meaning of any biblical text is not best understood in terms established by extra-biblical frames of reference. As Balthasar would have put it, the Gospels—and by extension the other books of the Bible—measure themselves. Accordingly, as biblical interpreters explore the intricate web of cultural borrowings evident in the Bible, Balthasar, along with his pre-modern forebears, would insist that the Bible itself sets the context within which these borrowings are properly understood. Only by accepting this hermeneutical convention will these interpreters be sufficiently attentive to the uniqueness of the texts and their subject matter.

▮ A fourth implication of Balthasar's emphasis on the wholeness of the biblical mediation of God's self-revelation finds its expression in his insistence that the Bible's spiritual sense cannot be divorced from its literal sense (understood as the grammatico-historical sense).[32] Here, once again, we find ourselves back in the thick of Balthasar's polemics against historical criticism. Historical critics are regularly upbraided for failing to see the spirit in the letter.[33] What might that mean? I would suggest two different, though not incompatible, ways of making sense of his criticism.

It can be understood in a way that emphasizes Balthasar's assertion that neither scripture as a whole, nor the work of a particular author or redactor, can be summed up adequately with abstract formulas.[34] It is true, of course, that he recognized that each biblical author or redactor brought to his work a unique perspective on God's self-revelation in creation and history. One can, for example, identify a typically Johannine emphasis in contrast to a typically Pauline one. And that, of course, can aid one's understanding, at least initially. But what Cleanth Brooks noted with respect to poems,[35] Balthasar maintained was true of the Bible: no paraphrase of it, or of one of its passages, is ever completely adequate. The danger of paraphrases, Balthasar seems to have thought, lies in our tendency to assume that they can replace the texts themselves. However true it may be that the letter is distinguishable from the spirit, the form of the text from the content it mediates, in the end, the content cannot be divorced from the form and is available to the reader only in this form. Realizing that means relinquishing any attempts to ascertain the meaning of the Bible with absolute certainty.

Balthasar's polemics against historical criticism on this score can also be understood in terms of the distinction, developed by Karl Barth and adopted by Balthasar, between reading the Bible as a self-involving witness to God's revelation and as a source of religious, sociological, political, historical, and linguistic information about ancient Palestine and its neighbors. Balthasar contended that historical critics read the Bible in the second way, as a source of information, while the faithful, at least when they hear the Bible as God's Word, read it in the first way.

By way of illustration, consider how an historical critic might interpret Ex 13.17–14.31, the deliverance at the Sea.[36] After addressing the difficult textual problems, the critic might seek to analyze the text source-critically, identifying on the basis of linguistic patterns (including questions of style and vocabulary) and theological perspectives its likely literary elements. Certain passages will be ascribed to J, others to P, still others to E, and so forth. Then the critic might try to answer the form-critical and traditio-historical questions. What is the probable oral prehistory of each literary strand? What are their likely settings in the life of ancient Israel? Should we treat the crossing itself as belonging to the Exodus event more narrowly construed, or to the traditions surrounding the wilderness wanderings?

It is true, of course, that if the critic concluded his or her work at this point, the final or received form of the text would be left in pieces. And it is equally true, as Brevard Childs has repeatedly insisted, that the real interpretive art lies in discerning the meaning, or a meaning, of the whole as we now have it. But notice that even to do that work can still be a matter of treating the text as a source of information (about the final redactor's various purposes in editing his sources just this way and no other), rather than as a witness to God's revelation that addresses the interpreter's own existential situation. The difference, then, between one sort of reading (as source) and the other (as witness, or more broadly, as the Word of God) lies in the purpose with which one reads, the use to which one puts the texts.

"Purpose" and "use" are not Balthasar's terms, but they can help us to understand his repeated polemics against historical critics to the effect that they misunderstand the text; that they make a hash out of what it is really saying; that they are seeing only the letter, and not the spirit in the letter.[37] They may be getting a textually defensible meaning from it, but because of their different purposes in reading the text, their meanings are different from Balthasar's. They do not read the text in order to hear it as personal address and, in so doing, to make the transition from the grammatico-historical to the pneumatic or christological sense.[38] They read it for other reasons. That, as I have already mentioned, introduces the question of use into the discussion and ties meaning to it. Nicholas Wolterstorff provides a brief summary of the hermeneutical upshot of such a move:

> Even in a metaphorical sense there is no such thing, for a text, as what it says. And so no such thing as discovering what it says. Interpretation, at bottom, is not a matter of discernment but of choice and habit. We human beings *adopt* interpretations of texts and *follow rules which assign* interpretations to texts—often without deliberation. But for every text it is possible to adopt other interpretations or follow other rules assigning interpretations. To arrive at an interpretation of a text one needs more than careful reading of the text. One needs a *purpose* which the interpretation is to serve or a *criterion* which it is to satisfy. Different purposes and criteria lead to different interpretations of the same text.[39]

So far as I am aware, nowhere in the *Theological Aesthetics* did Balthasar explicitly recognize the connection between the meanings one derives from a text and the purposes one has in reading it. But it is clearly implicit in the distinction between reading the Bible as a source of information and as a self-involving witness to God's revelation. That is to say, the distinction that I wish he had made does not conflict with, and indeed seems to be presupposed by, a distinction he did make. Had he acknowledged this presupposition, he might well have been able to temper his polemics against historical critics, which, on occasion, descended to the level of pointless invective.[40] He would have been able to recognize the legitimacy of their quite different purposes and, in so doing, more clearly to recognize the indeterminacy of the grammatico-historical sense of the text.

The foregoing has uncovered two more instances in which Balthasar's hermeneutics abides by pre-modern convictions that helped to nourish biblical literacy and imagination. In the first place, his refusal to allow paraphrases of biblical texts to supplant the texts themselves preserves the priority of the literal sense. To repeat the example provided by Hans Frei: when interpreting the Gospel narratives, this means accepting no doctrinal, creedal, or philosophical re-description of Jesus Christ as fully adequate. Such restraint would help to ensure that interpreters regularly reread the biblical texts in the hope of discovering new meanings to illumine new interpretive circumstances. Second, although Balthasar should be criticized for not recognizing the legitimacy of other purposes when reading the Bible, his own purpose is quite compatible with that endorsed by the classic hermeneutics. He read the Bible as authoritative for Christian life and thought. The ecclesial setting that Balthasar thought so important for the proper explication and application of the Bible will be examined in the third section of this chapter. Here I need simply to emphasize that along with most pre-modern Christian interpreters, Balthasar believed that through the ministrations of the Holy Spirit, the Bible will transform the lives of believers.

▌ A fifth hermeneutical implication of Balthasar's emphasis on the wholeness of forms concerns the importance of respecting the final or received form of the biblical text. At the outset, it must be acknowledged that Balthasar's uses of the phrase "final form" (*die Endgestalt*) and its cognates are ambiguous. He sometimes used it in reference to the biblical text itself in its canonical wholeness, as when arguing that "[o]nly the final results of the historical developments which lie behind a text . . . may be said to be inspired, not the bits and scraps which philological analysis thinks it can tear loose from the finished totality."[41] On other occasions, however, the final form referred not to the text, but to revelation generally, or to Jesus Christ himself.[42] This ambiguity is likely the result of Balthasar's conviction that the Bible, though a fully human document patient of historical-critical analysis, is at the same time the divinely inspired mediation of God's self-revelation in creation and history. He believed that both the final form of revelation (as that culminates in the God-man Jesus Christ) and the final form of its biblical mediation are authoritative for Christian life and thought. The final form of the Bible is the "guiding criterion for a new abundance of ecclesial thought which is still incalculable in temporal and historical terms."[43] But, as he went on to say, according such authority to the Bible is only possible "because the fulness of the Bible crystallises concentrically around a human and divine centre, a centre which is indeed expressed in Scripture and everywhere flooded by its light, but which essentially transcends Scripture and rests within itself as a sovereign reality."[44] He argued, therefore, that the Church is not ruled by a book, at least not by its grammatico-historical sense as abstracted from the spiritual sense. Rather, "the *pneuma* of Scripture is the *norma normans* for the entire form of ecclesial dogmatics. We say the *pneuma* and not simply the letter, even though this, of course, means the *pneuma* within the letter."[45] In short, the importance of interpreting the final redaction of the text, rather than its critically reconstructed constituent elements, and the importance of seeing this final redaction as the mediation of the whole sweep of revelation in creation and history were both—in theory—paramount for Balthasar.

In the remainder of this section, I examine the degree of consistency with which Balthasar followed this hermeneutical guideline. To that end, I present some examples of his exegesis, first of the Old Testament and then of the New (from volumes 6 and 7, respectively, of the *Theological Aesthetics*). Although Balthasar occasionally managed to abide by his commitment to interpret the Bible's final redaction, he rather more frequently did not.

One sees him following this rule in his exegesis of the various traditions surrounding Saul. "The tragedy of the first king, *Saul,* must be interpreted (no matter how difficult this may be) on the basis of the final redaction of the narrative, which has been painted over so many times."[46] What follows is a vivid illustration of Balthasar's familiarity with the philological, source- and form-critical, and traditio-historical issues with which one who seeks to interpret the text's final form must contend.[47] He seems especially keen not to harmonize the older and newer traditions, but to let the tensions created by their juxtaposition deepen the tragedy of the story and the theological issues at stake.

But such examples are quite rare in this volume. More typically, he based his exegesis on a critically reconstructed text. The most striking example of this is his exegesis of the book of Isaiah. He separated the discussion of the eighth-century prophet from that of the exilic deutero-Isaiah, and the discussion of the post-exilic trito-Isaiah from both.[48] When interpreting second Isaiah, he noted that it is "not for nothing" that the anonymous exilic prophet would choose to locate his message within the corpus of Isaiah proper.[49] But apart from a passing reference to their shared insight that God's salvation is to be worked out through judgment (which he knew is hardly unique to either), he made no attempt to elucidate the theological implications of second Isaiah's canonical position. The same is true of his work on trito-Isaiah. This material offers a good example of the way in which much of Balthasar's interpretation of the Old Testament in the *Theological Aesthetics* was guided, not by the final form of the text, but by the history of Israel and Judah as that has been reconstructed by historical-critical research.

It can be argued, of course, that in such cases his concern to take his interpretive cues from the final form of the text is overridden by a more pressing interest in tracking the development of ancient Israel's and Judah's understanding of divine glory. After all, such was his stated purpose in the sixth volume of the *Theological Aesthetics*. He expressly denied any attempt to present a complete theology of the Old Testament, preferring instead to dwell on the topic of glory in order to help restore it to what he regarded as its rightful place in theology.[50] None of this should be gainsaid. Moreover, after having criticized Balthasar for not acknowledging the legitimacy of different uses of the biblical text, I cannot complain if his purposes are not entirely compatible with those I wish he had undertaken.

Nevertheless, in light of his call for interpreters to abide by the final form of the Bible, it ought to be acknowledged that there is considerable irony in his having largely based his interpretation of the Old Testament on purported *Grundtexte*. And it must also be said that this approach comes with significant costs. First, the results of his exegesis are as fragile and tenuous as the reconstructed text itself. They reflect the particular biases of the various historical critics on whose judgments he depended. In some cases, these judgments are couched in terms that suggest a Christian triumphalism dubious about the theological merits of any post-exilic additions. To cite just one example, Balthasar dismissed "the petty prescriptions" of Ez 44.4–46 and the whole of chapter 48 on the grounds that they reflect "the attempt of Judaism to narrow down the breadth which had been attained in the exile and to bring it back to an earlier format."[51] He thereby missed the opportunity to note the ways in which the glory of God has not been unduly spiritualized in Ezekiel. Moreover, the irony of taking such a stance toward material written just prior to or during the time when the Old Testament canon was being finalized is palpable. Second, this dependence on a reconstructed text isolates him from the tradition with which he hoped to be in conversation when doing exegesis. The texts he interprets are not the canonical Hebrew or Greek texts treasured and interpreted in Jewish synagogues and Christian churches down through the ages. Rather, they are something completely different, particularly in the case of Isaiah. Third, Balthasar's approach largely ignores the synchronic dimension to the text. Admittedly, he was well aware of, and made frequent reference to, some of the ways the New Testament appropriated various parts of the Old Testament. But he seems almost entirely to ignore the ways different parts of a given Old Testament book interact. This is obvious with respect to Isaiah, but is also a feature of his exegesis of Ezekiel, Hosea, and Job, to name just three. With respect to the latter, on the basis of a judgment about the likely prehistory of the text, he concluded that Job's double answer to God (Jb 40.4–5 and 42.2–6) must belong together.[52] That this material likely originated as a single unit has long been noted. But Balthasar (along, to be sure, with most other interpreters of Job) failed to realize that regardless of the text's prehistory, the effect of the repetition is "to heighten the rebuke [and] to deflate Job's pretense of wisdom."[53] Notice that, once again, it is a hypothetical reconstruction of the text, rather than its received form, that constitutes the point of departure and "guiding criterion" for his exegesis.

Several differences and similarities become evident when comparing the ways Balthasar used scripture in the volume on the Old Testament with those he used in that on the New. First, Balthasar was less concerned when exegeting the New Testament to establish an *Ur-* or *Grundtext* upon which to base his interpretation. He often indicated an awareness of certain textual variants (the longer ending of Mark, say) or later additions (for instance, Rom 16.25–27 or 2 Cor 6.14–7.1). But his interpretation of such texts typically did not depend on choosing an earlier text as more authentic. Rather, he usually offered a theological explanation for either version. His brief discussion of the longer and shorter versions of 1 Cor 8.2f. provides an example. Interestingly, in this instance, in contrast to his treatment of the Saul traditions in 1 Sm, he sought to establish a fundamental agreement between the two variants.[54] With respect to Mark's endings, however, his several references to some of the verses in the later one stand in silent and unexplained contrast to his explanation of the shorter ending.[55] Just as often happened in the volume on the Old Testament, he did not seek to identify the final redactor's purpose in making such emendations or to discern the literary and theological implications of the interaction between earlier and later layers. The synchronic dimension to these texts he simply ignored.

Second, owing to the much more historically compressed process by which the New Testament came to assume its present form, Balthasar abandoned the attempt, characteristic of the Old Testament volume, critically to reconstruct the history of the way the New Testament uses the terms δόξα and its cognates. One result of this is that he never tried to present in a single synopsis a given New Testament book's notions of either. Instead, he ranged widely over the whole of the New Testament in order to summarize its understanding(s) of a given topic—say, the hiddenness of God's self-revelation in Christ, or the atonement, or faith—asking always, of course, how that bears on the question of God's glory and glorification. That procedure leaves him vulnerable to the charge of prooftexting, a concern of modern biblical scholarship he never adequately addressed, either in this volume or the earlier one.[56] It also raises the question whether he engaged in the sort of overeager harmonizations of divergent perspectives that make historical critics flinch. Answering that criticism with the sort of precision and detail it requires lies beyond the scope of this chapter. But I would offer one example of his approach that does not, in my judgment, make the mistakes of smoothing over tensions and ignoring significant differences among the New Testament authors in theological perspectives and rhetorical purposes. The passage is Balthasar's remarkable analysis of the New Testament's understanding of time. In particular, I will focus on his description of Jesus' so-called double temporal horizon.

From the beginning of the twentieth century until the 1980s there was widespread agreement among biblical scholars that the New Testament generally, and Jesus in particular, cannot be understood properly if divorced from an orientation to the end of the age. With the work of Johannes Weiss and Albert Schweitzer, the non-eschatological view of Jesus' ministry and preaching characteristic of the nineteenth century's liberal lives of Jesus was severely discredited. But it is not as though the question about Jesus' eschatology went into a kind of dormancy for eighty years until it was raised anew. Among those who accepted the importance of eschatology, there was vigorous debate over whether the end of the age should be seen as primarily a future, if imminent, event (Weiss and Schweitzer), or as a primarily realized state of affairs in Jesus' ministry and preaching (C. H. Dodd), or as something inaugurated by Jesus but still incomplete (Oscar Cullmann). Balthasar was satisfied with none of these views. He rejected both extremes and he rejected all attempts to mediate a compromise.

To understand why he did so, we need first to consider his assertion that Jesus knew himself to be "God's final Word of salvation" and "a proxy for the whole of mankind in the judgment of God."[57] This is backed by a claim that "the whole edifice of the Church's proclamation of faith in Jesus Christ and the portrayal of his earthly life" in the Bible would be brought down "at a single stroke" if one denied Jesus this self-awareness.[58] That, in turn, rests on the claim that there exists an "indissoluble nexus between event (Christ) and interpretation (Church)."[59] Thus, owing to Balthasar's belief that the Holy Spirit guided the early churches in the creation of the New Testament's diverse witness to the event of Jesus Christ, he was convinced that Jesus was aware of himself as God's final Word of salvation and as representative of humankind.

On the basis of this assertion, Balthasar concluded that Jesus was characterized by, and united, two distinguishable temporal perspectives: "the period of Jesus is an absolutely unique period—the divine-human period, into which indeed the time of the Old Testament flows, and in which the time of the Church can in a certain way participate, but which can never be identified with these."[60] From the human point of view, the time of Jesus is like that of any other mortal: it is embedded within a given epoch with its own historical peculiarities, it runs ineluctably toward death, and its limitations force Jesus to fashion his plans and actions accordingly. And yet from the divine perspective, the final reconciliation of the world with God is accomplished in the free self-abandonment of this one person, in the *kenosis* of his incarnation and of his death and descent. The eternal Word goes forth into creation as this human being and endures the timelessness of death and of hell itself: "precisely for this reason, the 'kingdom of God', which Jesus proclaims as 'near' and 'at the very door', is both already come, in so far as it is indeed present [in him], and yet also 'in process of coming', in so far as it is heading towards its own public and decisive end, its own 'hour'."[61]

Balthasar thus refused to choose between Schweitzer's immanent expectation and Dodd's realized eschatology. He insisted that given the uniqueness of Jesus' mission and identity, it is "theologically required" that we posit for him a double temporal horizon.[62] On the one hand, it is correct to say that Jesus foresaw a continuation of chronological time for his followers. On the other hand, Jesus undergoes the end of time in the bearing of sin on the cross and the descent into hell, only to enter into the eternal with the resurrection. In the latter case Balthasar was reluctant to speak of Jesus foreseeing any of this because that would impugn the fullness of his humanity. Jesus knew himself to be of definitive importance for the salvation of the world; he could not know (and still be human) how that would work itself out. Notice, too, that this double temporal horizon is to be distinguished from all mediating compromises between Schweitzer and Dodd. From the divine perspective, he is the fullness of the kingdom, in its entirety. But from the human perspective, which is contained and sheltered, so Balthasar said, within the divine, this fullness is drawn out chronologically. Christians speak, therefore, of his preexistence, his ministry, his death, his descent, his resurrection, and his return. But that is to speak from a "standpoint that projects on to the continuing time of the world that which is timeless . . . ; the time of the world is no longer the proper time of what is endless, and although it can be continuously present to it (Mt 28.20), this does not mean that for it itself Resurrection, Ascension, and parousia are separated by distances in time."[63]

Only thus—by shifting back and forth between the two temporal perspectives characteristic of, and united in, Jesus—can one see the integrity of the otherwise bewildering and, indeed, contradictory New Testament statements regarding time. How are believers to make sense of the Jesus of the Synoptics implying that the kingdom is present in him (Mk 2.19 and parallels) and yet urging his disciples to pray for the kingdom to come (Mt 6.10 and Lk 11.2)? On the basis of the foregoing, Balthasar would refuse to privilege either one or the other as more authentic. To do so, on his view, would be to eliminate the paradoxical unity of Jesus' double temporal horizon. From the human perspective, the kingdom's coming is projected forward as though it is to be concluded in the future, although its coming has the inevitability of the seed that sprouts and grows of itself (Mk 4.27): "Through the 'already' of his earthly presence (and only of *his* presence), the 'not yet' of the end that is drawing near receives its inexorability."[64] From God's perspective, the kingdom is fully present in each moment of the life of this man who freely allows God to fashion his future. The kingdom is present in Jesus, not as a timelessly true "idea" (in the Platonic sense of the term), "but in the going and passing away in time of this one's life."[65] According to Balthasar, this going and passing away is what constitutes both the not passing away of God's Word and the end of heaven and earth.[66]

My aim in the foregoing is neither to commend nor criticize the theological conclusions Balthasar reached with respect to the New Testament's understanding of time.[67] Instead, I want to highlight the degree to which Balthasar, in this instance at least, let the final form of the text be the basis for his "theological reflection on the biblical data."[68] Significantly, Balthasar did not resolve the tension between a realized and a futurist eschatology by distinguishing between earlier and later

forms of the text. But neither was he content simply to identify the differences and to leave them stand. The challenge he faced and met was
to find a way to appreciate the Bible's diversity and integrity that is consonant with Christian convictions about the unique God-manhood of
Jesus Christ. On his reading, the heterogeneity of material on time finds
its center in the hypostatic union of divine and human natures. In this
instance, then, the Bible's final form did provide the guiding criterion
for his exegesis.

Balthasar's exegesis of the New Testament passages on time provides two additional examples of his having abided by the classic hermeneutical conventions. First, in keeping with the priority of the literal
sense, Balthasar allowed the complex and seemingly self-contradictory
biblical uses of chronological expressions to set the terms by which to
understand Jesus' unique identity. The need to choose between a futurist and a realized eschatology, or find a mediating compromise, seems
obvious. But for Balthasar, doing so would have meant letting his exegesis be governed by the idea, foreign to the texts themselves, that Jesus
could not possibly have held that the end was both coming and yet already present in him. Balthasar refused to let this extra-canonical perspective on time determine the meaning of time in the New Testament.
However odd it may sound to some ears, Balthasar has here presented
an example of how a dogmatically informed reading of the Bible can
help historical critics (or, more precisely in this instance, redaction critics) determine the likely intended sense of the final redaction of these
biblical texts. For he would have insisted that the final redactor's use of
temporal terms is intentionally twofold, reflecting the redactor's Christian convictions about the identity of Jesus as fully God and fully man.[69]
Second, he read the various passages on time as self-glossing, although
in this case respecting the Bible's intra-textuality did not involve privi-
leging one set of passages, but allowing both to interpret the other.
The passages reflecting a realized eschatology and those reflecting a futurist one were each read in light of the other. Here we find Balthasar
advancing a synchronic reading that is measurably enriched by a diachronic one. This exegesis, then, provides an example of the sort of
constructive role he (sometimes) admitted historical criticism can play
in theology's responsibility to read the Bible as the Word of God. It
can serve, too, as an example of how historical criticism and dogmatic

theology can each aid the other. And, finally, it can provide a salutary reminder that abiding by certain features of the classic hermeneutics is not necessarily incompatible with, indeed on occasion may well help to correct, historical-critical investigations.

AUTHORIAL INTENT

A second major feature of Balthasar's hermeneutics is the claim that proper interpretation of a biblical text involves seeking to discern the intention of its author(s). Balthasar often wrote as though he thought that he, and theology in general, should be engaged in such an attempt. He urged interpreters to read the Bible as it is meant to be read, to understand it as it understands itself, to read it on its own terms. These are fairly common phrases of his.[70] They all suggest that to interpret the Bible correctly, one must read it in accord with, and take one's point of departure from, "God's manifest intention."[71]

This claim about discerning authorial intent actually has two dimensions that for Balthasar usually, though not always, overlapped. The Bible is a fully human document, so interpreting it means, among other things, discerning the intention of its human authors. But the Bible is also a medium of divine revelation fashioned by God the Holy Spirit. It is God's Word or God's divine art and, as such, has a divine author or creator whose intention also needs to be discerned. Balthasar seems generally to have supposed that the intention of God and those of the human authors were virtually identical. This is an implication of his belief that the Holy Spirit guaranteed the validity of the human authors' witnesses to the form of Christ. The Holy Spirit acts in such a way that their witnesses correspond to the Spirit's own witness to Christ.[72]

Several things suggest, however, that the two do not always overlap on his view, and therefore, that attending to authorial intent does have two distinguishable elements. First, Balthasar acknowledged that the human authors made mistakes; they distorted the witness they were to give.[73] Second, he acknowledged that the Catholic Church is a gathering of sinners that needs regular reform.[74] Since the early churches brought forth the scriptures, this further suggests that the scriptures may not always have been written in complete accord with the guidance provided by the Holy Spirit. Indeed, this freedom of the early churches vis-à-vis the Spirit in the act of creating the scriptures is one of the implications, so Balthasar held, of the Son's self-abandonment. Third, he asserted that it need not be assumed, however, that the human authors got it wrong for one reason or another in order to distinguish human and divine authorial intent. The following example makes clear that he also held that the meaning of the biblical writings exceeds the conscious intent of the human author. In his exegesis of Gn 1.26 ("Let us make man in accordance with our image. . . "), he took issue with Karl Barth for having rejected the idea, advanced by Gerhard von Rad, that the text refers to angels or other less than divine attendants who helped God in the act of creation.[75] Barth's point is that it seems ludicrous to suggest that God would need the assistance of such creatures when creating humans.[76] Balthasar proposed an interpretation of the text that is at once more defensible on historical-critical grounds and yet accepts the gist of Barth's complaint. There is a distinction, Balthasar claimed, between the partial sense of the text, namely, that consciously intended by the human author, and the fuller sense (the *sensus plenior* or *sens plénier*),[77] namely, that intended by God. Doing so allows one to acknowledge that the human author may well have had angels in mind when composing the text, since that would fit the sort of religious consciousness of the age. But it does not rule out the possibility that God intended to refer in this verse to an inner trinitarian conversation. This distinction between the human and divine authors of the Bible allowed him to defend the traditional trinitarian interpretation of the text while offering what he took to be a more credible reading of the likely human author's intended meaning.[78]

Granting that, on Balthasar's terms, it is possible to distinguish between human and divine authorial intent, what does attending to the *human* author's intent mean for him? His treatment of Gn 1.26 has shown one aspect of this: it involves an interpretation of the thought world of the age, developing a defensible notion of the likely religious consciousness or forms of thought and practice of the age, and judging on that basis what would be an appropriate form of remark for someone who belonged to such an age. This is a straightforwardly historical-critical undertaking. Therefore, his acceptance of the need for some historical-critical spadework as a feature of discerning the intention of the human author could not be clearer. But as I have indicated already,

Balthasar was unwilling to let the matter rest there. Establishing the most probable historical, sociological, and biographical background of a text does not yield its intended meaning, though it does help establish the meaning's likely parameters. One must also have, as he put it on one occasion, "a subjective empathy" for the author, "a loving comprehension [of his] whole person,"[79] and, on another, some sort of "interior communication."[80]

Such phrases offer apparently close parallels to the hermeneutical aims of Friedrich Schleiermacher and the Romantics, generally. We should not minimize the similarities, at least initially. In these two places, Balthasar indicated that the art of interpreting what the author intended to say involves a fellow feeling with the author, a shared experience. And to some ears that might sound rather like trying to recreate within oneself, as interpreter, the sort of experience that must have led the author to write what he or she did. Admittedly, there is nothing in Balthasar like the elaborateness of the means by which this should be achieved that there is in Schleiermacher's hermeneutics.[81] But the lack of elaborateness does little to distinguish him from Schleiermacher on the question whether proper interpretation involves reproducing the creative act by which the text came to be.

Balthasar's idea that the meaning of scripture is greater than that intended by the human author might seem to suggest an important difference from Schleiermacher. That would make him sound like the New Critics William Wimsatt and Monroe Beardsley who said a poem "is detached from the author at birth and goes about the world beyond his power to intend about it or control it."[82] Their insight is important, at least if limited to the notion that a writer is not in a uniquely privileged and authoritative position to interpret his or her own work.[83] But the difference it may suggest between Balthasar's and Schleiermacher's hermeneutics is illusory. Schleiermacher agreed that intention does not exhaust meaning. This is especially clear in his goal to understand the writer better than he did himself. For Schleiermacher, that meant seeking to bring to conscious reflection the myriad processes, some intended, some not, by which the work was created. He tried to reproduce the creation of the text in all its conscious and unconscious complexity. So establishing a text's meaning is not to be narrowed to divining the intent of the author. Rather, it is a question of divining the originating moment, of which the author himself is not completely aware. Whether those who appropriated Schleiermacher's dictum, or at least those Romantic expressivists against whom Wimsatt and Beardsley are polemicizing, would make this claim is doubtful.[84] Nevertheless, by contending that meaning cannot be restricted to conscious authorial intent, Balthasar, Schleiermacher, Wimsatt, and Beardsley are all (*mirabile dictu*) in agreement.

Setting the New Critics aside, let us suppose that Schleiermacher and Balthasar agreed on this one aspect of the interpretive enterprise: that it does involve getting back to the experience of the author in order thereby to reproduce it (at this point, of course, the New Critics would balk). However, this agreement is of quite modest scope because Schleiermacher and Balthasar disagreed over the centrality of that exercise in hermeneutics. For Schleiermacher, that is all it involved, or more precisely, the other interpretive work is strictly subordinated to this aim. The goal of reproducing the act of genius by which the text was created determines the use of the various hermeneutical tools that Schleiermacher identified. Even the subject matter itself fades from view, finally to be replaced by a common understanding between interpreter and author.[85] Even if Balthasar agreed with Schleiermacher that interpretation involves the reproduction of the originating experience (which is itself subject to doubts that I will address momentarily), he would not go so far as to elevate this aspect of interpretation over all others. For that would be to identify the subjective conditions for the production of a text with the objective evidence of its perception. It would collapse the distinction between understanding why an author was prompted to write what he did and understanding what he wrote (the subject matter). Balthasar's relentless polemic against purely subjective readings of scripture—for example, the "misreadings" of the immanentists—surely tell against such a collapse of the meaning of a text into its genesis. So one, if not the only, fundamental difference between Balthasar and Schleiermacher on this issue lies in Balthasar's accentuating the absolute priority of the subject matter in the act of perception and understanding. The fellow feeling that is sought with the author of a text is directed toward an understanding of the text's subject matter, which Gadamer correctly says Schleiermacher eschews as the object of interpretation-understanding.

Let me make my intentions in the foregoing clear. In effect, I have been giving full latitude to Balthasar's remarks about "subjective empathy" for, "loving comprehension" of, and "interior communication" with, an author. I have been allowing them to be interpreted in the most expressivist, Romantic sense possible. I am granting, that is to say, that Balthasar may well have thought that this was a feature of interpreting for authorial intent. But there are strong indications in his texts that he did not think that this was all that it involved, indeed, there are strong indications that it was not a particularly important element in discerning the intent of an author. Furthermore, there is some indication that the business of establishing a subjective empathy and a loving comprehension is more accurately understood less psychologically than has been suggested heretofore.

In the following two passages, Balthasar stressed that the importance of retracing the act of creation by establishing a fellow feeling with a text's author should not be exaggerated:

[W]e cannot assume that the work of art is intended in its author's mind, simply, to be an expression of himself. Quite the contrary, it is more often the expression of a world-view which the artist proposes as objective and valid for others as well. It is this world-view, and not himself, that he wants to fashion and make worthy of belief. For this reason, the artist will conceal himself in his work as much as he will reveal himself.[86]

[T]he analogy of human creation shows that, where a particular work is concerned, not everything and perhaps not even the main thing has been said when one comes to know the life and purpose of the artist. The work itself, where it has truly succeeded, possesses an objective, autonomous form and a meaning which is quite independent of its creator. This holds not only for technical works, in which the agent mostly remains anonymous since he has from the outset subordinated his personal spirit to a greater objective context that aims at a final product; it is true also of personal works such as a poem or a symphony, whose interior harmony is something quite different from the subjective 'aptitudes', from the knowledge and ability of its author.[87]

Both passages stress the independence of the text from the act by which it came to be and point out the considerable likelihood of an author having subordinated his or her self-expression to a more objective goal. In both instances, then, Balthasar placed strict limits around the importance of divining the interior processes by which a text came to be. Both quotations demonstrate that although Balthasar understood interpretation to involve the discernment of an author's intention, he did not intend it to be understood primarily to mean discerning the author's subjective experience.

Balthasar's assertion bears a close resemblance to T. S. Eliot's "impersonal theory of poetry."[88] "The progress of an artist," so Eliot maintained, "is a continual self-sacrifice, a continual extinction of personality."[89] As one commentator on Eliot observed, "the poem is about the experiences of the poet, which are 'objective' in the sense that others can and do have similar experiences, rather than about the subjective personality, unique to each individual, that undergoes the experience."[90] Balthasar shared with Eliot a view of texts as the description of a personal vision of a shared, public world. Although the personal dimension to a text is acknowledged, it is the public dimension that is emphasized. Accordingly, if one is to interpret aright the world depicted in the text, one's search for the intent of the author must not be confined—indeed ought to pay relatively scant attention—to the attempt to plumb the author's psyche in search of motives or personal experiences. Instead, the text itself must be able to mediate the splendor of this author's world in such fashion that it can be grasped in and through the texts themselves. In this way the text mediates a world that can become, through a subsequent act of *applicatio,* the reader's own. It is not necessary to get behind the text into the author's experience of creating it in order to understand it. A text mediates the author's vision of a shared, public world (in its most comprehensive sense). And it is primarily this, rather than the more or less overt expression of the author's private experience, that should be attended to when seeking to discern his or her intention.

A closer look at the places where Balthasar spoke of "subjective empathy" and "a loving comprehension of the author's whole person" and of an "interior communication" further suggests that he did not mean to endorse free-ranging speculation about why an author wrote what he or she did. First, the context from which the "interior communication" quotation is taken makes clear that, in this instance at least, establishing an interior communication has more to do with discerning the objective proportions of the text (or its subject matter) than with establishing a bond between the interpreter and the author. Not that the latter is dismissed as irrelevant, but in order to establish such a bond, the interpreter is called upon to become "interior to the work" and to "enter into its spell and radiant space."[91] The text itself sets the boundaries for an inquiry into authorial intent. Second, the full context of the "subjective empathy" quotation also emphasizes that such feelings should be guided by and take their measure from the objective features of the work. When seeking to discern an author's intention, the cues for establishing a fellow feeling must be provided by the work itself. The quotation in which the interpreter is urged to develop a "loving comprehension" of the author's whole person may strike readers as the most nearly Romantic sounding of the three. But there may be a way to interpret this passage that does not lead to the endorsement of reproducing within oneself the experiences by which a text came to be. My longstanding friendship with someone likely puts me in a better position than others less well acquainted with him to interpret his utterances. On hearing that this friend hurt someone's feelings at their first meeting, I might say: "I'm certain that Kirby would never have intended to hurt your feelings; he must have meant something else by that remark." There is no question here of my reproducing the experience that led Kirby to say what he did, though I have a strong sense that he is not the sort of person to hurl insults when introducing himself. If the analogy to textual interpretation holds, then this example may provide a way in which to understand Balthasar's urging us to develop a loving comprehension of an author without that becoming endlessly speculative. But in my example, discerning intention concerns establishing, not why a text was written, but what was the intended meaning of what was written. We will return momentarily to this important distinction, first made, to my knowledge, by Nicholas Wolterstorff.[92]

First, however, I ought to note that Balthasar's remarks about establishing a textually defensible fellow feeling with the author may serve as a warning against any thoroughgoing hermeneutical relativism that satisfies itself with an infinite play of textual meanings. Having a sense for what the author is concerned about, Balthasar seems to be saying, puts limits on how freely one should imagine what the meaning of a given text might be. (Such limits are irrelevant, of course, if one has already abandoned the idea that interpretation should at least take its cues from, without necessarily being utterly constrained by, authorial intent.) The term Balthasar often used for this basic orientation is pre-understanding. This term and its relatives, of course, have had very wide currency in hermeneutical discussions.[93] When appropriating the term, Balthasar was careful to insist that meaning not be collapsed into pre-understanding. For instance, in the article "Exegese und Dogmatik," he insisted that one's pre-understanding should provide nothing more than points of entry into the material. The subject matter itself eludes any attempt to interpret it strictly in terms of one's pre-understanding.[94] If we limit what the Bible can say to what we are already aware of, either thematically or unthematically, Balthasar feared that we will have simply closed ourselves off to what is most important in the text: what we cannot discover about God, our world, and ourselves on our own. This is the mistake he (following Barth, quite likely) thought Bultmann made by insisting on demythologizing the Bible. He maintained that we must not narrow the meaning of the Bible to "modern man's" horizon of understanding.[95] At bottom, his disagreement with Bultmann was christological: "if Christ is what he claims to be, then he cannot be so dependent on subjective conditions as to be hindered by these from making himself wholly understandable to man nor, contrariwise, can man, without his grace, supply the sufficient conditions of receiving him with full understanding."[96] Still, he granted Bultmann that one had to have some pre-understanding of love in order to be able to have any inkling at all about the sort of love enacted in Jesus Christ. But this pre-understanding, he asserted, is both transcended and fulfilled in the encounter of believers with Jesus Christ mediated by scripture. To understand Jesus Christ as "the love of God in the form of flesh, that is of human love" requires a "radical conversion; conversion not only of heart—and with it the admission that in the light of this love one has never loved—but also of the mind with the realization that one must start from the beginning to re-learn what love really is."[97] The hermeneutical point to be stressed is that Balthasar supposed that without some sense of what the author is likely talking about, one is liable to get his or her intention badly wrong.

It is time to put the question that has been lurking just beneath the surface of this discussion of authorial intent directly to Balthasar's texts. Does his version of the attempt to discern the author's intent, be that human or divine, fall prey to the intentional fallacy? Not if we define that fallacy in the way Nicholas Wolterstorff does. Wolterstorff argues, convincingly, that when interpreting someone's discourse, we must discriminate between asking why that person said or wrote something (an illegitimate or fallacious, because endlessly speculative, move) and asking what the person intended to say. In terms borrowed from J. L. Austin's speech-action theory, one ought to ask, not, "Why did someone perform a given illocutionary act?" but, "What illocutionary act did he or she intend to perform?" An example of Wolterstorff's will help clarify what is at issue.[98] The question, "Could you pass the salt?" can be an act of requesting salt or an act of inquiring whether someone is physically able to pass the salt. Of course it could function as other illocutionary acts as well, such as seeking an innocuous way to introduce oneself despite thinking one's soup is already rather too salty. If we want to know what the intended meaning of the sentence is, though, we must ask what illocutionary act the speaker intended to perform.[99] Did he or she intend to request salt, inquire about whether the salt was within someone else's reach, or introduce him or herself? We do not ask, that is to say, about what might have motivated the speaker to utter those five words.

Wolterstorff's distinction marks a significant refinement of the intentional fallacy as articulated by Wimsatt and Beardsley. They assume that one either engages in rank speculation (by doing historical and psychological and sociological investigations) or attends to the language of the poem, its structure, organization, etc. But that still involves a question of intention: What did the author likely intend to say when he used such language in such a configuration? One is claiming that the author likely intended to say this, not that, on the basis of the context in which the sentence being interpreted is located. Ironically, Wimsatt and Beardsley themselves appeal to this second sort of intention when responding to what they take to be a fallacious interpretation of a quatrain of

John Donne's.[100] They argue that what makes it fallacious is the attempt to link as motive to result Donne's interest in the new Copernican astronomy to verses that speak of the earth's movement. They contend in response that the texts themselves suggest that the earth's movement is better understood as referring to earthquakes. So it is not why Donne said something or other (because he was deeply influenced by the new astronomy) but what illocutionary act Donne intended to perform (comparing earthquakes to feelings of trepidation).

What, then, of Balthasar? I have indicated one way in which his concern to cultivate a sympathetic empathy with an author can, in theory, issue in endless speculation. I have also indicated several ways in which someone putting his hermeneutics into practice would not have to commit the intentional fallacy (as Wolterstorff defines it). Balthasar believed that the meaning of a text is greater than what is consciously intended by the author. He also believed that when texts succeed (a success he left undefined), they are descriptions of shared, public worlds. Trying, therefore, to discern the subjective motivations of such descriptions is to go around (or behind) the text, rather than to interpret it. Balthasar's insistence upon attending to the wholeness of a given work (with all that that entails) lends further support to my argument that he adopted a legitimate sort of intention-seeking interpretation. On balance, it seems appropriate to say that although Balthasar might be faulted for advocating (to a quite limited extent) a Romantic, expressivist version of intention seeking, all three of the aspects of Balthasar's hermeneutics just cited point to a different sense of intention from that criticized by Wolterstorff and, less precisely, by Wimsatt and Beardsley.

If concerns about Balthasar's attempts to discern the intention of the human biblical authors or redactors can be allayed, what about his efforts to interpret in order to discern God's intent? Did his proposals in that regard lead him to commit the intentional fallacy? That seems very unlikely, not only because the arguments marshaled above apply to interpreting God's discourse as well, but also because one can hardly suppose that Balthasar thought any biblical exegete capable of reproducing the act by which the texts were generated in the mind of God. So, just as with discerning the intent of the human author, discerning God's intention involves discerning what illocutionary act God intended to perform with the locutions of the text being interpreted. That will take all the work that looking for human intention does, plus something else. The scope of material under review is broadened beyond the boundaries of a particular human author's book or letter to embrace the whole of the canon, since all of it is, on his interpretation, God's Word.[101]

Balthasar did not often address this issue directly, at least not in such terms. Perhaps because of the imprecision with which he usually spoke of the relationship between God's discourse and the human author's discourse, he did not distinguish well between those times in which he thought he was articulating God's intention or that of the human authors or redactors. This raises problems for him, as I hope to demonstrate in the fifth chapter's analysis of his exegesis of Eph 5.23 ff. This failure to distinguish one sort of intention seeking from the other sometimes places him at odds with the prevailing historical-critical consensus regarding the likely authorship of a biblical book and the likely intent of a given passage. That, in turn, all too often leads even those otherwise sympathetic to his work to dismiss his exegesis as pre-critical or wildly speculative.

Before turning to the third element in Balthasar's hermeneutics, it is important to highlight those features of his conviction about the importance of discerning authorial intent that are compatible with the classic hermeneutics. Hans Frei and George Lindbeck do not discuss authorial intent when summarizing the classic hermeneutics, a fact that in Frei's case may reflect his indebtedness, especially in the years between the publication of *The Eclipse of Biblical Narrative* and his essay on the literal sense, to the New Critics' definition of the intentional fallacy. Be that as it may, de Lubac did at least allude to authorial intent when, for example, discussing "the whole gamut of senses" the Bible presents, an abundance that was held to reflect "the infinity of its Author."[102] In spite of this relative quiet on the part of our three guides to pre-modern exegesis, it is widely recognized that one of the features of patristic, medieval, and Reformation era exegesis was a shared belief in the divine inspiration of the Bible.[103] For example, despite their considerable differences, the Alexandrian and Antiochene schools were united by a common conviction that God the Holy Spirit has woven into the scriptural text a spiritual meaning that, depending on the passage, was distinguishable from the narrative sense.[104] For most of Christian history, believing that the Bible was the Word of God meant, among other

things, that the Holy Spirit had spoken to the prophets and other biblical authors, who wrote down what they heard.[105] Christians have tried
in a variety of ways to reconcile a belief in biblical inspiration with the
Bible's errors and inconsistencies. What should be emphasized here,
however, is that given this conviction about the Bible's authorship, pre-
modern biblical interpretation involved, among other things, attending
to what the Holy Spirit wished to say. Pre-modern exegetes interpreted
the Bible sure in the belief that God had spoken to its authors, who
faithfully rendered what God had said.[106] As we have seen, Balthasar
shared this conviction. He believed that interpreting the Bible entailed
trying to establish what God intended to say by means of it. More specifically, like his pre-modern forebears, he believed that it was imperative, in order accurately to discern the Bible's intended sense, to approach
it with mind and heart attuned to what God would likely be saying in
the text. To borrow an image from Irenaeus, unless we have some sense
of what God might wish to say in the Gospels, we will read the stories
about Jesus Christ and see a fox instead. And that would be to miss the
point(s) that God intends to make through these stories. And, again like
his pre-modern forebears, Balthasar scrutinized the text very carefully,
seeing, for instance, in Gn 1.26 evidence of God's own self-description
in the plural forms of a noun and a verb. That when doing so he sometimes distinguished between the intended sense of the divine and human
authors, unlike virtually all pre-modern exegetes, does not contradict the
more basic point of agreement. To interpret the Bible without attempting
to hear in it God's Word would have made no sense to either Balthasar
or the pre-moderns.

ECCLESIAL MEDIATION

A third major feature of Balthasar's hermeneutics is the importance of
ecclesial mediation. This can be distinguished into three basic parts—
tradition, the liturgy, and faith—which I treat in turn.

Since intention does not exhaust meaning for Balthasar, interpretation takes on the character of an ongoing argument about what God is
saying in and through scripture. This is not to dismiss the intention of

the original, human author, but to recognize the limits of its import. The point can be put, in Hans-Georg Gadamer's words, as follows: "The real meaning of a text . . . does not depend on the contingencies of the author and his original audience. . . . Not just occasionally, but always, the meaning of a text goes beyond its author. That is why understanding is not merely a reproductive but always a productive activity as well."[107] Admittedly, Balthasar did not describe biblical interpretation as a form of argument, preferring instead to think of it as a continual meditative reflection, or a plumbing of the limitless depths of triune love, or the continual development or articulation of the glory mediated by the texts. He believed that Christian churches, as long as they exist, will be called to reflect upon the central mysteries of the faith as they are normatively mediated by scripture. In this, they are responding to the offer of grace there made present.

It appears to some Protestants and Catholics alike that in Catholic exegesis the notion of ongoing *argument* is ruled out by the idea of a teaching authority. Two points can be made in response. First, Balthasar believed that the unity of the Catholic Church and the integrity of the kerygma depend upon, in part, the faithful adhering to the pronouncements of the magisterium. He cited Paul's having accepted the Jerusalem Council's decision respecting the observance of dietary laws as an example of valuing unity over personal convictions, however deeply held they may be.[108] And Paul's discussion of the strong and weak in 1 Corinthians and in Romans provided Balthasar additional textual support for his view that the strong must yield to the weak in order to preserve them in their faith.[109] It may seem odd to suggest that he believed that the magisterium could ever assume the role of the weak, as though their teachings must simply be tolerated or indulged in order to avoid misleading them with a superior, Christian gnosis. But that is one implication of Balthasar's criticisms of the Second Vatican Council for having written too much, much of which was "repetitive" and "amateurish."[110] Such criticisms, however, are extremely rare. Another way to understand the magisterium's pronouncements in terms of the distinction between the strong and the weak is this: the magisterium articulates positions relative to the kerygma that it knows are not fully in accord with the form of Christ in order thereby to preserve the weak in faith (and therewith, Church unity). In either case, on Balthasar's view, there is room for argument regarding the usefulness, appropriateness, and pertinence of the magisterium's interpretation of the gospel.

Second, Balthasar also seems to have thought that nothing prevents the magisterium being, on occasion, wrong. He believed that the magisterium was preserved from making irremediable error, but not error per se. This preservation is grounded, he claimed, in the Church being the spotless bride.[111] Although the Church remains spotless in Mary, there are times when, due to the sinfulness of those who make up and administer the Church, this spotlessness becomes practically unrecognizable. Citing Acts 20.29, Balthasar warned that wolves from without, and cowardly hirelings from within, will sometimes seek to destroy the flock. He believed (or hoped) that under such circumstances believers would have the capacity to discern which of the magisterium's teachings ought to be followed and which neglected. "[T]he Church has the anointing in herself (1 Jn 2.20ff.) which teaches her which precept and which 'manner of life' of those who 'preside over her' (Heb 13.7) she must follow."[112] This is the only place in the *Theological Aesthetics*, so far as I am aware, in which Balthasar appealed to a *sensus fidelium* over against the magisterium.[113] And this was done in the abstract, rather than in support of any particular theological proposal. Nevertheless, this view of the *sensus fidelium* is in keeping with his understanding of the body of Christ being subordinate to its head, not to the magisterium per se. It is subordinate to the magisterium solely to the extent that as it exercises its authority in the service of the gospel it "gives concrete expression to the Lord's obedience in love."[114] That is to say, from Balthasar's perspective, the magisterium is best able to perform its service to the whole Church when it least confuses itself with the Church's head. The best model for such transparency to the Lord of the Church is the saints.[115] Balthasar, therefore, can be described as adhering to the view developed in the tenth chapter of *Dei Verbum* that both the magisterium and the rest of the faithful participate in, and have a sense for, the tradition.[116]

In sum, Balthasar maintained that the authoritative teaching of the Catholic Church's hierarchy does not foreclose the possibility of continued discussion and civil argument on a given interpretation of scripture. In this regard, he was no strict conservative. Biblical interpretation is a form of argument, if by that we mean an ongoing reflection that then needs to be justified before believers as apt.

Having established that on Balthasar's view biblical interpretation involves argument, let us return to his contention that it is a never-ending enterprise. This is a very common theme in the *Theological Aesthetics*. On his view, theology is engaged in a historically extended conversation about the subject matter of the biblical texts. This follows from his view that the Bible's trinitarian-christological content can never be exhaustively interpreted since every approach to it is judged by its absolute superiority.[117] For Balthasar, there can be no question of ever comprehending the whole of the mystery of triune love, which remains a gift of the Spirit, of the Father, and of the Son.[118] Different epochs in the history of Christianity have favored one triune Person over the others, but each one of the divine Persons remains (or should remain) indissolubly bound to the others.[119] This "endless range of interpretability" is one reason for the "ecclesial teaching authority."[120] Because Balthasar maintained that the meaning of the Bible is always new, always opening itself up in diverse and unprecedented ways, it is appropriate, on his view, to think of the interpretive process as a continual, or at least continuing, conversation with the text about its subject matter.

This conversation does not go on in a vacuum. For Balthasar, the Christian interpreter enters into a conversation with the text that is shaped by the history of interpretation in and by the churches. Christian biblical interpreters stand within a history of tradition, a history of effect (*Wirkungsgeschichte*), as Gadamer put it.[121] Tradition mediates the text to the interpreter. Rather than confronting the interpreter as a static deposit of propositions to be believed truthful, tradition shapes the sorts of questions with which to approach the biblical text. It predisposes an interpreter to read the text in certain ways and to certain ends and not others. Over time, some forms of such predisposition or prejudice are deemed more significant and helpful than others. Thus there develops a community consensus or shared reading of the texts. Kathryn E. Tanner has called this the plain sense, a phrase with which I believe Balthasar's view is compatible.[122] The consensus of the community of faith as expressed in such conventional readings establishes the arena within which the ongoing task of interpretation is to be carried on. This constitutes another set of limits on the range of ecclesially apt interpretations besides the fellow feeling for the biblical authors discussed previously.

For Balthasar, Christian dogmas are a distillation of such conventional readings. He appealed to three different, though not contradictory, sets of metaphors in order to convey his view of the function served by the dogmas. First, he likened them to guidelines for theology's contemplative reflection on the scriptural mediation of triune love. After characterizing the Chalcedonian definition as "a methodological and heuristic principle for a Christology that must then be developed from it," Balthasar went on to ask, rhetorically, "would it not be true to say of the greater number of the Church's canons and definitions that they are . . . the solid guidelines that point the way for elaborating a theology, the guidelines that form the basis for a correct understanding and interpretation of the divine revelation?"[123] They act, according to Balthasar, as maps or signposts directing one to the relative significance of certain biblical passages and episodes and the relative insignificance of others. Balthasar's interpretation of the Gospels' views of time in terms of the hypostatic union discussed above stands as a particularly striking example of this approach. Second, he likened dogmas to the means by which the faithful protect the integrity of the gospel against misunderstanding and abuse. The achievement of the early ecumenical councils, on his view, was "to ward off the danger of the absorption of what was decisively biblical and Christian into a universal metaphysical schema."[124] Or, again, they can be understood as preserving some sense of the wholeness of the revelation of God against those who would split it into pieces. "It is here that the problem of heresy has its roots: *hairesis,* the selective disjoining of parts."[125] Finally (and I think the other two sets of metaphors coalesce in this one), he likened the dogmas to a form of service that points past itself to what is to be believed. They are not to be admired in themselves, Balthasar argued, for they have no autonomous form of their own, independent of the form of Christ. Rather, they "all point to something else, something different from themselves, something which is essentially superior to themselves and which lies at the level of divine revelation."[126] The dogmas are best understood, on his view, as standing in "a ministerial relationship to the primal form, which is what is to be rendered visible."[127] Above all, they do not pretend "to express better, more comprehensively and in a more modern way what the Bible has uttered in an awkward, fragmentary, purely unscientific, and popular manner which is essentially conditioned by time and, hence, in need of reform."[128] A lamentable "sluggishness in thought," he complained, is to blame for the notion that the gospel is a system of dogmas that must be believed rather than the living voice of God's love.[129]

Balthasar adamantly maintained that the conversation with the text in the light of the history of its effect or interpretation (understood in both its theoretical and practical dimensions) should not be one-sided. Proper interpretation does not amount to having a conversation with tradition about the text, which itself remains mute. Rather, the conversation goes on in the context of tradition (with its pre-understandings) between the interpreter and the text. There is a continual back and forth, a to and fro between the text and the interpreter. This is a clear implication of Balthasar's repeated insistence that the Bible can never be exhaustively interpreted. On his view, the interpreter does not turn to tradition, which, in its entirety, is supposed to have a fix on the whole meaning of the text. Rather, the text remains free, as it were, to confront the interpreter anew, each time he or she seeks to understand it. The text exerts its influence, provided the interpreter remains open to it doing so. Gadamer expresses this influence with the metaphor of the text asking the interpreter questions. The new hermeneuts (or Fuchs, at least) expressed it with the metaphor of the text interpreting the interpreter. Balthasar would likely not have objected to either formulation, though he spoke instead, in the *Theological Aesthetics,* of the absolute priority of the objective evidence. This reinforces a point made above in the discussion of intention seeking: from Balthasar's perspective, believers must not so limit what they get out of the text by their pre-understandings that they rob Jesus Christ and his Spirit of the power to effect new, unanticipated meanings.[130]

This discussion of the influence, as I have called it, of scripture on those who interpret it raises the question of Balthasar's understanding of the relation of scripture and tradition. In this connection, one remark in the *Theological Aesthetics* is particularly noteworthy: "In 'Scripture' [the Church] has a model of the mystery of love and of her relationship to it, but nothing more; in the theological tradition which finds its embodiment down through the ages, the Church has a continuous enrichment of the meditation. But this meditation must always adjust itself and correct itself afresh by means of the first model."[131] In the now classic formulation of Heiko Oberman, Balthasar is here advancing a "Tradition I" view, that is, one in which scripture constitutes "the canon, or standard, of revealed truth . . . [t]he history of interpretation [of which] is the Tradition of the Church."[132] Balthasar's view should therefore be contrasted with a "Tradition II" position in which tradition is regarded as an independent authoritative source for theology's ongoing reflection. In this, according to de Lubac, he is fully consistent with the practices of the pre-modern Church: "Nobody . . . ever spoke of two 'sources' of faith that would have been parallel and radically distinct—and, whatever authors who read its texts too quickly and superficially may say of it, the Council of Trent did not do so either. . . . Right from the beginning, in the very first generation of Christians, it was a matter of Scripture being read or the word of God being heard in Church and interpreted by Tradition."[133] Accordingly, there is nothing in the *Theological Aesthetics* of which I am aware that would threaten the material sufficiency of scripture.

Having completed the analysis of Balthasar's view of tradition, let us turn to a second basic part of his understanding of the ecclesial mediation of the scriptures, namely, his contention that biblical interpretation is shaped by the liturgy. Two points are worth making here, if only briefly. First, it is shaped by the way the liturgy uses the texts. As the faithful pray the Psalms, for instance, Balthasar believed that they participate in the Spirit-led glorification of the Son's love for the Father and the Father's love for the Son (and in and with that, their mutual love for the world). In this giving of praise, on his view, the movement from letter to spirit is enacted. The faithful participate in the transformation of a psalm written originally, say, for the coronation of an Israelite king (with its admittedly religious overtones) into a song of praise for God. Participating in this hermeneutical transformation alerts them to the ways in which the original intent of a passage has been transcended, if not altogether annulled. Further, it reinforces the particular use to which believers put these texts: they read them as an efficacious medium by which the Spirit of Christ makes Christ present to them, rather than as sources for an investigation of ancient Israel. In addition, the lectionary reinforces the notion that the various parts of the Bible are self-glossing. Typically, worshippers hear a reading from the Old Testament, from an epistle, and from a Gospel. If the sermon is expository, rather than topical, and if it is done well, the preacher will likely weave together references from among the three, attempting to read them in light of one another, to hear all of them as God's Word to the faithful.

Second, Balthasar stressed that in the celebration of the sacraments believers experience afresh the one whom the texts mediate. This reinforces the use to which the texts are being put in the liturgy more generally: "The unprecedented hardness and exacting nature of the corporeal form of the sacraments . . . call forth not only naked faith, but also the equally hard historical truth to which they owe their origin. . . . The image compels them to enter into the act by revealing to them the act which both instituted the image and is contained in the image."[134] In the Eucharist, Balthasar held, the faithful are conformed to Christ, who inserted "the content of the Cross into the form of the supper" both as a sign of sovereign freedom and of the "permanent validity of this form for the Church."[135] Participation in the liturgy deepens, particularly during the Church's reenactment of the events of Easter week, the believer's understanding of the identity of the one to whom the believer is conformed. On Balthasar's view, the Catholic Church, "basing herself first and last on the experience of the Lord's Mother in the flesh . . . can teach her children the Word of God and communicate to them from the heart of her motherly and bridal experience not only its meaning, but its taste, its smell, and its whole incarnational concreteness."[136] The worshippers are brought nose to nose, as it were, with the object of their devotion. Their minds *and* hearts are transformed by participating in the drama of crucifixion and resurrection. That in turn, shapes readings, since it deepens the faithful's affinity for the whole sweep of the biblical story and for the tradition that helps to mediate it. For instance, it will influence the sorts of questions that the faithful ask and avoid asking the text. In the context of the liturgical performance of the texts, it is simply jarring to ponder what sorts of plants the disciples would likely have encountered in the Kidron valley. In other contexts, of course, such questions are appropriate, but not during the liturgy.

The third part of Balthasar's convictions about the ecclesial mediation of the scriptures to the faithful concerns his view that proper interpretation requires that the interpreter approach the text with the appropriate attitude or cast of mind. On Balthasar's view, this is best il-lustrated by Mary, who is the supreme instance of an active contempla-tion of the form of Christ.[137] My argument here is twofold. First, this sort of contemplation, which Balthasar described as Marian-Ignatian, provides an additional justification for the theological appropriation of historical criticism, one Balthasar himself did not employ, but could have done without self-contradiction. Second, contemplation so under-stood indicates, that for Balthasar, understanding the Bible as the Word of God is a practical skill or capacity.

Balthasar asserted, with some frequency, that the contemplation of the form of Christ as mediated to believers in scripture involves the con-formation of the contemplative to Christ. It is, "as Paul says . . . the meta-morphosis of the beholder into the image he beholds (2 Cor 3.18)."[138] The less a person who seeks properly to interpret scripture resists this conformation, the more Christ's form will be im-pressed in him or her. The prime example of this is Mary. Her *fiat mihi* provides a model, Bal-thasar believed, for the way the faithful are bid to let the triune God impress Godself upon them. On his view, this occurs and must occur solely at the initiative and in accordance with the design of the triune God. Apparently concerned to dispel any suspicion of works righteous-ness, he summarized such goings on this way: "Allowing the Word its way in me is not an action, and is not, therefore, an accomplishment and a work; it is contemplative obedience that of its own passes over into the Passion in accordance with the law of the image which leaves its impress on it."[139] Balthasar has been criticized for such remarks on the grounds that he seems to leave no room for human freedom in relation to God. The pattern appears to be one of spiritual monergism, rather than a synergistic cooperation between infinite and finite freedoms.[140] Although there are certainly grounds for such a critique, in the *Theo-logical Aesthetics* such remarks are at the very least balanced against oth-ers that argue for a cooperation between the faithful and God's Spirit in the graced conformation to Christ:

> In no person does Christ's image become impressed as a result of that person's power, but equally it never occurs without the per-son's will and cooperation. This collaboration, however, cannot consist in the fact that here two people are working alongside and

with one another. . . . Nowhere do God and man work together on the same plane. Rather, the Marian *Ecce ancilla Domini* points to the distance between Lord and Handmaid, a distance expressed in the fact that in all things it is the Lord who commands and the Handmaid who obeys. This creaturely and Christian obedience . . . renounces all private ideas and objections in order to accept the entire work-plan from the Lord's hands and to place all one's own energies, both bodily and spiritual, at its disposal. This obedience is in this respect the opposite of a passivity that forsakes real cooperation so as to 'let God do what he will'.[141]

It should be acknowledged that on the very next page Balthasar seems to contradict himself by saying that the Christian life "is simply a life that lets God dispose of it as he will."[142] One could cite other passages where Balthasar seems to be riding two horses at once. But doing so would both subject the reader to an unnecessary tedium and miss a central point: because Balthasar wanted to affirm both the importance and the ultimate incommensurability of human and divine actions in the process of sanctification, he often sounded self-contradictory. Before going on to indicate what I take to be the important hermeneutical implications of this issue, let me indicate one way to resolve the seeming contradiction. This solution turns on bridging, with Balthasar, the seemingly unbridgeable chasm between action and contemplation: "While the Christian life ostensibly consists in alternate periods of action and contemplation, its aim should be to make the two interpenetrate more and more. With the saints they were no longer distinguishable. The saint in his activities can be in a perfect state of contemplation . . . and so, in the formula of Ignatius, he can be *in actione contemplativus*."[143] And so it was, Balthasar contended, with Mary. "Her 'waiting for the Lord' is her permanent attitude, which according to Christ's last parables suffices as Christian attitude provided it is truly lived out: this 'watchful waiting,' this 'active readiness' is the wet clay in which alone the Christ-form can become impressed."[144] The images clash: "wet clay" is a strange metaphor for "active readiness," the latter signaling the importance of human agency, the former seeming to deny it. But by juxtaposing them in this way, Balthasar expressed his conviction that accepting a vocation is not utterly passive; it involves an active cooperation.

Ignatius helps to elucidate this because he understood the importance for human freedom of Aquinas's teaching on the *analogia entis* and his distinction between divine and human causality.[145] As Balthasar observed in an essay on Ignatius in the *Theological Aesthetics*,

> The practice of indifference [*Indifferenz*], as understood by Ignatius, does not . . . mean the inevitable annihilation of man's own being and will. . . . No, the true mystery of Christian revelation is this: the perfection of the kingdom of God ('God all in all', 'it is no longer I who live, but Christ who lives in me') can be pursued as the universal operation of God in the active co-operation of the creature [*Allwirken Gottes im aktiven Mit-Wirken des Geschöpfs*]—in abandonment, surrender, service. This co-operation can no longer remain at the level of indifference in the sense of *merely* letting things happen; no, the particular will of God, which is to be actively grasped and carried out, must also be actively pursued.[146]

The last sentence in particular shows the degree to which, on Balthasar's view, the receptivity of the Christian life is imbued with an ardent, active expectancy.

Balthasar's view of the interpretive task involves just this sort of Marian-Ignatian cooperation. Indeed, if practiced as Balthasar would have one do, biblical interpretation is a primary instance of the Marian-Ignatian mode of contemplation. The contemplation he believed must characterize the Christian life includes (though is not exhausted by) ecclesially apt biblical interpretation. Although Balthasar held that the form of Christ can be contemplated in the saints and, in different ways, in works of art and in nature, the normative means of its mediation is the Bible.

The terms 'indifference' (*Indifferenz*) or 'disinterest' (*Interesselosigkeit*) can cause confusion in an interpretive context since they may seem to suggest an attitude free of bias or self-concern. It has become something of a commonplace since Gadamer's critique of the Enlightenment's discrediting of prejudice (*Vorurteil*) to assume that no reading is done with complete impartiality. To narrow the point to theological hermeneutics, it seems only natural to say that the faithful read the Bible in the hopes of hearing it as the Word of God. So there is inevitably a measure of self-interest, or self-concern, in any attempt at a faithful interpretation. Balthasar, too, recognized the futility of a purportedly presuppositionless exegesis. And he used that insight as a means of criticizing historical critics who trade on a view of science that presupposes such impartiality as its methodological watchword.[147]

The point he seems to have wished to make by using the terms indifference and disinterest is that a faithful reading of the Bible entails renouncing any pretensions to control the way God might speak through it. Or, in language more closely resembling his own, one has to let the glory of the Christ-form as mediated by the text irradiate one so that one sees the light coming from the form and not from oneself. "What, as the grace of faith, illumines the subject that approaches the phenomenon has to be the objective light that indwells it—its objective and radiant rightness. The illumined subject then—and ever increasingly— learns how emphatically that light derives from the object and indwells it."[148] One has to let the form be beautiful in itself and not merely in its relation to oneself. This, it will be recalled, is the force of Balthasar's complaint about the two misreadings of scripture, the one extrinsicist, the other immanentist, that were addressed in the previous chapter. He was concerned to avoid overt or covert utilitarian readings of the Bible that domesticate God's Word, treating it as something merely to serve personal ends. Still, from a believer's point of view, it is not as though the love of God has *no* bearing on his or her life. In the attempt not to manipulate the Bible, Balthasar argued that believers need not give up the hope of hearing themselves addressed by God. The requisite indifference and hopefulness cannot be set against one another, any more than can action and contemplation. Balthasar's point is, rather, that believers ought to try to read the Bible in such a way that their hopes do not foreclose the possibility of unhoped for results.

Two implications of this understanding of interpretation should be emphasized. First, and perhaps more controversially, the notion that discerning the will of God involves human enterprise provides an additional warrant for using the methods and findings of historical criticism. To my knowledge, Balthasar did not adduce this warrant when discussing the proper role and limits of historical criticism in theological exegesis. Yet here, in his view of the necessity of actively seeking, indeed pursuing, an understanding of God's will, lies a decisive reason for

Christians concerned to hear the Bible as God's Word not to fear, but to seek to integrate historical criticism into their exegetical practice. Historical criticism, when seen in this light, is one of the means by which the faithful ought to discern God's will in the Bible.[149] If his main argument for integrating historical criticism within Christian theological interpretation, as I noted earlier, is the double principle of a form being determined by its antecedents yet remaining an indissoluble whole, then this second argument addresses itself to the subjective side of the perception of the form of Christ in its scriptural mediation. Although this is not a case he made for the importance of historical criticism, it is compatible with his views. If contemplation of the form of Christ were sheerly passive, there would be no room for the critical methods, or even for any active interpretation that goes beyond mere repetition of the biblical words. Balthasar's way of putting it, stressing God's universal causality and the faithful's cooperation therein, does justice to his concerns to avoid fundamentalism while still giving the initiative in biblical interpretation to the Spirit who leads into all truth.[150]

Whenever one advocates the importance of historical criticism in biblical exegesis, there is a risk of seeming to commend a renewed form of scribalism. The worry about fostering a situation in which only a carefully (and expensively) trained elite can accurately interpret the Bible—a worry that Balthasar certainly had and took seriously—is in my judgment overworked.[151] There is an inevitable specialization among the faithful, as Paul's teaching concerning the *analogia pistis* already makes clear. And as Charles Wood once remarked, in practice believers have always understood that interpreting scripture requires a range of more or less specifiable skills.[152] There is no getting around the fact that historical criticism has, and will likely continue to have, a profound impact on the faithful's understanding of the Bible. The important point, then, is not that, as Balthasar himself put it, "the *habitus acquisitus scientiae* ought to be left behind and transcended by a *habitus infusus* and the *donum Spiritus*."[153] Rather, for the benefit of the Church, the infused *habitus* must inform the work of the acquired *habitus* right from the start "if the work [of the latter] is to bear theological fruit."[154] Historical criticism, he believed, will be of greatest service to the Church when the same Spirit that animates the texts themselves animates historical critics.[155] This view is propounded with particular vigor in "Exegese und

Dogmatik," an article that appeared half a dozen years after the completion of the *Theological Aesthetics*. Here one finds Balthasar urging historical critics to pursue their craft under the guidance of the Holy Spirit. This, he contended, is the only way to keep their work objective and free of compromise. To do otherwise, he believed, is to violate the very text they seek to interpret.[156] Insisting, along with Balthasar, on the continued importance of the historical-critical enterprise does not imply that God cannot speak through the Bible to those not so trained or to those who have not been exposed to those so trained. It is not necessary to hold that God cannot speak through the Bible to a fundamentalist who spurns the historical-critical method in order to stress the importance of doing historical-critical work on the text. Presumably God is free to use the Bible in whatever ways suit God's salvific purposes. It is certainly no threat to divine freedom to say that Christian churches ought to encourage biblical scholars to pursue their craft assiduously. My argument with respect to Balthasar's approach to the issue is simply that the rationale he provided for such encouragement could have depended, not only on his analysis of the objective evidence for belief, but on the subjective evidence, as well.

The second hermeneutical implication of Balthasar's understanding of the active passivity of contemplation to which I would draw attention is this: the proper interpretation of scripture is the exercise of certain capacities that are enacted in the texts. He contended that it is an act of imitating or participating in the archetypal God experiences of certain biblical figures (principally, though not exclusively, Jesus, Mary, Peter, John, Paul, and the Prophets).[157] So understanding the Bible as the Word of God is both a noetic and practical enterprise. But to put it in terms of that disjunction is already to miss Balthasar's point, since understanding is a capacity, a praxis, a doing something: "Christian life is not a second movement subsequent to contemplation, a practical corollary to *theoria*. For *theoria* can occur only as we spread out our existence under the image offered by God, which has shone within our darkness as God's light (2 Cor 4.6). The image unfolds *into* the one contemplating it, and it opens out its consequences in his life."[158] Granted, one can distinguish between *explicatio* and *applicatio,* but when one reads the Bible as the Word of God, the two condition each other to such a degree that they reflect a deeper unity. That is what Balthasar took to be the force of the author of John's insight concerning the existential or self-involving character of truth. One does the truth, as the Evangelist says (Jn 3.21).[159] The poor in spirit, Balthasar said, are those who understand the scriptures this way. They have been given the simple eyes of faith that are required to see the form of God's glory in Christ. And such "a simplicity of the eye, allowing the decisive perception, presupposes the unity of the act of seeing and the act of living, which Adolf Schlatter lays down as the fundamental postulate of the act of theological recognition, in that . . . the obedience to the revelation which is brought about in man through the revelation is the basis of the act of seeing."[160] So, for Balthasar, there is no seeing the form of Christ without being caught up in a movement, initiated and sustained by grace, of the whole person away from self and toward Christ. For the form is not established by God, so Balthasar asserted, simply to leave the faithful awestruck, but to kindle decision and action.[161] More specifically, it is to draw the faithful into creation's glorification of the triune God brought about by the Holy Spirit, a glorification that constitutes humanity's telos.[162]

In what ways might Balthasar's reflections on the hermeneutical importance of tradition, the liturgy, and faith comport with the principles of the pre-modern hermeneutics outlined in the introduction? I would cite two. The first concerns the priority of the literal sense. One aspect of this conviction to which I have not yet drawn much attention is the room it leaves for different interpretations of the same text. Since no interpretation can completely encapsulate the meaning of Jesus Christ, pre-modern exegetes generally accepted the idea that no single statement of a text's meaning would hold true for all times and places. Henri de Lubac has provided us with an abundance of quotations in support of this view, for instance: " 'Because there may be a variety of different meanings, Sacred Scripture can be understood as referring to one and the same thing in several modes.' "[163] Since, on the classic view, God uses the same texts to say different things in different circumstances, biblical interpretation remains an unfinished business. In contrast to the prevailing historical-critical aim to identify a single, fixed meaning of a given text (usually defined as the original sense of a text for its original audience), both pre-modern exegetes and Balthasar viewed interpretation as akin to exploring a vast, indeed limitless new world.[164] For guidance along the way Balthasar and the pre-moderns appealed to the rule of faith (with all its diversity), recognizing, for the most part, that doing so simply excluded certain faulty interpretations rather than specifying a single "true" or "correct" one.

Second, Balthasar and most pre-modern exegetes agreed that proper interpretation has a practical dimension. Interpreting the Bible as they would have one do affects not only one's ideas and emotions, but also one's behavior. The pre-modern custom of using the text within an ecclesial setting for theoretical *and* practical direction at the hands of the Holy Spirit finds a modern echo in Balthasar's view of the hermeneutical significance of both faith and the liturgy. Once again, de Lubac's work clarifies and supports the point. In his analysis of medieval exegesis, de Lubac noted that the term *disciplina* occurred repeatedly in descriptions of the Christian life: "This single word 'disciplina' was enough to evoke the notion of good morals and a whole panoply of solid virtues."[165] Although not utterly distinct from the Greek *paideia,* its roots in the biblical soil run much deeper. What distinguished it from both Graeco-Roman and Jewish practices was its *intentio,* its Christological orientation: "in yielding to it . . . we find Christ."[166] There was, de Lubac argued, a "natural link" between discipline so understood and "the exposition of the four senses of Scripture."[167] Interpreting the Bible in accord with the purpose of its divine author involved much more than simply trying to understand certain information correctly, though that was not insignificant. It was also a practical activity, an enactment of the truths offered and believed: "the most traditional typological exegesis, the one whose source is in the New Testament, does not necessarily rest on dogmatic content but includes, at least in principle, the moral and spiritual application. For the Christian mystery cannot be stopped short of the Christian life. . . . 'What has been done signifies something that is to be done in the Holy Church.' "[168] Balthasar would also have agreed with the following description by Rowan Greer of the patristic conception of the Bible's role in the liturgy and have urged contemporary Christians to adopt it as their own: "The liturgical use of Scripture was not understood primarily in terms of edification and instruction. Instead, it was designed to shape Christian lives by the constant reminder of the message of salvation and of the response required by that message."[169] As Greer notes, repeated exposure to the

Bible can clear the faithful's memory and imagination of pettiness, insincerity, and self-absorption, leaving them more willing to be conformed to the cross—a willingness, obviously enough, that is to shape their lives both during the liturgy and outside of it.

Conclusion

There are four basic assertions to be identified in summarizing Balthasar's theological hermeneutics. First, Balthasar thought biblical interpreters should respect the integrity of the form of Christ and its reflection in the scriptures. Second, he thought that exegesis should try to be true to the intent of the biblical authors and redactors, always bearing in mind, of course, that since God is the *auctor primarius,* the meaning of any given text is not exhausted by the intent of its human author. Third, he thought that biblical interpretation ought to be done in critical conversation with the traditions of the churches and shaped by their liturgical life. Indeed, its fundamental form ought to be the Church's manifold acts of glorifying the triune God. Finally, he thought that historical critics had an important role to play in the faithful interpretation of scripture, provided they abided by the guidelines set forth in the preceding three points. While he provided an important objective warrant for theology to appropriate historical-critical methods and findings, there is also another, subjective warrant that accords with his understanding of contemplating the form of Christ.

With respect to the question of Balthasar's fidelity to the premodern hermeneutical conventions outlined in the introduction, this chapter has shown Balthasar's concern to abide by the priority of the literal sense in several ways: he argued that Jesus Christ is his own, unique measure and therefore cannot be exhaustively explained in terms whose meaning is set by extra-biblical frames of reference; he refused to accept any paraphrase of the biblical texts as fully adequate to the sovereign subject matter it mediates; and he contended that biblical interpretation is an on-going task. This conviction about the priority of the literal sense animated his exegesis of the Gospel references to time, in which he let the seeming contradictions find their resolution in the hypostatic union of the God-man, Jesus Christ. Balthasar's work is also compatible with the pre-modern view of the Bible as a self-glossing, christologically focused whole. We saw this enunciated somewhat confusedly in his polemic against historical criticism's supposed inability to read the Bible synchronically. His examination of what he called Jesus' double temporal horizon provided a vivid instance of how he, on occasion, was able to advance a synchronic reading of diverse biblical texts without ignoring their diachronic dimensions. Finally, Balthasar's work demonstrates his conviction that the Bible should serve as an authoritative guide to Christian life and thought rather than, for example, as a source of information about the ancient Near East. This entails, so he argued, listening attentively to what God intends to say by means of these texts. The faithful can develop such an ear for the Word of God by steeping themselves in the traditions of the Church and by being incorporated into the body of Christ through the liturgies. Doing so can shape their identity, transforming what they hope to receive from the texts and, therefore, the questions they put to it and the answers (and questions) they hear from it in return.

3

THE UNITY OF SCRIPTURE

Since the moment of its inception, the Church has wrestled with the question of how to understand itself in relation to Israel. One dimension of this question has been whether and how to make use of the Old Testament when doing theology. Increasingly, contemporary theologians are wary of answers that might further the Church's lamentably frequent practice of denigrating the theological significance for Christians of Israel's scripture.[1] Balthasar's approach to the issue is generally consistent with this trend. "Whoever accepts Jesus," he maintained, "must accept the unity of the Old and New Testaments."[2] But while wishing to emphasize the integrity of the revelation of God witnessed to by the Old and New Testaments, the Church has tried to articulate the relationship of the Testaments in ways that do not compromise its conviction that the unique and unsurpassable fulfillment of God's plan for salvation is Jesus Christ. It has affirmed, at least since the Jerusalem Council's decision denying that Gentiles are bound by the ritual observances of the Torah, that something absolutely new has occurred in Jesus Christ.

Finding the right set of categories to express this unique relation of continuity and discontinuity between the Testaments has proven extraordinarily difficult. Although Balthasar used the more common ones (type and anti-type, latency and patency, figure and reality, letter and spirit, and promise and fulfillment) at various places and for various purposes in the *Theological Aesthetics,* he did so with reservations. He believed that all of them, though in different ways peculiar to each, can undermine the uniqueness of God's self-revelation in Jesus Christ, or to Israel, or both.[3] For the same reason, on Balthasar's view, even the seemingly innocuous concepts 'continuity' and 'discontinuity' are problematic.[4] He was convinced that these or other conceptual pairings have to die, as it were, to their original, extra-biblical meanings in order to be better suited to describing the complex relations of the Testaments. And even then, no one set of categories struck him as fully adequate to the task.[5] Each throws a single shaft of light on something that, in order to be understood, must be lit up from all directions.

For my argument, the chief consequence of Balthasar's conceptual eclecticism is organizational. Rather than contending that a certain way of relating the Testaments is especially Balthasarian, I will adopt the following procedure. I begin by identifying three features of the Old Testament witness that Balthasar argued call out for a transcendent fulfillment. This Jesus Christ provides, a claim for which Balthasar believed there are two distinguishable forms of 'proof'. In the second section, I outline both and identify the sort of unity they suggest Balthasar believed the Bible to have. By way of conclusion, I note some of the strengths and weaknesses of Balthasar's uses of the Old Testament in the formulation of these 'proofs'. I also indicate the ways in which Balthasar's views and uses of scripture described herein are consistent with those features of pre-modern exegesis, outlined in the introduction, that helped to nourish the *sensus fidelium.*

FRAGMENTATION

One aspect of the Old Testament witness to God's revelation that Balthasar thought reflected the need for a fulfillment outstripping its own categories is the mutual irreconcilability of its various conceptions of both the covenant's fulfillment and the means by which that fulfillment is to be effected. To note some of the examples he provided in support of this view: The "today" of the cultic reenactment of creation and the Exodus is distinguished from the "today" of the apocalyptic visions. The prophets' summons to discern and respond faithfully to God's will in history differs from the contemplation of the cosmos's immanent order that characterizes much of the wisdom literature. The eschatological images of the apocalyptic seers are at odds with the earthy eroticism of the Song of Songs. The image of a messiah descending from the house of David as a political savior stands in tension with that of God's suffering servant. And both of these latter images, which depict the salvation of Israel being mediated by a human being, contrast with the Danielic Son of man coming down from above and with Ezekiel's vision of the heavens opening to reveal God's glory descending in a raging storm.[6]

In keeping with his principle methodological interest in *The Glory of the Lord*, Balthasar usually enunciated this observation in aesthetic categories. The Old Testament remains formless on its own terms.[7] There is no integrating form that would draw all the disparate elements into a comprehensive unity. Because of the contrasts and tensions among the diverse forms of Israel's hope for salvation, it is impossible to draw lines linking them all together.[8] The messianic, apocalyptic, and sapiential theological trajectories of the post-exilic period defy any attempt to coordinate them on their own terms. They and the other images of salvation mentioned above converge around a midpoint that remains open and indeterminate.[9] The exact contours of the fulfillment they anticipate cannot be ascertained within the confines imposed by the Old Testament's own theological axioms. For Balthasar, this meant that the transcendent form of the new and eternal covenant could be portrayed only after the seemingly absolute boundary of death had been breached and the abyss dividing God from creature had been bridged. But to do that would mean stepping outside of the old covenant's notions of what is conceivable, something that Balthasar believed would have been both psychologically and theologically impossible.[10]

Thus, on Balthasar's view, the Israelites and Judeans were inspired by God to fashion the elements of a transcendent form that they could not perceive by means of these elements. When evaluated on Christian presuppositions, the Old Testament's forms are merely 'formal', that is, they await the transcendent 'material' that God's trinitarian self-revelation in Jesus Christ provides. The cultic sacrifices, the celebration of the Passover and Day of Atonement, and circumcision—which Balthasar collectively called "the blood event"—provide one instance of what he meant by this formal emptiness.[11] These rituals were based on the correct understanding of YHWH's absolute dominion over life. God has rights both to the firstlings of the flock and to the first fruits of the harvest. These rights are God's, not only as creator, but also, in an age of sinfulness, as "the judge and the one who calls in the debt of expiation."[12] The sacrifices were therefore a principal means by which both parties to the covenant could ritually reaffirm the existential seriousness with which their agreement ought always to be regarded. When correctly understood, the sacrifices also acknowledged the compenetration of YHWH's justice and mercy. YHWH is the merciful one who acts to ensure that the rights of the weak and the oppressed are restored. But it is not the case that laying low the strong and the oppressors is an act of justice while lifting up the weak and oppressed is an act of mercy. The judgment of one is a function of the redemption of the other. Whenever God judges, "he does so only in connection with his redemptive act of salvation."[13] None of this is superseded in the new covenant. And yet "nothing expresses so clearly the provisional character of the old covenant as the bloody sacrifices."[14] Why? Because, Balthasar contended, although the formal element of sacrifice will remain in place, the material content is completely different. The sacrificial lamb has been replaced with someone who is both creature and creator, judged human and judging God.

The dialogue between Israel and God carried on in the Psalms offers another example of what Balthasar meant by the formal emptiness of the Old Testament.[15] Israel attained in its prayers of confession (in the twofold Augustinian sense of professing praise for God and one's own need for grace) an obedience that it would never surpass.[16] In the Psalms, God's chosen people come to understand that their mission is to return to God the word of grace God has uttered to the whole world. Because it is the very word of grace they return that enables Israel to confess in the first place, God stands, as it were, on both sides of the dialogue. Consequently, the exchange is formally trinitarian; it resembles the dialogue of mutual love between Father and Son occurring in the Spirit. That dialogue will be revealed 'materially', however, only later, especially in the prayers of Jesus to the Father. There is, on

Balthasar's reading, a "far-reaching preparation for what is distinc-
tively Christian through the praise found in the Old Testament."[17] What
will happen between Jesus and the Father, a dialogue after which Christians are to pattern their own lives and praise, is foreshadowed in Israel's prayers. And yet, since in the Old Testament God relates to God's
people as Lord to servant, even the Psalms must await the coming
transposition of its songs into a trinitarian key. With the full, 'material'
revelation of the Trinity witnessed to by the New Testament, the relation between God and humanity (in Jesus Christ) is transformed into
the trinitarian relation in which Jesus is at once Lord and servant, or
better, the lordly servant and the serving Lord.[18]

A second feature of the Old Testament witness that Balthasar
thought indicated the need for a transcendent fulfillment is its eschatology. Two related aspects of this bear particular mention: death and
final judgment. For Balthasar, each remains an "unfinished problem"
in the Old Testament.[19]

With respect to the former, Balthasar observed that for Israel death
meant, not only an end to bodily existence, but also, and more importantly, the end of relations with YHWH.[20] In the "cold, clayey depths"
of Sheol, the dead are "without strength, without activity, without
enjoyment, without knowledge of what takes place on earth, without
praise of God, without return."[21] They exist without purpose, comfort,
or power in a realm of empty silence, of "nothingness and oblivion."[22]
Sheol therefore stands as the absolute and impenetrable boundary beyond which the whole old covenant must not pass.[23] By accepting the old
covenant, Israel is obliged to stand patiently in "the waiting-room before
the closed door," believing in God's promises, hoping for their consummation, yet all the while "staring death in the face," without solace.[24]
This is a nearly impossible situation to bear. Israel must trust and hope in
YHWH as the God of the living, as the one who is able to bring forth
life and bring it to an end, as the one who can cast down into Sheol and
raise back up. Yet all the while, Israel is forbidden the consolation of the
promise of eternal life.[25] This is what makes the Old Testament's view of
death an "unfinished problem" for Balthasar: "Here we can see at once
the inner impossibility of the entire old covenant: how can a covenant
of the immortal with mortals have any meaning?"[26] How can Israel bear
the contradiction of a covenant allowing mortals to see, hear, and touch

the God of the living without hope of life everlasting?[27] Does it not ask too much of finite humans, Balthasar wondered, to expect us faithfully to uphold a covenant with an eternal partner? For isn't doing so like planting an oak in a flowerpot?[28]

However that may be, Israel's scriptures indicate that, by and large, it was not terribly disturbed by this. Its remarkable and, on Balthasar's view, praiseworthy reticence about death is characteristic of what he called "the classic theology of the Old Testament."[29] Save for a few exceptions, Israel successfully resisted the temptation to embellish its conceptions of Sheol with ethical or mystical speculations up through the age of the prophets.[30] This consensus about the reserve with which to speak of the dead began to unravel after the exile. Prompted by Persian and Hellenistic sources, the more vocal elements in the theological chorus of Second Temple Judaism could not resist imagining what might lie on the other side of death's boundary. Balthasar was thinking especially, in this connection, of the florid images of apocalypticism. The flood gates, he said, were opened by Daniel's vision of heaven, though Ezekiel's vision would also play its part in stimulating the morbid curiosity about what is to befall the elect and the damned that Balthasar contended dominates the apocryphal and pseudepigraphical apocalyptic literature.[31] Although inspections of heaven are elaborated here, it is especially hell that fascinates.[32] The apocalypticists want to know what will become of the reprobate; they want to see how God's judgment will be upheld and his righteousness preserved.

Such speculations indicated to Balthasar that the problems with Israel's eschatology pertain, not only to death, but also to a final judgment. The two are related, as he saw things, by an understanding of death as the moment of definite judgment on one's life. No matter how sanguine we may be at the thought of dying, death nevertheless "writes the final word."[33] This is reflected in Israel's "classic" view of death, which he saw as a clear manifestation of the "clarity and sharpness of judgment in the Old Testament."[34] Few would contest Balthasar's assertion that judgment is a dominant motif in Israel's scriptures. But what about it did Balthasar think constitutes an "unfinished problem"? The fluency, the sheer rhetorical power of the prophetic condemnations of Israel and Judah raises the question of how to understand the relation of this critique, which, after all, is affirmed as the Word of God, to God's promises of salvation. How, Balthasar wanted to know, should God's righteous indignation be related to God's profound affection for God's people?

There was no question in Balthasar's mind that the Old Testament presents God as the one Lord of the covenant who is both enraged by, and smitten with, "the lascivious whore Jerusalem."[35] The Marcionite practice of distinguishing between an Old Testament God of anger and the New Testament God of love is rightly condemned by the Church as a heretical misreading of the texts.[36] God's *sedek* (righteousness) and *mishpat* (mercy) belong together, as the great prophets always understood.[37] The divine judgments presupposed grace; they made sense only when directed beyond themselves to a greater future: "everything points to a new order which is what imparts any meaning to the order of judgment."[38] On Balthasar's telling, the nearly incessant divine "No" of the Old Testament prepared the way for the same God's ultimately triumphant "Yes" uttered in Jesus Christ.

Precisely because, on Balthasar's view, it is the New Testament that bears witness to the full, concrete revelation of the absolute unity of God's judgment and mercy in Jesus Christ, it cannot be denied that God in the Old Testament seems to present a double visage. In Hosea, YHWH's willingness to humiliate himself seems boundless, while in Jeremiah, YHWH so despairs of his people that he forbids the prophet to pray for them and abrogates the old covenant. These two moments in the drama between the free and loving God and God's free and obdurate people stand in a tension so striking it "almost amounts to [divine] self-contradiction."[39] The "exaltedness of the free God and the humiliation of the loving God" threatens to split in two what must remain united and, in the "classic" period, largely remained so.[40] Once again, on Balthasar's reading, it is the apocalypticists who went too far. In their zeal to comprehend the final judgment, they drove a wedge between God's righteousness and mercy. But their radical division of the lost and saved, their hardening of the tension between God's anger and tenderness into a "cosmological system" simply extended lines of thought already pursued in the canonical literature.[41]

Israel's and Judah's views of death and a final judgment further illustrate, so Balthasar maintained, that the Old Testament witness demands a transcendent fulfillment. The vault of the covenant could not be supported when one of its pillars was finite, fallible humanity.[42]

From this perspective, the apocalypticists' speculations and the hopes of the Judeans who came to share their belief in an afterlife are quite understandable. They were storming the barrier of death because of the "inner impossibility of the entire old covenant." Their patience with God had simply run out.[43] However explicable this rebellion may be, rebellion it remains. Under the terms established by the old covenant, the hope in an afterlife and a final judgment are in vain. The barrier of death remains intact and the question of how to reconcile God's righteousness and mercy persists. The old covenant "owe[s] us" a resolution to these problems that it cannot provide on its own terms.[44]

The third feature of the Old Testament witness that Balthasar believed pointed toward a transcendent fulfillment is the limitation placed by the old covenant on YHWH's solidarity with his covenant partner. Balthasar identified two aspects of this issue: sin and death.

With regard to sin, he maintained that in order for God's righteousness to be established on earth, Israel must return without reserve the same measure of devotion shown to it by YHWH. It must freely walk in his ways, pouring itself out in praise and heartfelt obedience. But Israel staggers under the burden of this responsibility; it cannot support the vault of the covenant on its own shoulders. True, Israel attained a measure of perfection in the Psalms when it praised the grace of God and acknowledged its own wickedness. And in so doing, it helped to bring forth an inspired word of scripture.[45] But was anyone in Israel able completely to pattern his or her life after the righteousness praised in the Psalms? Balthasar was convinced that not even Israel's most graced representatives were able to bear the burdens of the old covenant. None of them could make the required self-sacrifice. Even the suffering servant, the Old Testament figure who Balthasar believed came closest to fulfilling this charge, stumbles under its weight. His vicarious death in expiation of the sins of the oppressors is inadequate because he himself is not utterly without sin. His death could not be completely selfless because he stood to benefit from the very expiation of humanity's sins that he sought to effect by dying. The boundary between sinner and sinless, between oppressor and oppressed, cannot be crossed even by one such as he.[46] All of us, no matter how selfless, remain "incapable, by [our] own strength, of contributing a righteousness other than [our] own—and in the presence of God's requirements, this righteousness is insufficient, indeed in its depths [it is] a righteousness that fails."[47]

The question then arises whether God will let the rubble of broken promises fill the space over which the vault of the covenant ought to span. Unless God is willing to let sin have the last word, God must do something to ensure that God's righteousness is established on earth. God must somehow support both the divine and the human sides of the covenantal arch without compromising the gift of freedom bequeathed to us; God must somehow stand in our place without thereby displacing us. How could such a solidarity of God with humans be effected without imperiling the absolute distinction between creator and creature on which the entire old covenant is based?[48]

YHWH, of course, had always taken on the cause of orphans and widows, of the aggrieved, persecuted, and outcast. After the exile, when all of God's people found themselves humiliated, dispossessed, and downtrodden, God took up their cause in an unprecedented manner.[49] But was this solidarity sufficient to support the covenant? It is true that by siding with Israel, YHWH was taking on the lot of his chosen people. And since Israel's history is marked by a series of willful infidelities, it is clear that by doing so YHWH agrees to side even with sinners. But what of the dead? Does God's identification with the lowly and powerless extend to those in the utter oblivion of Sheol? Israel knew that YHWH did not need to fight to exert his authority among the dead.[50] He retained a certain "mobility" over Sheol that was simply a function of his sovereign freedom to do what he wills. And Israel knew that although YHWH was gloriously enthroned on high, he had always been willing to descend from heaven in order to be with those whom he favored. He had gone down with his people into Egypt and brought them back up again. And some of the (late) Psalms extend this promise of divine solidarity to all those who suffer. What, then, of those in Sheol? Would he not do the same for them? Would he not be with them in their isolation, shed light in their darkness, draw them out of death into eternal life? "Does not God owe it to himself," writes Balthasar, "'to glorify' his glory even there (Ezek 39.21) and 'to sanctify' his holiness even there (Ezek 28.22, 25) where all glory has been extinguished since all is empty unholiness?"[51] Israel knew that YHWH could do this, but would he? And if he did, how would it be done?

On Balthasar's reading, this is a conundrum the Old Testament never resolves. It makes preliminary sketches of the one who embodies God's righteousness on earth and the one who suffers in obedience. But the two cannot be brought together. Nor can it conceive how the one who dies vicariously for the sins of others could be identified with God's descent into the abyss of Sheol. How humanity (and the whole of creation) might be given a share in the divine life without abridging the difference between creator and creature or encroaching on human freedom remains an insuperable obstacle. The longing for such a solidarity between YHWH and his people—a longing seemingly felt by both sides—is palpable in the Old Testament. But the distance remains; it has to remain so long as the barrier of death has not been breached and a means for bridging the gulf between God and humans without compromise to either side is not forthcoming.

INTEGRATION

According to Balthasar, anyone who wishes to defend the unity of the Old and New Testaments can do so by contemplating the person and work of Jesus Christ and by contemplating the relationship between the old and new covenants. Although the former is held to be superior because it is more direct,[52] both demonstrate to the eyes of faith the theological aesthetic necessity[53] of God's definitive self-revelation in Jesus Christ and, therewith, the unity of scripture. The first, vertical proof turns on seeing the connection between Jesus Christ's death and resurrection, on the one hand, and the salvific will of the Father, on the other, while the second, horizontal, or historical, proof depends on seeing in the new covenant the fulfillment of the various promises uttered in the old.[54] If the latter proof points to a dimly conceived figure who will fulfill the covenant, the former demonstrates that Jesus Christ is this figure. This section describes Balthasar's version of both proofs and sets forth some of the ways in which he believed that, by focusing on the fulfillment of the covenant, they help to unify the scriptures. My goal is more readily achieved by treating the historical proof first.

Despite his deep reservations about the limitations of historical criticism, Balthasar felt bound by many of its findings. Accordingly, he tried to recast the old *argumentum ex prophetia* in a way that was not incompatible with historical criticism.[55] The once widespread practice of arguing for the credibility of the gospel on the basis of Jesus Christ having fulfilled specific prophecies has been discredited for most Christians. But acknowledging the limitations of that approach does not vitiate all other applications of Old Testament texts to Jesus Christ. Balthasar argued that the naïve apologetics of an older era actually depends on a perfectly cogent and defensible theological insight: the new covenant is the surpassing fulfillment of the old. As witnesses to this fulfillment, the two Testaments exhibit "a certain harmony" or "general correspondence" that the pre-critical apologists saw clearly, however inadequately they may have articulated it from time to time.[56] The harmony is not the fruit of this now dubious application of Old Testament texts to New Testament events; it is the presupposition for this application. The application itself is secondary. So to dispense with it as historically and philologically suspect in no way jeopardizes the harmony that an earlier era thought it reflected. On Balthasar's view, the historical-critical demolition of the rickety superstructure of an earlier apologetics actually cleared the ground for a "much more important and splendid" edifice.[57] Although based on the same foundational insight regarding the correspondence between the Testaments, it is an attempt to demonstrate that correspondence by appeal to the prophetic (or typological, or figural, etc.) character of the entire covenant-history of Israel and YHWH.[58]

In the *Theological Aesthetics,* Balthasar chose to retell this story by tracing the changes in the way the Old Testament uses the multitude of Hebrew words that the Greek translators of the Septuagint rendered δόξα (or its cognates),[59] a project to which he devoted nearly the whole of volume 6. The most expedient means to outline this project is to begin where he thinks the biblical witness concludes, namely, with what he took to be the fourth evangelist's most important and enduring insight: the glory of God, which the Old Testament had tried to depict in innumerable ways, attained its definitive form in the life, death, and resurrection of Jesus Christ.[60] In him the seemingly disparate, fragmented Old Testament images of God, of the covenant, and the means of its fulfillment are thoroughly integrated into a concrete, (tri-)personal unity. This integration, though, does not start with Jesus Christ. However much Balthasar wanted to deny that Jesus Christ is simply the final phase of an evolutionary development, he contended that the integration that Jesus Christ is and represents begins already in the Old Testament. That view of the Old Testament's connection to the New is only reasonable, since from "the historical viewpoint, Israel's understanding of God must be deepened by the fact that, in God's active word, God's inner being is disclosing itself ever more richly. . . . [T]he different aspects [of God's self-revelation] become integrated as they converge through time . . . towards a point . . . which will have to lie beyond the Old Testament in the new clarity of Jesus Christ."[61]

On Balthasar's reading, therefore, there is a discernible transformation in the Old Testament's view of God's glory (understood in the extraordinarily broad sense Balthasar would have us do) from something quite abstract and dialectical to something much more concrete and integrated.[62] This is apparent, to cite one example, when one compares the theophanies of the Elohist and Jahwist traditions with the Deuteronomist's understanding of God's covenantal fidelity. In the Elohist tradition, God is manifest as "a deep, oppressive, and threatening darkness" that creates panic among his people, who then have to be reassured by Moses (cf. Ex 19.16, 20.18–20). In the Jahwist tradition, God is manifest as a " 'consuming fire' " that so attracts his people that they need to be warned not to approach (cf. Ex 19.12, 18, 21).[63] The sovereign subject manifesting himself in such contradictory sensory phenomena remains deeply enigmatic.[64] Is God better understood as a menacing dark cloud or a blinding, yet mysteriously attractive light? Even when taken together, these images bespeak a God who, though at once terrifying and enthralling, nevertheless remains relatively abstract.

In Deuteronomy, by contrast, God's self-revelation has taken on a more concrete, which is to say, integrated content. Here, under the influence of Hosea, God is manifest primarily as Israel's devoted, yet jealous, covenant partner.[65] To be sure, Deuteronomy makes use of sensory images, depicting God speaking to Israel "out of the fire" (Dt 4.12). And already in the Jahwist we find God described as "a jealous God, punishing children for the iniquity of parents . . . but showing steadfast love to . . . those who love [God] and keep [God's] commandments" (Ex 20.5–6).[66] Deuteronomy's contribution is to convey with greater clarity than its forebears the unifying center holding the sensory and personal dimensions of God's glory together. The fire of divine wrath is kindled by a consuming love for Israel. The Deuteronomist interpreted the sensory images of the earlier theophanies from the standpoint of the free election of Israel by a sovereign who demands from it complete devotion. True, Hosea knew YHWH to be a jealous lover, but he did not explicitly link this to the notion of God's *kabod* (glory).[67] This was to be the Deuteronomist's achievement. "From Deuteronomy onwards, the true kernel of glory emerges from the *kabod Yhwh:* absolute love."[68]

Although Balthasar tended to run them together, there are really two distinguishable processes at work here. One concerns the transformation of God's glory from a sharply dialectical set of sensory images to a more nearly integrated image of an admittedly still incomprehensible, but profoundly personal divine agent who freely loves and expects love in return. The other concerns the transformation of God's glory from the stateliness befitting an exalted, utterly transcendent Lord to the self-squandering humiliation of a jealous lover. This second sort of transformation is evident in Balthasar's contention that YHWH exposes the prophets to the hate and scorn of his beloved Israel in order that he himself might penetrate more deeply into the realm of what is opposed to him.[69] In the prophets, God divests Godself of the prestige and majesty associated with the Lord of creation or heavenly king. As YHWH strips himself of the appurtenances of power, the meaning of his *kabod* changes. By opening his heart to Israel in the prophets, by throwing himself at Israel seemingly without self-restraint, YHWH reveals that what "is divine in God, his glory, [is] understandable as love."[70]

The transition from this to the New Testament's view of glory will not be smooth. Jesus Christ will not only fulfill, but transcend the prophetic model of obedience. Although the prophets are to be "the vessel in which God's *'anawa,'* his 'condescension' . . . is received,"[71] God's glory still retains a measure of inalienability in the prophets. God has not yet broken open the vessel of his condescension, let God's own heart be pierced on the cross. Further, as God's glory descends what Balthasar called the stairway of prophetic obedience, it still draws up short of Sheol.[72] Although "God himself . . . uncovers his heart to blows in the prophets,"[73] and though the prophets must die in God's service, God has not taken on the lot of the dead themselves. Since the barrier of death remains intact, the extent to which YHWH appears willing to identify himself with what is opposed to him is limited. Nevertheless, the lines of continuity are readily apparent: "God has begun to do something here that will not come to a stop until Golgotha."[74] What appears as utter foolishness on YHWH's part will not be confirmed as wisdom until Jesus Christ is raised from the dead.

What I have described as the transformation of God's glory from relative abstraction to relative integration and from relative splendor to relative lowliness is, on Balthasar's reading, the means by which God's *dabar,* his "active Word of Wisdom . . . seeks to establish his righteousness upon earth in the chosen people."[75] Balthasar argued that there is a corresponding transformation in the way Israel glorifies YHWH in return, which can also be understood as an integration. Two features of Israel's response to God need emphasis in this regard: its liturgy and the obedience of its representatives. With respect to the former, Balthasar divided his discussion into four parts: the Psalms, the Lamentations, the Torah or "speech event," and the cultic sacrifices and circumcision or "blood event."[76] His treatment of the Psalms alone, however, conveys the gist of his argument. With respect to the obedience of Israel's representatives, Balthasar's discussion was even more extensive. Again, in order to understand what he meant by the integration of Israel's glorification of YHWH, we need only address ourselves to the mysterious figure in whom, Balthasar maintained, Israel's response to God came most nearly to represent perfection: the suffering servant.[77] I begin with the Psalms.

"Israel is happy when it sings."[78] In spite of all its infidelities, Israel continually longed to be faithful to God. It longed to be the image of God that the "Primal Maker of Images" intended it to be. It satisfied this longing by singing about God's righteousness and mercy and therewith confessing its own need for God. This is the double-sided confession in the Psalter to which I alluded earlier. By glorifying God in song, Israel was, as Balthasar put it, returning God's word to God. Whatever may have been the original *Sitze im Leben* of the various Psalms (and Balthasar was well aware of the diversity of Israel's cultic practices), they all lay the world bare before God.[79] In the Psalms, Israel stripped itself of pretense. Its longing for God, for the final consummation of God's promises, reached the same febrile pitch there as the love YHWH expressed for his people in Hosea. The Psalms spring from a piety that maintained that all wisdom proceeds from fear of God and that although our days are numbered, God's are without end. They are, therefore, songs that act like mirrors, reflecting back pure answers to God's word, pure light to God's light.[80] The transparency to God's will thus attained (by grace) in these "dialogues of mutual blessing" constitutes Israel's perfection; it constitutes the supreme integration of its glorification of God: "all the facets of Israel's existence meet in this point, overlap and become identical. Just as the fullness of the God who is to be praised can be separated into its individual components . . . only to be reunited in the one statement 'kingdom for ever' (Ps 145), so the fullness of human dispositions is integrated in the will to give glorification."[81]

Naturally, Israel recognized that its glorification of YHWH ought to extend beyond the temple walls. To be completely integrated it ought to embrace, not only its liturgical celebrations, but the full round of its activities. This is why Israel prayed for the steadfastness of heart and soul that would enable it to return God's word in everything it undertook. From the time of the covenant on Horeb/Sinai, however, Israel had sought the aid of a mediator who would present its case before YHWH, a go-between who would intercede on its behalf. Accordingly, Balthasar looked to the history of these various representatives for indications of the way in which Israel further integrated its glorification of God. As I have already noted, Balthasar regarded the suffering servant as the supreme Old Testament representative of the sort of prophetic existence through which God wished to be glorified. The suffering servant has the shadowy outline of a bipartite form uniting the role of Israel's personal representative with that of the sacrificial beast.[82] The lines connecting the servant with Ezekiel and Jeremiah, with the Deuteronomist's Moses, even with Joseph, are strong and deep. All offered themselves as willing sacrifices for the sins of others.[83] But the transparency of the servant to God's will surpasses that of anyone else in the Old Testament: "The sharp struggle between the divine 'I' and the human 'I' in Jeremiah and Job, and the lordly gesture with which God took hold of Ezekiel's spirit and body, have given place here to a mystery of penetration that finds nothing in the old covenant with which it can be compared, no category into which it can be fitted."[84] In response, the servant contributes only his desire to let God dispose of him as God will. This is the supreme act of faith: "the perfect disposition of sacrifice which allows God to make the one who believes the perfect sacrificial beast, the lamb that is led to the slaughter without opening its mouth."[85] This transparency is reflected in the fact that we do not know who this figure is. All we know is that he sought to become the embodiment of his calling. Only his commission matters; his identity does not.[86] God will glorify himself in this one who surrendered his name and his life to God. And in so doing, God will glorify the servant, however much that will remain inexplicable to the servant himself. According to Balthasar, this image of God glorifying his name in the nameless one brings salvation history[87] to a stop lasting half a millenium.[88]

Just as with the summary of how God's glory in the Old Testament becomes progressively integrated, it needs to be said here, too, that the transition between these old covenant forms of glorifying God and their new covenant counterparts will not be smooth. Whatever may be the extent of the perfection of obedience the Psalms reflect, Jesus Christ's prayers to the Father, as we have seen, will fill their forms with a surpassingly new material content. Similarly, the glorification of God uttered in the silence of the servant's suffering, although likewise formally trinitarian, does not yet have the sinlessness of Jesus Christ at its foundation. It cannot, therefore, embody with complete adequacy the chosen people's glorifying response to God's word of glory. Still, the lines of continuity are readily apparent here, too. The forms are in place; the space has been cleared. All that remains is for God to fill these forms with his full, trinitarian self-revelation.

The image of the old covenant as a great arch supported by two pillars, one divine, the other human, helps to summarize my argument thus far and to indicate what lies ahead. The centuries-long process by which God's glory is transformed from a relatively abstract self-manifestation of an exalted Lord to the more concrete, self-squandering devotion of jealous lover constitutes the means by which God supported God's side of the covenantal arch. For its part, the chosen people sought to hold up its side by glorifying God in the cult and in the obedience of its representatives. Over the course of centuries a form of glorification emerged that attempted to integrate the expiatory sacrifice of the cult with the function of Israel's personal go-between. This comes into focus most clearly for the old covenant in the figure of the suffering servant. But since no fallen creature,[89] as such, can contribute the righteousness necessary to establish God's kingdom on earth, there emerges a dilemma:

It was impossible for man alone in his intercession and his suffering for others to establish God's own and entire righteousness upon
earth. But it was likewise impossible for God's *dabar* alone to take
this upon itself, for he cannot bypass or overtrump the God-given
freedom of man (the freedom which ennobles him to the image of
God). But this could be achieved by a form which was the absolute
identity of God's Word and a man who in free obedience took on
himself the sin, now not merely of the people, but of the world. In
his atoning death, judgment and mercy came together, so that the
final judgment that should bring doom became a function of the
final mercy that wished to establish God's new and eternal covenant
with the world.[90]

Here we have, in a highly compressed form, Balthasar's version of the
horizontal, or historical, proof of scriptural unity. Of course, the centerpiece of the proof, the one toward which the entire movement has
aimed, is missing, or at least remains anonymous. It is the task of the
so-called vertical proof to demonstrate that this mysterious figure, who
is the unthinkable identification (at least from the perspective of the old
covenant's absolute distinction between creator and creature) of God's
dabar with a human being, is Jesus Christ.

The vertical proof rests on what Balthasar called "the analytical connection" between the words of Jesus and what he did and suffered.[91]
There is, he contended, a paradoxical congruence between Jesus' claim
to authority and his absolute poverty to which the entire Bible, in different ways, bears witness.[92] My aim here is not to assess the cogency of
Balthasar's christology, but simply to present his picture of Jesus Christ
in order then to draw out the implications that has for his understanding
of the unity of scripture. The picture can be drawn in three quick strokes.

First, Jesus is distinguished by his claim to authority. This is evident,
to begin with, in his attitude toward the Law. Whether or not he rejected
it *in toto* or discriminated among its various precepts, or identified its
essential core, "it is certain that he took it upon himself to make a judgment about the whole law, and thereby set his own authority alongside . . . that of Moses."[93] But for a rabbi to place himself on a par with
Moses is to cease to be a rabbi; it is in fact to place himself above the
authority of Moses.[94] Jesus' claim to authority is also evident in his

capacity to see into the hearts of those whom he encounters. He knows the thoughts and intentions of his friends and enemies alike. They lie exposed and undisguised before him. These are not two distinct capacities, but one: "seeing into men's hearts is one with his seeing into the heart of the Law."[95] Therefore, the decision he makes about men and women, about whether their hearts hold faith or not, is indistinguishable from the final judgment of God. Whether he identified himself with the coming Son of man or not, the claim being made is that the destiny of those around Jesus is determined by their attitude toward him.[96] In order for God's creatures to lie transparent before him this way, Jesus must be equally transparent before God.[97] And this transparency is not to be understood along the lines of prophetic inspiration. Rather, the "judging transparence of Jesus" and the authority to preach, interpret the Law, and cast out demons that goes with it, "makes him the incarnate Word of God."[98]

When this claim is juxtaposed to the second fundamental characteristic of Jesus, his absolute poverty, then the paradox of his life and mission comes more sharply into focus. We find in Jesus the paradoxical combination of "the claim to be more than a prophet with the complete attitude of poverty."[99] The requirement he lays upon his followers to be poor and to leave everything makes them completely vulnerable. They stand before the future without defense, having to trust completely in God's providence. But to ask his followers to bear the weight of this requirement would be inconceivable had Jesus himself not also done so. In order to ask this of them, he must have "first accomplished this archetypally, representatively and inclusively."[100] This means that Jesus' poverty is above all else an act of solidarity.[101] He aligns himself with those who are dispossessed, suffering, and on society's fringes. More importantly, he also sides with those who have repented of their sins. Although there is no question of Jesus consorting with sin per se, "there does exist a bond of sympathy with the one who knows that he is a 'poor wretch', one whose tears flow much more quickly than those of the hard, righteous Pharisee (Lk 7.44f.), and whose melting heart makes directly for the melting heart of God."[102] Just as Jesus was transparent to the Father in his claim to authority, so too is he transparent to the Father in his poverty. In his complete openness to what the future may bring and in his solidarity with the poor and repentant, Jesus is clearing a space for the Father to act in him. He is allowing the Father to draw from him, who is the Word, the not-word of the cross and the descent that fulfills the new and eternal covenant.[103]

Third, the paradoxical unity of Jesus' absolute claim and absolute poverty is at once preserved and transcended in his self-abandonment on the cross. In one sense, this is fairly obvious: both because of his presumption regarding the Law and his solidarity with (among others) those who have transgressed it, Jesus is condemned and willingly submits to being crucified.[104] But, more deeply, the unity with which Balthasar was concerned is that between Jesus' obedience to the Father and the Father's self-revelation in that very obedience. The majesty of the Father is already evident in Jesus' claim to authority, or, as the author of John puts it, in his claim to be the Word of the Father who sent him. And it is also evident in Jesus' poverty, which is to say, in his freely personifying the Father's commission and in his refusal to seek his own glory by using the authority at his disposal to seize control of his future. However, the ultimate unity of divine humiliation and divine majesty of which Jesus' ministry is a foretaste reveals itself paradigmatically on the cross. It is there, so Balthasar contended, that the majesty of the Father definitively blazes forth in the utter humiliation of the Son. In the "servant form [of the Son] is manifested—really manifested—the Father's form of Lordship."[105] Balthasar sometimes spoke as though this revelation of the Father in the Son took place in stages, as though the Son were first obedient in order for the Father then to lay upon him the sin of the world.[106] The danger with that formulation, as Balthasar recognized, is that it can turn Jesus into a second God or into the monstrous neither/nor of Arian subordinationism.[107] Rather, owing to the unity of divine nature, what must be affirmed is that "the humiliation itself is already in essence the glorification of the Father and, hence, also of the Son himself."[108]

For Balthasar, Jesus Christ's descent into hell is implicit in the humiliation of the cross.[109] Jesus' absolute solidarity with humanity has to involve a journey to the dead, since death is the fate that awaits all of us. In so doing, the Son carries out the saving will of the Father to its conclusion.[110] This is the deepest point of God's descent of the stairway of obedience. Of course, it is not just the loss of life with which the Son is confronted, but death understood in terms of the old covenant as that state into which God's glory does not venture and in which the dead cannot glorify God.[111] As the Son breaches this boundary, he crosses from the old to the new covenant.[112] The Son's descent brings God's glory to what had been without glory. But it is " 'glory' in the uttermost opposite of 'glory', because it is at the same time blind obedience that must obey the Father at the point where the last trace of God seems lost (in pure sin)."[113] So the obedient Son is "led by the Father" into the state of utter forsakenness, to confront " 'sin in itself' in the whole formless chaotic momentum of its reality."[114]

Unless one understands this leading of the Son by the Father in terms of their mutual love, "the idea of the 'severe vengeance of God' " predominates, throwing the whole form of Jesus Christ out of balance.[115] Therefore, on Balthasar's view of the Trinity, there is another dimension to the unity of Father and Son revealed on the cross. Two steps will take us there. First, bearing in mind that the glorification of the Father by the Son is the Son's transparency to the Father's will, the Son's self-abandonment for the salvation of the world, which is predicated on the Father's having surrendered the Son for that same salvation, is the definitive revelation of both the Father's and the Son's love for the world. But second, the cross reveals, not only the love of the Father for the world, and not only the love of the Son for the world, but *in this* their love for each other.[116] The salvation of the world is the fruit, that is to say, of the mutual love of Father and Son. And that love is the Holy Spirit, who, proceeding from the Father and the Son, does not simply reveal, but *is* the Spirit of their mutual love.[117] The Spirit alone is able to exhibit the unity of "the highest majesty and the deepest descent" because the Spirit is itself the Spirit of love uniting the Father and the Son.[118]

This completes the brief outline of how Balthasar understood the concordance of Jesus Christ's words and deeds to be revelatory of the Father, Son, and Holy Spirit. What ought to be accented is the fact that, on his reading, what appears initially to be a christocentric understanding of the Bible's unity opens up to reveal, at its heart, a trinitarian theocentricity.[119] One cannot understand the Christ-form as it wants to be understood (as Balthasar put it), unless one sees it in relation to the Trinity. This has one very important implication for any attempt to elucidate Balthasar's view of scriptural unity. It means that his treatment of the Church's Spirit-led glorification of the triune God cannot be ignored without distorting his understanding of what unifies the scriptural witness. The Church is integral to the form of Christ when that form is understood, as it should be, from this larger trinitarian perspective: "Christ . . . can be what he wants and ought to be only in the faith of the Church and the Church . . . comes to be what she can and must be only ἐν Χριστῷ."[120] To put this another way, while it is true that the covenant has been fulfilled in Jesus Christ, on both the divine and human sides, the incarnation of the righteousness of God in Christ requires from God's people a fitting and utterly faithful response.[121] Only so, argued Balthasar, is "the righteousness (*sedek*) of the Old Testament, as a relatedness affecting the whole of man's being . . . transcended and deepened to a communication to the creature of the relationality of the triune life which affects the whole of being within the Godhead."[122]

The Church's glorification of God evinces, on Balthasar's view, a fourfold structure: Petrine, Pauline, Johannine, and Marian. Without wishing to minimize the importance of the other three traditions, Balthasar contended that they are "sustained and undergirded" by the Marian one because it lies "at a level deeper and closer to the centre."[123] In view of the fundamental character of this dimension of the Church's glorification, it is appropriate to focus on Balthasar's mariology, confining the inquiry to just three of its aspects.[124] First, Mary constitutes the bridal perfection of God's people. In her graced *fiat*, "the faith of the covenant partner finds its embodiment . . . , with its pure hope set on God, for therein is only 'poverty' and 'lowliness', so that this faith is also pure obedience to God's word of instruction."[125] This is reflected with particular clarity in her song of praise, the Magnificat, with its echoes of the spirituality of YHWH's *anawim* (poor ones) and of the attitude of humility and chastity characteristic of the daughter of Zion.[126] In Mary, the Church fulfills the Old Testament image of the people of YHWH, who freely respond to his gracious initiatives with obedience and praise. She is the perfect realization of its glorification of God. Thus understood, Mary constitutes the Church's "personal center" and its "full realization."[127] Second, Mary is the "believing and remembering womb of the Church."[128] In her, the early Church, fructified by the Holy Spirit, brought forth the scriptures.[129] And the unity of poverty, virginity, and obedience that she incarnates (as the synthesis of the evangelical counsels)[130] helps to guarantee the unity of those scriptures.

Third, the basis of her graced *fiat,* and thus of her being both the bridal perfection of God's people and the meditative womb of the Church, lies in the second Person of the Trinity's prior kenotic *fiat.*[131] This divine decision, through which the preexistent Son consented out of love for the world and for the Father to the humiliation of the incarnation, cross, and descent, constitutes Mary's pre-redemption.[132] Thus, according to Balthasar, the Church's glorification of God is thoroughly trinitarian, both in the inspiration of its written witness and subsequent praise, and in its foundation in the prior redemptive decision of Father and Son.

The foregoing analysis of the Marian foundation of the Church's glorification of God lends further support to the idea that what initially appears to be a Christocentric construal of biblical unity turns out, on closer inspection, to be embraced within a fuller, trinitarian theocentricity. Clearly, the climax of the form of revelation for Balthasar is the divine Word's incarnation in Jesus Christ and his death and resurrection. He is the crown and unifying center of the biblical witness. But, as we have seen, Balthasar maintained that the form of Christ cannot be rightly perceived if it is taken in abstraction from the Trinity. This entails seeing the actions of the Father and the Spirit, not only in the *triduum mortis,* but also in the glorification of the Trinity in Israel's and in the Church's archetypal experiences of God.[133] Israel and the Church stand, as it were, on either side of Christ. Both point to him, though Israel does so blindly, without knowing the one in whom it believes and for whom it hopes, while the Church, having beheld him as in a mirror, longs for the face-to-face vision promised in the age to come. In both cases, however, the act of pointing—the glorification of God—is enabled and sustained by the very God to whose glory they point.

Three different aspects of Balthasar's construal of the unity of scripture, which I have just described as trinitarian, need to be highlighted. First, the Bible is unified in virtue of the unity of its subject matter or content. On Balthasar's view, the various forms of the Old and New Testaments crystallize around the *triduum mortis.* At the center of the biblical witness stands the cross, or more exactly, the cross seen in its trinitarian relation to the descent into hell and the resurrection. So a great rift opens up between the two Testaments that, paradoxically, bespeaks its "single and indivisible content: salvation through judgment."[134] Without setting aside either God's will for salvation or the need for divine judgment on the sin of humanity, in fact by uniting them "through a synthesis possible for God alone" the covenant has been fulfilled.[135] By doing this, God demonstrates that it is in God's nature to do it.[136] God proves that God's glory is self-squandering, yet finally victorious trinitarian love and that the glorification of God involves nothing less than being drawn into this same, selfless love. In *The Glory of the Lord*, as we have seen, Balthasar elucidated this content in terms of aesthetics. As the admittedly diverse elements of the Old Testament's witness crystallize around the form of Christ, they appear to the eyes of faith, together with their divine-human center, possessed of an exquisite and compelling beauty. Like a gemstone, one cannot take it all in at a single glance, and yet the total effect, as one turns it around and around, is breathtaking.

Balthasar insisted, as I noted in the second chapter, that the unity of the Bible's subject matter cannot be summed up in a few abstract concepts. In order to interpret it aright, we must be willing to surrender "all abstract short-hand formulas about the 'essence' of Scripture or the 'essence' of the Synoptic, Johannine, or Pauline principles (for in the realm of Scripture there are no legitimate abstractions)."[137] In one sense, this is not at all surprising. The fullness of the Trinity eludes any attempt to grasp it with a few abstract "fundamental thoughts."[138] The Fourth Lateran Council's dictum regarding the ever greater dissimilarity between God and creation echoes in the background of Balthasar's concern. But then why would Balthasar have said that "salvation through judgment" is the Bible's "single and indivisible content"? Doesn't that sound like one of the very "abstract short-hand formulas" that Balthasar would have us eschew? Understanding why it is not requires realizing that Balthasar defined both 'salvation' and 'judgment' in terms set by the *triduum mortis*. Salvation is the fruit, realized in the Spirit, of the judgment on sin rendered by the Father in the Son. The meaning of calling the Son the savior because he is the object of divine judgment is determined by this eschatological event of cross, descent, and resurrection. It is not as though Balthasar first defined these terms in abstraction from the Christ-event and then applied them to it. Rather, the predication works the other way around. The subject of the predicates 'judged' and 'savior' is Jesus Christ. He does not get his meaning from them; they get their meaning from him, from what he said, did, and suffered. This unique event governs the meaning of the otherwise abstract universals 'salvation' and 'judgment'. They derive their sense in their application to this particular, concrete individual.

A second aspect of Balthasar's construal of the unity of scripture concerns the common focus of its authors, or at least its final redactors, upon its transcendent subject matter.[139] It is important to realize that that is not the same thing as claiming that the Bible is unified by a single, self-consistent theology. Although he did refer to the Old Testament as having a "classic theology," at least on the issue of death and final judgment, he nevertheless maintained, as we have seen, that when read on its own terms, the Old Testament fragments into numerous irreconcilable theological perspectives. Nor, on his view, does the New Testament present anything like a carefully worked out systematic theology. Were it otherwise, if it were possible to create "a harmony of all the New Testament theologies in the sense of a system, then gnosis would have won the victory over agape, and anthropology would have swallowed up theology into itself."[140] To say that the Bible is unified in virtue of its redactors reflecting upon the self-revelation of the triune God does not entail, therefore, positing a rigorously systematic theology of the Old and New Testaments.

Nor does it entail ascribing to the redactors of the Old Testament a fully formed ecclesial faith. They were faithful, yes; it is they and the faithful remnant generally who, in concert with the Holy Spirit, "faithfully carried God's Word . . . and allowed it to mature into that figure which . . . it achieved as 'Old Testament'."[141] Yet the faith of the Old Testament believers, including Abraham, though justifying, is nevertheless a *figura* of Christian faith. It is an existence *in typo* when compared to the *inchoatio vitae aeternae* (beginning of eternal life) with which Christians are blessed.[142] But in order for Old Testament faith to be a genuine foreshadowing, it "must already in advance live on the grace of what is to come."[143] Of course, finding the right word for such an existence is difficult. Can one describe the *figura* while doing justice to the newness of the *res,* and vice versa? Three motifs common to Balthasar's descriptions of both Old and New Testament faith suggest that he thought it possible: emptying oneself or being poor for God, being transparent to or a reflection of God's will, and being obedient to God.[144] All are meant to suggest an acceptance of what God wills, a willingness to be expropriated by God to serve God's salvific purposes. And "[t]his "willingness is called *faith*. . . . "[145] When Isaiah's eagerness to be chosen is compared to Jeremiah's begrudging acknowledgment that God is in the right, it is clear that the term "willingness" has a broad range of applications.[146] Nevertheless, it is this willingness to be open to God's self-revelation that Balthasar believed is common to all the various biblical authors and redactors.[147]

In fairness to Balthasar, he never explicitly articulated the claim I am here ascribing to him. Or, to be more precise, he never explicitly articulated it with respect to the Old Testament authors and redactors. Of the New Testament authors and redactors, he clearly said that their product is united by a common, contemplative beholding of the center of all theologies, namely Jesus Christ as the revelation of the triune God.[148] Yet I think extending this claim to embrace the unity in faith of the entire Bible is an implication of two ideas of Balthasar's with which we are already familiar. One is that the Old and New Testament faithful, together with the Holy Spirit, produced the scriptures out of a contemplative reflection on God's self-revelation.[149] My discussion of Balthasar's hermeneutics in the second chapter has shown that he believed it impossible for a person without faith to engage in that sort of contemplation. The act of self-surrender to the object of faith, an act empowered, to be sure, by that object, is a necessary condition of seeing the object in the first place. Second, on Balthasar's view, Christians need not, indeed must not, choose between regarding the Bible as a mere product of the faith of its authors and as a word from God. God wants to make Godself known through the medium of faith, whether that be the faith of the Old Testament or of the New. In fact, he said that the evidence for faith being an essential aspect of the formation of scripture is nowhere "more impressively clear than in the textual history of the Old Testament, where the Word of God is carried in a millennial pregnancy by the believing meditation of the people."[150] So while rejecting any effort to channel the variety of biblical writings into a single theological stream, and while recognizing that within each Testament faith takes a multitude of forms, Balthasar seems to have believed that the Bible's diverse theological perspectives are linked, not only by their common divine object, but also by the medium of faith through which this object makes itself manifest.

Finally, the Bible is unified for Balthasar in virtue of its telling the story of the triune God's dealings with creation. It is important, once again, to be clear about what this does not mean. Balthasar insisted that the Bible does not possess a literary unity. There are simply too many different genres in the Bible to claim otherwise: "To the view of a purely literary analysis the writings especially of the New Testament fall apart into a collection of diverse forms of literature which coexist alongside each other without any particular intrinsic relationship and which together do not form a rounded whole."[151] Since that may sound like an outright contradiction of the point I am trying to make, it will be useful to indicate what prompted his remarks. He was concerned to distinguish himself from those who maintain that the unity of scripture is evident to all who look upon scripture's "well-wrought form" with an eye schooled in an inner-worldly aesthetics.[152] Historical criticism in its literary and philological incarnations has succeeded in cutting the ground out from underneath anyone who might wish to advance such a view. My point is, rather, that when Balthasar construed the various biblical writings as diverse witnesses to the form of Christ, he treated them as constituting different episodes in the story of how God's glory became integrated in its slow descent to the dead. Of course, only the eyes of faith are able to recognize this descent as the fulfillment of the covenant and to appreciate its impact on humanity. That is not the sort of thing that is patient of literary analysis. Still, on Balthasar's account, there is a narrative movement to the various biblical witnesses when considered as a whole. As he said, "the canonical image of Scripture . . . tells a story [*Geschichte*] and tells it in a mode which is itself historical [*geschichtliche Weise*]."[153] The Bible "bears witness to the fact that in God something akin to a drama is played out between the sovereignty of his judgment and the humiliation whereby he allows himself to be judged, and that these two voices in God are both united and kept distinct by a third . . . voice," which is soft, ineffable in the Old Testament and louder, if not yet completely audible, in the New.[154] Theology's "supreme object [*das Oberste*]" is understood as "the form of divine revelation in salvation-history, leading to Christ and deriving from him."[155] Although the rightness of this form "for one long moment" can and should "be regarded as a static order," nevertheless, "this firm and not fluid measure between God and man" is, as such, "living, dynamic, dramatic—an event whose subject is God and which subsequently, within God's subjectivity, allows man too to 'happen' before God."[156] Accordingly, the form of divine revelation culminating in Christ "is the revelation of [the] final dramatic action between God and the world."[157] The next chapter will address the issue of whether in the *Theological Aesthetics* Balthasar primarily conceived of scripture, when construed as a drama, to be narrating identities or illustrating paradigmatic lives. In the meantime, we should simply note that he regarded the Bible as unified in virtue of its relating the story of God's interactions with creation.

CONCLUSION

The principal strengths and weaknesses of Balthasar's uses of the Old Testament in the formulation of the two proofs of the fulfillment of the old covenant in the new can be identified by asking three questions.

Did Balthasar regard the Old Testament as bearing a unique witness to the Christ-event? Research into the history of near eastern religions demonstrated to Balthasar's satisfaction that "all the essential categories of Israel's religion" have parallels in the beliefs and institutions of its neighbors.[158] Kingship, prophecy, priesthood, sacrifices, even the idea of a covenant, can all be traced back to the political, legal, or religious environment out of which the Old Testament arose. He found these parallels "enlightening" and the methodological presuppositions underlying their discovery "both acceptable and necessary."[159] While acknowledging the obvious challenge such discoveries pose to the uniqueness of the Old Testament, Balthasar saw in these shared forms a means by which God is able to deliver over to Christ "the general religious heritage of all mankind. . . . Thus, by fulfilling in himself Israel's message of promise, Christ at the same time makes historical contact, through Israel, with mankind's religious forms, and in this way, too, he fulfills not only Israel's expectation but the longing of all peoples."[160]

Balthasar further maintained that although everything constituting Israel's witness to the Christ-event can be explained at the level of human or, perhaps, near eastern religiosity, the eyes of faith can nevertheless discern this witness's uniqueness.[161] While the forms of Israel's witness link it to its neighbors, the spirit animating them, as he put it, refuses to be bound by such connections.[162] To be sure, historical criticism can identify certain aspects of Israel's religious life that are peculiar to it. For example, Balthasar accepted von Rad's contention that Israel gradually weaned itself from the mythical understanding of the divine-human relation characteristic of its neighbors in favor of a much more pessimistic assessment of human capacities.[163] Although the eyes of faith may see in this process one of the ways in which the Holy Spirit adapted available forms to suit God's purposes, it certainly does not require faith to be persuaded that Israel engaged in this quite radical and "wholly unique de-mythologisation."[164] So the uniqueness of Israel's witness that faith alone can perceive lies, as Balthasar would put it, at an entirely different level. For instance, he affirmed that only faith can see that Abraham's belief in God is more and other than "a symbol of a universal human attitude."[165] Its uniqueness lies, not in Abraham's subjective state, but in his unique election by a unique God, something which historical criticism is simply unable to discern. Similarly, while it can be "humanly" demonstrated that Israel's diverse forms of salvific expectation are mutually incommensurable, only the eyes of faith can see that they coalesce around their transcendent center in Jesus Christ.[166]

In sum, then, in Balthasar's hands the Old Testament bears a unique witness to the Christ event that is not compromised by that borne by the New. I touched upon three aspects of this witness: Israel is unique among the world's religions in virtue of its role as the bearer of the religious aspirations of humanity, in virtue of the faith of Abraham, and in virtue of the way the diverse forms it generated crystallize around Jesus Christ. I will have more to say about the nature of this witness. Here my point is simply that, on Balthasar's view, the Christ-event does not flatten out the unique contours of the witness borne the triune God by the Old Testament.

Does the Old Testament, according to Balthasar, have its own distinctive theological voice? It might seem that the foregoing provides us with our answer. But it is possible to affirm without contradiction both that the Old Testament bears a unique witness to Jesus Christ and that its principal characters were blessed with a full-blown, if necessarily future-oriented, faith in this particular historical person. My question is directed to the second of these affirmations. Balthasar's answer is clear:

although the faith of all those biblical figures whose experience of God Balthasar called archetypal obeys the logic of the incarnation (a point to which we will return in the following chapter), the Old Testament faithful did not believe that Jesus of Nazareth was the Son of God. One of the more important hermeneutical implications of this conviction is that a given Old Testament type prefigures a New Testament person or event only if one does not offend against the type's unique significance in the history of God's dealings with God's people. Balthasar insisted that the various Old Testament images must not be cut loose from their historical moorings. To seek to illumine something in the New Testament by lifting an Old Testament type out of its place in the story of God's dealings with Israel would eviscerate the very analogical relation to the New Testament on which the figuration depends. The various Old Testament types "bear their meaning in themselves only as history that has happened between God and Israel, and it is only thus that they form an analogy to the definitive event of Christ."[167] Because their significance as figures of New Testament realities rests in their being part of the story of the covenantal God's relations with the chosen people, Old Testament types must remain rooted in their Old Testament soil. As we saw when examining his versions of the horizontal and vertical proofs, on Balthasar's view, Jesus Christ does not absorb or dissolve the images crystallizing around him; he constitutes a form together with them.[168] Each one "in its *own place* [is] indispensable" to the anti-type.[169]

As James Preus has argued, preserving the theological value of the Old Testament's distinctiveness makes tropological applications of the Old Testament easier and more persuasive. The Old Testament faithful do not constitute a kind of spiritual elite who, by the gift of the Holy Spirit, are able to glimpse in their own age what remains hidden behind an *umbra, figura,* or *signum* for their audience. Accordingly, Christians are not asked to identify themselves with someone "elevated in prophetic isolation from among his contemporaries," but with one who, like themselves, is firmly rooted in a particular place and time and seeks to discern and obey God's will therein.[170] By leaving the Old Testament figures in their Old Testament setting, Balthasar avoided treating them as New Testament figures in Old Testament dress. This means, among other things, that as they exhibit faith, they do so as genuinely Old Testament figures. The Old Testament is thereby allowed to have, in its own right, a positive theological value. In the *Theological Aesthetics*, the New Testament does not drown out the Old Testament's distinctive theological voice.

Did the Old Testament witness serve for Balthasar as a foil for that offered by the New Testament? Rosemary Radford Ruether traces back to the Fathers this practice of treating the Old Testament as a means of throwing into better light the New Testament.[171] More important for my purposes, however, is the argument put forward by Jon D. Levenson that most Old Testament biblical theology since the days of Wellhausen "is, in fact, often really the modern continuation of the ancient *adversus Judaeos* tradition in which the New Testament writers and the church fathers excelled."[172] On Levenson's persuasive view, Old Testament theology in the critical era has generally regarded Israel's religion as having attained its most theologically profound expression in the pre-exilic and exilic prophets. The post-exilic traditions, especially those pertaining to the law and the cult, are pale reflections of the prophetic brilliance. Walther Eichrodt's *Theology of the Old Testament* offers a case in point. His view of what he called classical Israelite religion can be likened to the high point of a bell curve that depicts the increasing immediacy of YHWH's personal presence up through the exilic prophets, only to have that process reverse itself after the exile, when YHWH again becomes much more remote and abstract.[173] On Eichrodt's view, in contrast to the classical theology beginning with Moses and extending through the exilic prophets, the priestly theology, as well as the beliefs and practices of Second Temple Judaism generally, are laced with works righteousness.[174] In all of this Levenson finds "an intense anti-Semitism" that, sadly, is not limited to the works of Eichrodt.[175]

There are certainly some similarities between this and Balthasar's construal. Balthasar regarded the pre-exilic and exilic prophets, especially the suffering servant, as paradigms of a faithful response to God. One finds in them a previously unheard of and subsequently unsurpassed experience—until the incarnation—of God's freedom and sovereignty: "This prophetic concept of God emerges as the most exalted and living reality which could be attained by a pre-Christian religion."[176] It is also true that the intimacy of divine-human relations in prophecy becomes, in Balthasar's work, a yardstick by which to measure the supposed estrangement of the post-exilic period.[177] God, he said, veils Godself after the exile, leaving "late Judaism"[178] groping after God's glory in a half-millennium-long twilight.[179] During this "empty time," "the force and evidentness of [God's glory] decline with the frequency with which it is named and the urgency with which it is demanded."[180] Although he thought it would be an exaggeration to speak of a genuine abandonment by God of the Judeans, their threefold reaching out for an assurance of God's lordship (messianicly, apocalyptically, and sapientially) could only be the result of a great sense of deprivation.[181] This sense of loss, Balthasar maintained, also drove the post-exilic faithful to adhere to the Torah so fervently: "the Law and its observance had become a kind of abstract substitute for the living intercourse of God with his people."[182] The same held true for the extravagance of the blood sacrifices: "It is as if the flowing blood calmed the tormenting uncertainty: are we still in the covenant?"[183] Indeed, Balthasar went so far as to assert, at least on one occasion, that "everything that the Jew might have undertaken" in order to fill the void created by God's withdrawal would prove futile:

> he was an obstacle in the path of God's plans, merely taking up the place that God wanted empty, in order to fill it himself. So terrible was God's judgment in the destruction of the holy city and the abandonment of the holy land, so decisively had his fist smitten what remained into fragments, that man, for all the energy that he devoted to sacrifices and observance of the law, to looking out for the return of God's glory by examining the future, the heavens, and the creation, was not able to mend the broken pieces, but could only make what was dreadful yet more obvious.[184]

Balthasar contended that this is exactly what the Old Testament ban on images was supposed to forestall. It was to prevent the chosen people trying to fill the space that God wanted left open.[185] It was to keep them yearning for a future consummation of God's promises, to keep them expectant, hopeful, and ready. The theology and practices of Second Temple Judaism, from this perspective, constitutes a centuries-long assault on this ban and therewith a repudiation of the chosen people's proper mission.

On Balthasar's view, much of the canonical literature from this period reflects this supposed attenuation of God's presence and the theological superficiality of Second Temple Judaism's efforts to interpret it: "The echoes of post-exilic prophecy are insignificant, petering out in the concerns of the priesthood (Zechariah) and the cult (Malachi). The silence that takes the stage after the prophetic voice has fallen still is ominous."[186]

> At first, the attempt is made to interpret the poor fare of the events after the return from exile as a continuation of sacred history: we find this in Nehemiah and Ezra. This is like a brook in the process of drying up. The Books of Chronicles merely adapt past sacred history to the ideology of Judaism and of the Levitical service in the temple. The Books of Maccabees do not succeed in portraying anything other than the secular history of a religious war carried out with pious enthusiasm and heroic idealism.[187]

Although he accepted these books as inspired and authoritative for the Church, it was clear, to Balthasar at least, that "from the perspective of salvation history, they lie a whole level lower down."[188]

The foregoing has made sufficiently clear that there are some striking parallels between Balthasar's periodization of the history of Israelite and Judean religion and that of modern Old Testament theology.[189] There is considerable textual evidence to support the argument that in the *Theological Aesthetics*, Balthasar depended heavily on its generally appreciative view of pre-exilic and exilic prophecy and on its generally critical view of post-exilic prophetic, priestly, messianic, apocalyptic, and sapiential traditions. And to that extent, his treatment of these traditions of Second Temple Judaism bears some resemblance to the anti-Semitic features Levenson associates with much Christian Old Testament theology.[190] So viewing the Old Testament as a unique witness and viewing the diversity of that witness as rooted in particular times and places, as Balthasar did, does not necessarily ensure against treating it, at least in part, as a foil to the New Testament. Balthasar was, therefore, guilty of this; he did treat the Old Testament witness as putting that offered by the New Testament in a comparatively better light.

Yet Balthasar did not simply consign the Old Testament to the role of warning sign. Although he may sometimes have regarded the Old Testament in part, or in its entirety, as providing a flattering contrast to the New, he nevertheless saw in it more than a set of markers indicating ideas and practices faithful Christians imitate at their peril. That is to say, Balthasar regarded the Old Testament as not merely of negative, but also of positive theological value for the Church. In light of Levenson's criticisms of Old Testament biblical theology's tendency to slight the law and the cult in Second Temple Judaism, two features of Balthasar's use of these materials are especially noteworthy.

First, Balthasar was far from unreservedly critical of either the law or the cult during this period. With respect to the former, he held that there is something "immensely moving" in the attempt of post-exilic Judeans to remain within the covenant by devoting themselves to following God's ethical, juridical, and cultic directives:[191] "Such existence means hanging on God's lips, trusting in his commandments, walking in the path of his instruction, and loving the word, the directive and prescription, the decree and the command, the order and the promise unconditionally with the same love one has for God himself: and seeing in this pure grace, sheer goodness."[192] By thus clinging to the law, the Judeans sought to effect the harmony between God's word and the human response that God wished to hear. Could this be properly interpreted as an arrogant and ultimately self-defeating effort by the Judeans to reassure themselves of God's love and presence despite the lack of concrete saving acts in history? Balthasar gave some credence to such an interpretation, especially with respect to their attempt to anchor all the details of the post-exilic forms of Torah observance in the patriarchal and Sinaitic covenants. But he cautioned that "one must not overlook the possibility that this could take place in good faith."[193] The self-justification that so many Old Testament biblical theologians have seen in this and other aspects of the law is, from this perspective, "unconscious." It should not dilute, therefore, an appreciation for the Judeans' "confidence in the promise of the Lord of the covenant, in whose word the holy community . . . put its trust."[194] On Balthasar's view, Martin Noth went too far when declaring that from the exile on the law became an instrument of works righteousness, replacing the covenantal understanding of the priority in all things of God's grace with a rigid system of human achievement and divine reward.[195] Rather, the faithful remnant understood that "the original covenant with God was the presupposition of every law."[196] For Christians, therefore, the law serves, not merely to convict them of sin, nor merely to warn them of the temptation of self-righteousness, but to remind them that judgment always presupposes mercy, that the law is only an expression of the covenantal fellowship for which God and humans both long.

One has to look a bit harder to find Balthasar offering an irenic interpretation of the cultic life of Second Temple Judaism. Admittedly, he held the Psalter in very high regard, as we have already observed. And he readily acknowledged that post-exilic Judeans never gave up singing God's praises. "The Psalms are a book of love" that helped to sustain the remnant during "all the experiences of night and through all judgments."[197] But the blood sacrifices are the more common target of polemics against the so-called religion of the priests. Paralleling his discussion of the law, Balthasar credited the view that they were in part an attempt to reassure the faithful of God's love and presence despite the catastrophe of the exile and its aftermath. Amid the dreadful silence of the long twilight, "one's own persevering 'action' remains the foundation of hope."[198] But he also regarded them as a faithful attempt to acknowledge the validity of the prophetic denunciations of their abuse while—in deference to Deuteronomy, Ezekiel, and the priestly theology—rejecting any effort to disincarnate and spiritualize the sacrifice God required.[199] Above all else, the blood symbolized the absolute seriousness of the covenant, the uncompromising universality of the commitment God demanded.[200] "True seriousness," as he put it, "means commitment of one's entire bodily existence, and therefore includes the blood."[201] Balthasar contended that this element of "bloody existential seriousness" lay behind all of the chosen people's sacrifices, from the time of Abraham forward.[202] Hence, the post-exilic sacrifices were more than the attempt to placate the Judeans' fears of having been abandoned by God. They were ritual enactments of the faithful giving of themselves utterly, even blindly, to the Lord of the covenant. That they may have been abused, as Amos, Hosea, and Isaiah indicate, does not militate against their importance in the old covenant or the faithfulness with which they were sometimes carried out. On Balthasar's view, therefore, they function for Christians, not merely as examples of a sterile and self-satisfied ritualism, but as reminders of faith's necessarily existential and therefore bodily and public dimensions.[203]

Second, and more broadly, Balthasar understood the Old Testament as providing a host of images that are crucial for understanding Jesus Christ in his relation to the Trinity. This, of course, is one of the lessons he would have Christians learn from the horizontal proof of scripture's unity. A principal vocation of the chosen people was to prepare a set of images that were then placed at the Spirit's disposal. By developing over the course of centuries distinct, if mutually irreconcilable, images of salvation and its bearer, they were able to polish, as it were, the facets of Christ's form one by one.[204] Even the seeming rebellion of Second Temple Judaism's threefold attempt to call forth the glory of God had a providential purpose to serve in this regard. Their messianic, apocalyptic, and sapiential reflections served to open the historical form of Israel into the future, the heavens, and the cosmos.[205]

Two brief examples will suffice to indicate how Balthasar made use of some of the Old Testament images in the *Theological Aesthetics* to deepen his understanding of the Christ-event. His view of the prophets as vessels of divine condescension constitutes one of the more common means by which he was able to accord the Old Testament a positive theological value. Recall that when describing YHWH's self-humiliation in Hosea, he said that God had undertaken something in him that would not stop until Golgotha. God's work on behalf of the chosen people in and through the prophets enhances an understanding of who God is and the depth of God's affection for Israel (and through it, the world): "It is only when we come directly from these scenes between Israel and Yahweh that we will realise the extent of what God is determined to reveal and confide about himself in the New Testament."[206] Balthasar also contended that any attempt to understand the atonement that minimizes the importance of the lines that converge on it from the Old Testament "is doomed from the outset to error."[207] However true it may be that the Old Testament's notions of, say, sin offering, expiation, sacrifice, divine wrath, divine mercy, or covenantal fidelity do not, of themselves, yield the form of Christ, Balthasar insisted that in order to see the atonement in its fullest dimensions, one must attend to the way the Old Testament witness uses such terms. It is no longer defensible to dismiss the New Testament references to the Old Testament as arbitrary prooftexting, nor is it enough simply to note in passing that such terms have their roots in the old covenant.[208] What is required is a thorough-going analysis that is sensitive both to the Old Testament's diverse us-ages and to the ways in which these usages remain the same and change in their various New Testament settings.[209]

Despite their brevity, these two examples help to clarify why Bal-thasar spoke of there being "a kerygmatic need" to present the form of Jesus Christ in the historical and theological context provided by the Old Testament.[210] Although he took pains to remind his readers that Jesus Christ cannot be subsumed within any developmental scheme, not even that of the Old Testament's history of God's dealings with Is-rael, he nevertheless insisted that "the God-Man, as a form in the midst of creation, *cannot* be an isolated entity without historical con-nections."[211] However true it may be that the Spirit moves some to be-lieve in Jesus Christ apart from a thorough familiarity with the Old Tes-tament, Balthasar asked whether its "frame of reference" did not provide the means to understand the object of belief "at least more adequately, sharply and completely."[212] This enduring, positive theological value for Christian theology of the Old Testament is symbolized, to Balthasar's great satisfaction, in the twenty-four elders of Rv 4.4, twelve from the old covenant and twelve from the new, seated without apparent dis-tinction or hierarchy around the throne of God.[213]

It is clear that Balthasar's uses of the Old Testament show significant similarities to the sorts of uses Levenson quite rightly decries. To say that the Jews of the Second Temple period were "an obstacle in the path of God's plans, merely taking up the place that God wanted empty, in order to fill it" themselves is indefensible. Moreover that sort of remark does not square with Balthasar's own appreciative comments about the moti-vations behind and uses of the law and the cult, on the one hand, and the importance of the images of salvation and its bearer generated after the exile, on the other. Nor do they comport with his contention that the Law and the cult are of positive theological value for Christians because they reflect important lessons about the corporate, social, and incarnate dimensions of the faithful life.

But my concern is not to carp about Balthasar's inconsistency. In a work as sprawling and unsystematic as the *Theological Aesthetics,* occasional inconsistencies ought not to surprise. Rather, it seems important to note the degree to which Balthasar was able to break free of the quite widespread anti-Semitism in the historical-critical work on which he so heavily relied. It is plausible that his Catholic heritage disposed him more favorably to ceremony, to ritual, to law, to just those features of Second Temple Judaism that a predominantly Protestant Old Testament theology, with its deep suspicions about work righteousness and priestly mediation would be most likely to denigrate. Having worked without the benefit of more recent and more sympathetic treatments of Second Temple Judaism, by both Protestants and Catholics,[214] the degree to which Balthasar managed to transcend the basic anti-Semitic stance of much of the historical-critical material he worked from is remarkable.

There are four additional instances in the foregoing where Balthasar's views and uses of scripture echo the pre-modern hermeneutical convictions characterized in the introduction as having helped nurture the biblical literacy and imagination of the faithful. In two places I provided evidence of Balthasar having abided by the priority of the literal sense. As will be recalled from the introduction, giving priority to the literal sense concerns itself in the first place, not with the facticity of what is reported about Jesus (though traditionally, that has simply been assumed), but with the relationship of such reports to the one to whom they are ascribed. It means giving priority to the ascriptive subject Jesus as the one in whom that which is predicated of him finds its meaning. The clearest instance of this is Balthasar's contention that the meaning of the phrase "salvation through judgment" is parasitic on the form of Christ. Absent a thorough familiarity with the latter, the former inevitably will be misunderstood. Less obvious, perhaps, is his reluctance to choose any single pair of terms to sum up the diverse ways in which the Old and New Testaments interact. Balthasar believed that when used in the service of explicating God's self-revelation, all concepts must undergo a christological transformation. They have to die to their original extra-biblical meanings in order to fit the uniqueness of the form borne witness to by the Bible. We also saw that Balthasar conceived of the Bible being unified in virtue of several factors, one of which is its depicting the drama of God's sovereign freedom humiliating itself out of love for creation. Although it is true that in the *Theological Aesthetics* Balthasar favored static metaphors, like that of a jewel, to portray the unity of the Bible, this did not prevent him following the pre-modern practice of construing the Bible's unity in terms of a story. (In the *Theo-Drama* such static metaphors are thrown into the shadows as the dramatic interaction of divine and human freedoms moves to center stage.) Finally, in the discussion of the extent to which Balthasar was able to allow the Old Testament to sound its themes in its own key, we learned of his reluctance to lift Old Testament figures out of their time and place. However well intended, doing so inevitably undercuts the Church's ability to use the Old Testament—and the New Testament, *mutatis mutandis*—as a guide to contemporary thought and action. It is that use, which George Lindbeck would call the application of biblical imagination, which is currently imperiled in the Church and which Balthasar's work may help to restore.

4

THE AUTHORITY
OF SCRIPTURE

This chapter describes and critically assesses the logic of Balthasar's claim that the Bible is authoritative for the life of the Church.
The Bible was, for Balthasar, both a fully human document patient of
historical-critical inquiry and a divinely inspired witness to the Word of
God that, while not revelation per se, mediates God's presence among
the faithful. I argue that Balthasar's attempts to ensure the priority of
the literal sense in the Gospel narratives would have been better served
had he construed the divine presence more frequently than he did in the
mode of an agent whose identity is rendered by those narratives. I also
indicate the chief difficulties associated with Balthasar's content-based
account of biblical authority and argue that had he cast his assertions
about the scriptural mediation of God's presence in terms of a functionalist account, they would have been less misleading.

CORPUS TRIFORME

Scripture is the Word of God that bears witness to God's Word. The one Word therefore appears at first as though divided into an attested [*bezeugtes*] and an attesting [*bezeugendes*] Word. . . . But this appearance is deceptive. Both forms of the Word are ultimately the one Word of God bearing witness to itself in the one revelation.[1]

So begins the opening essay in the first volume of Balthasar's *The Word Made Flesh: Explorations in Theology*. As the German title more clearly suggests, he conceived of this work as a collection of tentative sketches (*Skizzen*) that did not pretend to finality. Still, this way of putting the relation between the Bible and the second Person of the Trinity would become definitive for him, informing his subsequent discussions of this and allied topics in the *Theological Aesthetics*.[2] By using the term *Bezeugung,* which means attestation or bearing witness, Balthasar sought to distinguish his position from those of two sets of adversaries: those who equate the Bible *simpliciter* with revelation and those who see it as nothing but an expression of faith's self-understanding.

Not all readers of Balthasar recognize that his view of the Bible differed significantly from that of an older theology, tracing its lineage back at least as far as Origen, that viewed the Bible as but one mode of the body of Christ. As I indicated in the introduction, Joseph Fitzmyer, S.J., contends that Balthasar's description in "The Word, Scripture and Tradition" of the Bible as the body of Christ marks his exegesis as naïvely pre-critical.[3] Prescinding from the question whether Balthasar's, or anyone's, view of scripture is best understood merely as the fruit of exegesis, there remains the charge that he viewed the Bible as a living embodiment of the divine Logos. Fitzmyer seems to think that speaking of the Bible in this way implies that it is itself revelation, rather than a fully time-conditioned witness thereto. Although Balthasar wished to distance himself from such a perspective, the evidence against him seems straightforward: on occasion he did refer to the Bible, without qualification, as the body of Christ or as the Word of God. For example, in his essay "The Place of Theology" there is this: "The Word that is God took a body of flesh, in order to be man. And because he is Word, and, as Word, took flesh, he took on, at the same time, a body consisting of syllables, scripture, ideas, images, verbal utterance and preaching."[4] Later in the same essay we find the following: "The flame of worship and obedience must burn through the dispassionateness of speculation, as it always does through the entire Word of God: the Word that was Christ, and that gave itself to be consumed in this same fire; the Word that once again is Christ and is called 'scripture'."[5] In both of these cases, the relation between the second Person of the Trinity and the biblical texts does verge, at the very least, on identity.

Nonetheless, passages in which Balthasar equated scripture and the second Person of the Trinity without mediation are relatively rare. More often, one finds sentences like the following from the *Theological Aesthetics*: "Although ever since Luther we have become accustomed to call the Bible 'God's Word', it is not Sacred Scripture which is God's original language and self-expression, but rather Jesus Christ."[6] Or, again, later in the same volume he claimed that "Scripture is not identical with revelation, but is rather the testimony [*Zeugnis*] about revelation established by God."[7] On those occasions when Balthasar did not employ the terms testimony or attestation to describe the relation of the divine Logos and scripture, he was far more likely to describe the two in analogical, rather than univocal, terms. Because of Fitzmyer's particular objection to the *corpus triforme* doctrine (that is, treating the Bible as one of the forms taken by the body of Christ), I will elucidate the point in reference to Balthasar's qualified acceptance of this Alexandrian teaching. But the argument also applies to those occasions when Balthasar identified the Bible directly, not with Christ's body, but with the Word of God. Just as in the former case, he was speaking analogically, not literally. For instance, in the context of an argument against what he saw as misunderstandings of God's ineffability, he declared: " 'Word' expresses God's power to disclose what is within himself for others—this is free, and thus it was hitherto concealed—and to make it accessible to them as a gift. In this comprehensive (analogous) and not univocally philological sense, God's salvation history and its writing-down is God's word."[8] It is in this analogical sense that he understood the witnessing word and the witnessed Word to be "ultimately the one Word of God bearing witness to itself in the one revelation."

In the very essay that drew Fitzmyer's fire, Balthasar never actually called scripture the body of Christ. Instead, he acknowledged that "body of Christ" can have many different uses and went on to identify the two most significant: Jesus' historical, fleshly body and his mystical body, the Church.[9] Scripture and the Eucharist, on his view, are means whereby the Holy Spirit incorporates the faithful into the historical, now risen, and mystical body of Christ, the Church. By the power of the Spirit, scripture and the Eucharist both mediate (albeit in different ways) the one, incarnate Word of God.[10] Balthasar made the same point when discussing the Alexandrian view of the Bible in the *Theological Aesthetics*. He maintained that through the vehicles of scripture and the Eucharist, the Holy Spirit makes present the historical, risen Christ and impresses his form upon the hearts of those gathered to worship. Indeed, "Church" for Balthasar is the event when "the power of the Christ-form [*Christusgestalt*] expresses and impresses itself [as] the community is gathered in its Eucharist memorial listening to the Word."[11]

Scripture can be called the body of Christ, then, only by analogy to its "basic and primary" sense as the historical body Jesus received from Mary, which was crucified, raised from the dead, and whose concrete particularity is spiritually universalized as Church through the power of the Spirit.[12] On Balthasar's view, to equate the Bible directly with Christ's body, as Origen did when he compared submitting the scriptures to the tools of philology with handing Jesus over to the Romans to be tortured, is simplistic and easily misunderstood.[13] On this point, at least, he and Fitzmyer agree. From Balthasar's perspective, the doctrine of the *corpus triforme* should be understood as a way to express the fact that the form of Christ is mediated to humanity in multiple ways. To be sure, scripture and the Eucharist are preeminent among these mediating forms. But neither is a self-sufficient instantiation of this body; they are both instruments directed to the incarnation of the risen Christ in the hearts of believers. As such, they should not be confused with the incarnate, risen Lord whose crucified form or 'body' they mediate.[14]

By Balthasar's own admission, however, these mediating realities are difficult to describe: "on the one hand, they are the Christ-form itself, but, on the other hand, in their communication to the world, they are thus already necessarily affected in their very form by the world that receives them."[15] It seems likely that precisely this difficulty led Balthasar occasionally to express himself, without sufficient qualification, on the relation between scripture and the body of Christ, between scripture and the Word of God, and between scripture and revelation. When Balthasar spoke of scripture in terms that seem incompatible with an understanding of the Bible's human dimension, he was simply voicing one side of a dialectic. For him, the Bible is neither simply the Word of God, nor simply a human word to God. It is both at once. To speak of such things, however, almost inevitably leads to a certain rhetorical one-sidedness. In highlighting one dimension of scripture, it is possible to slight the other.[16]

BIBLICAL INSPIRATION

A principle reason for Balthasar's reluctance simply to equate scripture and revelation is his conviction that no words can do full justice to the incomprehensible revelation of God's glory in the concealment of the cross.[17] Here the Word of God utters a cry of dereliction and falls silent. This wordless Word of God, the one who silenced himself for all humanity, demands, as it were, a corresponding silence. All subsequent proclamation that seeks to understand this event in the light of the resurrection is an attempt to utter the unutterable, to proclaim the "density and fullness that hold within themselves God's final and most mysterious turning to man."[18] Although God's revelation in hiddenness (*enthüllende Verhüllung*) reaches its climax in the cross and resurrection, all of God's dealings with humanity, from creation to eschatological consummation, elude conceptual grasp. As Balthasar's frequent protests against the Hegelian synthesis (and Gnosticism, generally) make plain, he vigorously opposed any attempt to master in thought the ever greater and, therefore, ever-more-hidden God.[19]

Balthasar maintained that despite the insurmountable obstacles to giving fully adequate expression to the divine majesty, mute adoration is by no means the only appropriate response to God's acts of covenantal fidelity.[20] He regarded the commissioning of the apostles at Easter to preach the gospel as but one example of the diverse ways in which the Holy Spirit impels God's covenant partners to give voice to their encounter with the divine. What cannot be expressed must be.[21] Although human words fail to do justice to what they are supposed to convey, nevertheless they can be a valid (which is to say, salvifically efficacious) expression of God's ineffability.[22] To suppose otherwise, to think that the biblical witness to God's self-revelation is nothing but an obscuring integument, underestimates God's power to create self-revelatory forms and condemns it to "a tragic futility" that implies the collapse of the covenant.[23] God, as sovereign freedom, chooses to fashion the biblical literature into the "proper" (if not fully adequate) means for proclaiming all that must be said about the incomprehensible triune God.[24] Thus, despite the fact that the Bible is "affected through and through by very far-ranging human relativities . . . , God's absolute Word to mankind becomes expressed within this fully human medium."[25]

One can distinguish between the christological and the trinitarian warrants that Balthasar provided for this claim. Such distinctions are provisional, however, because the warrants necessarily overlap. With that in mind, we can begin with the christological aspect of his argument. Balthasar contended that the "identity of Christ's person in his two natures as God and man is the guarantee of the possibility and rightness of the reproduction of heavenly truth in earthly forms."[26] Faith is able to see in Jesus Christ that God has taken up and perfected the form of the human without doing violence to it in order to express God-self therein.[27] By doing so, however, God does not just transform humanity. Rather, God determines and establishes the entire created order as irrevocably oriented about its center, Christ.[28] Like so many iron filings swung round by the pull of a magnet, the world of natural and cultural forms reorients itself around the Christ-form.[29] What is reoriented to the eyes of faith, though, has in fact always been centered on Christ. It is the blindness of sin that prevents one seeing this in the first place. In fidelity to God's christologically centered creation, God always mediates God's self-revelation in natural and cultural forms.[30] This is as true of the revelation witnessed to by the Old Testament as by the New. Although God's glory is not to be identified with such media, it is nevertheless visible solely through them. As we have already noted, Balthasar contended that the perennial temptation to flee the world of forms in order immediately to experience God is fruitless and self-defeating. It bypasses the incarnation, which is at once the pinnacle and the unshakable foundation of God's self-communication. What appears initially as an obstacle to God's self-revelation—the particularity of any finite human being—becomes, in God's hands, the normative means to demonstrate that God is freely self-sacrificing, trinitarian love.

The logic of the Son's absolute self-abandonment entails that he not glorify himself. He is to do nothing other than interpret the Father by being transparent to him. As a consequence of the Son's complete *kenosis,* he cannot rely on himself to reveal who he is. He therefore hands over the responsibility of his own interpretation to others.[31] With this claim, we begin to turn toward the trinitarian dimension of Balthasar's argument for why scripture can be an efficacious medium of God's self-revelation. On his view, the glorification of the Son, that is, his being interpreted and made known to the world, takes three forms: that of the Father, of the Holy Spirit, and (through the Holy Spirit) of the believing Church. The Father's glorification of his Son principally takes the form of vindicating the Son's obedient self-sacrifice by raising him from the dead. This act demonstrates that the Father has allowed the self-sacrificial love of the Son to bear fruit. All that the Father has achieved for the sake of the world through the Son's mission has as its foundation the Son's absolute obedience to the Father's command. The Holy Spirit's glorification of the Son takes the form of exhibiting the personal identity of the Son's love for the Father and the Father's for the Son. For Balthasar, the Son's love for the Father is enacted and revealed in his obedient self-sacrifice for the salvation of the world. The Father's love for the Son is enacted and revealed in the Father allowing the Son to become utterly forsaken, to die, and to pass over into Sheol, in order thereby to fulfill the new covenant.[32] The unity of their love for each other, which is "lived out in the distance of the Passion" and the descent into hell, is achieved in, and exhibited by, the Holy Spirit.[33] Neither the Son nor the Father is able to manifest their love for each other alone. That must fall to the Spirit, who, as we noted in the previous chapter, proceeds from the Father and the Son, and does not simply reveal but *is* the Spirit of their mutual love.[34] Naturally, the ways in which the Spirit glorifies the Son are indescribably diverse. Stated briefly, the Spirit exhibits the mutual love of the Father and the Son by creating a dwelling place for that love among the faithful, who are initiated into it.[35] So on Balthasar's telling, the Church glorifies the Lord by bearing within it the Spirit of the eternal, triune love of Father and Son. This it does by writing, editing, and interpreting the scriptures; teaching;

proclaiming the gospel; celebrating the Eucharist; praising the Lord in song and prayer; sacrificing itself for his glory; loving others more than itself.[36] The Spirit is present and active in all of these activities of the Church, though in ways that are unique to each. In all of them, the Spirit makes present, testifies to, interprets, glorifies, and/or reveals the triune God, for the Holy Spirit is "the exegesis of the mortal-immortal 'Head' within the 'Body' of the Church."[37] Thus the Spirit glorifies the Son in and through the inspired activities of the Church and the Church glorifies its Lord in and through these same inspired activities.[38]

How, then, did Balthasar conceive of biblical inspiration and how did it bear on his assertion that the Bible is authoritative for the Church? What needs highlighting is his contention that the formation of the Bible by the people of God is a means by which they, with the help of the Holy Spirit, glorify their creator and savior.

From time to time, Balthasar described the inspiration of the biblical authors and redactors in terms that sound decidedly monergistic. The following passage from the first volume of the *Theological Aesthetics* offers a case in point: "And, just as the Holy Spirit was in their eyes so that the image should spring into view, so, too, was he in their mouth and in their pen so that the likeness which they drew up of the original image should correspond to the vision which God's Holy Spirit himself possesses of God's self-representation in the flesh."[39] Balthasar was thoroughly familiar with the objections, both theological and historical, with which anyone seeking to advance such a view of biblical inspiration must contend. As a consequence, he typically did not describe the biblical authors as virtually inert instruments pushed about by God, because that would imply that in fashioning the definitive testimony about the mystery of trinitarian love, the Holy Spirit violated human freedom and the integrity of the created order. More often than not, Balthasar stressed the freedom of the biblical authors and redactors. "Is not Scripture Christ's authentic interpretation by his own Holy Spirit, who works freely not only from above but also freely within God's free children, within God's free Church as a whole?"[40] Although Balthasar himself did not describe the biblical authors and redactors as enacting the Marian-Ignatian cooperation that I described in the second chapter, it is consistent with his views of biblical inspiration to think of them as having done so. The same active-passivity, the receptive alertness and availability (*disponibilité*) needed for ecclesially useful biblical interpretation is precisely the attitude required of the Bible's writers and editors. Certainly on balance, then, Balthasar acknowledged that his doctrine of biblical inspiration ought not to undercut human freedom. He also recognized that even if one managed successfully to defend the freedom of the biblical authors while conceiving of them as mere mouthpieces of the Holy Spirit, this view of their role would be unacceptable on historical-critical grounds. He explicitly rejected the notion, once prevalent, if not universal, in the Church, that the "human author [was] a secretary of God, one who was, of course, free and intelligent but who basically simply wrote down what was dictated to him."[41] Such a conception, he said, has been forever discredited by historical-critical research into the intricacy of the Bible's oral prehistory and subsequent literary development.

It is true, then, that Balthasar occasionally employed a form of speaking about biblical inspiration that is redolent of an earlier, pre-critical understanding of the ways in which the human authors and redactors were involved in the formation of scripture. But that is not, in my judgment, his considered opinion. Balthasar's more monergistic- and pre-critical-sounding statements about the inspiration of the biblical authors and about the Bible being the Spirit's glorifying testimony regarding the Word should be read with the two foregoing countervailing sets of remarks in mind. Doing so provides a response to those who assert that Balthasar's view of scripture (prescinding from his uses of it) is of little use to contemporary theology because of its essentially precritical stance regarding inspiration. More importantly, it allows an examination of the means by which Balthasar defended his claim that the Bible is both an inspired Word from God and faith's word about God. As I have already indicated, Balthasar sought to steer a path between what he regarded as the Scylla of treating scripture as a purely divine document and the Charybdis of treating it as a purely human one. The principle mechanism he used to that end was to assert that the biblical witness to God is the fruit of an inspired theological reflection.

In accord, therefore, with his twofold concern to preserve the freedom of the biblical authors and to take account of the findings of historical criticism, Balthasar likened the creation of the biblical writings to the Church's ongoing process of contemplative theological reflection upon the revelation of God in creation and history. "[T]heology in the Bible can have no fundamentally different form from later theology in the Church: each is an interpretative act of standing and circling around a midpoint that can indeed be interpreted, but is always in need of interpretation and has never been exhaustively interpreted."[42] Although Balthasar usually expressed this conviction, as he did in this instance, in the context of an argument regarding the formation of the New Testament, the Old Testament is, on his view, the result of a similarly inspired interpretive process.[43] Although there are differences between the two that result from the New Testament authors having beheld the incarnation of the new covenant in Jesus Christ, both Testaments reflect a meditative gestation out of which the human authors, in the power of the Spirit, gave birth to an authoritative witness to God's self-revelation. Before going on to cite some of the instances in which Balthasar saw this process reflected in the Old and New Testaments, the image of gestation, which is Balthasar's own, bears some scrutiny since it conveys well why Balthasar believed that the Bible is both a human word about God and, at the same time, a divine Word from God.

In order to see these two conceptions of the Bible in their unity one must realize that God "wants to be received, borne and brought into the world by . . . the womb of human faith, a faith effected by the grace of revelation."[44] It is only through the medium of the gift of faith that God's revelation can be understood. Only so can God make Godself known to God's people. Because the Spirit's glorification of the Son in the formation of the Bible bespeaks an "indissoluble nexus between event (Christ) and interpretation (Church),"[45] it is theologically shortsighted to debate whether the Bible is better understood as the product of faith's response to revelation or as God's Word to God's people. On Balthasar's view, it is both at once. God's Word of revelation comes to fruition in the faith of God's people. "In the very form in which it addresses man, the Word of God already wants to include the form of man's answer to God."[46] To be sure, this formulation overcomes the dualism at the price of a certain circularity of thought. The faith in Jesus Christ that the revelation of God in the resurrection is said to effect must have been given in and with that act of revelation in order for the witnesses to have recognized it as such. And that implies, paradoxically, that faith presupposes faith. But Balthasar disagreed that that circularity cripples theological reflection, as Langdon Gilkey famously suggested.[47] Balthasar would reply to Gilkey's charge that this is how God has freely chosen to deal redemptively with God's creation. The gift of faith, he said, is the presupposition, not only for being able to see God's revelation, but also for God's revelation letting itself be seen.[48] Since God wants to be received in faith, God enables humans, by grace, so to receive God.

In the following section I analyze Balthasar's twofold explanation of how these texts mediate God's self-revelation. First, however, it is necessary to examine some of the ways in which Balthasar believed the spiritually guided theological meditation of the faithful is reflected in the composition of the biblical texts. It is important to bear in mind that Balthasar wanted to give a theological explanation for states of affairs that if not always discovered by, are at least plainly visible to, historical-critical inquiry. This accords with his concern to articulate and defend a doctrine of biblical inspiration that at once preserves human freedom and is compatible with the findings of historical criticism. It also reflects his belief that the formation of the Bible, although a fully human process, is not merely human. God's Spirit was at work in the centuries-long gestation of scripture in order to ensure that the Bible is a salvifically efficacious attestation of God's Word.

With respect to the New Testament, Balthasar asserted that the glorification of the Son by the Holy Spirit began with the disciples' dawning awareness, before the crucifixion, of Jesus' identity.[49] But as the Gospels themselves indicate, the disciples did not really understand who Jesus was during his ministry. On Balthasar's reading, only after the resurrection, once the crucified Jesus had breathed forth his Spirit (following John), did the various images of Jesus begin to coalesce around a common center. The contours of the Christ-form, particularly in its relation to the promise of salvation recorded in the Old Testament, took shape in the disciples' understanding "together with the coming of the Spirit."[50] On analogy to the way one can neither hear nor identify the entire structural coherence of a symphony until after the last note sounds, the disciples could not see the totality of the Christ-form until after the resurrection.[51] With the aid of the light shed backward by the Easter event, they were able to see the necessity of the cross and its relation to God's promise of salvation with a clarity that earlier escaped them.

On Balthasar's reading, this retrospective theological meditation on God's self-revelation in Jesus Christ suggests itself in the way the biblical authors and redactors fashioned their descriptions of Jesus' person and work. Consider the following two examples. First, it is a commonplace among biblical scholars that in an attempt to give voice to this developing understanding of Jesus, the early Church adapted a host of available titles to fit the peculiar pattern of his life, death, and resurrection. Jesus became identified with the Danielic Son of man, the son of God, the suffering servant of Isaiah 52 f., the high priest, the messiah, the Davidic king, the Lord, etc.[52] Balthasar believed that this reworking of material is prompted and guided by the Holy Spirit.[53] That is not to imply, however, that he supposed that the christologies of the New Testament were created piecemeal, from above or from below, in either Docetic or Ebionite fashion. Notwithstanding the fact that he repeatedly spoke of the development and deepening of the New Testament's own theological reflection, Balthasar seems to have believed that the eyewitnesses' original affirmations came as a lightning flash of realization that occurred in the power of the Spirit, whose presence bestowed the sensorium, the simple eyes of faith, required to see Jesus as the Christ.[54] Under the inspiration of the Spirit, the eyewitnesses then set about shaping to their particular purposes whatever common linguistic stock was available.[55] On Balthasar's view, the Spirit-guided reworking begun by the disciples and furthered by the New Testament authors and redactors was not limited, however, to a series of christological titles. It also involved Jesus' parables and miracles.[56] The Gospels, Balthasar knew, do not necessarily present the *ipsissima verba et acta Jesu.*[57] Balthasar contended that in order to glimpse the historical Jesus, one has to "depaschalize" the evangelists' stories about him.[58] Jesus of Nazareth, even as the hypostatic union of divine and human natures, would not have anticipated his glorification by the Father in the way the evangelists said he did.[59] For him to have done so, according to Balthasar, would have run counter to the central thrust of his existence, namely, being transparent to the salvific will of the Father. Although the evangelists are not afraid to report that the disciples failed to understand who Jesus was until the resurrection, it proved impossible for them entirely to eliminate the post-Easter perspective from their literary depiction of some pre-Easter events.[60]

It is perfectly clear, then, that Balthasar was aware of the different purposes characteristic of each of the three stages in the gospel tradition.[61] He was not disturbed by the historical-critical consensus regarding the development of the traditions about Jesus because he saw this development as part of the Spirit's glorification of the Word. The evangelists' reworking of the teachings and acts of the historical Jesus is theologically tenable—indeed necessary—because the New Testament authors believed that the truth of the crucified one had been revealed to them in the risen, spiritual Christ.[62] They are further justified, on Balthasar's account, because of the divine imperative to free the life and teachings of Jesus from the "terrible isolation of their unique historical situation."[63] Only by transforming what Balthasar, in keeping with the Jesus research of his day, believed was the predominantly eschatological emphasis of much of Jesus' parables into an ecclesial teaching, could the evangelists address a broader audience. The essential hiddenness or obscurity of Jesus' ministry and death is illuminated in this transformation (the legitimacy of which finds its basis in the movement from cross to resurrection) of his life and work from the time of Jesus to that of the Church. Only so, contended Balthasar, is this material "brought . . . into the sphere within which [it can] be grasped in the Holy Spirit."[64]

Naturally, if one accepts the notion that there are three distinguishable stages in the development of the traditions about Jesus, then one accepts, as Balthasar did, that each evangelist shaped those parts of the Church's *memoria* available to him in ways that suited his particular rhetorical purposes. Apart from the obvious parenetic and apologetic advantages to including a fourfold witness to the life of Jesus, Balthasar maintained that there was a christological imperative at work in the Church's decision. The Spirit's hand, Balthasar believed, can be seen in this feature of the biblical testimony about God's revelation, too. The diverse perspectives of the Gospels, and by extension of the Epistles and the Apocalypse, serve to remind the faithful of the fundamental impossibility of comprehending the fullness of the mystery of Christ: "the unique and divine plasticity of the living, incarnate Word could not be witnessed to other than through this system of perspectives which, although it cannot be further synthesized, compensates for this by offering a stereoscopic vista."[65] The implication, which Balthasar endorsed, is that the divine content of the New Testament (and, indeed, that of the entire Bible) transcends the particular forms of expression its various human authors and redactors employed.[66] Not that the literary forms are to be stripped away in order that the divine content might shine forth in all its unmediated glory. Such an approach would violate Balthasar's oft-repeated dictum concerning the indissolubility of form and splendor. But that unity subsists under the priority of the content. Although the content appears solely in the form, it is not identified with the form. With respect to the Bible, this means that for believers, "a most essential gap has opened up between the testimony and that to which it points, and this in such a way that the testimony is seen to belong unconditionally to the thing it attests as an actual part of it, while the thing itself, as that which is attested, essentially transcends the testimony."[67] This gap, as Balthasar observed, has been measurably widened by the findings of historical criticism. But that should not unsettle the faithful; quite the contrary. On Balthasar's view, rather than diminishing the Church's confidence in the Bible's testimony, historical criticism, when properly practiced and understood, actually accords with a doctrine of biblical inspiration.

Balthasar maintained that a similar, Spirit-filled contemplation of the data of revelation lay behind the composition of the Old Testament. And as a consequence, it too shows evidence of development and different theological perspectives. One finds repeatedly in the Old Testament that "one Word of God is joined to another and together they bear a new Word of God, and all of this without prejudice to the 'inspiration' of the Prophets and the meditation of the pious."[68] On Balthasar's telling, historical criticism has helped illuminate this process with particular clarity in the book of Deuteronomy. Here the event of the Sinai covenant is brought forward into the seventh century, "so that the 'today' of which [Moses] continually speaks is both the 'today' of Moab—in which the 'today' of Sinai becomes actuality—and the 'today' of the Samaria which faces its destruction, and also the 'today' of the king Josiah who reads it 'at the pillar' in the temple of Jerusalem."[69] Balthasar asserted that this daring attempt to render contemporaneous a past event of revelation indicates that the Deuteronomist believed—rightly, on Balthasar's view—that subsequent interpretation belongs essentially to the fullness of the original historical event of God's self-revelation.[70] It neither attenuates nor obscures, but broadens and deepens the people of God's understanding of that event. Balthasar identified the same meditative process in the reinterpretation and handing on of the words of the prophets. Although the prophets addressed themselves to particular historical circumstances, because their words were believed to be events in human speech of divine revelation, later generations of the faithful, who sought to hear themselves addressed by God, amplified or refocused the original prophetic message.[71] The practice rested on the belief that once uttered, the words of the prophets could not become irrelevant.[72]

Because the inspiration of both the Old and New Testaments, on Balthasar's view, involved this centuries-long, reinterpretative transmission of earlier oral and literary sources, layers of the received text that have been identified as later additions are not, for all that, any the less inspired than earlier material. It is not as though the later developments dilute an earlier, and therefore purer, spiritual pedigree. In fact, Balthasar believed that later additions can provide the interpretive lenses through which the earlier material is to be viewed. For instance, he spoke approvingly of the later Wisdom literature for having, through "strenuous interiorization" of the patriarchal narratives, furnished an important theological corrective to these earlier, mythopoetic accounts that allows subsequent generations to perceive God's supernatural revelation within, rather than simply alongside, natural forms.[73] And he showed a consistent preference for John's more "mature" interpretation of the Jesus traditions over those of the Synoptics.[74] Neither example is meant to suggest, however, that Balthasar believed that whatever is shown to be later is, for that very reason, necessarily more theologically astute. The pre-Pauline Christ hymn of Phil 2, surely among the earliest elements in the New Testament, provides an essential link in the chain of argument that Balthasar constructed to support his view of the atonement. The point is rather that Balthasar conceived of the creation of the biblical texts on analogy to the way the Church, down through the centuries, has tried to interpret God's self-revelation in the light of that revelation. And just as some of those interpretations are more perceptive than others, on his view (and this is by no means a unique judgment), some of the biblical texts stand relatively closer to the "midpoint" than do others.[75]

In sum, on Balthasar's construal, the writings of both the Old and the New Testament, though thoroughly human and therefore subject to the entire range of historical-critical methods, are nevertheless and as such the Word of God. This is warranted by the claim that God freely chooses to reveal Godself in and through created forms, a decision paradigmatically enacted in the incarnation. And it is warranted by the claim that under the guidance of the Holy Spirit, the people of God brought forth from the meditative womb of their theological reflection a means by which God makes Godself present among the faithful. This inspired guidance does not eliminate error; it does not eliminate misjudgment. But it does ensure that the Bible, despite its shortcomings, is a salvifically efficacious medium for God's self-revelation. It is therefore theologically defensible to call it the Word of God. Although this Word, as the Spirit's glorification of the Son, is to be distinguished from the second Person of the Trinity, Balthasar believed the Bible should be viewed as part of God's objective revelation to the faithful. The seeming equivocation in this claim—Do the faithful contemplate in the scriptures revelation or the various witnesses to it?—is overcome if one remembers that form and splendor are inseparable for Balthasar. To view the Bible either as revelation per se or as a merely human artifact violates this fundamental aesthetic principle. The splendor of God's revealed presence is mediated by and through natural and artistic forms. There is no getting around (or behind) the sheer contingency and particularity of the history of God's traffic with humans.[76] That the biblical witness to God's self-revelation is itself revelatory, then, comports with God's decision always to reveal Godself in and through the created order.

By way of conclusion to this section, I should mention a difficulty with one of the ways Balthasar tried to defend the claim that the Bible is at once a fully human document and the Word of God. At the beginning of this chapter, I cited a passage in which Balthasar said the Bible is the Word of God that bears witness to or attests the Word of God. There and throughout the *Theological Aesthetics*, Balthasar spoke of the Bible being a witness to divine revelation and, as such, the Word of God. Nicholas Wolterstorff has identified a problem associated with speaking of the Bible as the witnessing Word of God. He argues persuasively that to call the Bible the Word of God because it attests or bears witness to the Word of God is to stretch the concept "word" to the snapping point.[77] If you make a promise to me and I bear witness to this fact in written form, you are not *prima facie* the author of the document. The words I write are *prima facie* my words, not yours. The situation changes somewhat when we introduce the idea of inspiration. But it does not change things the way one might suppose. If you inspire me to write, the words I use are still not *prima facie* yours. To think otherwise is to fail to realize that "the phenomenon of X inspiring Y to say such-and-such is not the same as X saying such-and-such."[78] This is because when you inspire me to write, it becomes an open question whether what I have written are my words or yours or somebody else's. This has nothing to do with the degree or extent of inspiration. Even if you dictate every word to me, the question as to whose words they are remains open until one or the other of us, or someone else, lays claim to them as his or her own. That is to say, inspiration answers the question of how some words came into existence. It does not answer the question of whose words they are.[79]

To apply the point to Balthasar's formulation, he confused attesting or bearing witness to God with God speaking. If, in his defense, we say that the Holy Spirit inspired the biblical authors and redactors to write what they did, we have merely replaced one confusion with another. Saying that the Holy Spirit inspired the Bible does not answer the question why the Bible should be called the Word of God. Something must happen subsequent to the inspiration in order for the inspired words to become God's own.

It is Wolterstorff's contention that the subsequent something that God does to make the Bible the Word of God has an analogue in human discourse. When an executive dictates to his or her secretary the words of a letter, those words do not become the executive's until he or she lays claim to them, usually by signing the dictated letter. The letter, then, is an example of what Wolterstorff calls appropriated discourse.[80] There is no need, of course, for the appropriated discourse to be inspired. I can appropriate what someone else has said without any influence from me by saying something like, "That goes for me too." By the same token, I can appropriate discourse that I did not explicitly dictate, but for which I offered guidance and suggestions. The theological analogue for this appropriation, Wolterstorff asserts, occurs during the process by which the Church closed the canon. This act coincides with, if not constitutes,

God's appropriation of the Bible as God's Word.[81] So, on Wolterstorff's view, the Bible is both a human document (patient of historical-critical analysis) and the literal Word of God.

From Wolterstorff's perspective, the problem with Balthasar's view of the Bible is the reverse of what most contemporary readers would suppose. It is not that he called it the Word of God. By holding that the Bible is literally the Word of God (not analogically, as Balthasar did) Wolterstorff has, in effect, done Balthasar one better. Rather, the difficulty is that he adopted (probably from Barth) a means for explaining why Christians are justified in calling this human document the Word of God (the concept 'witness') that is acutely ill-suited to the task. Although, so far as I am aware, Balthasar never acknowledged having borrowed the concept 'witness' from Barth, it seems likely that he did so. If that is the case, then there is an irony in that decision because, when looked at in the wider context of his thought, this borrowing was unnecessary.

The lack of necessity is apparent when one remembers that Barth used the concept of witness both to protect God's sovereign freedom from the limitations placed upon it by calling the Bible the literal Word of God, and to account for the fact that the Bible is a fully human document subject to historical-critical inquiry.[82] Balthasar, however, operated with a different notion of divine freedom that could have allowed him to honor the results of historical criticism without having to appeal to Barth's formulation. As we have seen, one of the implications for Balthasar of Jesus Christ's utter self-abandonment on the cross is that he handed himself over to the Church in order there to be glorified through the Spirit. This reverbalization (*Rückauswortung*)[83] of the divine Word was carried out by finite human beings firmly rooted in particular cultures and times. That is an inescapable feature of God's having freely chosen to work within God's free creation to fashion a suitable vehicle of God's presence. Balthasar, then, was more willing than Barth to think of God having surrendered, or at least limited, God's freedom by submitting God's Word to the Church's inspired theological reflection. The Bible's humiliated form, with its historical errors and stylistic infelicities, is an analogue of Jesus Christ's humiliation on the cross. In short, Balthasar did not need to appeal to the concept 'witness' to protect God's sovereign freedom because he believed that God has already limited that freedom in the *kenosis* of the eternal Son. Since God's freedom does not need to be protected in the way Barth thought it did, and since the Bible can be subject to historical-critical inquiry without necessarily offending against its character as an analogous form of the Word of God,[84] Balthasar did not need to use Barth's notion of the Bible as a witness.[85]

BIBLICAL AUTHORITY

This section assesses in two stages Balthasar's uses of scripture as authoritative for the Church. First, I examine two different ways in which he construed scripture in the course of his exegesis. In the *Theological Aesthetics*, he usually conceived of the Bible as mediating God to the faithful in the mode of ideal existences to which they, by grace, are conformed and as having the wholeness of a beautiful work of art that enraptures and transforms those who behold it. Less commonly, at least in the *Theological Aesthetics*, he conceived of the Bible mediating God to the faithful in the mode of an agent and as having the wholeness of a story that, by relating the creative and redemptive acts of God on behalf of humanity and the world, provides an identity description of the triune God. I then make a case for why his concern to preserve the uniqueness of Jesus Christ would have been better served had he favored the latter approach over the former. In the second subsection, I examine two different means Balthasar provided for understanding the basis of biblical authority. Typically, he maintained that scripture's authority rests on its having preserved a divinely revealed content. But on occasion he asserted that it is based on the way God uses these texts in the common life of God's people. Had Balthasar preferred this second means, his view of biblical authority would not have been hamstrung by several significant problems characteristic of the first.

Two Construals of Scripture

Balthasar's understanding of the Bible as an authoritative witness to God's self-revelation rests on two distinct and logically prior construals of the mode of that self-revelation and on two correlative construals of the Bible's wholeness. In *The Uses of Scripture in Recent Theology,* David H. Kelsey has provided the conceptual machinery that I will deploy in demonstrating this.[86] Kelsey identifies three different ways that contemporary theologians have conceived of God's presence among the faithful in the life of the Church, including, but not limited to, the Church's uses of scripture. God might be conceived of as present ideationally, that is, in the teaching and learning of doctrines or concepts about God that are imparted in scripture. Or God might be conceived of as present agentially, that is, in the encounter of the faithful with the divine actor whose identity is rendered narratively in the Bible. Or God's presence might be conceived of ideally, that is, in the imitation of certain biblically described forms of life that are shown to be paradigmatically graced.[87] In the *Theological Aesthetics,* Balthasar tended to conceive of God's presence among the faithful as mediated by biblically portrayed ideal existences. To put it in language more closely resembling Balthasar's own, God mediates Godself to the faithful through their graced conformation to the archetypal God-experience (*urbildliche Gotteserfahrung*) of certain Old and New Testament figures. This is not the only way in which he construed scripture, but it is certainly the dominant one.

In order both to explain how these experiences mediate God in the mode of an ideal existence and how they relate to Balthasar's understanding of the Bible as authoritative, I will examine his various uses of the phrase "archetypal experience of God." At the outset, Balthasar's insistence that God relates to the people of God in diverse ways must be emphasized. He maintained that one cannot abstract from the particular, concrete circumstances of those biblical figures whose experiences are described as archetypal in order to isolate a universally applicable concept of archetypal experience.[88] There is, of course, an anthropological reason for this. Each human being is unique and God relates to us as such: "God's exchanges and dialogue with man (who is always particular and non-interchangeable) . . . can be understood and contemplated only historically and concretely in place and time, in the unrepeatability of my personal situation."[89] But there is also a more nearly theological reason: the diversity of archetypal experiences of God reflects the fact that different members of the people of God have been given different spiritual charisms. Accordingly, Balthasar used "archetypal experience of God" in correspondingly diverse ways.[90] On his reading, the experiences of the patriarchs differ one from the other and from those of the prophets. The prophets, in turn, all have unique experiences that are, nevertheless, distinguishable as a group from those of the Writings and the apocalyptic seers (with all of their respective diversity). The New Testament accounts of archetypal experience likewise reflect a certain multiplicity. Mary's experience of God in Christ differs from that of the Twelve, within which the experiences of Peter, James, and John are also distinguished. And Paul's experience of God in Christ contrasts with the experiences of both Mary and the other apostles.[91]

Still, at bottom, the archetypal experiences of God recorded in the Bible, whether in the Old or New Testament, are linked in virtue of their being determined by a common object: the inherently invisible God has taken form in this world, manifesting the triune Godhead through the medium of the created order. The conclusion to be drawn from this is that the various archetypal experiences of God portrayed in the Bible all obey the logic of the incarnation. "[A]s 'standing over all' (Jn 3.31)[,] Jesus' experience furnishes the form that conditions all other experiences, both before and after it."[92] God the Father relates to God's people in the Son through the power of the Spirit of love shared by the Father and the Son. The form of the archetypal encounter between God and God's people is christological.[93] Notwithstanding the fact that Jesus' experience of God is unique and unrepeatable, it provides the archetype against which are measured the other (secondary and derivative, though still for faith foundational) archetypal experiences of God in the Bible.[94] Accordingly, to say that the God-experiences of the patriarchs, the psalmists, or the apostles are archetypal means, among other things, that they participate in Christ's archetypal experience of God.[95]

What, according to Balthasar, are the contours of this christological form? What are the characteristics of Jesus' archetypal experience of God that are reflected throughout the various subordinate archetypal experiences of God? One need not rehearse Balthasar's entire Christology to isolate the salient features of his answer to that question. It suffices to attend instead to what Balthasar said about the christological structure of the biblical experiences of God (including Jesus') in the first volume of the *Theological Aesthetics*.[96] Over the course of his discussion, a number of characteristics of the archetypal experience of God emerge. I will focus on what I judge to be the five most important.

First, the archetypal experience of God comes at God's initiative.[97] An encounter with God is possible because of God's prior act of gracious, self-revelatory condescension. As we saw in the first chapter, in contrast to the relation that obtains between Being and its formal manifestations, "God's invisibility and his visibleness in his historical revelation are not connected by a natural necessity that he reveal himself."[98] The revelation of God in the archetypal experience is a free act on God's part. It is not occasioned by any natural capacities to which the creature might lay legitimate claim.[99] Even a cursory examination of the evidence demonstrates that the subjective conditions of those favored with an epiphany of God in the Bible vary enormously.[100] What is significant about each epiphany has, therefore, much less to do with the subjective conditions of its occurrence than with the objective one, namely God's prevenience.[101] God offers Godself "precisely when and in so far as the person renounces his own ability to grasp and to comprehend, and surrenders and delivers himself over to what is to be believed."[102] God's covenant partners, therefore, do not call forth God's self-revelation; it is bestowed upon them.[103]

Second, an archetypal experience of God involves the whole person, body and mind. God does not encounter God's covenant partners as disembodied centers of consciousness, but as organic unities of sensate self-reflection and intentional action. The God of the Old Testament archetypal experiences is thoroughly sensible. YHWH is seen, touched, heard, smelled, and tasted.[104] God thereby discloses Godself as sovereign Lord of all existence, both spiritual and corporeal.[105] The archetypal experiences of God recorded in the New Testament also involve the body and mind. It is true that under the influence of a Platonic aesthetics Christians have often supposed that the sensibility of God's self-revelation in the Old Testament is superseded in the New.[106] This is usually couched in terms that treat the New Testament experiences of God as purer because they are less corporeal and more spiritual.[107] Given his understanding of the indissolubility of form and splendor, it is not surprising that Balthasar rejected such a view out of hand: "The best aspects of [the Old Testament forms of experiencing God] are not surpassable: these are the earnestness and also the joy of the whole man's encounter with God, of his seeing, hearing and touching God. . . . "[108] As we have seen, Balthasar was persuaded that for Christians to adopt a platonizing approach to the biblical accounts of archetypal God-experience is self-contradictory because it is anti-incarnational. Jesus Christ experienced (and thereby revealed) God with his entire existence. It is not just what Jesus said, but also what he did and suffered that is revelatory of God. Because his God-experience provides the measure for all others, the archetypal experiences of God in both Testaments are unashamedly corporeal and spiritual.

Third, archetypal experiences of God are proleptic. They are a living anticipation of the final consummation of the covenant relationship in the *eschaton*.[109] This is, perhaps, more easily recognized in reference to the Old Testament archetypal God-experiences. It will be recalled from the previous chapter that as every seeming fulfillment of the covenant with Israel eventually showed itself to be partial and thus inadequate, Israel's faith was driven forward in anticipation of a wholly unpredictable consummation of God's promise. Each stage in the development of Israel's experience of God is therefore to be understood as opening up into an unimaginable future. But this eschatological teleology is not unique to the Old Testament encounters with God.[110] Even Christ's experience of God is proleptic, in two senses: first, because the Holy Spirit will continue and perfect Christ's incarnation in his resurrected body, the Church; and second, because the Son and his bride are to return at the end of time to usher in the Kingdom of the Father.[111] If Jesus Christ's experience of God is proleptic, so much the more is that of Mary and the apostles. They experienced Christ both as fully present (i.e., as Emmanuel, God-with-us) and as the God who will return in glory.

Fourth, the archetypal experience of God is a form of obedient service wholeheartedly committed to God's plan for salvation. Once again, Christ's God-experience constitutes the unique measure for all other, derivatively archetypal experiences of God. The faithful see in Jesus Christ one whose entire existence is devoted to the mission given him by the Father. All that Jesus Christ said, did, and endured was expropriated for the salvation of the world. "There is in him no unaffected residue of subjectivity which has not been assumed into his task as redeemer: everything down to the foundation of his person has been put at the disposal of his ministry and made available for his work."[112] Balthasar repeatedly asserted that Jesus Christ is incomprehensible if this basic and enduring salvific functionality is ignored. And he maintained that the same holds true of the archetypal experiences of those who bear witness to him.[113] Neither the God-experience of Christ nor those of his witnesses (including those in the Old Testament) are fully explicable in terms other than functional ones. There is an "intrinsic teleology" to these experiences of God, though of course the particular role played in achieving that telos varies from person to person.[114] Stated broadly, for Jesus, it involved suffering on the cross, while for the others, it involved a graced participation in that suffering. But in both cases, the suffering service constitutes their respective archetypal experiences of God. In their ready openness to being put to use by God, they reveal (again, uniquely in Jesus' case and derivatively in that of his witnesses) that God is self-sacrificial love.

Finally, the archetypal experience of God in Christ is "inseparably divine and human."[115] In his divinity, Jesus Christ comes to know humanity, while in his humanity he comes to know God. This is what Balthasar referred to as the dialectic of Christ's archetypal God-experience.[116] "Christ, the full and perfect man, has . . . the experience of what God is. . . . And, as God-become-man who reveals God to man, Christ, even as God, has the experience of what man is."[117] Although just as in the discussion of the other features of the archetypal God-experience, so here too must it be stressed that this is uniquely and unrepeatably true of Jesus Christ, nevertheless, humanity has been called to participate in the experience of the incarnate God. Notice that the genitive phrase is both subjective and objective. *Experientia Dei incarnati* refers to God's experience as incarnate and to humanity's experience of the incarnate God: "Something is being affirmed here both about God and about man—first about God and then about man."[118] Naturally, archetypal experiences in the Old and New Testaments evince this christological dialectic differently. Mary and the apostles actually saw, heard, and touched the incarnate Son, while the Father (through the Son) saw, heard, and touched them.[119] But in the Old Testament, the christological dialectic still obtains. Not only do the prophets, for example, experience God,[120] but God experiences humanity in them when descending the "stairway of obedience" through the prophets on the way to the incarnation.[121]

It is now time to draw together the various threads of the nature of the relationship between the God-experience of Jesus Christ and that of his assorted witnesses discussed in the foregoing. The relation with which I am here concerned is not that between the archetypal experiences described in the Bible and the subsequent, imitative experiences of God enjoyed by later generations of believers. I will address that topic momentarily after describing the nature of the relationship between the archetypal God-experience of Jesus Christ and what I have been calling the secondary, or derivative, archetypal God-experiences of his witnesses.

I have argued that these two forms of the archetypal experience of God share a fivefold christological structure. This may lead one to suppose that it is possible to identify a form of life called "christological" in which both Jesus and his witnesses participate. But that would imply that Jesus Christ's form of life is but one instance of a more general category of human existence. Balthasar insisted (along, to be sure, with other theologians) that such a supposition undermines the Christian conviction about Jesus Christ's uniqueness: "if he is the 'Unique One', then no universal and external measure suffices to measure him; essentially he can be measured only by himself."[122] The christological structure of archetypal experiences of God, then, is not something standing, as it were, apart from Jesus that he uniquely fulfilled. Rather, to say that Jesus is the Christ, on Balthasar's view, means (among other things) that Jesus' existence *is* this christological structure. He is not the perfect exemplar of something that could have been dreamed up apart from its occurrence in Christ. His life defines the adjective "christological" rather then being defined by it.

This assertion of Balthasar's is by now quite familiar. It is one of the more common ways in which he abided by what Hans Frei called the priority of the literal sense. And by having done so, Balthasar once again appears to have accepted this feature of the pre-modern hermeneutical conventions I outlined in the introduction. But at this juncture it also raises a question: If Jesus' archetypal God-experience is unique, how can the archetypal experiences of those who are witnesses to him be called revelatory? How can they be called the Word of God? Clearly, the witnesses' God-experiences are not simply patterned after some abstract and universal standard. Instead, Balthasar asserted that they participate in Christ's own archetypal God-experience in virtue of their being drawn, by grace, into the life of Christ. They "merely participate," as he said, because the God-experience of Jesus Christ is unrepeatable.[123] And yet it is a full participation involving all five of the characteristics of Christ's own God-experience summarized above. Balthasar sometimes likened this participation to imitation, at other times he compared it to discipleship, at still others he blurred this classic distinction by referring to the witnesses' imitative discipleship.[124] Probably the most common way for Balthasar to describe the relation in the *Theological Aesthetics* is in terms of Paul's notion of the faithful being conformed to Christ. Whatever terms are employed, however, the essential point remains the same: the witnesses could not partake of that experience on their own. Through the power of the Holy Spirit, the secondary and derivative archetypal God-experiences of Jesus Christ's witnesses partake of his God-experience by living, as Paul put it, ἐν Χριστῷ.

Having analyzed Balthasar's uses of the phrase "archetypal God-experience" and his understanding of the relationship between the God-experience of Jesus Christ and the derivative, though nevertheless authoritative, God-experiences of his witnesses, it is time to examine Balthasar's contention that there exists "a real and vital relationship" between the archetypal God-experiences recorded in scripture and the contemporary experience of God in the Church.[125] What is his view of the nature of that relationship? In keeping with Balthasar's recognition of the diversity of forms Christian discipleship takes, he identified four figures whose lives provide distinguishable, if overlapping, models that mediate the experience of the mediator to those who wish to participate in it. They are Peter, Paul, John, and Mary.[126] According to Balthasar, these four and the traditions they represent afford later generations "different modes of access" by which to encounter the risen Lord of the Church.[127]

A word about the christological and pneumatological conditions for the possibility of such subsequent participation in Christ's God-experience is in order. As I have already noted, Balthasar contended that the life of Christ is at once inimitable and that which must be imitated.[128] The faithful cannot, strictly speaking, reproduce Christ's God-experience because what he did for the salvation of the world cannot be repeated. And yet the *disponibilité* of his life is open to imitation. Indeed, the terms Balthasar used, namely, imitation, discipleship, and conformation, are each different means of expressing the way in which the faithful allow themselves to be expropriated by God to serve God's ends. The lives of the faithful are "functionalized" for the sake of the Church and, through it, the wider world. This happens through the power of the Spirit, who "is poured out creatively from Christ's generative Passion (and Resurrection) over the creatureliness that stands over against it."[129] The members of the Church are thereby united by the Spirit of Christ to Christ and, through him, to each other. They enjoy a "privileged participation" in Christ's archetypal God-experience and in the archetypal God-experiences that have been deposited along with his "in the common treasury of the *Communio Sanctorum* for the common use."[130]

On the basis of the foregoing, what conclusions can we draw respecting Balthasar's understanding of the role played by the Church's uses of scripture in this process? The Bible depicts a variety of God-experiences in which subsequent generations participate through the power of the Spirit of Christ. It provides the faithful with different forms of ideal existences on which they are to pattern their understandings of, and actions in regard to, themselves, their world, and God. To be sure, Balthasar recognized that the Bible also depicts those whose thoughts and behavior are eminently unworthy of imitation. His treatment of Ecclesiastes indicates that he believed it served primarily as a negative example, an object lesson illustrating an unfaithful pursuit of divine and human abstractions.[131] And the apostolic God-experiences can serve the same purpose. An essential feature of their archetypal experience is their failure to have sufficient faith during Jesus' ministry, climaxing in their denial, their flight, and their slumber at the crucial hour.[132] Yet these failures, too, are authoritative. They stand as a part of the "permanent archetype of the apostolic Church with her *fides ex auditu,* a Church which indeed manages the *auditus* but often enough stops there."[133] The faithful see a variety of models of faithful and unfaithful existence depicted in scripture—often in the same person. The faithful's participation in, or avoidance of, such experiences is the work of the Holy Spirit. Balthasar believed the Spirit fortifies the faithful against temptation and enables them to allow themselves to be expropriated by God in order to serve God in ways that are up to God's determination.

To characterize in such fashion the role of scripture in the lives of the faithful may seem unnecessarily to limit the possible range of ways one might be faithful to just those sorts of faithful God-experiences described in the Bible. Does Balthasar's view of these matters remain too rooted in the times of that book? Is he saying that the faithful should pattern their lives after the thoughts and behavior of Christians, Jews, and Israelites who lived roughly two to four millenia ago? Has he wound up, despite himself, advocating a view of theological exegesis that is limited to a "retrospective reflection which elaborates the past revelation?"[134] Would that not be tantamount to violating his own convictions regarding the open-endedness of biblical interpretation, the multivocity of God's Word, the ever new eventfulness of God's presence to the faithful in and through their uses of these texts?

Balthasar's understanding of Paul's archetypal experience points the way toward the resolution of this issue.[135] Paul bridges the gap between the apostolic experiences of God in Jesus Christ and those of the later Church. Because his experience is not that of an eyewitness, at least not an eyewitness of the historical Jesus, he is forced to defend his gospel against those who question his authority. In order for Paul to be accepted as an authoritative witness, he must prove that beyond the fleshly experience of Christ, there is a pneumatic one that does not spiritualize Christ (in the sense of stripping him of his connections to the historical Jesus), but rather "shows him to be the one who has truly risen with his body."[136] Paul's proof of this experience is functional: the warrant he provides for his private revelation is his personal sanctity. "For Paul there is no other legitimation than that of his own turning from the Old to the New Covenant and to the new man."[137] This is not, at least as Balthasar would have us read it, a warrant for collapsing the distinction between the object of faith and faith's own self-understanding. The Spirit that shapes Paul's sanctity does so according to the love made manifest in the incarnate Son. Paul's authority, then, confirms itself in virtue of the way in which his life accords with the sort of self-forgetting love enacted by Jesus Christ. It is the concordance that matters. The same concordance is found, though worked out in different ways in response to different circumstances, in the other apostles and in Mary.[138]

At the very least this would seem to suggest that, for Balthasar, faithfulness involves the patterning of the life one leads within one's own circumstances after the sort of love exhibited in their respective circumstances by Jesus Christ and those who bear witness to him (both proleptically and retrospectively) in the Bible. To suppose otherwise would be to transform Christianity into a religion bound to a set of particular times and places. It would be to constrain the freedom of God's Spirit to continue to fashion new ways in which God is glorified by creation. And that, so Balthasar maintained, would be to ignore one of the lessons of Paul's graced existence. For Paul helped to transform Christianity into "a religion of the freedom of God himself, a freedom in which God's whole manifestation in Christ" has been opened to the wider world.[139] The derivative, or subsequent, archetypal God-experiences portrayed in the Bible are not, therefore, intended to circumscribe within a more or less narrow range what constitutes genuinely faithful forms of Christian life. Rather, to return to Balthasar's own language, they provide "different modes of access" to the God-experience of Christ who, through the Spirit, remains the author of the innumerable host of ecclesial charisms.[140]

According to Balthasar, then, the faithful are confronted in scripture with a set of faithful and unfaithful forms of life that they are to emulate or avoid in the power of the Spirit. Naturally, Balthasar did not suppose that the scriptural depictions of archetypal God-experience are ever approached without some form of pre-understanding. That much is clear from the discussion in chapter 2 of the role played in scriptural interpretation by Church dogmas and the history of interpretation. "Tradition emerges here as the reality through which the archetypal experience is connected to the imitative experience."[141] But, as we saw there, scriptural readings are no less shaped by the liturgical life of the Church. Above all else, for Balthasar, this means that the ecclesially mediated links between archetypal and imitative experience are unashamedly sensory. The faithful are confronted in the liturgy (in word and sacrament considered as a whole) with the risen Lord such that he can be seen, heard, touched, tasted, and smelled.

So far I have described the relation that obtains between the scriptural depictions of archetypal experiences of God and the subsequent God-experiences in the Church as one of graced participation. I have also warned against misconstruing that too narrowly to mean that later forms of participation in the archetypal God-experiences are limited by the specific ideas and behavior exhibited or described by those whom Balthasar understood to have had such experiences. Rather, the normative model of love that the faithful are to imitate is found in the life, death, and resurrection of Jesus Christ and (derivatively) in those who bear witness to him. And, finally, I have indicated that it is Christ, through the power of his Spirit, who enables the faithful to emulate the archetypal God-experiences and be conformed to him thereby.

The foregoing discussion has explained how Balthasar conceived of the mode of God's presence among the faithful in their uses of scripture as an ideal existence. As I indicated above, such a conception of God's presence can be correlated with one of Balthasar's construals of the Bible's wholeness. When Balthasar construed scripture as mediating God to the faithful through the archetypal God-experiences described therein, he attributed to scripture a certain sort of wholeness. What was this wholeness and how did it, together with his construal of God's presence, figure in his uses of the Bible as authoritative?

David Kelsey's analysis of the uses of scripture by contemporary theologians again provides the requisite analytical tools to proceed. He identifies different determinate patterns within the Bible to which different theologians appeal when authorizing their theological proposals.[142] The patterns characterize the particular sort of whole each theologian takes the biblical texts to constitute. Just as when construing God's presence, so here too, a theologian will appeal to different patterns in the course of elaborating different theological proposals. Less frequently, a theologian will appeal to different patterns when seeking exegetical support for a single proposal. Generally speaking, a theologian will tend to favor one pattern over the others—as we will see is true of Balthasar. On this account, then, the authority of scripture is not solely a matter of the mode of God's presence to the faithful in the Church's uses of the biblical writings. It also concerns the determinate patterns with which a theologian ascribes a certain sort of wholeness to the texts. Together, in their mutual interaction, a theologian's judgments about the mode of God's presence and the sort of wholeness the Bible exhibits constitutes the *discrimen* by which he or she uses scripture to help authorize theological proposals.[143]

According to Kelsey, what guides a theologian's decisions regarding the determinate patterns to which appeal is made is a judgment about what is central to the manifest heterogeneity of the biblical texts.[144] And that is shaped, in turn, by how he or she tries imaginatively to describe, as Kelsey puts it with disarming simplicity, "what 'the Christian thing' is basically all about."[145] In Balthasar's case, determining what he believed lies at the heart of the gospel is less difficult than one might suppose given the sprawling and unsystematic quality of his *Theological Aesthetics*. Near the end of the introduction to the first volume, we find the following: "For the object with which we are concerned is man's participation in God which, from God's perspective, is actualized as 'revelation' (culminating in Christ's Godmanhood) and which, from man's perspective, is actualized as 'faith' (culminating in participation in Christ's Godmanhood)."[146] This synoptic judgment about what in an earlier era would have been called the essence of Christianity can be linked to the two *discrimens* Balthasar used when interpreting scripture. Together they are decisive for understanding how the Bible functioned authoritatively for him.

The first and, judging from the frequency with which it is employed, obviously more important *discrimen* (at least in the *Theological Aesthetics*) is reflected in his extended examination of the biblical archetypal experiences of God reviewed above. We will be able to isolate its distinctive features by borrowing from Kelsey the four diagnostic questions he puts to the theologians whose uses of scripture he examined.[147]

First, what aspects of the Bible did Balthasar take as authoritative when discussing archetypal God-experiences? Not surprisingly, he dwelt upon the accounts of the experience of the biblical figure(s) in question. As I demonstrated earlier, what Balthasar described as the christological quality of such experiences exhibit a fivefold set of characteristics: they come at God's initiative; they involve the whole person, body and mind; they are living anticipations of the covenant's consummation; they take the form of whole-hearted, obedient service; and they are inseparably human and divine.

Second, what about these accounts of archetypal God-experiences made them authoritative for Balthasar? They provide descriptions of faithful forms of life in which one participates through the power of the Holy Spirit. Specifically, it is the self-forgetting love that the biblical figures instantiate in myriad ways that Balthasar believed authoritative for later generations of Christians.

Third, what logical force did Balthasar ascribe to scripture in the course of his appeal to the authority of such accounts of archetypal experiences? In the *Theological Aesthetics* generally, and particularly in the section on archetypal God-experiences, Balthasar construed the Bible as having the wholeness, integrity, and compelling beauty of a sculpture or a gemstone. But as I argued in the previous chapter, the musical or dramatic analogies with their temporal movement were never far from his mind. In either case, the Bible is taken to have the logical force of a work of art, the beauty of which is such that one who beholds it is enraptured, drawn into the world it depicts, and transformed thereby.

Finally, how did Balthasar bring scripture so construed to bear on theological proposals in order to authorize them? Initially, it appeared as though Balthasar expected Christians to model themselves directly after the sets of attitudes and behavior exhibited by the various biblical figures whose experience of God he called archetypal. It was almost as though Balthasar were urging Christians to mimic the acts and feelings of the biblical figures. But on closer inspection, it became clear that what was authoritative about the archetypal experiences was the self-forgetting love they enacted. Self-forgetting love as it came to expression in what the various biblical figures said, did, and suffered—this is what Balthasar would have Christians pattern their lives after. The normative model for such love is Jesus Christ. So on Balthasar's view, a theologian who wishes faithfully to interpret the scriptures has first to clarify just what this love entails as it comes to expression in the event of Jesus Christ. Only on the basis of that would he or she then be able to articulate a given theological proposal. Put in other words, it is in the light of the glory of the crucified and risen Lord that theologians do their work. Their proposals are not more or less apt recapitulations of the biblical materials so much as they are responses to Jesus Christ who is made present by the power of the Holy Spirit. The responses are based on a contemplative reflection on the data of revelation, but they are not an attempt simply to reproduce it in an idiom more congenial to the modern ear. In that sense, then, scripture bears on theological proposals indirectly.

To sum up so far, one *discrimen* with which Balthasar operated when using scripture in the *Theological Aesthetics* to authorize his theological proposals is characterized by a conception of God's presence among the faithful in the mode of an ideal existence when and as they use scripture construed on analogy to a work of art whose beauty draws one into its world, thereby transforming oneself and one's relations to others. If we were to link this *discrimen* to Balthasar's synoptic judgment about "the Christian thing," then it would be associated with humanity's participation in God as that is realized in the faithful's participation in Jesus' Godmanhood.

The second *discrimen* that Balthasar employed in the *Theological Aesthetics* is much less common than the first. It is perhaps best illustrated in his interpretation of Jesus as the unique coincidence in utter self-abandonment of an absolute claim and an absolute poverty. Again, Kelsey's four diagnostic questions equip us for an analysis of this.

First, what aspects of the Bible did Balthasar attend to when describing Jesus' claim, poverty, and self-abandonment? In the first case, an examination of Jesus' interactions with others led Balthasar to contend that during his ministry Jesus was possessed of a unique authority or power (ἐξουσία) that was self-evident to those around him. In the case of his poverty, it is above all else Jesus' identification with the powerless, the dispossessed, the repentant, etc., as reflected in his conduct toward them and in certain of his parables (the prodigal son, the lost sheep, and the drachma), that prompted Balthasar to argue that Jesus relinquishes his power in order to make himself transparent to that of the Father. And finally, once again, it is the storied depiction of Jesus' having repeatedly handed himself over in acts of self-forgetting love—a pattern that climaxes in the crucifixion, is foreshadowed in the last supper, and reflected in the creation of scripture—that formed the basis for Balthasar's assertion that the claim to authority and absolute poverty are united in Jesus' absolute self-abandonment. In each instance, though in various ways, Balthasar turned to the narrative depiction of Jesus' words, deeds, and sufferings when describing his claim, poverty, and self-abandonment.

Second, what made the narratives authoritative for Balthasar? It is not, at least not primarily, that they illustrate an archetypal experience of God. Rather, the narratives serve to identify this particular person as the unique subject of the predicates ascribed to him. He emerges in Balthasar's discussion as an individual in his own right about whom certain more or less puzzling words and deeds are predicated. He does not symbolize a mode of behavior whose essential characteristics are defined on the basis of a logically prior analysis of, say, human religious capacities. Even in his acts of solidarity with the powerless, when he identifies himself with their lot, it remained clear for Balthasar that precisely as Jesus Christ represents the poor of YHWH, he remains a unique and unrepeatable individual. So what made the narratives authoritative for Balthasar is not their having described a graced mode of being, but their having identified just who this person Jesus is. Or, to be more accurate, Balthasar believed that what makes them authoritative is God's acts in the Holy Spirit to make present among the faithful the person they identify.

Third, the scriptures so construed have the logical force of a story in which the identities of the central characters are rendered cumulatively by the way they interact with their social circumstances, by the way they speak with and act toward others, by the way they respond to what others say, and by the way they undergo what others do to them. When Balthasar construed the biblical narratives in this fashion, they functioned in much the same way as the biblical narratives did for Karl Barth in certain exegetical passages in the *Church Dogmatics,* which Kelsey says served to "render a character [or] offer an identity description of an agent."[148] In Balthasar's case, they did this by means of recurring patterns in the way Jesus interacted with and disposed of himself toward others that Balthasar described in terms of Jesus' claim, poverty, and self-abandonment.

Finally, just as with the previous *discrimen,* so here, too, scripture so construed more often than not authorizes theological proposals, not directly, but indirectly. It is not the business of theology simply to repeat what scripture says, but to reflect upon the one whose identity is definitively established in the Gospels (though by anticipation in the stories of God's relations with Israel) and to tease out the theological, christological, and ecclesiological implications of his person and work.

When pursued as it should be, theology constitutes the intellectual aspect of faith's response to this divine agent. And that will involve making a host of claims that are only indirectly authorized by the actual concepts or stories of the Bible.

On the basis of the foregoing analysis, it is apparent that as we seek to describe this second *discrimen,* we are no longer dealing with a view of God's presence among the faithful in the mode of an ideal existence. Rather, it entails a conception of God's presence in the mode of a personal agent when and as the faithful construe scripture as narrating the identity of this same agent. And if we were to link this *discrimen* to Balthasar's synoptic judgment about what Christianity is all about, then it would be associated with humanity's participation in God as that is realized in God's incarnation in the person Jesus Christ.

I do not wish to imply that these two *discrimens* are the only two with which Balthasar operated. But they are the most prevalent.[149] Of the two, at least in the *Theological Aesthetics,* the first *discrimen* is much the more dominant way in which he construed scripture as authoritative. By favoring this *discrimen* over the other, Balthasar unnecessarily exposed himself to certain dangers of which he was acutely aware. Reading scripture as an aesthetic whole, whose depictions of religious experience are sufficiently compelling to elicit (in the power of the Spirit) imitation, discipleship, or conformation, carries with it the risk that Jesus Christ will become identified as the archetype of a set of more or less hypostasized dispositions. When that happens, Jesus becomes identified by the dispositions, rather than they by him. The dispositions themselves usually get defined on the basis of a logically prior philosophical anthropology. Under such circumstances, the stories about Jesus serve normatively to illustrate how these dispositions ought to function in the course of human interaction. The disadvantage of this approach, as I noted in the introduction, is that the fact of Jesus having existed loses significance relative to the sort of ideal existence he is held to represent in storied form. At its logical extreme, this completely severs the Christ of faith from the Jesus of history. Why? Because the story could continue to evoke the desired response among the faithful quite apart from whether its central character ever was as he is described, or, for that matter, ever *was* at all. It is the dispositions that matter, not the person who illustrates them.

There is much to indicate that Balthasar was well aware of this problem. He regularly criticized what he regarded as the Bultmannian legacy in Protestant theology whereby the object of faith gets dissolved within faith's self-understanding. And, as I have shown, he insisted on the importance of not violating the priority of scripture's literal sense. I noted many instances in which it was apparent that Balthasar wished to have his uses of a given concept, or set of concepts, be guided by their application to the particular subject Jesus Christ. In such cases, at least, Jesus Christ is treated as the subject of the predicates ascribed to him rather than as an archetype of their expression or enactment.

To Balthasar's credit, he regularly spoke out against such a reduction. This is in keeping, of course, with a conviction basic to the *Theological Aesthetics,* namely, that the Spirit's universalization of the incarnate Word is not an act of abstraction that leaves the corporeal behind in a flight to a realm of allegedly pure spirit. And this comports with his view of beauty as a dynamic interaction between a form and its inner, radiant light. To break apart a beautiful form into its supposedly more fundamental constituents is to destroy it. These convictions, which I would argue are themselves dependent on Balthasar's doctrine of the incarnation, largely prevent Balthasar from falling prey to the temptation to hypostasize Jesus' dispositions. This appears, then, to be another case—the seeming Cartesianism of his anthropology discussed in chapter 1 being the other—when his theological aesthetics helped him avoid the pitfalls many of his contemporaries did not.[150] But if the rules of Balthasar's theological aesthetics are not applied with absolute rigor, then the unity of the "primal phenomenon" falls to pieces and the inner (in the case of anthropology) or the general (in the case of Christology) gets priority. In the latter case, what Emil Brunner called the scandal of Jesus Christ's particularity is neatly eliminated.

Balthasar's concern to preserve the uniqueness of Jesus Christ would have been better served had he reversed the relative dominance of these two *discrimens.* This is because the second *discrimen* with which he operated is considerably less vulnerable to the danger of rendering superfluous the role of Jesus Christ in salvation. When reading scripture as providing an identity description of the irreducibly unique person Jesus Christ, the chances of treating the dispositions ascribed to him in the narratives as other than being defined by him are slight. To do so would be to force the texts (so construed) into doing something they do not naturally do. By contrast, when reading the stories of Jesus for a description of the archetypal experiences they illustrate, it is only too easy to reduce him to an instance of the dispositions associated with such experience.

Of course, making this change would have entailed backing his contention that the Bible is God's authoritative Word less with a view of God as present in the Church's uses of scripture in the mode of an ideal existence and more with a view of God as present in the mode of a personal agent. But that would not have materially affected his claim that the Bible is authoritative. Furthermore, for Balthasar to have made this change in priority is entirely compatible with his conviction, repeatedly voiced in the *Theological Aesthetics*, that Jesus Christ is unique and therefore irreducible to a generalizable mode of being in the world. In the light of such considerations, I argue that making this change would have better served Balthasar in his efforts to elucidate this uniqueness within the context of a theological method that respects the analogies between beauty and divine glory.[151]

Two Views of Biblical Authority

I have shown that Balthasar believed the Bible functions authoritatively either as the Spirit enables the faithful to participate in the God-experience of Christ or as the Spirit makes the divine agent whose identity the Bible renders present among them. In both cases, the faithful encounter the risen Lord and are conformed to him as they use the Bible in their life together. This subsection will answer the question: What view of biblical authority does this understanding of the relation between scripture and later generations of the faithful entail?

Balthasar's answer is an amalgam of two distinguishable conceptions of how scripture might authorize the lives of the faithful. One of these conceives of scriptural authority in terms of it bearing a divine content that has the power to enrapture those possessed of the simple eyes of faith and to transform their lives into a visible image of Christ. This content is nothing less than the glory of God, paradigmatically revealed in Jesus Christ. For Balthasar, as we saw in the last chapter, glory is a cipher. It has the requisite elasticity to serve as a kind of logical placeholder for the extraordinarily diverse ways that God manifests Godself to God's people. Glory is the name given to God's self-revelation in creation and salvation history as both attain their fulfillment in Jesus Christ.[152] Scripture is authoritative in virtue of its mediating to the faithful the divine glory. In some sense, then, scripture "contains Christ."[153] What gives scripture its authority is the divine δόξα manifest through it. In fact, on Balthasar's view, divine authority and glory "are but one in so far as in both of them God's divinity approaches the believer."[154] On this view, scripture preserves the content of an ever new divine revelation with which the faithful are confronted and to which theology will respond in a more or less systematic way. As we have seen, the warrant for this ability of scripture so to preserve this content is provided by a doctrine of biblical inspiration. The human authors and redactors of scripture were guided such that their witness to divine glory (in the Old and the New Testaments) accords with God's own self-witness.

As many have pointed out, this picture of the Bible's authority resting on its revealed divine content is not without its difficulties.[155] By emphasizing revelation in this fashion, Balthasar traded on the common, but nonetheless dubious, assumption that it can adequately embrace the diversity of ways in which God communicates to God's people. Certainly, one of the ways God is depicted in the Bible as communicating with God's people is by speaking to them. On Balthasar's view, divine speech is a form or instance of divine self-revelation. But Nicholas Wolterstorff has argued persuasively that it is erroneous so to conflate speaking and revealing: "If we assume that illocutionary actions, such as asserting, commanding, promising and asking, are a species of revelation, they will elude our grasp. It's true that in promising someone something, one reveals various things about oneself. But the promising does not itself consist of revealing something—does not itself consist of making the unknown known."[156] So while it may be true that God reveals Godself in (and through) the Bible, a theologian is ill-advised to treat all the forms of God's communication as different species of the genus revelation.

Furthermore, revelation is also unable to account fully for the variety of ways in which the Bible depicts God dealing with God's people. Since the beginning of modernity's preoccupation with epistemological questions, datable rather precisely to John Locke's decision to examine our understanding in an effort to settle what objects it is and is not "fitted to deal with,"[157] the doctrine of revelation has assumed an enlarged, indeed inflated, role in Christian theology. As the epistemological question became more pressing, the doctrine of revelation, construed as an answer that preserves divine prevenience, became correspondingly dominant.[158] For Balthasar, divine glory is the solution to the problem posed by the modern theological concern to justify faith's knowledge of God while preserving God's freedom: "The freedom . . . that appears in Christ is that of the God whom nothing can compel, who is absolute and sufficient in himself, but who nonetheless, of his free graciousness, binds himself to his creature in the hypostatic union forever and indissolubly, *with the purpose of making his appearance and offering himself to view in the creature.*"[159] Although he clearly recognised the one-sidedness of such formulations,[160] that did not prevent Balthasar asking, rhetorically, "[W]hat is the creation, reconciliation, and redemption effected by the triune God if not his revelation in and to the world and man?"[161] As Carl Braaten has observed, when revelation is made the leading explanatory concept of Jesus Christ's mission, then other aspects of the Christ-event risk being eclipsed.[162] The reconciliation of humanity to God in Jesus Christ is not something revealed that had been true all along, though hidden. Rather, it is an entirely new thing, a new creation and unique event acted out in history. Significantly, Balthasar was keenly aware of the importance of stressing the newness of the life in Christ made possible in the atonement. But it has to be said that his considerable efforts toward defending that claim cut right across the grain of the scaffolding he erected in the *Theological Aesthetics* to support the centrality of the doctrine of revelation. It is true that in reconciling the world to God, God reveals that God is able to do this wondrous thing, but the reconciliation is not itself an act of revelation. And to call it such, as Balthasar would have us do, is to confuse one divine act with another.

In light of these and other problems, a less misleading account of biblical authority rests on a claim about the way God fashions new individual and corporate identities by using the Church's uses of scripture. Kelsey can once again be our guide. As he puts it, the Bible's authority derives, not "in the first instance from [its] 'content,' but rather from the *end* to which [it is] used."[163] On this construal, God's relation to the

Bible, rather than some divine content of the Bible, is the source of biblical authority.

Notwithstanding Balthasar's adherence to a content-based view of scriptural authority, there are several passages in the *Theological Aesthetics* that indicate Balthasar also thought of scriptural authority in functional terms. For example, he called scripture "an instrument of the Holy Spirit who . . . through this humanly active form, impresses the form of Christ pneumatically upon mankind."[164] Elsewhere he spoke of the Holy Spirit "wielding this instrument" in order to effect within the hearts of its hearers and readers the christological transformation of the literal sense to the spiritual, i.e., to bring about the personal, existential appropriation of the Christ-event.[165] He also called scripture "a vehicle that impresses the Christ-form in the hearts of men."[166] Admittedly, this last quotation can be interpreted as supporting a content-based understanding of scriptural authority. Scripture would bear sacramentally the Logos, who is impressed on the hearts of the faithful by the Holy Spirit. It is certainly true that Balthasar drew attention to the similarities between scripture and the sacraments.[167] But he more frequently insisted that scripture and the sacraments should not be confused: "Scripture is not . . . a sacramental icon within which the thing—grace itself—lies substantially hidden and imprisoned."[168] Rather, scripture serves as a monstrance of God's self-revelation as and when God uses it to that end: "the believing person who seeks Christ . . . will indeed encounter Christ here in a theological remembering which through grace makes Christ present."[169]

Balthasar's affirmation of the freedom of God to make Christ present to the faithful through scripture's "theological remembering" suggests that his remarks should not be interpreted to the effect that scripture contains the divine glory in a flat-footed, substantialist sense. As we saw in this chapter's second section, Balthasar held that the content of scripture, its subject matter, essentially transcends the scriptural witness. While it is true that the scripturally mediated divine glory is available to the faithful only through the letter, it is not held captive, as it were, by the letter. The Bible "contains Christ" at God's good pleasure, and only then. That way of putting the point about scripture's content and its authority for the life of the Church looks rather functionalist. Scripture mediates the divine glory as and when God uses it to do so. So while it is evident that Balthasar operated with two distinguishable conceptions of biblical authority and that the much more dominant one (measured by the frequency with which it was invoked) viewed the source of biblical authority as the divine content it mediated, it is not incompatible with his views to reverse this priority by understanding the content-based conception in terms of the functionalist one.

This prioritizing of the functionalist account of scriptural authority has certain advantages over Balthasar's own formulation.[170] First, because it emphasizes God's uses of scripture to fashion new corporate and individual identities, it does not make the mistake of couching all of God's activities in terms set by a doctrine of revelation. The acts of God as creator, redeemer, and sanctifier do not all have to be understood as instances of God's self-revelation. To repeat an earlier point, it may well be that in God's ongoing acts of creation, redemption, and sanctification, God reveals Godself. But these acts do not in themselves consist in acts of revelation.

Second, this approach has the further advantage of locating a doctrine of scripture in the context of discussions about the third Person of the Trinity. That is to say, the conceptual home for reflections on the authority of scripture is not within a doctrine of revelation (as we saw is true of the *Theological Aesthetics*), which has traditionally been ascribed to the work of the divine Logos, but within discussions of the ways in which the Holy Spirit transforms the lives of the faithful, individually and collectively. A doctrine of scripture, then, belongs within reflections on the Church or, more broadly, sanctification. This is less misleading than Balthasar's own approach, not only because it coheres better with his emphasis on the importance of the Holy Spirit's uses of scripture to conform the faithful to Christ, but also because it fits better with his view of the importance of the Church in the formation and interpretation of the Bible.

Third, a functionalist account of scriptural authority denies the seeming necessity of backing the authority of scripture with a claim about its inspiration. In contrast to a content-based account of scriptural authority, a functionalist account does not need to be backed by a doctrine of inspiration. It can be, but it does not have to be. The functionalist account does not necessarily deny that scripture is inspired, it merely distinguishes between that claim and the claim that scripture is authoritative. It holds that God is free to use this text quite apart from whether its contents are free of error or whether the experience of the biblical authors and redactors is peculiarly graced. All that the functionalist account claims is that at God's good pleasure, the triune love of God will be present in the Church's faithful uses of scripture.[171]

These remarks about biblical inspiration raise one possible objection to a functionalist account of scriptural authority. Does not the content-based view of scriptural authority have an advantage over the functionalist one, namely, that it can provide an explanation for why God would choose to use this collection of texts rather than some other? If scriptural authority derives not primarily from the content of the Bible, what would keep God from using Melville's *Billy Budd* to authorize new corporate and individual identities? Kelsey would likely respond that there is absolutely nothing to prevent this. And he would be right, since God is free to use whatever means God chooses to effect the salvation of the world. But, as I understand him, Kelsey would also insist that God's decision primarily to use the Bible to that end rather than some other text is not mere happenstance. But the reason he gives for why God has chosen to use the Bible is not the same as that provided by Karl Barth, or Paul Tillich, or any of the other theologians whose exegesis he examined in *The Uses of Scripture in Recent Theology*. And their respective reasons are as distinct from each other's as his is from theirs. The explanation for the differences lies in the different ways in which they try to summarize what lies at the heart of Christianity. Although scripture is not decisive in the formation of this judgment, it is important. This is because one makes a judgment about "the Christian thing" in the context of one's experience of the Church's use of the Bible in the diverse forms of its life. Over the course of time, Kelsey argues, the "particularities of the concrete use of scripture peculiar to the common life of the church as [one] experiences it will shape which images strike [one] as most apt" for describing the full round of the miracle effected in Jesus Christ.[172] Although Billy Budd might offer an important analogue of the sort of innocent death one finds in Jesus Christ,[173] it would be foolish to suggest that one can provide a synoptic judgment about the whole of "the Christian thing" on the basis of Melville's story. It is clear, therefore, that the functionalist account of scriptural authority does answer the question why God has chosen to shape new identities through the Church's uses of the Bible rather than some other text.

In view of this and the advantages of a functionalist account already cited, I contend that Balthasar's conception of scriptural authority in the *Theological Aesthetics* would have been strengthened had he more consistently articulated his claims about the divine content of scripture in terms compatible with his own functionalist accounts.[174]

5

THEOLOGICAL EXEGESIS

In what follows I examine some of the ways Balthasar used scripture in the course of elaborating his doctrine of the Church. I do this for several reasons. I want further to illustrate some of the claims I made in the second chapter's analysis of Balthasar's hermeneutics; to continue my assessment of the consistency with which he followed his own hermeneutical guidelines, especially those that provide for a constructive role for the fruits of historical criticism; and to indicate those features of his exegesis that are compatible with the classic hermeneutics outlined in the introduction. My thesis is that the example of Balthasar's exegesis analyzed in this chapter has some serious, but nevertheless illuminating, flaws. This exegesis provides an important warning to those who might suppose that contemporary Christian theologians can, without careful deliberation, appropriate the hermeneutical conventions of the pre-modern era. Nevertheless, I contend that readers would be rash to dismiss Balthasar's views and uses of scripture simply because his exegesis sometimes offends against the most likely intended sense of the human author. For his exegesis can be reconstrued to accord with his own hermeneutical principles and, if the necessary changes are made, to not contradict explicitly a consensus among centrist historical critics.

MARY AS A TYPE AND AS THE BRIDE OF THE CHURCH

Balthasar's mariological reflections dwell at length upon Mary's graced response to the Holy Spirit at the Annunciation. On his view, by consenting to the incarnation Mary not only allowed the second Person of the Trinity to be brought into this world, she also let the triune form of the divine life impress itself upon her. She thereby became, along with the apostles and the rest of the saints, although preeminent among them, the measure of Christian faith. Her disposition toward God finds its standard in that of Jesus Christ, who, as obedient all the way to the cross and beyond, allowed his experience of God to be shaped by God. Mary's *fiat*, as Balthasar understood it, indicates that she, too, like her son, let her own form of life wane as God's triune form waxed within her. As I indicated in the second chapter, despite Balthasar's occasionally having used images like this one that suggest otherwise, he regularly insisted that Mary's response to the Spirit was not utterly passive. He tended rather to think of it as an expectant obedience best understood in terms of the Ignatian doctrine of *indiferencia*.[1] He believed that Mary's open readiness for divine revelation provides the Church, not simply a model for the Christian life, but an incalculable treasure that, by grace, all believers can draw upon.[2] As they do so, the faithful participate through Mary in Christ's God-experience. Naturally, Balthasar realized that her experience of God in Christ is not the only one portrayed in the Bible. Still, he maintained that all the other forms of what he called archetypal God-experience, including those of Peter, Paul, John, and the faithful of the Old Testament, are themselves undergirded and made fruitful by Mary's.[3] Thus understood, Mary is more than just an historical figure, or even exemplar. In her, Balthasar said, "The Church flowing forth from Christ finds her personal center . . . as well as the full realization of her idea as Church."[4] In Mary, and only in her, the Church is at once the immaculate mother of Christ as well as his spotless bride.

In my examination of how Balthasar used scripture to authorize this view of Mary and the Church I will focus on the bridal, rather than the maternal, dimensions of Balthasar's understanding of Mary. This comports with Balthasar's relatively greater emphasis on Mary's bridal character. Not surprisingly, therefore, considerable attention will be given to Balthasar's exegesis of Eph 5.23–33, the *locus classicus* for speaking of the Church as the bride of Christ. But since it is part of the nature of Balthasar's interpretive procedure to juxtapose passages from different books of the Bible that bear on the theme he wished to explicate, it will be necessary to examine, at least in passing, his treatment of other texts.

Balthasar's argument that the Church attains its bridal perfection in Mary can be broken down into four stages. In the first stage, Balthasar asserted that the Old and New Testament conceptions of God's covenant partner are, despite continuities, fundamentally different. The predominant self-understanding of Israel, of course, was as the chosen people of God. To be sure, Israel is often spoken of as a singular subject who acts in particular ways and has specifiable relations with its neighbors. Yet, on Balthasar's reading, the predication remains one of analogy. In the Old Testament, Israel is not understood as an individual center of consciousness or intentional agent, but as a people or a nation. He believed that the first verse of the letter to the Hebrews gives a christological reason for this state of affairs. So long as the Word of God remained at the level of instruction and promise, addressing Israel "in many and various ways," God's people understood itself primarily as a collective subject whose unity and relation to God were understood as grounded in a shared loyalty to the one who had chosen them, freed them from slavery, and given them the Law, the Davidic kingdom, and the Prophets.[5]

With the incarnation of God's Word in Jesus Christ, a previously unheard of intimacy now prevails between God and God's covenant partner that Paul conveyed in the image of the Church as Christ's body.[6] Balthasar saw hints of this Pauline insight in the contrast drawn by the author of Hebrews between Moses' faithfulness *in* God's house and Christ's faithfulness *over* God's house (Heb 3.3–6): "Because Christ, as the Word of God (and simultaneously high priest), has become *immanent* in the people of God, this people receives a *transcendent* head that stands above it: this it did not possess in the old covenant."[7] Notice that by using the term "head" in reference to Christ, Balthasar was, in effect, using the Pauline image to interpret Hebrews. There is nothing in

Hebrews about Christ being the head of his body the Church, at least not in those exact words. The author of Hebrews articulates the Christian conviction about Christ's simultaneous immanence and transcendence differently. Christ is described as having become "like his brothers and sisters in every respect" (Heb 2.17) in order to "destroy the one who has the power of death, that is, the devil" (Heb 2.14). Having done so, Christ is distinguished from the people as, among other things, the sanctifier of those sanctified and as the liberator of those made free (Heb 2.11, 15).[8]

By reading Hebrews in light of the Pauline imagery, Balthasar believed that he was simply making explicit what he saw as an implied corrective that the author of Hebrews wished to give to the Old Testament images of Israel as the people of God or as God's dwelling place.[9] Neither of these, on Balthasar's view, does full justice to the New Testament notion of Christ being at once identified *with* and Lord *over* his Church.[10] Balthasar believed that this insight was sufficiently central to the ecclesiology of Hebrews, but that when the letter is understood correctly, its view of the Church as God's house and Paul's image of the Church as the body of Christ appear linked by "an interior logic."[11] He therefore maintained that a close reading of Hebrews propels the reader into the orbit of the Pauline simile.

At first glance, Balthasar's treatment of Paul's bodily imagery yields exactly what one might expect. Without Christ, the Church is a lifeless torso. Accordingly, the Church is not to be understood as self-sufficient, as though possessed of an independence that allows it to stand over against the risen Lord. But there is more to Balthasar's analysis than this. One of its unusual features is his contention that when the image of the body of Christ is treated in isolation from the bridal imagery with which it is paired in Ephesians 5.23 ff., it becomes impossible to answer the question concerning the subjectivity of the Church in anything other than negative terms.[12] The comparison of the Church to Christ's body expresses the belief that the Church is not autonomous, but this much, Balthasar believed, is conveyed better by the analogy of the vine. There is nothing fruitful in the branches that does not come from the divine life flowing outward from the roots and stock. And any act independent of the stock causes withering and desiccation leading inevitably to death.[13] To give a more substantive answer to the question of the

Church's identity requires reading the metaphor of head and body in light of the bridal imagery.[14] Thus, on Balthasar's view, although the two symbols of the Church are bound together inseparably, the latter is given hermeneutical priority.[15] Only if we interpret the image of the head and body of Christ nuptially, and therefore personally, can we give a positive answer to the question: Who is the Church? This assertion marks the second stage in Balthasar's argument to identify Mary as the bride of Christ.

How is the picture of the Church as Christ's body altered when seen through the lens of the bridal imagery? To answer that we need to look at Balthasar's exegesis of Eph 5.23–33. In this passage, Paul[16] likens the head of the body to the husband, whom Balthasar calls the "ruling partner" in marriage, while the body is understood as the wife.[17] Setting aside the question of whether such a view of marriage is any longer tenable or even widely held in our day, we can say that Balthasar believed this refocusing of the imagery once again preserves Christ's transcendence over, and immanence in, or unity with, his Church. But how does it answer the question of the identity of the Church as a singular subject? In fact, does it not make answering that question more difficult by confronting us with a paradox? On the one hand, we have the notion of a Church whom Christ loved and for whom he sacrificed himself. On the other hand, we see the Church described as a spotless, youthful bride who owes her existence to what Christ did for her on the cross. Eph 5.25–27 puts it this way: "Husbands, love your wives, just as Christ loved the Church and gave himself [up] for her, in order to make her holy by cleansing her with the washing of water by the word, so as to present the Church to himself in splendor, without a spot or wrinkle or anything of the kind—yes, so that she may be holy and without blemish." Balthasar believed that Paul put forward in these verses two divergent notions of the Church: one as preexisting the passion and the other as owing her origins wholly thereto.

The contrast between these two notions of the Church, while easy enough to understand in the abstract, may strike some as less clearly expressed in Ephesians than Balthasar would have us believe. Perhaps because Balthasar recognized that these verses convey the Church's preexistence more clearly than her origin in Christ's obedient self-sacrifice, he sought to buttress his argument by adverting to the traditional patristic interpretation of Jn 19.34. In affirming, with many of the Fathers, that the Church originated in the pierced side of Christ on the cross, Balthasar was careful to locate the ecclesiological significance of this verse within the context of the events immediately preceding it: the abandonment, as he saw it, of Mary by her son in order that she might accompany him into "absolute foresakenness," and Christ's surrender of his spirit to the Father. By the same token, Balthasar contended that when speaking of the birth of the Church on the cross, we must also not forget what happened afterward. The cross and resurrection are inseparable events.[18] The effect of these hermeneutical decisions is to nuance, and therefore make more persuasive, the traditional view of the Church as coming from the side of Christ (*Ecclesia ex latere Christi*). Later, I will examine Balthasar's reading of Jn 19.34 more closely. For now, however, the point to be accented is that his appeal to the Johannine texts serves to sharpen the contrast between the notions of the Church as preexistent, on the one hand, and as born in the Christ-event, on the other—a contrast he believed Paul expressed in Eph 5.

So Paul's reworking the bodily imagery in terms of the marriage of Christ and his Church obliges us, Balthasar insisted, to hold together two seemingly contradictory statements regarding the origin of the Church.[19] Can this tension be sustained? On Balthasar's reading, the answer lies in Paul's theological anthropology, which is based on Gn 2.20ff. Paul alluded to this story of the creation of Eve out of one of Adam's ribs in verse 31 of our passage from Ephesians. After seeing Eve, Adam describes her as "bone of my bones and flesh of my flesh" (Gn 2.23). The account in Genesis concludes with the verse Paul cited: "Therefore, the man will leave his father and his mother and will cleave to his wife, and the two will become one flesh" (Gn 2.24). Prescinding from the question as to the appropriateness of Paul's interpretation of Genesis, his view of the relation between the sexes as one of hierarchy embraced by unity provided him with a metaphor for the relation between Christ and the Church.[20] Just as the woman is born of the man, and so dependent upon him, the Church owes her existence to Christ's death and resurrection. And just as the man marries the woman, who is a person in her own right for whose sake the man leaves his parents, Christ loved the Church and gave himself up for her on the cross.[21]

It has long been noticed, however, that the analogy between Adam and Eve and Christ and his Church does not quite work, since, if we take the story strictly on its own terms, Adam and Eve, as the first human beings, were without parents. To resolve the problem, Balthasar again appealed approvingly to patristic exegesis. Following many of the Fathers, Balthasar said of this passage: "since this twofold statement of Genesis, to which Paul refers, is inapplicable to Adam and Eve, since Adam had no parents to leave, it must have to do with the future. And so Paul . . . is . . . undoubtedly thinking of the simultaneous realization of both aspects in the relationship between Christ and the Church."[22] Those Fathers who spoke of Christ leaving God the Father and Mother Jerusalem (that is, the heavenly Zion) to descend to earth in order to rescue his bride from her enslavement to sin, and those Fathers who spoke of the bride, soiled by her harlotry, being purified by the blood of the cross and rendered thereby glorious, without spot or wrinkle, merely, as Balthasar put it, "make fully comprehensible Paul's statement."[23] On Balthasar's reading then, Paul resolved the apparent contradiction between the notion of the Church as preexistent and as born on the cross by appeal to the theology of gender relations he saw elaborated in the Genesis account. Putting the point in terms that Balthasar believed were consonant with Paul's intent, these two, seemingly contradictory notions of the Church find their resolution in the view of the bride of YHWH having died to sin in the baptismal font in order, now purified, to rise with Christ.[24]

With this Balthasar has moved closer to identifying Mary as the bride of Christ. But before examining the last two steps in his argument, there is a question to be asked: Did Balthasar, by highlighting in this fashion the continuities between the Old and New Testament bridal imagery, undercut his claim that while the Old Testament conceives of God's covenant partner as a collective subject, in the New Testament it assumes a more nearly personal, singular subjectivity? In order to answer this objection, Balthasar asserted that the relation of YHWH and his spouse was conceived in ethical or juridical terms.[25] That is to say, it primarily concerned the behavior of the two partners: Israel's infidelities and YHWH's steadfast loyalty.[26] However vivid and theologically fruitful the Old Testament imagery of YHWH longing for his adulterous bride may be, Balthasar maintained that nowhere in the

Old Testament do we find YHWH and his spouse as closely tied as Paul would link Christ and the Church in Eph 5. When, following Paul, we read the bodily imagery in nuptial terms, what emerges is an understanding of the Church and Christ on the analogy of a couple, bound in marriage, becoming one flesh. To have understood the relation of Christ and his Church in such terms, Balthasar maintained, was one of Paul's great contributions. By contrast, on Balthasar's reading of the Old Testament, "Israel, as Yahweh's spouse, is indeed a kind of subject, but nothing in the nature of a 'body' of God."[27]

Up to this point in the argument, Balthasar has asserted that the Church must be understood as a singular subject and that the New Testament bridal imagery should be given hermeneutical priority over other biblical symbols for the Church. This leaves Balthasar with the Church understood primarily as the bride of Christ, but does not yet carry him over the threshold of explicitly identifying Mary as Christ's spouse. The next stage in his effort to do so follows from his claim, itself derived from his interpretation of Eph 5.27f., that the bridal character of the Church involves being of one flesh with her bridegroom. Balthasar argued that because God's Word became incarnate in Jesus Christ, the human response to this Word must likewise become incarnate. "[T]he nuptial character of the subject that receives the revelation must necessarily accomplish an incarnation that is analogous to the Incarnation of God's Word."[28] At first blush, this can sound as though Balthasar is impugning the humanity of Jesus Christ. But he did not mean to suggest that Mary, or anyone else for that matter, had somehow to make up a deficiency in the reconciliation of God and humanity effected by Christ's death and resurrection. The covenant has been fulfilled, for both the divine and human partners, in the God-man Jesus Christ. Nevertheless, Balthasar believed that when viewed from the human side of this fulfillment, Jesus Christ "appears as the 'sanctifier' (and thus as the representative of the divine husband)."[29] What is required of those sanctified is a concrete, particular someone, who is "undeniably a human, feminine bride," to correspond to the unity of the one sanctifying.[30] On Balthasar's view, then, if we think through to its logical conclusion the requirement for an incarnate subject to receive God's Word in Jesus Christ, we are led straight to the notion of the bride of Christ without spot or wrinkle that Paul described in Eph 5.27.[31] But that image is now seen in a new light. Where earlier it had referred to the Church as by analogy to a single center of consciousness or intentional agent, here it also refers to a particular, historical individual.

The final step of the argument looks like this: God wants neither to receive a fragmented or piecemeal response to the offer of grace in Jesus Christ nor to receive a response that is in any respect partial, approximate, or defective.[32] In fact, God's Word goes forth precisely in order to receive a perfect response. Balthasar found scriptural warrant for this in Is 55.11: "My word . . . shall not return to me empty, but it shall accomplish that which I purpose, and succeed in the thing for which I sent it."[33] Since the righteousness of God has become a man, humankind is required to give to this Word an appropriate and incarnate response in the form of a woman's graced and yet utterly free, self-less "Yes."

When taken together, these four postulates "converge," as Balthasar put it, on Mary the mother of Jesus.[34] She gave the only appropriate response when she said, in the place of all humanity, "let it be done with me according to your word" (Lk 1.38).[35]

An Analysis of Balthasar's Exegesis

Having explicated Balthasar's exegetical case for identifying Mary—in her function as a type of the Church—as the bride of Christ, I now turn to summarizing some of the techniques and conclusions of his exegesis that stand in tension with his own hermeneutical principles, especially those that govern the proper contributions and limits of historical criticism.

On two occasions in the examples presented, Balthasar cited isolated biblical verses as part of a theological argument. He appealed to Heb 1.1 to warrant his claim that one of the ecclesiological implications of the incarnation is that the Church ought to be understood on analogy to a particular person, rather than as a collective subject like a people or nation. And he saw in Is 55.11 grounds for arguing that the incarnate Word requires of humanity an unwavering "Yes" in response to the offer of salvation. This pattern of theological argument had largely fallen out of favor until being revived by Karl Barth.[36] It is widely rejected by historical critics because of the ease with which such citations do violence to the verse's wider context. The fear is that by lifting an individual verse out of the pericope within which it has its textual home, one almost inevitably ignores the ways in which that setting shapes the verse's meaning. Heb 1.1, for example, is typically seen as the beginning of a four verse introduction celebrating "the Christian confession that the exalted Jesus is God's eternal Son."[37] There is nothing in the text that even suggests that the point of the passage concerns how the Church should or should not be understood. Balthasar's use of Heb 1.1 would seem to typify precisely the sort of prooftexting that drives historical critics to distraction. To put a better face on it, however, one might say that Balthasar heard in the first verse echoes of a much later one (Heb 13.3) that may seem to suggest some familiarity with a body ecclesiology.[38] It is suspect, however, whether these verses can be taken as definitive of the letter's doctrine of the Church, as Balthasar seemed to suppose.[39] Accordingly, Balthasar's use of Heb 1.1 does, at the very least, verge on the arbitrary selection of a text with little regard for the likely intended meaning of the verse in its original context and the application of it to a wholly unrelated issue. As such, it ignores two of his hermeneutical guidelines. It offends against the aesthetic concern to respect the integrity of the relations between parts and wholes. And it shirks the exegete's responsibility to determine the most likely intended meaning of the text's human author. It should be clear that neither rule prohibits the use of proof texts altogether; they simply place limits around the ways in which proof texts are employed.

I also examined two occasions when Balthasar used a passage from one biblical author to interpret a verse or verses from another one. He used Paul's notion of the Church as the body of Christ to interpret the image of the Church as God's house in Hebrews and he used a nuanced version of the traditional reading of Jn 19.34 (the piercing of Jesus' side) to sharpen the contrast between the Church as predating Christ and as born on the cross that he believed Paul was wrestling with in Eph 5.25–27. In terms of the hermeneutical discussion of chapter 2, Balthasar's use of the Pauline body of Christ imagery, Heb 1.1, and Jn 19.34 to explicate Eph 5.23 ff. provide examples of his having treated the Bible as self-glossing. It also provides an instance of the sort of undue harmonizing of theological perspectives that Balthasar's aesthetic sensibilities ought to have prevented. In particular, I am concerned that the letter to the Hebrew's ecclesiology stands in greater tension with that of the author of Ephesians than Balthasar would have us suppose. It may be that his eagerness to identify a single biblical image of the Church as taking precedence over all others led him, on this occasion, to flatten the distinctive contours of the biblical texts that his theological aesthetics should have led him to preserve.

As we have seen, Balthasar contended that one of the interpretive goals of the biblical exegete is to discern the human author's intended meaning. In this, at least, he and most historical critics agree, since the latter, despite considerable variations in method, are generally allied in seeking the intended meaning of the biblical writer or final redactor.[40] When measured by this aim, the example of Balthasar's exegesis we have reviewed has four serious shortcomings.

To begin, Balthasar's assumption that Paul wrote Ephesians is no longer widely credited. Although there remains a significant minority who defend a genuine Pauline authorship, the critical consensus has shifted behind the view of the text as the creation of an anonymous author, whom some, though not all, argue belonged to a "Pauline school."[41] This is by no means the only instance in which Balthasar's convictions about the identity of a biblical author parted ways with the critical consensus. He defended the authenticity of Colossians, too.[42] Even more controversially, he also seems to have ascribed Hebrews to Paul, 1 and 2 Peter to Peter, and the Apocalypse to John.[43] This dismays Louis Dupré, who correctly observes that most "Protestants and many Catholics refuse to follow [Balthasar] in this regard."[44] Significantly, however, in virtually every instance, one can find other texts in which Balthasar either explicitly or by implication denied the apostolic authorship of these very books. It is not as though, as he became more familiar with the relevant biblical scholarship over the years, he grew to accept the critical consensus. With respect to the authorship of Hebrews, for instance, in volumes 1 and 7 of the *Theological Aesthetics* he seems both to have accepted and denied its Pauline authorship.[45] The same pattern of both accepting and denying apostolic authorship repeats itself with respect to the other biblical books just mentioned.[46] Naturally, one can put all of this down to the haste with which Balthasar wrote these volumes, but I do not think this inconsistency has anything to do with sloppiness. Since he clearly indicated that he accepted the findings of historical critics respecting the authorship of these books, it seems reasonable to say that when he ascribed them to their traditional authors, he was simply following a long-standing habit in the Church of so doing. The traditional ascriptions may function, then, not as claims about the historical individuals themselves, but as a way of reading the books that respects their canonical integrity. They may signal his concern, certainly more evident in his volume on the new covenant than in that on the old, to read the biblical texts in their received or final form. On this view, the biblical figures Paul, Peter, and John (to name just the three we have discussed) become representative archetypes or theological styles. They instantiate ways of reflecting on the central mysteries of the faith that are normative for the Church's ongoing theological reflection. So despite an initial impression that suggested otherwise, Balthasar's ascription of Pauline authorship to the letter to the Hebrews and Johannine authorship to the Gospel of John did not necessarily function for him as an historical claim (though it likely did with respect to the letter to the Ephesians), but as a theological-hermeneutical one. That neither violates his own hermeneutical guidelines nor ought it to disturb historical critics, provided they recognize the legitimacy of different interpretive purposes when reading these texts.

A second issue of concern is Balthasar's having sided with a minority of historical critics (again) by asserting that Eph 5.25 ff. is indicative of an understanding of the Church as predating the cross. The apparent tension in the text upon which Balthasar based his entire reading is, on the majority's view, simply not there. It is not that Balthasar engaged in a flight of pure fancy, however. His reading was influenced by those who, like Heinrich Schlier, saw in the letter to Ephesians a reworking of the Gnostic redeemer myth in which the soul, originally united with the redeemer in heaven, longs for her bridegroom and is eventually reunited with him in the bridal chamber.[47] While not denying that there are echoes of this myth in the letter, Rudolf Schnackenburg, whose views are representative of the majority, argues that "the idea fundamental to that myth of the *pre-existent* Church cannot be confirmed in Eph."[48] For one thing, such a view can only with some difficulty be squared with Eph 2.11 ff., where Gentiles and Jews are said to have been made through the cross into one race in Christ. (We know how Balthasar would respond to this objection: Eph 5.25 ff. is a paradox that can only be resolved in light of the Genesis citation in Eph 5.31.) More generally, however, on Schnackenburg's reading, to speak of a preexistent Church badly misconstrues the author's pastoral purposes. He believes that the letter was written from the perspective of a later generation of believers for whom the Church is quite clearly an existing, objective entity whose foundation lies in Christ's sacrificial death. Eph 5.2 speaks of Christ having given himself up, just as does Eph 5.25, but in Eph 5.2 it is said to have been for "us," that is, the original author and addressees, rather than for the Church. It is Schnackenburg's contention that by using the terms "Church" and "us" interchangeably, the author of Ephesians wished to convey the idea that later converts to the faith are incorporated, through baptism, into an ongoing, living community that is of one flesh with its Lord. It is not that the Church predates the cross, but that for the later, post-apostolic community of the author and addressees, the Church predates their baptism.[49] If we assume that Schnackenburg is correct, then Balthasar failed correctly to identify the human author's intended meaning. That would mean he violated one of the guidelines governing what he believed to be not just critically defensible, but also theologically sound exegesis.

A third difficulty with Balthasar's exegesis of these passages concerns his treatment of Jn 19.34. Here he is more isolated from the prevailing historical-critical opinion than in either of the other two instances I have examined. It should be noted that this is one instance of his having exegeted a biblical passage in light of the history of interpretation. The traditional patristic interpretation is endorsed, but not uncritically. That is to say, Balthasar tried to nuance the older view by locating it within the broader context of the scene beneath the cross with Mary and the beloved disciple, on the one hand, and the resurrection, on the other. Still, he claimed of this verse that "[t]here can be no doubt that, for John, water and blood represent all the sacraments."[50] We can set aside the obvious problem of the authorship of the fourth Gospel. The traditional view, which, as I have indicated, Balthasar usually, though not always, seemed to uphold, has seriously eroded in the last century and a half. The question is simply whether or not the evangelist, whoever he was, intended the issue of blood and water from Jesus' side to refer to "all the sacraments." The general consensus is that he did not. This view is often based, as in Leon Morris's commentary, on the contention that the other uses of "blood" and "water" in the Gospel are not consistent with an intentional allusion to the Eucharist and baptism.[51] It would therefore seem still more difficult to follow Balthasar in arguing that the evangelist had in mind "all the sacraments" when writing this verse.[52] If we assume that the majority view is correct, then Balthasar's exegesis once again failed to identify the most likely intended meaning of this passage's human author.

A fourth area in which Balthasar's exegesis paddles against the mainstream of biblical scholarship is his identification of Mary as the referent of the bridal imagery in Eph 5. Again, one needs to bear in mind that the issue here is whether or not the author of Ephesians intended this reference to be to Mary. In fairness to Balthasar, he nowhere explicitly stated that Paul (whom he supposed wrote Ephesians) had Mary the mother of Jesus in mind when he wrote or dictated these lines. And yet the whole exegesis is undertaken in conversation with Paul. Phrases such as, "Paul . . . is . . . undoubtedly thinking of. . ." indicate clearly that Balthasar believed himself to be following Paul's line of argument.[53] It is safe to say that the majority of scholars would not accept this view.[54]

My purpose in the foregoing has been to demonstrate that when exegeting Eph 5.23 ff., some of Balthasar's methods and conclusions both violate the hermeneutical guidelines we identified in the second chapter and part ways with the reigning historical-critical consensus. We seem to be left with a choice. One option is to reject his work on this passage as sheer speculation, a nearly textbook case of eisegesis. Most of his readers, at least those who maintain that historical criticism can make significant contributions to the Church's biblical interpretation, would be inclined to do just that. This book opened with a list of biblical scholars, theologians, and Christian philosophers who would likely take this course. But I would argue for a different option, one that upon examination has considerable merit, not the least of which is that it provides a check against over hasty dismissals of *all* Balthasar's views and uses of scripture on the basis of those instances when he appears to ignore the lessons of historical critics and the guidelines of his own theological hermeneutics. This option involves reconstruing what he was doing in terms other than his own in order to render it compatible with the hermeneutical rules he advocated, including those that provide for a constructive role for historical criticism. Two relatively recent interpretive models suggest themselves as plausible means by which to do that.

ALTERNATIVE DESCRIPTIONS OF BALTHASAR'S EXEGESIS

The first interpretive model, called "performance interpretation," was proposed by Nicholas Lash. It was later adapted, with two significant modifications, by John Riches to describe at least one instance of Balthasar's exegesis.[55] Before indicating what changes Riches has made, let me briefly summarize Lash's proposal. On his view, Christians perform the scriptures (though he oddly refers solely to the New Testament) as they seek "to share [Jesus'] obedience and hope" by means of "the life, activity and organization of the believing community."[56] A performance interpretation is fundamentally a practical affair; it is an ongoing discipleship in which the faithful try to be true to the story of the one in whom they believe God has acted and continues to act in ways that are of ultimate and salvific significance for oneself and the universe. This view of interpretation accords well with all four of the aspects of Balthasar's hermeneutics that we identified in chapter two. First, it seeks to take the wholeness of the Bible seriously. One cannot excise a significant part of the biblical story and credibly claim to be performing the same story as someone who has not. Drop the Pauline *pro nobis*, for example, and the import of Jesus' life, death, and resurrection is fundamentally altered. Second, a performative interpretation model also accords well with Balthasar's understanding of the proper role and limits of historical criticism. As Lash points out, the skills required to perform one of Beethoven's late string quartets are considerable, but they are not the same as those required by "the textual critics who make the score available through scholarly research and the critics and musicologists who have their own contribution to make to the continuing history of Beethoven interpretation."[57] Yet the skills of the various critics are indispensable, Lash contends, because "the players cannot do whatever they like with the score" but must seek to have their creativity constrained, in some measure, by what the composer intended the piece to sound like.[58] Thus, third, on Lash's view, performance interpretations of the Bible must take the intended meaning of the author(s) into account. The creativity of an interpretation is bounded by the aim of remaining true to the words, deeds, and sufferings of the one whose story the biblical authors intended to tell.[59] Once again, historical critics play a crucial role in uncovering the likely intended meaning of the biblical depiction of Jesus, but the actual performance of the text, through faithful imitation or response, is something quite different. Significantly, Lash does not distinguish between discerning the intent of the human authors and redactors and God's intent in authoring the Bible. But there seems no reason why one could not use Nicholas Wolterstorff's helpful suggestion that discerning divine intent would involve all the efforts of human intention seeking, plus the additional one of taking the whole of the canon into account. Fourth, the performance interpretation model is fully compatible with Balthasar's threefold assertion regarding the importance of tradition, liturgy, and practical application. In fact, on Lash's view, the three come together paradigmatically in the celebration of the Eucharist, where they are inextricably entwined: "Here, that interpretative performance in which all our life consists—all our suffering and care, compassion, celebration, struggle and obedience—is dramatically distilled, focused, concentrated, rendered explicit. In this context, the principal forms of discourse are 'practical': in praise, confession, petition, they seek to *enact* the meanings which they embody."[60]

As pertinent as Lash's proposal appears to be, there are two difficulties with using it to describe our example of Balthasar's exegesis. First, although Balthasar may have thought he was discerning the human author's intended meaning in Eph 5.23 ff., most historical critics disagree that that is in fact what he did. In this respect, Lash's proposal is a considerably better fit with Balthasar's hermeneutics than it is with his actual exegetical practice, at least in this instance. And it is the latter for which I am seeking a suitable description. Lash's emphasis on practical application creates a second difficulty. If interpreting a text requires performing it in the sense that Balthasar and Lash have indicated, then what Balthasar was doing with respect to Eph 5.23 ff. in the *Theological Aesthetics* and the essay, "Who Is the Church?" is not a performance interpretation. A highly original means of coaching others to perform the text in ways true to what sense Balthasar has made of it, perhaps, but not an actual performance.[61]

One way to resolve this problem would be to employ a different definition of performance interpretation, such as that proposed by John Riches. While seeming to allude to Lash's work and the interest it has sparked,[62] Riches does not conceive of performing the scriptures as an act of practical application. He contrasts Luther's search for Paul's intended sense in the letter to the Romans with Balthasar's "virtuoso performance" of the Gospel accounts of Jesus' death and resurrection.[63] It seems to be the way Balthasar emphasized the importance for Christian theology of Holy Saturday, even though the biblical texts themselves pay relatively scant attention to it, that strikes Riches as indicative of a performance. So performance interpretations of the Bible, according to Riches, look like embellishments on a given theme or set of themes. They are a form of theological extrapolation, an attempt to puzzle out and enunciate what must be the case given the intended meaning of the biblical authors. Riches holds, however, that such fealty to authorial intent distinguishes Balthasar's exegesis from performative interpretations per se. That is to say, unlike Lash, Riches does not think that performance interpretations are chastened by authorial intent and insists, quite rightly, that Balthasar believed his exegesis was so chastened.[64] This is the second major modification of Lash's view of performance interpretation Riches makes. For that reason, then, Riches thinks his own definition of performance interpretation as a literary arabesque does not quite hit the mark. In one respect it seems to fit what Balthasar thought he was doing with the biblical texts, but in another it does not.

For this section's purposes, however, that is not as important an objection as it might first appear. I am concerned, after all, to describe what Balthasar actually did with scripture, not what he thought he did. And as we have seen, if the critical consensus regarding the intended meaning of Eph 5.23 ff. is to be accepted, he did not always follow his own hermeneutical guidelines. It seems appropriate, therefore, to conceive of Balthasar's exegesis as an exercise in performance interpretation, provided that is not understood to entail practical application. Furthermore, performance interpretations need not necessarily consist in the sort of thematic embellishments characteristic of Balthasar's reflections on Holy Saturday or the bride of Christ. They may do so, but they need not. They may be more like Oscar Peterson's renditions in the *Songbook* series of Gershwin's music than Brahms's variations on themes from Handel. That is because Peterson's performances more closely follow Gershwin's scores (prescinding from the question of Gershwin's intent with respect to those scores) than Brahms's do Handel's. In other words, interpretive performances of the Bible may be characterized by the sort of close, attentive readings of the text evident in Balthasar's discussion, summarized in the second chapter of this book, of Jesus' double temporal horizon. Notice that what Balthasar did with those New Testament texts is not a matter of straightforward description,[65] since there is no biblical author who ascribed such a view to Jesus. But it does take into consideration the variety of New Testament understandings of time in order to make sense of the whole.

To sum up thus far, Nicholas Lash's view of interpretive performances accurately describes Balthasar's hermeneutics. But both because Balthasar did not always attend to the biblical authors' intended meanings the way he said he would, or thought he was, and because Balthasar's exegesis is not an instance of communally enacting the text's meanings, Lash's proposal is considerably less well suited to describing Balthasar's actual exegetical practice. In this regard, John Riches's definition of performance interpretation as thematic embellishment that pays little heed to the intended meaning is preferable. But this relatively narrow definition needs to be broadened in ways that I have suggested to accommodate those occasions when Balthasar was either more successful at identifying the original author's intent, or engaged in a much closer reading of the text(s), or both.

An obvious problem with this construal of biblical interpretation presents itself. What checks are there against freewheeling rhapsodies that bear no relation to the text they claim to be interpreting? The metaphor of performing texts provides some idea of the kind of constraints under which biblical interpretation thus understood would have to operate. Although great musical performances are not limited to how the original composer wanted a piece played, there must be at least some, call it analogous, relation between that intent and the present performance. Otherwise, two questions go unanswered: Why bother claiming to be performing it? And how would an audience recognize what piece is being performed? Similarly, good interpretations of the Bible are not sheer equivocation, bearing no resemblance to the original. Yet neither are they univocal, slavishly faithful repetitions of the text themselves. So while biblical performances are rightly disciplined or chastened by historical-critical reconstructions of the likely intended meaning, they are not limited thereto. Just as an audience well versed in Cole Porter's "All of You" can render a reasoned and defensible judgment regarding the relative merits of Miles Davis's improvisations on it, so too can the Church assess the strengths and weaknesses of a given interpretation— provided, of course, its ear for what is ecclesially apt has been trained through frequent exposure to good, close readings of the Bible and participation in the liturgies.

One way of making such an assessment would be to gauge the usefulness of an interpretation for achieving some end. In this case, the question would become how well does the identification of Mary as the bride of Christ advance the interests of ecclesiology? Balthasar's proposal does a good job of conveying the unity of the Church. And in that regard at least, it does seem superior to the image of the people of God. The bridal imagery alone, that is, apart from its identification with Mary, can do much the same, of course. But the Marian connection enriches it a great deal. The Church is seen as overshadowed by the Holy Spirit and uttering, in Mary, its graced "Yes" to God. But by that very token, this image for the Church is less well suited to express the Church's relations with Israel and Judah. It is simply not satisfactory to say that the bride of YHWH died in the baptismal font to be reborn in Christ as stainless and without wrinkle. That formulation puts Balthasar well down the road toward Christian triumphalism. One of the consequences of such an approach is to make it difficult for Christians to hear the Church's historical and contemporary failings prefigured in the stories and images of Israel's infidelities. Although Balthasar maintained that the prophetic denunciations of Israel's waywardness applied to "members of the Church,"[66] it becomes hard, on his reading of the bridal imagery, to understand how they could be so applied to the Church as a whole. To his credit, when discussing this symbol, Balthasar was at pains to speak of the Church as bearing within her breast both saints and sinners. But "at her core," as he phrased it, the Church remains in Mary "unspotted and a pure bride."[67] To make such a claim is to go beyond saying that the Church, through grace, is kept from making any irreformable error, or that when the pope promulgates dogma *ex cathedra,* he does so infallibly. And it also risks making

Paul's warning in Rom 11, that the engrafted branches can be cut off from the root, unintelligible in other than individualistic terms. Accordingly, I think it can be argued that in this regard the image of the people of God is superior to the image of the bride.

In summary, if Balthasar's own self-understanding is taken as normative, then the conclusion is likely to be reached that his exegesis of Eph 5.23 ff. is an inadequate attempt to discern the intended meaning of the original author. Many, though not all, of his interpreters have done just that. One alternative is to describe what Balthasar was up to in different terms, namely, as giving the Church interpretive performances of these texts. Although any assessment of such performances will have to involve more than a judgment of their efficaciousness, on this score at least, Balthasar's interpretation of the Church as the Marian bride of Christ is commended by its ability to convey the unity of the Church. Such a view falters, however, when it comes to providing the Church the means for speaking of its continuities with faithless Israel and Judah—and, correlatively, for hearing the Old Testament in all its full-throated theological vigor.

A second, more recent model for understanding biblical interpretation that has been proposed by Nicholas Wolterstorff also holds promise for describing Balthasar's exegesis. In the course of this book, I have already alluded to certain features of this proposal, which is known as authorial-discourse interpretation, in connection with the discussion of Balthasar's hermeneutical remarks about authorial intent: it is necessary to distinguish between the intended meaning of the various human authors and redactors of the Bible and God's intended meaning. As we saw in the second and again in the fourth chapter, on Wolterstorff's view, the most appropriate means for describing the way in which God is the author of scripture is to say that God has appropriated as God's own discourse the great variety of discourse found in the Bible. On analogy to the way I can appropriate my wife's spoken words by saying, "That holds for me, too," or by signing my name to a letter she has written, God can be thought of as appropriating the words of the Bible in the course of the closing of the Church's canon.[68] And just as it is crucial for one who seeks to discern my intended meaning in appropriating my wife's words first to establish my wife's intended meaning, so too must a biblical interpreter first identify the intended meaning of a given human author or redactor before trying to do the same for God's intended meaning.

Wolterstorff identifies three elements in this procedure. I summarize them briefly because the particulars of how to discern the intended meaning of a biblical passage are less important at this juncture than the fact that it needs to be done. First, one establishes the noematic content of the biblical verse under examination. This typically involves "considerations about the meanings of sentences, considerations about tropic uses established in the linguistic culture, and considerations of probability and improbability as to what the discourser had and didn't have as his intention to say."[69] The last set of considerations involves having a sense for the various linguistic options available to a discourser and a sense for which of these options the discourser is most likely to have chosen.

Second, the designative content of the verse to be interpreted must also be established. The difference between noematic and designative content can be illustrated with a brief example.[70] Imagine that a historian of American civilian life during times of war discovers two identical sentences ("The war is over!") in two different diaries. Imagine further that the historian can accurately determine that the writers of these sentences were speaking literally and that in each case the illocutionary stance taken toward the sentence is assertion. Under these circumstances, the noematic content of these sentences is identical. Now imagine that the historian says that one diary dates from April 14, 1865, and the other from August 15, 1945. It immediately becomes clear that these two writers were referring to the end of different wars. On Wolterstorff's terms, the designative content of each sentence is different. The first one predicates of the American Civil War that it is over; the second of the Second World War that it is over. Notice that in making that judgment, it was necessary to cease asking questions whose answers determine a sentence's noematic content in order, as Wolterstorff puts it, to enter the real world of events. The dates of the journal entries are of decisive importance, of course, though we still need to know that these wars were fought and that they ended on these dates in order accurately to determine the sentences' designative contents. By the same token, we have to know what "hyssop" is in order to understand (or begin to understand) the designative content of Ps 51.7.

Finally, it is necessary to establish the likely illocutionary stance a discourser takes toward the piece of discourse to be interpreted. One very large clue is the mood of the sentence, be that indicative, subjunctive, or imperative. Is the discourser stating a fact, expressing a wish, asking a question, or giving a command? Establishing a sentence's mood, though important, is not decisive. We can be sure that the mood of the sentence, "The war is over!" is declarative. But if the same person wrote the sentence, "The war is over!" in a diary and also in a novel, it is clear that his or her illocutionary stance toward the sentence in the diary is different from that taken toward the sentence in the novel. Establishing the genre of a biblical verse or the pericope in which it is found is no easy task, of course. But it remains of vital importance. As Hans Frei pointed out, there seems good reason to suppose that when we read the Gospel narratives as factual reports, we misunderstand what illocutionary stance the evangelists took toward their own writing.[71] Establishing a discourser's illocutionary stance also involves the same sort of considerations about the likely linguistic options he or she might have chosen as is true of establishing noematic content.

Turning to the question of determining God's intended meaning in the Bible, we should repeat that it entails first establishing the intended meaning of the discourse God appropriated as God's own. Unless there is good reason to do otherwise, the interpreter begins with the assumption that God's intended meaning is the same as the intended meaning of the human author whose discourse has been appropriated. When that becomes improbable for one reason or another (say, for example, if the intended meaning of the human author is to assert that the sun stood still in the sky), the interpreter turns to the next most likely illocutionary stance and content that God could have intended:

> It follows that we do our interpreting for divine discourse with convictions in two hands: in one hand, our convictions as to the stance and content of the appropriated discourse and the meanings of the sentences used; in the other, our convictions concerning the probabilities and improbabilities of what God would have been intending to say by appropriating this particular discourse-by-inscription.[72]

Before summarizing the sorts of convictions about God that Wolterstorff identifies as fundamental to biblical interpretation, I should repeat a point made in the second chapter about the implication for biblical interpretation of the claim that God has appropriated the Bible as a whole as God's own discourse. If I seek to interpret the intended meaning of a sentence in a letter, I would be foolish to ignore the likely intended meanings of the other sentences in the same letter. The same holds when I seek to interpret discourse that has been appropriated: "when someone appropriates for his own the discourse-by-inscription of others, we as interpreters have to interpret parts of what he appropriated in the light of the totality of what he appropriated."[73] By the same token, it is incumbent upon biblical interpreters who seek to determine God's intended meaning in a given biblical verse to do so bearing in mind God's likely intended meanings in the whole of the canon. That requires a juggling act of sorts. The interpreter has to hold in his or her head numerous possible intended meanings of various verses until arriving at the most probable intended meaning of the entire text under consideration. Once again, arriving at that determination involves certain convictions about what God would or would not likely intend to say in these individual verses and the Bible as a whole.

Wolterstorff notes several such convictions that have been basic to Christian biblical interpretation. The first is that God does not contradict Godself; the second is that what God says in scripture is conducive to love of God or neighbor and does not conflict with Christian dogmas; and the third is that God attends in the scriptures to matters of faith and morals. An example in which the first principle would be brought to bear is the seeming conflict between James and Paul on the importance of works. The Christian interpreter cannot abide by God seeming to say one thing by appropriating Paul's discourse and another by appropriating James's. Resolving the conflict, if that is possible, entails distinguishing between the way they argue their points and those points themselves. One can then claim, as Balthasar did, that they are making the same point with different conceptualities (though "compatible points" would be more accurate).

That is but one of the strategies identified by Wolterstorff for relating the human and the divine discourses when they are in conflict.[74] In addition, it is a commonplace that one illocutionary act of a speaker can count as another. When God appropriates biblical discourse, God may well change this relation of counting as by generating a new illocutionary act. Wolterstorff cites the Song of Songs as an example.[75] A final strategy I shall mention is to recognize that "often there is a relation of *specificity/generality* between the noematic content of the appropriated human discourse and that of the appropriating divine discourse."[76] What God says by way of appropriating a given human discourse may have wider application than was intended by the original author. Or it may have narrower application, as could be the case with 1 Tim 2.12, cited by Wolterstorff, in which the author bids women not to speak or have authority over men.

How can the authorial-discourse interpretation model for biblical interpretation, which lays such emphasis on interpreting the human author's intended meaning, be applicable to Balthasar's exegesis of Eph 5.23 ff.? As we saw with Lash's version of performance interpretation, this model seems better suited to describing Balthasar's hermeneutical proposals than his actual exegetical practice. Is not the very failure of Balthasar accurately to discern the human author's intended meaning part of what prompted this search for alternatives to his own hermeneutical self-descriptions? True enough. It may be that Balthasar's having failed to discern the intended meaning of the human author of these verses means that this model should not be used as a means to describe the way Balthasar interpreted the Bible.

On the other hand, what if the interpreter is fairly clear about the likely intended meaning of Eph 5.23 ff.? What if the interpreter accepts Schnackenburg's centrist analysis? Could Balthasar's exegesis then be thought of as an instance of interpreting for divine discourse? In that case, we would say that the human author's illocutionary act in Eph 5.27 (" . . . the church . . . without a spot or wrinkle or anything of the kind.") has been appropriated by God such that it counts as a description of Mary. Admittedly, this is not an ideal solution. At a minimum it seems to unravel the important connections between the human and divine intended meanings. But as Wolterstorff has taught us, the relations between these two are highly varied. They are so varied that they elude any attempt to sum them up in a sweeping generalization. So it may well be that Balthasar, having done a pretty bad job of discerning the human author's intended meaning, was able, *mirabile dictu,* to enunciate God's.

It may chill one's spine to make claims about God's intent when interpreting scripture, but as I showed when discussing the performative interpretation model, one way to guard against the sort of free flights of interpretive fancy that Balthasar rightly saw offend historical critics[77] is to evaluate the usefulness of a given assertion about divine intent toward some specified end. Wolterstorff would disagree. He contends that "once one has opted for discourse interpretation, then the issue is not whether one's interpretation is valuable in one way or another—exciting, original, imaginative, provocative, beneficial—but whether it is true."[78] On this point, Wolterstorff seems unpersuasive. He appears to exclude the biblically warranted possibility ("by their fruits you shall know them") that one means for determining whether or not one's biblical authorial-discourse interpretation is true is to evaluate its practical implications for the life of the Church. As we saw in the earlier discussion of Balthasar's Marian ecclesiology, one of its weaknesses is that it makes Paul's analogy of the root and the graft in Rom 11 impossible to interpret in other than individualistic terms, which provides strong evidence that God is not likely to have intended to identify Mary as the bride of Christ. Thus one way to judge the probability of a certain interpretation being God's intended meaning is by assessing its implications for interpreting other biblical passages, bearing in mind our convictions about God's relations with God's people.

CONCLUSION

This chapter has presented what amounts to a worst-case scenario. When exegeting Eph 5.23 ff., Balthasar managed to violate at least three of his own hermeneutical guidelines. By illegitimately prooftexting, he brushed aside what his aesthetics say about the importance of respecting the integrity of the relations between, and the mutual influence on, parts and the wholes to which they belong. When trying to use the ecclesiology of Hebrews to support his reading of the ecclesiology of Ephesians, he unduly harmonized two distinct theological perspectives. An aesthetically tuned appreciation for genuine differences among the parts of an integrated whole should have prevented that. And in several instances, he failed to identify what the likely intended meaning of a given biblical author or redactor was.

This chapter also provided additional examples of Balthasar having abided by some of the pre-modern hermeneutical conventions outlined in the introduction. But in contrast to the examples discussed in previous chapters, these do not necessarily commend themselves to contemporary Christians concerned to learn from their pre-modern heritage without abandoning the lessons of the hermeneutics of suspicion. For instance, when discussing Jn 19.34, Balthasar was at pains to engage the tradition in an effort better to understand what the passage means. That he did so in a relatively nuanced and not uncritical way is laudable. But he nevertheless failed to identify what the author of John likely meant when speaking of the issue of blood and water from Jesus' side. And that is what he claimed to be doing. Balthasar also followed the pre-modern approach when he treated Eph 5.23 ff. as part of a self-glossing whole. This was evident in his appeals to Gn 2.20ff., Is 55.11, Lk 1.38, Jn 19.34, Heb 1.1, and Heb 3.3–6. It is true that some of these are less problematic than others, at least when measured by his own and historical criticism's aim to discern the human author's intent. But as we have already noted, his interpretations of Jn 19.34 and Heb 1.1 are dubious, at best, to say nothing of his reading of Is 55.11.

Three responses are in order. The first is to urge contemporary readers not to dismiss Balthasar's doctrine of scripture because of these shortcomings. I have outlined two ways in which his exegesis of this and other passages can be reconstrued to no longer offend against his hermeneutical principles, including those regarding historical criticism. My interest is not to paper over the exegetical problems, but to suggest that those who use these problems to reject all of Balthasar's views and uses of scripture do so unnecessarily. Second, those who advocate a contemporary reappropriation of some of the hermeneutical conventions characteristic of the pre-modern era must do so fully recognizing that at least some of these conventions are open to abuse. There should be no place for a naïve repristination of patristic, medieval, or Reformation era exegetical methods. Although they can measurably enrich a reading of scripture, they can also mislead because they are not sufficient to prevent one either ignoring or misjudging the likely intent of the human author. There are also dangers attending any attempt to treat the Bible as self-glossing. By interpreting the unknown or obscure in terms of the known or clearly understood, we run the distinct risk of forcing a coherence upon the biblical texts that they lack. For these reasons, and in order to avoid having their exegesis lampooned by historical critics, it is imperative that when Christian theologians exegete the Bible, they state clearly what their interpretive goals are. If a general lesson can be drawn from Balthasar's failings in exegeting Eph 5.23 ff., it would be that interpreters must know when they are interpreting for the human or divine author's intended sense. That entails, among other things, determining if there is a consensus among historical critics regarding what the human author intended to say. If the conclusion is reached, in light of that, that God wishes to say something else by appropriating the discourse, then interpreters should be willing to evaluate the merits of their interpretation in light of long-standing convictions about God's identity and will for God's people.

CONCLUSION

I undertook to fulfill two aims in this book. First, I examined and assessed five features of Hans Urs von Balthasar's work in his seven-volume *Theological Aesthetics*: his criticisms of modern biblical interpreters for having largely lost the skills and sensibilities characteristic of most pre-modern exegetes; the hermeneutical implications of the theological aesthetics he maintained would help recoup these losses; his construal of the unity of scripture; his accounts of the authority of scripture; and his uses of scripture when developing a Marian ecclesiology. Despite Balthasar's conviction that theology must be authorized by the scriptural mediation of the Word of God as that is faithfully interpreted in the Church, and his frequent appeals to scripture throughout these volumes, his views and uses of scripture are typically either ignored or dismissed as hopelessly pre-critical. Both responses are mistaken. My second aim was to contend that Balthasar's doctrine of scripture, when modified in ways that are consistent with his own principles, exemplifies an approach to the Bible that, while remaining conversant with historical criticism, is compatible with certain aspects of pre-modern approaches that helped to nurture and sustain the capacity of Christians to understand themselves and their world in terms of the stories, concepts, and images of the Bible. The two aims are linked by the conviction that an interpreter's views and uses of scripture can be measurably enriched by historical-critical inquiry without abandoning significant hermeneutical conventions that predate the development of the modern critical apparatuses.

As the argument has unfolded, I have pointed out those aspects of Balthasar's hermeneutics and exegesis that are compatible with the premodern conventions outlined in the introduction and supplemented in chapter 2. In the first place, he accepted the hermeneutical consensus regarding the priority of the literal sense, as was evident in his criticism of two misreadings of scripture and in his distinction between aesthetic theology and theological aesthetics. Further instances of this compatibility included his contention that Jesus Christ's uniqueness means he cannot be explained exhaustively in terms whose meaning is set by extra-biblical frames of reference; his refusal to accept any paraphrase of the biblical texts as fully adequate; his insistence that biblical interpretation is a continuing task for Christians; his refusal to describe the relation between the two Testaments in terms that have not undergone a christological transformation; and his contention that the abstract universals 'salvation' and 'judgment' are to be defined in terms of their embodiment in the event of Jesus Christ. This conviction was likewise at work in his assertion that the christological structure of archetypal experiences of God should be understood in terms of the life, death, and resurrection of Jesus Christ. I argued that Balthasar's concerns in this regard would have been better addressed had he (in the *Theological Aesthetics*) more frequently construed scripture as narrating the identity of Jesus Christ rather than paradigmatically illustrating his God-experience.

I indicated numerous places where Balthasar treated the Bible as a christologically focused, self-glossing story relating the triune God's creation and redemption of the world. I examined the implications of Balthasar's repeated assertion that biblical interpreters must take the wholeness and integrity of the biblical mediation of God's revelation as their starting point and guiding criterion. He enunciated this in a somewhat misleading polemic against historical criticism's supposed inability to read synchronically and put it into practice in his exegesis of New Testament passages relating to Jesus' views of time. I showed that one of the ways in which Balthasar conceived of the Bible's christologically focused trinitarian theocentricity was in terms of its narrative, or dramatic, movement. My analysis of his actual uses of the biblical narratives showed that he construed them in two quite different ways, namely, as illustrating sets of graced dispositions and as rendering the identities of particular divine and human agents.

Balthasar also accepted the pre-modern concern to interpret the intended sense of the biblical authors. I contended that although authorial intention seeking was an important feature in his hermeneutics, his actual exegesis, as I showed in relation to his mariological reflections, sometimes fell short of his goal.

Finally, it was clear from several examples that Balthasar accepted the pre-modern view of scriptural interpretation finding its proper home in the Church and its proper purpose in the development of lives conformed to Christ. These examples included the role he assigned to Church teachings and traditions, to the liturgy, and to faith; his preference for a typological application of the Old Testament that, though distinct from that employed by most pre-critical exegetes in at least one important way (he did not uproot biblical types from their own historical circumstances), nevertheless was based on the shared conviction that the Old Testament provides types of New Testament (as well as contemporary) persons, institutions, and events; and his conviction, which he shared with most pre-critical exegetes, that typological applications of the Old and the New Testament when carried on in the Church's common life are one of the means by which, through the power of the Holy Spirit, Christians are transformed, edified, and strengthened.

On the basis of these findings, I am persuaded that Balthasar's views and uses of scripture in the *Theological Aesthetics,* while remaining conversant with historical criticism and generally abiding by its fruits, are compatible with those features of the pre-modern approaches to the Bible that helped sustain the sort of biblical fluency and imagination among Christians that today is in such short supply. To the extent that the *sensus fidelium* was traditionally nourished by such readings of the Bible, a contemporary version of this approach that retains the correctives provided by modernity's hermeneutics of suspicion may help to counteract its current disintegration. If Balthasar's approaches to scripture constitute such a contemporary version, then the rapprochement between Catholics and Protestants over the doctrine of scripture discussed at the start of this book is more significant than it initially appeared. That is because one of its most welcome results is to have increased the likelihood that Protestants will take seriously what this Catholic theologian has to say about scripture and what he actually does with it in the course of developing his theological proposals. More than at any time since the Reformation, then, one can reasonably hope that the lessons Balthasar might have to teach the wider Church about biblical interpretation will likely find an appreciative audience among Protestants and Catholics alike.

NOTES

Titles and publications in brackets refer either to the original version of translated works or to an English translation thereof.

1. These include Georges Chantraine, S.J., "Exegesis and Contemplation in the Work of Hans Urs von Balthasar," in *Hans Urs von Balthasar: His Life and Work*, ed. David L. Schindler (San Francisco: Ignatius Press, 1991), pp. 133–49; Brian McNeil, "The Exegete as Iconographer: Balthasar and the Gospels," in *The Analogy of Beauty: The Theology of Hans Urs von Balthasar*, ed. John Riches (Edinburgh: T. & T. Clark, 1986), pp. 134–46; Edward T. Oakes, S.J., "The Wave and the Sea," chap. 7 in *Pattern of Redemption: The Theology of Hans Urs von Balthasar* (New York: Continuum, 1994); John Riches, "The Biblical Basis of Glory," in *The Beauty of Christ: An Introduction to the Theology of Hans Urs von Balthasar*, ed. Bede McGregor, O.P., and Thomas Norris (Edinburgh: T. & T. Clark, 1994), pp.56–72; idem, chaps. 10 and 11 in *A Century of New Testament Study* (Valley Forge, Pa.: Trinity Press International, 1993); and Volker Spangenberg, "Von Balthasars Auseinandersetzung mit der historisch-kritischen Exegese. Ein Beispiel," section 3.2.1 of chap. 3 in *Herrlichkeit des Neuen Bundes: Die Bestimmung des biblischen*

Begriffs der "Herrlichkeit" bei Hans Urs von Balthasar (Tübingen: J.C.B. Mohr [Paul Siebeck], 1993).

2. Brian McNeil notes, for example, that Edward Schillebeeckx in his two volumes on New Testament christology nowhere mentions the work of Balthasar, despite having canvassed over eight hundred "studies of real significance." See Schillebeeckx, *Jesus: An Experiment in Christology* (London: Collins, 1979) [*Jezus. Het verhaal van ein levende* (Bloemendaal: Nelissen, 1974)], p. 62; and *Christ: The Christian Experience in the Modern World* (London: SCM, 1980) [*Gerechtigheid en liefde. Genade en bevrijding,* (Bloemendaal: Nelissen, 1977)]. See McNeil, "Exegete as Iconographer," p. 134.

3. See Joseph A. Fitzmyer, S.J., *Scripture, the Soul of Theology* (New York and Mahwah, N.J.: Paulist Press, 1994), p. 91 n. 70. The essay from which this quotation was taken, "Word, Scripture, and Tradition," was reprinted in Balthasar, *Explorations in Theology,* vol. 1, *The Word Made Flesh,* trans. A.V. Littledale and Alexander Dru (San Francisco: Ignatius Press, 1989) [*Skizzen zur Theologie,* vol. 1, *Verbum Caro* (1960; Einsiedeln: Johannes Verlag, 1965)], p.15.

4. Fitzmyer, *Scripture,* p. 91 n. 70; Fitzmyer's emphasis.

5. John O'Donnell, S.J., "Truth as Love: The Understanding of Truth according to Hans Urs von Balthasar," *Pacifica* 1 (1988): 210.

6. Stephen Happel, review of *The von Balthasar Reader, Religious Studies Review* 10:4 (October 1984): 356.

7. Louis Dupré, "The Glory of the Lord: Hans Urs von Balthasar's Theological Aesthetic," *Communio: International Catholic Review* 16:3 (fall 1989): 408.

8. Christoph Schönborn, O.P., "Hans Urs von Balthasar's Contribution to Ecumenism," in Schindler, ed., *Life and Work,* p. 255.

9. Riches, "The Biblical Basis of Glory," p. 59.

10. "I think it would not be going too far to say that the whole value and validity of Balthasar's theology for the Church in the coming millennium will hinge on the validity of his approach to the Scriptures, especially because to some extent it stands in such tension with the historical-critical method (though hardly naïvely)." Oakes, *Pattern of Redemption,* p. 185.

11. One reader of a draft of this book, herself an historical critic, objected to the term "post-critical" on the grounds that the Church's reading of the Bible must remain, as the Greek root of criticism suggests (κρινω: to choose, question, separate), an act of reasoned discernment, judgment, and choice. She could also have mentioned that to call pre-modern exegesis "pre-critical" is misleading, as anyone familiar with Origen or Augustine can attest. In spite of these disadvantages, I use the term both because of its currency in recent discussions and to signal my conviction that while modern biblical scholarship has an essential role to play in the life of the Church, its purposes are distin-

guishable from the ongoing attempt by the faithful to read the Bible as an authoritative guide to their life and thought.

12. Avery Dulles, S.J., "Scripture: Recent Protestant and Catholic Views," in *The Authoritative Word: Essays on the Nature of Scripture,* ed. Donald K. McKim (Grand Rapids, Mich.: Eerdmans, 1983), pp. 239–61.

13. James D. Smart, *The Strange Silence of the Bible in the Church: A Study in Hermeneutics* (Philadelphia: Westminster Press, 1970). See especially the preface and chap. 1. Although Smart does not address the question of the scope of his investigations, his account appears to be limited to North America.

14. James Barr, *The Bible in the Modern World* (New York: Harper & Row, 1973), p. 10. Barr acknowledges that his expertise on the topic is limited to English-speaking countries. He mentions the related, though distinguishable, concern on the European continent about the mode of biblical authority (in contrast to its legitimacy). See Barr, *The Bible in the Modern World,* p. 8f. I ought also to mention that the situation has changed, at least in one respect, since Barr's book was published. The ideological critique of the Bible, particularly as it has been advanced by some feminists, has led some to take precisely the step of rejecting the Bible's authority.

15. Ibid., p. 8.

16. George A. Lindbeck, "The Church's Mission to a Postmodern Culture," in *Postmodern Theology: Christian Faith in a Pluralist World,* ed. Frederic B. Burnham (San Francisco: HarperCollins, 1989), pp. 37–55.

17. A friend of mine recently received this counsel from his priest: "Well, as Shakespeare said, 'Do unto others as you would have them do unto you.' " When my friend pointed out that these words are from the Sermon on the Mount, his priest, upon reflection, kindly but firmly disagreed.

18. Its demise is recounted in Hans W. Frei, *The Eclipse of Biblical Narrative: A Study in Eighteenth and Nineteenth Century Hermeneutics* (New Haven: Yale University Press, 1974).

19. Rowan A. Greer notes that in antiquity the various "methods" of biblical interpretation, including moral proofs, proofs from prophecy, typology, and allegory, "do not always appear in a pure form, nor do we find writers adopting one of these approaches in isolation from the others." See "The Christian Bible and Its Interpretation," pt. 2 of James L. Kugel and Rowan A. Greer, *Early Biblical Interpretation,* ed. Wayne A. Meeks (Philadelphia: Westminster Press, 1986), p. 127.

20. Frei, *The Eclipse of Biblical Narrative,* p. 10. Having grown increasingly wary of deploying any explanatory theory in defense of a literal reading of the biblical narratives, Frei would later worry that speaking of the biblical narratives as "realistic" implied that they are an instance of a more general class of literary texts called "realistic narratives" that are understood to mean

in relation to human experience in a way true of all members of the species. While not denying that the biblical narratives are like realistic ones, he argued in an essay that appeared twelve years after *The Eclipse of Biblical Narrative* that the analogy is incomplete, especially when applied to the question of the meaning of the incarnation. Accordingly, in his last years Frei contented himself with the more modest aim of describing, albeit "thickly," the interpretive practices of Christian communities. Persuaded by Frei's arguments, I am using "realistic" and "literal reading" in this more limited, analogical sense. See Hans W. Frei, "The 'Literal Reading' of Biblical Narrative in the Christian Tradition: Does It Stretch or Will It Break?" in *The Bible and the Narrative Tradition,* ed. Frank McConnell (New York: Oxford University Press, 1986), pp. 36–77. This article was reprinted in Hans W. Frei, *Theology and Narrative: Selected Essays,* ed. George Hunsinger and William C. Placher (New York: Oxford University Press, 1993), pp. 117–52.

21. Frei, *The Eclipse of Biblical Narrative,* p. 13.

22. Frei, "The 'Literal Reading,' " p. 39.

23. As will become clear momentarily, the terms "typology" and "figuration," to say nothing of "literal reading," are given quite different senses by different authors.

24. Frei, *The Eclipse of Biblical Narrative,* p. 7 and passim. Frei, of course, was by no means unique in this understanding of typology. Brian McNeil notes that "[t]ypology is distinct from allegorical interpretation of the OT [sic] which claims that the 'real' meaning of the OT text is something with no continuity with the historical intention of its writer (cf. e.g., Philo, the Qumran *pesher* on Hab., and Paul's exegesis of Deut. 25.4 at 1 Cor. 9.8–10)." See McNeil, "Typology," in *A Dictionary of Biblical Interpretation,* ed. R. J. Coggins and J. L. Houlden (London: SCM; Philadelphia: Trinity Press International, 1990), p. 713. Still, remembering the warning sounded by Rowan Greer about the frequency with which ancient biblical interpreters jumbled together approaches to the Bible that might preferably have been left distinct, we need to realize that not all typological applications of texts respected the historical integrity of the Old Testament. By the same token, not all scholars of ancient biblical interpretation agree that allegory necessarily offends against the literal, historical sense of the texts. Andrew Louth, for instance, argues that allegorical interpretation "was a way of freeing the text of scripture from the confines of its original context of utterance so that it could be a vehicle for the word of Christ to the contemporary church. It is not that the literal historical meaning of the text of scripture is ignored—the church has a history and needs to be faithful to that history—rather it is that the literal meaning does not exhaust for all time the meaning of the scriptures for the church" (Louth, "Allegorical Interpretation," in ibid., p. 14). And as we will see, Henri de Lubac took strong exception to any Platonizing definitions of allegory, insisting that in its Pauline form allegory is an

essential ingredient in the Church's uses of the Bible. In light of that, I do not wish to imply that all allegorical interpretation is problematic or that all typological interpretation is welcome. My concern, rather, is to avoid interpreting either Testament in ways that treat its literal meanings, to steal a line from Quodvultdeus, "like husks that are fed to swine" by the spiritually astute.

25. Frei, *The Eclipse of Biblical Narrative,* p. 34 ff. Frei is here describing Calvin, but cites Erich Auerbach's *Mimesis* in support of his claim that this feature was once true of Western Christian interpretation in general. See Auerbach, *Mimesis: The Representation of Reality in Western Literature,* trans. Willard R. Trask (Princeton: Princeton University Press, 1953) [*Mimesis: Dargestellte Wirklichkeit in der abendländischen Literatur* (Bern: Franke, 1946)], pp. 73 f. and 195 f.

26. See George A. Lindbeck, "Scripture, Consensus, and Community," *This World* 23 (fall 1988): 5–24, especially p. 6. This article was reprinted in Richard John Neuhaus, ed., *Biblical Interpretation in Crisis: The Ratzinger Conference on Bible and Church* (Grand Rapids, Mich.: Eerdmans, 1989), pp. 74–101.

27. Hans W. Frei, *Types of Christian Theology,* ed. George Hunsinger and William C. Placher (New Haven: Yale University Press, 1992), p. 137 and passim.

28. Ibid., p. 141.

29. Ibid., p. 142.

30. Ibid., p. 140 f.; cf. Frei, *The Eclipse of Biblical Narrative,* p. 3 f.

31. Jaroslav Pelikan, *Jesus through the Centuries: His Place in the History of Culture* (New Haven: Yale University Press, 1985).

32. Rowan Greer refers to this as the "flexibility" of patristic exegesis in "The Christian Bible and its Interpretation," p. 197 f.

33. Lindbeck, "Scripture, Consensus, and Community." p. 20 n. 9. The allusion is to Lam 3.23.

34. Lindbeck, "The Church's Mission to a Postmodern Culture," in Burham, ed., *Postmodern Theology,* pp. 43, 50.

35. See Brevard S. Childs, "The Sensus Literalis of Scripture: An Ancient and Modern Problem," in *Beiträge zur Alttestamentlichen Theologie: Festschrift für Walther Zimmerli zum 70. Geburtstag,* ed. Herbert Donner (Göttingen: Vandenhoeck & Ruprecht, 1976), pp. 80–93.

36. See George A. Lindbeck, "Barth and Textuality," *Theology Today* 43:3 (October, 1986): 361–82, especially p. 365.

37. Frei, "The 'Literal Reading,'" p. 64.

38. One modern example of the intratextual approach is Karl Barth. Paul McGlasson points out, however, that Barth was far from consistent on this score. See McGlasson, *Jesus and Judas: Biblical Exegesis in Barth,* AAR Academy Series, vol. 72 (Atlanta: Scholars Press, 1991). Origen provides a premodern example of how philosophical commitments can obscure rather than

illuminate the biblical text being interpreted. In fairness to Origen, however, just as with Barth, he did not pursue any one program of exegesis single-mindedly and, on balance, probably tilted more toward an intratextual, rather than intertextual, approach. My views on Origen's exegesis owe much to the vigorous defense of his genuinely "Pauline" use of allegory mounted by Henri de Lubac in *Medieval Exegesis*, vol. 1, *The Four Senses of Scripture*, trans. Mark Sebanc (Grand Rapids, Mich.: Eerdmans; Edinburgh: T. & T. Clark, 1998) [*Exégèse médiévale*, vol. 1, *Les Quatre sens de l'Ecriture* (Paris: Éditions Montaigne, 1959)]. It is very likely that these studies by Balthasar's one time teacher also influenced his treatment of the Alexandrian. See *Origen: Spirit and Fire*, ed. Hans Urs von Balthasar, trans. Robert J. Daly (Washington, D.C.: Catholic University of America Press, 1984) [*Origenes: Geist und Feuer. Ein Aufbau aus seinen Schriften*, trans. and with an introduction by Hans Urs von Balthasar (Salzburg: Otto Müller Verlag, 1938)].

39. I use "translate" advisedly. As David H. Kelsey contends, although it represents the standard picture of the relation between the Bible and biblically authorized theological proposals, it is simply inadequate to describe the variety of ways in which the Bible is actually used in doing theology. See his *The Uses of Scripture in Recent Theology* (Philadelphia: Fortress Press, 1975), especially p. 192.

40. Lindbeck, "The Church's Mission to a Postmodern Culture," in Burnham, ed., *Postmodern Theology*, p. 38.

41. De Lubac, *Medieval Exegesis*, vol. 1, p. 263.

42. Ibid., p. 265; cf. p. 227.

43. Ibid., p. 265.

44. Ibid., p. 75; cf. p. 31.

45. Ibid., p. 227.

46. Ibid., p. 77.

47. Ibid., p. 247f.

48. Ibid., p. 256. Following Gregory the Great and "the whole Latin tradition" that subsequently adopted it, de Lubac found this ably illustrated in the "two golden cherubim with spread wings, who faced each other within the Dwelling Place of Yahweh at the two ends of the mercy seat, their gaze turned toward him. . . . Do not the two Testaments in some respect frame the Mediator, since one of them prophesies what the other shows as having been fulfilled? The pure gold of the cherubim is the pure truth of the two Testaments" (ibid., p. 255).

49. Henri de Lubac, "Typology and Allegorization," in *Theological Fragments*, trans. Rebecca Howell Balinski (San Francisco: Ignatius Press, 1989) [*Théologies d'occasion* (Paris: Desclée de Brouwer, 1984)], p. 129. This article first appeared in *Recherches de science religieuse* 35 (1947): 180–226. Daniélou's article, "Traversée de la mer Rouge et baptême aux premiers siècles," in

which he argues for the antiquity of typological interpretations and their prefer-ability over allegorical ones, was published the previous year in the same jour-nal, pp. 402–30.

50. De Lubac, *Medieval Exegesis*, vol. 1, p. 259

51. De Lubac, "Typology and Allegorization," in *Theological Fragments*, p. 151.

52. Ibid., p. 134.

53. Ibid., p. 132.

54. De Lubac, *Medieval Exegesis*, vol. 1, pp. 16, 258.

55. Ibid., p. 16.

56. De Lubac, "Typology and Allegorization," in *Theological Fragments*, p. 158.

57. Ibid., p. 152.

58. Frei, *The Eclipse of Biblical Narrative*, p. 29.

59. De Lubac, "Typology and Allegorization," in *Theological Fragments*, p. 156. Remembering that Frei and Auerbach spoke of the pre-modern domi-nance of "literal-figurative" interpretations, which by definition respect the integrity of the literal sense, one can see why the debate can so easily get muddled.

60. Ibid., 154. As I have already indicated, de Lubac admitted that this approach to the biblical texts, particularly those of the Old Testament, proved too great a temptation for some pre-modern Christians.

61. Ibid., p. 159 n. 162.

62. St. Hilary, *In Ps. 134*, n. 18, cited in Henri de Lubac, "Hellenistic and Christian Allegory," in *Theological Fragments*, p. 169. This article first ap-peared in *Recherches de science religieuse* 47 (1959): pp. 5–43.

63. Augustine, *De diversis quaestionibus octaginta tribus* 83, q. 65; cited in ibid., p. 170, quoted from *Patrologiae cursus completus: Seria Latina*, ed. J. P. Migne, vol. 40 (Paris: n.p., 1844–64).

64. De Lubac, "Hellenistic Allegory and Christian Allegory," in *Theologi-cal Fragments*, p. 185f., quoting J. Pépin, *Mythe et allégorie: Les origenes grecques et les contestations judéo-chrétiennes* (Paris: Aubier, 1958).

65. De Lubac, "Typology and Allegorization," in *Theological Fragments*, p. 144.

66. Auerbach, *Mimesis*, p. 73f.

67. Ibid., p. 74.

68. Ibid., p. 195.

69. Frei, *The Eclipse of Biblical Narrative*, p. 30.

70. Auerbach, *Mimesis*, p. 195f.

71. De Lubac, *Medieval Exegesis*, vol. 1, p. 239; emphasis his.

72. Ibid, p. 240.

73. Ibid., pp. 251, 241f.

74. De Lubac, "Hellenistic Allegory and Christian Allegory," in *Theological Fragments,* p. 176.

75. De Lubac, *Medieval Exegesis,* vol. 1, p. 226.

76. Ibid., p. 233f.

77. Ibid., p. xixf.

78. Ibid., p. 265; see also pp. xx, 227, 263.

79. Roger Aubert, *La Théologie catholique au milieu du XXᵉ siècle* (Paris: Casterman, 1954), pp. 11–28.

80. Robert Murray, S.J., "Revelation (*Dei Verbum*)," in *Modern Catholicism: Vatican II and After,* ed. Adrian Hastings (New York: Oxford University Press, 1991), p. 80.

81. Sandra Schneiders, "Does the Bible Have a Postmodern Message?" in Burnham, ed., *Postmodern Theology,* p. 58.

82. Ibid.

83. Denis Farkasfalvy, "The Case for Spiritual Exegesis," *Communio* 10:4 (winter 1983): 332.

84. For a concise, informative account of the liturgical changes associated with Vatican II, see Aidan Kavanagh, O.S.B., "Liturgy (*Sacrosanctum Concilium*)," in Hastings, ed., *Modern Catholicism,* pp. 68–73. The use of the vernacular for some rites had already been "grudgingly" allowed by Pius XII in *Mediator Dei* (1947). See ibid., p. 71.

85. Murray, "Revelation (*Dei Verbum*)," in ibid., p. 79.

86. Ibid., p. 78.

87. Schneiders, "Does the Bible Have a Postmodern Message?" in Burnham, ed., *Postmodern Theology,* pp. 65–73.

88. Denis Farkasfalvy, "In Search of a 'Post-critical' Method of Biblical Interpretation for Catholic Theology," *Communio: International Catholic Review* 13:4 (winter 1986): 301. Cf. Farkasfalvy, "The Case for Spiritual Exegesis," p. 335.

89. Frei, "The 'Literal Sense,'" p. 74.

90. See Schneiders, "Does the Bible Have a Postmodern Message?" in Burnham, ed., *Postmodern Theology,* p. 58.

91. See William C. Placher, *Unapologetic Theology: A Christian Voice in a Pluralistic Conversation* (Louisville, Ky.: Westminster & John Knox, 1989), especially in chap. 7.

92. Lindbeck, "Scripture, Consensus, and Community," p. 17 and passim.

93. This is not to invoke one model of conversation among Christians and another for conversations between Christians and non-Christians. The difference is one of degree, not kind. The revival of the classic hermeneutics might help provide a more comprehensive idiom, but even under the best of circumstances there will be elements of the "common Christian language" that not all Christians share.

CHAPTER 1. THEOLOGICAL AESTHETICS:
A METHODOLOGICAL AND HISTORICAL ORIENTATION

1. Balthasar, "Theologie und Heiligkeit," *Wort und Wahrheit* 3 (1948): 881–96; revised and reprinted in Balthasar, *Skizzen zur Theologie*, vol. 1. ["Theology and Sanctity," in *Explorations in Theology*, vol. 1. See also from this volume "The Place of Theology" and "Spirituality"; the phrase "fatal cleavage" is taken from the latter, p. 213.] Balthasar, "The Unity of Theology and Spirituality," in *Convergences: To the Source of Christian Mystery*, trans. E. A. Nelson (San Francisco: Ignatius Press, 1983) [*Einfaltungen: Auf Wegen christlicher Einigung* (Munich: Kösel Verlag, 1969)]. And, finally, Balthasar, "Theology and Holiness," *Communio: International Catholic Review* 14:4 (winter 1987): 341–50. Antonio Sicari, O.C.D., locates the topic in relation to Balthasar's larger theological program in "Hans Urs von Balthasar: Theology and Holiness," *Communio: International Catholic Review* 16:3 (fall 1989): 351–65. For an equally sympathetic, though much longer, treatment, see Jutta Konda, "Das Verhältnis von Theologie und Heiligkeit im Werk Hans Urs von Balthasars" (dissertation, Rheinische Friedrich-Wilhelms-Universität, 1990).

2. One critic, Thomas J. A. Hartley, laments the neoscholastic "cerebral bias, the simplistic non-historical approach to Christian dogmas, the failure to emphasize the mystery of things, the negative attitude in the face of the modernist crisis, etc." See *Thomistic Revival and the Modernist Era*, St. Michael's in Toronto Studies in Religion and Theology Dissertation Series, vol. 1 (Toronto: Institute of Christian Thought, University of St. Michael's College, 1971), p. 43f. A more comprehensive assessment of neoscholasticism is provided by Gerald A. McCool, S.J., *Nineteenth-Century Scholasticism: The Search for a Unitary Method* (New York: Fordham University Press, 1989). This book is a reissue of *Catholic Theology in the Nineteenth Century: The Quest for a Unitary Method* (New York: Seabury Press, 1977). I have drawn on McCool's work, especially pp. 217, 225, 236–40, in the following paragraph.

3. In an autobiographical essay, he complained of "languishing in the desert of neoscholasticism" as a student in Munich. See Balthasar, *My Work: In Retrospect*, trans. Brian McNeil, C.R.V., et al. (San Francisco: Ignatius Press, 1993) [*Mein Werk—Durchblicke*, (Einsiedeln: Johannes Verlag, 1990)], p. 89.

4. Balthasar, "Peace in Theology," *Communio: International Catholic Review* 12:4 (winter 1985): 398–407 (p. 405).

5. In his obituary of Thomas Pègues, O.P., M.-D. Chenu complained of Pègues's "indifference to the enrichment that, by nature, Christian theology seeks in an ever renewed study of the revealed *datum* and its permanent virtualities in the most varied climates of the Church" ("Le R. P. Pègues, O.P.," *Bulletin Thomiste*, 4 [1936] cited in Hartley, *Thomistic Revival and the Modernist Era*, p. 43). As Hartley noted, these are "[h]ard words for a necrology."

6. The distinction is Balthasar's, elaborated in a discussion of Origen's doctrine of faith. See *The Glory of the Lord: A Theological Aesthetics,* vol. 1, *Seeing the Form,* ed. Joseph Fessio, S.J., and John Riches, trans. Erasmo Leiva-Merikakis (San Francisco: Ignatius Press, 1982) [*Herrlichkeit: Eine theologische Ästhetik,* vol. 1, *Schau der Gestalt* (1961; Einsiedeln: Johannes Verlag, 1967)], p. 137. Hereafter, *Glory* 1.

7. The phrase "conclusion theology" is Johannes Baumer's. See *Theologie als Glaubensverständnis* (Würzburg: Echter, 1953), pp. 228–29, cited in McCool, *Nineteenth-Century Scholasticism,* p. 225.

8. See Balthasar, "The Place of Theology," in *Explorations in Theology,* vol. 1, p. 155.

9. Balthasar's distinction between kneeling [*kniende*] theology and sitting theology has become, to borrow his cousin's description, "proverbial." See Peter Henrici, S.J., "Hans Urs von Balthasar: A Sketch of His Life," in Schindler, ed., *Life and Work,* p. 26. Balthasar first articulated this distinction in his 1948 essay, "Theologie und Heligkeit" (see n. 1). He knew, however, that this sentiment long predated him. For instance, when describing Anselm's "monastic . . . contemplative reason," he said: "It is the contemplation, above all, of a praying reason which only hopes to find insight in dialogue with the eternal truth, and therefore ever again passes over from the form of meditation to that of prayer." Balthasar, *The Glory of the Lord: A Theological Aesthetics,* vol. 2, *Studies in Theological Style: Clerical Styles,* ed. John Riches, trans. Andrew Louth et al. (San Francisco: Ignatius Press, 1984) [*Herrlichkeit: Eine theologische Ästhetik,* vol. 2, *Fächer der Stile,* pt. 1, *Klerikale Stile* (1962; Einsiedeln: Johannes Verlag, 1969)], p. 212. Hereafter, *Glory* 2. Or, again, in his summary of Bonaventure's aesthetics, Balthasar applauded the Franciscan's contempt for those theologians who would have " 'reading without unction, speculation without devotion, research without wondering, prudence without exultation, hard work without piety, cleverness without humility.' " Bonaventure, *Itinerarium prol.* 4 (Quaracchi edition [1882–1902], vol. V 296a), cited in *Glory* 2, p. 268.

10. Thomas F. O'Meara, O.P., speaks of Balthasar having been appropriated by "an intellectually conservative minority" as a result of his criticisms of Rahner and Küng. See O'Meara, "Of Art and Theology: Hans Urs von Balthasar's Systems," *Theological Studies* 42:2 (June 1981): 272, cited in Edward T. Oakes, *Pattern of Redemption: The Theology of Hans Urs von Balthasar* (New York: Continuum, 1994), p. 5 n. 9.

11. See Stephen Happel and Susan A. Ross's reviews of *The von Balthasar Reader* by Hans Urs von Balthasar, *Religious Studies Review* 10:4 (October 1984): 354–56 and 358–60, respectively. I do not dispute that these are conservative positions. My complaint is rather that on the basis of such views the judgment is made that Balthasar is a conservative theologian or that his work as a whole is conservative.

12. See his "Two Modes of Faith," in *Explorations in Theology*, vol. 3, *Creator Spirit*, trans. Brian McNeil, C.R.V. (San Francisco: Ignatius Press, 1993) [*Skizzen zur Theologie*, vol. 3, *Spiritus Creator* (Einsiedeln: Johannes Verlag, 1967)], especially p. 85. For another brief discussion of *aggiornamento* in relation to reform, see Balthasar, *My Work*, p. 51 ff. Finally, see Balthasar, *Herder-Korrespondenz* 21 (January 1967): 1–30.

13. Balthasar, *My Work*, p. 105. A similar point is made in the following: "Theologie, insbesondere Dogmatik hat als Anstrengung des Verstehens immer die gefährliche Tendenz, die entscheidende Synthese und Integration selber zu vollbringen und darzustellen, deshalb Schrifttexte als 'geschlossene' zu lesen und Definitionen mit erschöpfenden Sätzen zu verwechseln. So betriebene Dogmatik erzeugt praktische Integralisten, die wenn sie ihre Position extrem verstehen, ihr integrales, das heißt lückenloses System an die Stelle des unendlich offenen Systems Gottes setzen müssen." Balthasar, "Exegese und Dogmatik," *Internationale Katholische Zeitschrift* 5 (1976): 390.

14. "Patience would be the central disposition with which the theologian has to approach the hardening of the fronts and its immediate danger of schism. The hardening of the 'right' must therefore be the most dangerous, since with its recourse to the tradition it almost always appeals to the letter of yesterday, which, according to Paul, can kill if it is not animated, illuminated, and clarified by the spirit blowing today." Balthasar, "Peace in Theology," p. 402.

15. Balthasar, *The Glory of the Lord: A Theological Aesthetics*, vol. 7, *Theology: The New Covenant*, ed. John Riches, trans. Brian McNeil, C.R.V. (San Francisco: Ignatius Press, 1989) [*Herrlichkeit: Eine theologische Ästhetik*, vol. 3, pt. 2, *Theologie*, pt. 2, *Neuer Bund* (Einsiedeln: Johannes Verlag, 1969)], p. 113 f. Hereafter, *Glory* 7. See further the section "Pistis and Gnosis" in *Glory* 1, p. 131 ff.

16. This is not the place to evaluate in any detail Balthasar's critique of transcendental Thomism. Although there remains much work to be done in this area, Rowan Williams has made a significant contribution. See his "Balthasar and Rahner," in Riches, ed., *The Analogy of Beauty*, pp. 11–34. For a more recent account of the differences and similarities between Rahner and Balthasar that scrupulously tries to avoid tipping in favor of one position or the other, see Eamonn Conway, *The Anonymous Christian—A Relativised Christianity? An Evaluation of Hans Urs von Balthasar's Criticisms of Karl Rahner's Theory of the Anonymous Christian*, European University Studies Series 23, vol. 485 (Frankfurt am Main: Peter Lang, 1993).

17. Balthasar, "Theology and Sanctity," in *Exploration in Theology*, vol. 1, p. 190. Balthasar's view of the Spanish spirituality of the baroque is more ambivalent than I am able to convey here. He described it as "primarily, not a mysticism in service of the Church" (p. 190). But he recognized that Teresa, at least, was encouraged to adopt the more self-centered form of description by

her confessors (p. 192). And in another essay he contradicted himself by claim-
ing that Teresa's visions were regarded as given for the preservation of the
Church in its fight with the Reformation. See Balthasar, *Elucidations*, trans.
John Riches (London: SPCK, 1975) [*Klarstellungen: Zur Prüfung der Geister*
(Freiburg im Breisgau: Herder Verlag)], p. 127.

18. Balthasar, "Theology and Sanctity," in *Explorations in Theology*, vol. 1,
p. 192. Balthasar's insight, which is more asserted than argued for, gains considerable credence when read in the light of an excellent study of pre-modern
mystical theology by Denys Turner. He maintains that its theology and practice
should be distinguished from contemporary Christian mysticism in large measure because of the latter's preoccupation with mystical experience. See Turner,
The Darkness of God: Negativity in Christian Mysticism (Cambridge: Cambridge University Press, 1995).

19. Balthasar, "Theology and Sanctity," in *Explorations in Theology*, vol. 1,
p. 208.

20. Balthasar, "Current Trends in Catholic Theology and the Responsibility of the Christian," *Communio: International Catholic Review* 5:1 (spring
1978): 85.

21. Balthasar, *Razing the Bastions: On the Church in this Age*, trans.
Brian McNeil, C.R.V. (San Francisco: Ignatius Press, 1993) [*Schleifung der Bastionen: Von der Kirche in dieser Zeit* (Einsiedeln, Johannes Verlag, 1952)].

22. I will take up the first of these concerns in more detail below. Balthasar expressed his reservations about the second with typical acerbity: "When
everything goes so well with anonymity, it is hard to see why a person should
still be a name-bearing Christian." *My Work*, p. 56. See also Balthasar, "Current Trends in Catholic Theology," p. 79f. and 85.

23. Balthasar, *Convergences: To the Source of Christian Mystery*, trans.
E. A. Nelson (San Francisco: Ignatius Press, 1983) [*Einfaltungen: Auf Wegen
christlicher Einigung* [Munich: Kösel Verlag, 1969)], p. 39; see also p. 35. The
quotation is actually part of a polemic against Bultmann's existential reductionism. Later in the same essay Balthasar examines, briefly, political theology
(p. 40ff.). See also "Current Trends in Catholic Theology," pp. 83–85; "Liberation Theology in the Light of Salvation History," in James V. Schall, S.J.,
Liberation Theology in Latin America (San Francisco: Ignatius Press, 1982),
pp. 131–46; and *Theo-Drama: Theological Dramatic Theory*, vol. 4, *The Action*, trans. Graham Harrison (San Francisco: Ignatius Press, 1994) [*Theodramatik*, vol. 3, *Die Handlung* (Einsiedeln: Johannes Verlag, 1980)], pp. 482–87.
Hereafter, *Theo-Drama* 4.

24. *Glory* 1, p. 149.

25. See Balthasar, *Love Alone: The Way of Revelation*, ed. Alexander Dru
(London: Burns & Oates, 1968) [*Glaubhaft ist nur Liebe* (Einsiedeln: Johannes
Verlag, 1963)], especially chap. 2, "The Anthropological Method." It is the in-

cipient hominization of dogmatics that, in my view, ties these quite sophisticated theological movements to the more naïvely sentimental work of many of modernity's spiritual writers.

26. Ibid., p. 58.

27. As Balthasar did; ibid., p. 43.

28. Henri de Lubac described the disintegration of the bonds uniting theology, biblical exegesis, and spirituality in the first chapter of his *Medieval Exegesis*, vol. 1. He does not link this disintegration to the transformation of the relations among the transcendental attributes of Being that, following Balthasar, I am about to describe.

29. I discuss the merits and limitations of Balthasar's use of the term "witness" to describe scripture's relation to revelation in chapter 4.

30. For this paragraph, see *Glory* 1, pp. 147–50.

31. *Glory* 1, p. 178.

32. See Jeffrey Ames Kay, *Theological Aesthetics: The Role of Aesthetics in the Theological Method of Hans Urs von Balthasar*, European University Papers Series 23, vol. 60 (Bern: Herbert Lang; Frankfurt am Main: Peter Lang, 1975), p. v. Cited in Oakes, *Pattern of Redemption*, p. 144 n. 16.

33. See *Glory* 1, pp. 148–50, 177.

34. See *Glory* 1, p. 150f.

35. For the discussion of Plotinus's aesthetics see, *The Glory of the Lord: A Theological Aesthetics*, vol. 4, *The Realm of Metaphysics in Antiquity*, ed. John Riches, trans. Brian McNeil, C.R.V., et al. (San Francisco: Ignatius Press, 1989) [*Herrlichkeit: Eine theologische Ästhetik*, vol. 3, pt. 1, *Im Raum der Metaphysik*, pt. 1, *Alterium* (Einsiedeln: Johannes Verlag, 1965)], pp. 280–313, especially p. 307. Hereafter, *Glory* 4. Thomas's aesthetics are discussed in the same volume, pp. 393–412. See also *Glory* 1, pp. 10, 118. Since, on Balthasar's reading, Thomas's aesthetics do not successfully break free from their philosophical framework, it can reasonably be argued that I should not give him the attention I do in what follows. Thomas's failure to present his aesthetics as "the unfolding of a theology based on the biblical revelation," prompted Balthasar to omit him from his volume on clerical theological aesthetic styles (*Glory* 2, p. 21). Still, Balthasar acknowledged that Thomas often got things just right; he put them with a force and clarity that escaped so many others. For this reason I amplify his voice in ways Balthasar might have found troubling, or at least a bit misleading, if that prominence were taken to reflect the relative theological profundity of Thomas's aesthetics when compared to those of others. The discussion of Bonaventure, for whom Balthasar voiced no such misgivings, indeed from whom Balthasar seems to have appropriated the basic ideas for his own theological aesthetics, can be found in *Glory* 2, pp. 260–362.

36. *Glory* 1, p. 20. What P. F. Strawson says about the concept of person being "primitive" provides a formal parallel to the view of the beautiful

Balthasar advocates: "We are not . . . to think of [the concept person] as a secondary kind of entity in relation to two primary kinds, *viz.*, a particular consciousness and a particular human body." Strawson, *Individuals: An Essay in Descriptive Metaphysics* (London: Methuen, 1959), p. 104 f.

37. *Glory* 1, p. 119.

38. In order to avoid misunderstanding, it is important that the reader bear in mind my argument in the introduction to the effect that although de Lubac would not likely have described this hermeneutical convention in terms of the *priority* of the literal sense, he clearly endorsed the implications that Frei and Lindbeck seek to highlight by means of that phrase.

39. *Glory* 1, p. 313 f.

40. *Glory* 2, p. 273. See also, in the same volume (pp. 47 f., 60 f.), Balthasar's discussion of Irenaeus, who obviously shared this anti-Gnostic conviction with Bonaventure.

41. *Glory* 2, p. 318. To anticipate what is to come in later chapters: Bonaventure, "advancing beyond Denys' *apophasis,* always understands the *ablatio* of this experience of ecstasy in a nuptial sense" (*Glory* 2, p. 269).

42. The attacks, that is, of the early Kierkegaard. Balthasar argued that by the time he wrote *Stages on Life's Way,* Kierkegaard's concern to harmonize the aesthetic with the ethico-religious had given way to a rigid marking off of the boundaries between the two (*Glory* 1, p. 49 f.).

43. Søren Kierkegaard, *Either/Or,* vol. 1, trans. David F. Swenson and Lillian Marvin Swenson (1944; Princeton: Princeton University Press, 1972), p. 301.

44. Balthasar, "Revelation and the Beautiful," in *Explorations in Theology,* vol. 1, p. 96.

45. *Glory* 4, p. 19.

46. For examples, see *Glory* 4, p. 20.

47. *Glory* 4, p. 374. Note the qualification, "when at his most competent." As I indicated earlier, Balthasar expressed doubts about the degree of success with which Thomas was able to translate his philosophical aesthetics into a theological idiom. See *Glory* 2, p. 21.

48. Balthasar, *The Glory of the Lord: A Theological Aesthetics,* vol. 5, *The Realm of Metaphysics in the Modern Age,* ed. John Riches, trans. Oliver Davies et al. (San Francisco: Ignatius Press, 1991) [*Herrlichkeit: Eine theologische Ästhetik,* vol. 3, pt. 1, *Im Raum der Metaphysik,* pt. 2, *Neuzeit* (Einsiedeln: Johannes Verlag, 1965)], p. 12 f. Hereafter, *Glory* 5.

49. *Glory* 5, pp. 16–21, 91.

50. *Glory* 5, pp. 29–47.

51. "Rahner hat Kant, oder wenn Sie wollen, Fichte gewählt, den transzendentalen Ansatz. Und ich habe Goethe gewählt—als Germanist. Die Gestalt, die unauflösbar einmalige, organische, sich entwickelnde Gestalt—ich denke an

Goethes 'Metamorphose der Pflanzen'—, diese Gestalt, mit der Kant auch in seiner Ästhetik nicht wirklich zu Rande kommt." From an interview entitled "Geist und Feuer," *Herder-Korrespondenz* 30 (1976): 76.

52. *Glory* 5, p. 362.

53. *Glory* 5, p. 363.

54. *Glory* 5, p. 372. The degree to which Balthasar's attitude toward the critical biblical disciplines was influenced by such convictions, or at least paralleled them, will become apparent in the next chapter. For a discussion of Goethe's reactions to Newtonian mechanism, see chap. 3 in Edward T. Oakes, *Pattern of Redemption*, especially pp. 83–88, 94–98.

55. *Glory* 1, p. 29. On Balthasar's account, in Bonaventure's writings we find "for the last time within Christian theology, the doctrine of the *world* [being] considered in very close relationship to the doctrine of the scriptural revelation. For Adam the 'book of the creatures' sufficed, that he might learn thereby 'to contemplate the light of the divine Wisdom'. . . . If the world is interpreted in light of Scripture, it once more gives its proofs of God, as it did at its origin" (*Glory* 2, p. 309f., citing Bonaventure's *Breviloquium* 2, 12 [Quaracchi edition (1882–1902), vol. V 230b] and *Hexaemeron* 10, 10–18 [Quaracchi edition (1882–1902), vol. V 378–379]). On the loss of this view among most contemporary Christians, see also *Theo-Drama: Theological Dramatic Theory*, vol. 1, *Prolegomena*, trans. Graham Harris (San Francisco: Ignatius Press, 1988) [*Theodramatik*, vol. 1, *Prolegomena* (Einsiedeln: Johannes Verlag, 1983)], p. 48f. Hereafter, *Theo-Drama* 1.

56. *Glory* 1, p. 25.

57. Søren Kierkegaard, *Either/Or*, vol. 2, trans. Walter Lowrie (1944; Princeton: Princeton University Press, 1972), p. 10. See "Revelation and the Beautiful," in *Explorations in Theology*, vol. 1, p. 103 and *Glory* 1, p. 49f. Although Balthasar was occasionally quite critical of Kierkegaard's work, especially his "incredibly false" analysis of Mozart's *Don Juan*, he evidently had a great deal of respect for the Dane. See Balthasar, "Geist und Feuer," p. 73 and *Love Alone*, p. 41f.

58. "When beauty becomes a form which is no longer understood as being identical with Being, spirit, and freedom, we have again entered an age of aestheticism, and realists will then be right in objecting to this kind of beauty" (*Glory* 1, p. 22).

59. *Glory* 1, p. 70.

60. *Glory* 1, p. 74ff.

61. *Glory* 1, p. 38.

62. *Glory* 2, p. 283. Consider, too, the following. Finite being for Bonaventure is grounded in God's will to expression "in a double way: first, in as much as the archetype in God [i.e., the divine Word] is itself an expression, and

second in so far as the individual being is the goal of a particular intention of expression on God's part, *expressissime* and *distinctissime* chosen to be as it is, and addressed by God with this intention" (*Glory* 2, p. 296).

63. Thomas Aquinas, *Summa Theologiae* (London: Blackfriars, 1964–76), Ia, 13, 2. Thomas here discussed the perfection goodness, but the point remains the same, *mutatis mutandis*.

64. The same *docta ignorantia* is evident, as Balthasar knew, in Anselm: " 'For I hold that it must be enough for the one who seeks to understand an incomprehensible matter if by reasoning he arrives at the conclusion that he knows most certainly that it is, even if he cannot penetrate by his understanding how it is.' " (*Monologion*, 64, in *Opera omnia,* ed. F. S. Schmidt, O.S.B., vol. 1 (Secovii, 1938–), p. 75, cited in *Glory* 2, p. 228.)

65. *Glory* 1, p. 38. Cf. *Theo-Drama: Theological Dramatic Theory,* vol. 3, *The Dramatis Personae: Persons in Christ,* trans. Graham Harrison (San Francisco: Ignatius Press, 1992) [*Theodramatik,* vol. 2, *Die Personen des Spiels,* pt. 2, *Die Personen in Christus* (Einsiedeln: Johannes Verlag, 1978)], p. 39 f. Hereafter, *Theo-Drama* 3. Without meaning to ignore its biblical roots, Balthasar traced this conviction back to Irenaeus, whose work "marks the birth of Christian theology," and whose notion of recapitulation led him "to note the continuity above all between reality and ideal, between nature and grace, the work of the Father (creation) and the work of the Son and Spirit (the order of salvation), between Adam and Christ, Old and New Covenant, world and Church" (*Glory* 2, pp. 31, 44; see also p. 80 f.). A similar assessment of Anselm's work appears in the same volume, p. 235.

66. *Glory* 1, p. 432.

67. *Glory* 1, p. 69.

68. *Glory* 1, p. 432.

69. *Glory* 1, p. 25.

70. *Glory* 1, p. 36; see also *The Glory of the Lord: A Theological Aesthetics,* vol. 6, *Theology: The Old Covenant,* ed. John Riches, trans. Brian McNeil, C.R.V., and Erasmo Leiva-Merikakis (San Francisco: Ignatius Press, 1991) [*Herrlichkeit: Eine theologische Ästhetik,* vol. 3, pt. 2, *Theologie,* pt. 1, *Alter Bund* (Einsiedeln: Johannes Verlag, 1967)], p. 87 ff. Hereafter, *Glory* 6.

71. Balthasar, "Revelation and the Beautiful," in *Explorations in Theology,* vol. 1, pp. 114–16. There are conspicuous parallels between the way Balthasar phrased all three of the sub-points or "threads" I have just noted and Bonaventure's formulations. This is especially true of the last, kenotic one, where Balthasar contended that we see Bonaventure's Franciscan heritage most clearly. See, for instance, *Glory* 2, pp. 292 f., 345 ff., 352 ff.

72. Balthasar held that Bultmann's errors in this regard are paradigmatic. "The idea of the beautiful is of no significance in forming the life of Christian faith, which sees in the beautiful the temptation of a false transfiguration of the

world which distracts the gaze from 'beyond'. . . . [I]t is true for the Christian faith that it is not art that discloses the depths of reality . . . but rather that this is grasped in *suffering.* . . . The beautiful . . . is therefore, as far as the Christian faith is concerned, always something that lies beyond this life." Rudolf Bultmann, *Glauben und Verstehen,* vol. 2, 2d ed. (Tübingen: Mohr, 1958), p. 137, cited in *Glory* 4, p. 27 n. 11. Perhaps above everything else that Balthasar would find objectionable in this assertion is the opposition of beauty and suffering. The aesthetic sensibility for wholeness is precisely what allows one to see and affirm life's meaning in the midst of suffering. And as I have just noted, in the suffering self-sacrifice of Jesus Christ on the cross Balthasar finds God's glory shining most brightly.

73. *Glory* 4, p. 24.

74. To the extent that this has once again become possible in our day, Balthasar believed the credit was due to the pioneering work of Henri de Lubac, whose patristic and medieval research helped discredit the two-storied view of the relations of nature and grace that has hobbled Catholic thought since the sixteenth century. See Hans Urs von Balthasar, *The Theology of Henri de Lubac: An Overview,* trans. Joseph Fessio, S.J., Michael Waldstein, and Susan Clements (San Francisco: Ignatius Press, 1991) [*Henri de Lubac: Sein organisches Lebenswerk* (Einsiedeln: Johannes Verlag, 1976); and with George Chantraine, S.J., *Le Cardinal de Lubac: L'Homme et son oeuvre* (Paris: Éditions Lethielleux, 1983)], especially pp. 63–73. Both theologians agreed that only if nature be regarded as distinct from, yet suffused with, grace will revelation not be threatened by the perennial Gnostic heresy that revelation's concrete forms are but accidentally related to God's essence. To the extent that Protestant theology, operating to be sure with different conceptualities, is able to enunciate this insight, it will have placed itself within what used to be, on Balthasar's account, the mainstream of the theological tradition. To demonstrate that one major Protestant theologian had made at least great strides in that direction was Balthasar's aim in writing his analysis of Barth's theology. See Balthasar, *The Theology of Karl Barth: Exposition and Interpretation,* trans. Edward T. Oakes, S.J. (San Francisco: Ignatius Press, 1992) [*Karl Barth: Darstellung und Deutung seiner Theologie* (Cologne: Jakob Hegner Verlag, 1951)].

75. *Glory* 1, p. 10.

76. *Glory* 1, p. 38.

77. *Glory* 1, p. 41.

78. Ibid.

79. *Glory* 1, p. 45–48. Developing a theology of the Word of God was of paramount interest to Balthasar, too. He remained critical of those theologians, however, who in seizing upon that Word, seemed to have forgotten that it was sent into the world. Thus where Luther fell short, on Balthasar's view, was in

overemphasizing the dialectic of Christ's death and resurrection at the expense of ignoring virtually all analogies between nature and grace. See *Glory* 4, p. 243.

80. *Glory* 1, p. 468.

81. *Glory* 1, p. 119.

82. *Glory* 1, p. 38. Cf. the following: "By [theological aesthetics] we mean a theology which does not primarily work with the extra-theological categories of a worldly philosophical aesthetics (above all poetry), but which develops its theory of beauty from the data of revelation itself with genuinely theological methods" (*Glory* 1, p. 117).

83. "To engage in a theological aesthetics does not mean to transpose the categories of a realm essentially foreign to theology (as, for instance, the Greek religious understanding of the world) uncritically into the sphere of Christian revelation." *Glory* 1, p. 607.

84. Balthasar, "On the Tasks of Catholic Philosophy in Our Time," *Communio: International Catholic Review* 20:1 (spring 1993): 148f.

85. *Glory* 1, p. 119; cf. p. 607.

86. *Glory* 1, p. 34.

87. Balthasar, *The Theology of Karl Barth*, p. 84.

88. Obviously, the importance of analogy for theological reflection was seen well before that. By speaking of God creating humanity in God's own image and likeness, the first account of creation in Genesis presupposes analogy. Still, in part because Aristotle more carefully worked out his theory of analogy than did Plato, it was not until Thomas's confrontation with Aristotelianism that the full impact of biblical monotheism upon the Greek notion of analogy made itself felt. On this last point, see Oakes, *Pattern of Redemption*, p. 30.

89. Przywara did not advocate, Barth's judgment to the contrary notwithstanding, a theological procedure based upon a neutral concept of Being within which could be fit both God and creation. Such a simplistic view of the analogy of Being bears no relation to Przywara's own formulation and should be dismissed, according to Balthasar, as "fraudulent." Balthasar, *The Theology of Karl Barth*, p. 382.

90. See, for example, Louis Dupré, "The Glory of the Lord," p. 389f.; cf. an earlier version of this essay, "Hans Urs von Balthasar's Theology of Aesthetic Form," *Theological Studies* 49 (1988): 303.

91. Balthasar, *The Theology of Karl Barth*, p. 382.

92. Balthasar, "On the Tasks of Catholic Philosophy," p. 149. He did not try to say in what that synthesis consisted for all time, of course, because the conceptual tools available to theology and thus the synthesis created with them vary from one age to the next. But he did believe that it remains a perennial responsibility of Christian theology to fashion anew for each generation such a synthesis between an extra-biblical metaphysics and biblical theology. See *Glory* 4, p. 25.

93. Dupré, it should be noted, would not disagree, though I think he is mistaken when asserting that Balthasar, unlike Barth, did not admit of a definitive *caesura* between philosophical and theological aesthetics. See Dupré, "The Glory of the Lord," p. 389. I take the existence of such a *caesura* to be the force of Balthasar's repeated insistence that one cannot simply appropriate philosophical categories into theological discourse without in some way transposing them into a new key. See *Glory* 1, p. 460f., where he expressed the relation between philosophical and theological aesthetics in terms of death and resurrection.

94. The phrase is Gottlieb Söhngen's, cited in Balthasar, *The Theology of Karl Barth*, p. 290.

95. Ibid., p. 269.

96. *Glory* 4, p. 35.

97. For examples, see *Glory* 1, pp. 21, 442.

98. As Michael Waldstein correctly observed. See Waldstein, "An Introduction to von Balthasar's *The Glory of the Lord*," *Communio: International Catholic Review* 14:1 (spring 1987): 25. Balthasar made this point in *Glory* 1, p. 119, where he alluded to his longer discussion of it in chap. 3 of *Theo-Logic: Theological Logical Theory*, vol. 1, *Truth of the World*, trans. Adrian J. Walker (San Francisco: Ignatius Press, 2000) [*Theologik*, vol. 1, *Wahrheit der Welt* (Einsedeln: Johannes Verlag, 1985)].

99. *Glory* 1, p. 21. Balthasar frequently developed analogies between God's glory and the beauty of the plastic, musical, dramatic, and literary arts.

100. *Glory* 1, p. 29. Cf. *Glory* 7, pp. 104, 379f., 455. See also Balthasar, "God Is His Own Exegete," *Communio: International Catholic Review* 13:4 (winter 1986): 280–87, and *Does Jesus Know Us? Do We Know Him?* trans. Graham Harrison (San Francisco: Ignatius Press, 1983) [*Kennt uns Jesus — Kennen wir ihn?* (Freiburg im Breisgau: Herder Verlag, 1980)], pp. 73–79. This (Johannine) notion of Jesus Christ as the exegesis of God will be developed in chapter 4.

101. "[T]he realm of human relationships no doubt constitutes the privileged place where we can grasp what is meant by divine revelation in Jesus Christ." Balthasar, *Truth Is Symphonic: Aspects of Christian Pluralism*, trans. Graham Harrison (San Francisco: Ignatius Press, 1972) [*Die Wahrheit ist symphonisch: Aspekte des christlichen Pluralismus* (Einsiedeln: Johannes Verlag, 1972)], p. 32. In keeping with his characteristic caution in such matters, Balthasar went on in the next paragraph to say: "Naturally, there is also a danger here. . . . "

102. Balthasar fought shy, at least on occasion, of saying Being expresses *itself* in created forms. This was out of concern that such phrasing would leave the mistaken impression that Being itself is personal, self-subsisting, and capable of self-explication. He preferred to say that something of the fullness of Being is made manifest, or is expressed, by individual existents who participate

in this fullness. See *Glory* 5, p. 620. Such reservations notwithstanding, he said the image of "expression" remains the most important one, whatever its inadequacies. See *Glory* 5, p. 623.

103. Balthasar, *Truth Is Symphonic*, p. 31.

104. Given his fight with Valentinian Gnostics, Irenaeus was an early and vigorous opponent of such dualism: "for Irenaeus the body does not bear just a trace of God and the soul the image of God, as the Platonising Fathers will later say, but the whole man, made up of body and soul, is created as the image and likeness of God" (*Glory* 2, p. 65). Doubtless this is one of the main reasons Balthasar included him in his survey of pivotal clerical exponents of sound theological aesthetics.

105. Gilbert Ryle, *The Concept of Mind* (Chicago: University of Chicago Press, 1949), p. 15 f.

106. This concise formulation is Wolfgang Treitler's. See his "True Foundations of Authentic Theology," in Schindler, ed., *Life and Work*, p. 171.

107. *Glory* 1, p. 21. As the context of this quotation makes clear, Balthasar understood that the temptation to get behind a given phenomenon to a purportedly more primal soul or spirit can be traced back at least as far as Plato.

108. Hans W. Frei, "Theological Reflections on the Accounts of Jesus' Death and Resurrection," *The Christian Scholar* 49 (1966): 283.

109. *Glory* 1, p. 26.

110. *Glory* 1, p. 20. In the following, Balthasar neatly blended the analogies to God's glory in works of art and in persons: "Great works of art appear like inexplicable miracles and spontaneous eruptions on the stage of history. Sociologists are as unable to calculate the precise day of their origin as they are to explain in retrospect why they appeared when they did. Of course, works of art are subject to certain preconditions without which they cannot come into being: such conditions may be effective stimuli but do not provide a full explanation of the work itself. Shakespeare had his predecessors, contemporaries and models; he was surrounded by the atmosphere of the theatre of his time. He could only have emerged within that context. Yet who would dare offer to prove that his emergence was inevitable?" Balthasar, "Why I Am Still a Christian," in *Two Say Why: Why I Am Still a Christian by Hans Urs von Balthasar and Why I Am Still in the Church by Joseph Ratzinger,* trans. John Griffiths (Chicago: Franciscan Herald Press, 1971) [Balthasar, "Warum ich noch ein Christ bin," in *Zwei Plädoyers, Hans Urs von Balthasar and Joseph Ratzinger* (Munich: Kösel Verlag, 1971)], p. 20. My thanks to Edward T. Oakes, S.J., for this reference.

111. Balthasar, *Truth Is Symphonic*, p. 31.

112. *Glory* 1, p. 442; cf. pp. 27 f., 445.

113. However tempting it may be to declare that beauty is an event, doing so risks falling into what Balthasar—with some justification, given Luther's preoccupation with the dialectic of law and Gospel—deemed the characteris-

tic Protestant trap: "from the standpoint of Protestantism, beauty has to be transferred wholly to the sphere of event. For from the Protestant perspective, any kind of regularity, of immanence which is seen as a perduring, inherent *qualitas,* as Being-in-repose, as *habitus,* as something that can be manipulated, is already by that very fact identified with demonic corruption" (*Glory* 1, 67).

114. For this paragraph, see *Glory* 1, pp. 117ff., 152f., 464f. Tributaries of intellectual influence are often difficult to chart, particularly in the thought of someone as well-read as Balthasar. Nevertheless, his definition of beauty's objective evidence parallels quite closely the threefold structure characterizing Bonaventure's view of beauty as *expressio et impressio.* On Balthasar's reading, these are "the basic concepts that characterise the whole of Bonaventure's aesthetics, distinguishing him from the tradition" (*Glory* 2, p. 271). For the Franciscan, the beauty of an expressive form is seen in the harmony of relations among the parts constituting a whole as together they refer "to the unity of the divine wisdom and idea" (ibid., p. 344); in the form's revelation of the light or depth of Being, which self-expressive power constitutes the resemblance of created things to God, without thereby forgetting that "it is rather he who expresses himself in them" (ibid., 346); and in its free, gratuitous, "disinterested self-giving," which impresses itself on those who see it as such and which, when redescribed in theological terms, is the "aspect of the Holy Spirit" (ibid., 348).

115. Not that Balthasar rejected outright all attempts to establish connecting lines between biblical revelation and the religious and philosophical institutions and insights of Israel-Judea's and early Christianity's ancient conversation partners. He was quite critical of the postwar Protestant biblical theology movement's overriding interest in proving the uniqueness of Israel-Judea and early Christianity because, in his judgment, it overlooked or suppressed data suggestive of their indebtedness to their neighbors, particularly the Greeks. See *Glory* 1, p. 607ff. But he was just as worried about denying the uniqueness of the ways in which both Israel-Judea and early Christianity transformed what they borrowed from their surroundings. And he was particularly concerned to point out the ways the early Church reworked the categories of Greek philosophy better to suit its own purposes. It was his conviction that the more clearly one discerned the parallels between biblical and non-biblical modes of thought and practice, the more clearly loomed the distinctiveness of God's revelation in Jesus Christ. Both of these attitudes of Balthasar's, as I have tried to show, are in keeping with his interpretation of the relationship between God's work as redeemer and as creator.

116. Balthasar argued that the form of Jesus Christ must be understood within a threefold context: the truths of his preaching, the historical events of his life that partially determine his identity, and the mediating ecclesial realities by which he sought to lead humanity to himself: "A statue can be placed anywhere; a symphony can be performed in any concert-hall; a poem of Goethe's can be understood and enjoyed without any knowledge of its biographical

context. The form of Jesus, however, cannot be detached from the place in space and time in which it stands" (*Glory* 1, p. 198).

117. See Burton L. Mack, *A Myth of Innocence: Mark and Christian Origins* (Philadelphia: Fortress Press, 1988).

118. See J. D. Crossan, *The Historical Jesus: The Life of a Mediterranean Jewish Peasant* (San Francisco: HarperSanFrancisco, 1991).

119. See Marcus J. Borg, *Jesus: A New Vision* (San Francisco: Harper & Row, 1987). To his credit, Borg eschews any one model or historical type with which to compare Jesus. In his view, Jesus is best characterized with four distinct, though related images: he was a charismatic healer or "holy person," he was a subversive sage or teacher of countercultural wisdom, he was a social prophet, and he was the initiator of a movement to revitalize Israel.

120. See E. P. Sanders, *Jesus and Judaism* (Philadelphia: Fortress Press, 1985).

121. To see Jesus Christ as Balthasar would have us do, not surprisingly, requires an ecclesially shaped faith, for only the eyes of faith are able to see him as the God-man. I will say more about such contemplative vision when discussing the subjective dimension of the analogies between revelation and beauty. And I take up the topic again in the third section of chapter 2 on the ecclesial mediation of the forms of revelation.

122. Balthasar, *Does Jesus Know Us? Do We Know Him?* p. 67.

123. Ibid., p. 68. Cf. the following: "If . . . essential portions are excluded, what is left is such a paltry construction (such as Renan's historical Jesus, or Harnack's, or even Bultmann's) that its academic provenance may be detected at a distance, and then one is still left with the problem of explaining how so slight a kernel could become such a full-powered and seamless form as is the Christ of the Gospels" (*Glory* 1, p. 486 f.).

124. *Glory* 1, p. 172.

125. *Glory* 1, p. 486. Both this and the previous quotation are congruent with (if not the fruit of reflection on) Anselm's view of the balance, proportion, and beauty of the orders of creation and redemption. As Balthasar put it, "Anselm contemplates the highest rectitude (*rectitudo*) of the divine revelation in creation and redemption; he discerns its truth from the harmony, from the faultless proportions, from the way in which it must be so (*necessitas*), something at once dependent on the utmost freedom and manifesting the utmost freedom, and this vision reveals to him absolute beauty: God's beauty in the freely fashioned form of the world" (*Glory* 2, p. 211; cf. p. 233 f.).

126. "If the aesthetic forms which come from God are in all their expressions complete and authentic, then we must accept them without question. Querulous responses only attempt to manipulate God. . . . When the principle of critical acceptance has been removed from the reader or the hearer, will the presence of the Other not appear linguistically one-sided, an oracular series of statements to be taken by the reader as gift or to be refused

only at the expense of guilt and peril to the reader's salvation? There is a certain violence about this kind of rhetoric, however subtle; it does not invite, but, rather, forces receptivity." Happel, review of *The von Balthasar Reader*, p. 356.

127. See *Glory* 1, pp. 467, 495.

128. See *Glory* 1, p. 532. I will discuss Balthasar's view of scripture and its inspiration at greater length in chapter 4.

129. "[T]hrough the inspiration of the Spirit, the writers find appropriate images and symbols in which to express the historical events in a way that can speak to men. They cannot be reduced to something 'underlying' them, nor can they be distilled into some general abstract truth. They are limbs of the living body of Scripture and can only participate in the life of the whole if they are left intact. It is the final form that is normative." *Theo-Drama: Theological Dramatic Theory*, vol. 2, *The Dramatis Personae: Man in God*, trans. Graham Harrison (San Francisco: Ignatius Press, 1990) [*Theodramatik*, vol. 2, *Die Personen des Spiels*, pt. 1, *Der Mensch in Gott* (Einsiedeln: Johannes Verlag, 1976)], p. 106. Hereafter, *Theo-Drama* 2.

130. Balthasar took a similar approach with Homer's work: "The question of what traditional religious material he made use of here is far less important than the question of what he formed out of his material, theologically and artistically" (*Glory* 4, p. 63). According to Arthur Quinn, outside of Germany, the documentary hypothesis in Homeric studies is no longer given much credence at all. See his "Rhetoric and the Integrity of the Scripture," *Communio: International Catholic Review* 13:4 (winter 1986): 329. As I seek to demonstrate in chapters 2, 3, and 4, however, in actual practice, Balthasar frequently violated his own rule about the final form setting the norm for biblical interpretation. His treatment of the Old Testament, in particular, owes much more to von Rad's *traditionsgeschlichtlich* approach than to the received text's canonical ordering.

131. *Glory* 1, p. 31.

132. See *Glory* 1, pp. 516–22, the quotation appears on p. 519.

133. *Glory* 1, p. 440; see also, p. 153.

134. *Glory* 1, p. 457.

135. *Glory* 1, p. 460. I have altered the translation slightly; cf. *Herrlichkeit*, vol. 1, p. 442.

136. Here, again, it may be useful to indicate something of the extent to which Balthasar's views reflect those of Bonaventure: "Bonaventure speaks continually of this *condescensio* of God: creation, revelation, grace, and Incarnation are all God's humble act of adapting himself to the increasingly diminishing dimensions of the creature. . . . This *humilitas Dei* is the most profound thing that God reveals of himself in his Incarnation and especially in his cross. The cross is absolutely the key to everything: *omnia in cruce manifestantur*, not only sin, not only man, but God himself" (*Glory* 2, p. 353, citing Bonaventure). "Thus it is God's going forth into the danger and the nothingness of the creation that

reveals his heart to be at its origin vulnerable; in the humility of this vulnerability lies God's condescension (*condescensio*) and thus his fundamental readiness to go to the very end of love on the cross. This entire immeasurable concealment becomes precisely the highest expression of God. . . . The stigmatisation of the father of the Franciscan Order forbids even the least doubt of the power of expression of what God said through the cross: for in it the final word about God and man has been uttered" (*Glory* 2, p. 356). See also Balthasar's discussion of Irenaeus's and Anselm's theologies of the cross in *Glory* 2, pp. 69, 236 ff., respectively. He gave his most comprehensive account of his own and others' soteriology in chap. 3 of *Theo-Drama* 4, and in *Mysterium Paschale: The Mystery of Easter*, trans. Aidan Nichols, O.P. (Grand Rapids, Mich.: Eerdmans, 1990) [*Theologie der drei Tage* (Einsiedeln: Benziger Verlag, 1983)].

137. Cf. *Glory* 1, p. 188.

138. Ibid.

139. *Glory* 1, p. 546.

140. *Glory* 1, p. 546 [*Herrlichkeit*, vol. 1, p. 525]. Cf. *Theo-Drama* 2, p. 106.

141. *Glory* 1, p. 31.

142. See, for example, *Glory* 6, p. 92 n. 15 and *Glory* 7, p. 112 n. 5.

143. *Glory* 1, p. 32.

144. *Glory* 1, p. 549.

145. *Glory* 1, p. 541. The discussion in the second section of chapter 4 amplifies these remarks and sets them in the context of Balthasar's arguments for viewing scripture as the product of the inspired theological reflection of the Church.

146. *Glory* 1, p. 609.

147. Ibid.

148. For this paragraph, see *Glory* 1, pp. 118, 152 f., 313.

149. *Glory* 1, p. 18; the translators wisely preferred "disinterest" to the more literal "indifference," which would have failed to convey the absence of selfish motives that is the main point Balthasar sought to make.

150. *Glory* 1, p. 220; cf. p. 247.

151. Balthasar, *Love Alone*, p. 44.

152. See *Glory* 1, p. 535 ff.

153. *Glory* 1, p. 178. Cf. the following: "A great work of art has a certain universal comprehensibility but discloses itself more profoundly and more truly to an individual the more attuned and practiced his powers of perception are. Not everyone picks up the unique inflection of the Greek in a chorus of Sophocles, or of the German of *Faust, Part II*, or of the French in a poem of Valéry. Subjective adaptation can add something of its own, but that objective adequacy which is able to distinguish the noble from the commonplace is more important." Balthasar, "Why I Am Still a Christian," p. 21 f.

154. *Glory* 1, p. 153.

155. Not that this seeing, even for the *beati,* involves complete understanding of God in God's aseity. As so often happened, Anselm and Bonaventure sounded the right note for Balthasar. See *Glory* 2, pp. 233, 267f.

156. Here once again we can see the influence of Bonaventure on Balthasar's theological aesthetics. "The joy of the senses, with its three levels [*pulchrum, suave, salubre*], has therefore its theological equivalent in the beholding of the truth, in the experience of intimacy, and in the receiving of the satisfying fullness (*veritas, intimitas, plenitudo*). But all this takes place no longer on the basis of a relationship *between* man and God, but through man's participation by grace in a proportion and joy within the Godhead; for man experiences thereby 'that the true *delectatio* which is the source of joy is in God alone, and that all other pleasures are for us a signpost, so that we may seek that joy'" (*Glory* 2, p. 342, quoting Bonaventure's *Itinerarium* 2, 1–9 [Quaracchi edition (1882–1902), vol. V 299b-302a]).

157. *Glory* 1, p. 153.

158. *Glory* 1, p. 139. For a fuller discussion of Balthasar's reservations about the ways in which Christians have appropriated this classical Greek concept, see his "Action and Contemplation," in *Explorations in Theology*, vol. 1, pp. 227–40.

159. See *Glory* 1, p. 311.

160. *Glory* 1, p. 610.

161. Marc Ouellet exaggerates the role played by these analogies in Balthasar's work when asserting that the experience of beauty provides an "anchoring point for an objective vision of revelation" and that the encounter with a loving Thou "facilitates a prior comprehension of the gratuitousness of divine love." Marc Ouellet, "Hans Urs von Balthasar: Witness to the Integration of Faith and Culture," *Communio: International Catholic Review* 18:1 (spring 1991): 123. It is more in keeping with Balthasar's description of both experiences as providing one "at the most . . . with a pointer, a signpost suggesting the direction in which to look for the specifically Christian" to think of them as analogous to an encounter with the forms of God's self-revelation rather than as providing anchoring points or an occasion for a prior comprehension of God's love. See Balthasar, *Love Alone*, p. 43.

162. As Balthasar asserted in ibid., p. 43ff.

163. *Glory* 1, p. 316.

164. Ibid. Once again, Balthasar found the point made convincingly by Irenaeus in his battles with the Gnostics. "[T]he Greek categories of matter and spirit must be assimilated to the Biblical paired concepts of flesh and spirit without suppressing or falsifying them. In other words, the body is not an obstacle to man's true spiritualisation" (*Glory* 2, p. 66, citing Irenaeus's *Against Heresies*).

165. *Glory* 1, p. 123f. John O'Donnell, S.J., is quite right, then, to assert that for Balthasar, "the way of negative theology is the supreme temptation for any serious philosophy of religion." O'Donnell, "The Logic of Divine Glory," in McGregor and Norris, eds., *The Beauty of Christ*, p. 167.

166. See, for instance, *Glory* 1, p. 490.

167. *Glory* 1, p. 319.

168. Just as with my earlier observation concerning the priority of the literal sense, it is important here, too, that the reader recall my argument in the introduction to the effect that although de Lubac accepted the term "typology" only grudgingly (preferring "Christian allegory"), he affirmed the centrality in pre-modern Christian exegesis of the interpretive realism regarding the literal sense that Frei and Lindbeck wish to emphasize with this term.

169. *Glory* 1, p. 44. See also *Theo-Drama* 1, p. 128, and *Theo-Drama* 3, p. 146.

170. *Glory* 1, p. 432.

171. *Glory* 1, p. 44.

CHAPTER 2. THEOLOGICAL HERMENEUTICS

1. That would not constrain God's freedom, since, on analogy with the freedom of an artist, God is free to create whatever form God chooses. See *Glory* 1, pp. 164, 488.

2. *Glory* 1, p. 203.

3. Cf. the following summary of Irenaeus's views: "If we keep to the canon of faith, 'all Scripture given to us by God will be found to be harmonious (*symphônos*). . . . ' Irenaeus is not here describing a literary work made up of different writings and chapters, but the symphony of being and history which is expressed in Scripture and has as its supreme law the recapitulation of mankind through the God-man" (*Glory* 2, p. 73).

4. See *Glory* 7, pp. 229–35. See also Balthasar, *Mysterium Paschale*, pp. 148–88.

5. Cf. 1 Pt 3.18–19, 4.6, Eph 4.8–10, and Rom 10.6–7. On the descent into hell, see Raymond E. Brown, S.S., *The Death of the Messiah: From Gethsemane to the Grave. A Commentary on the Passion Narratives in the Four Gospels*, vol. 2 (London: Geoffrey Chapman, 1994), pp. 1127–29.

6. *Glory* 1, p. 126.

7. See *Glory* 1, p. 204.

8. The terms synchronic and diachronic are used differently by different authors. I use synchronic to mean those readings that treat the Bible as self-glossing. Diachronic readings, by contrast, seek information in the texts reflecting their genesis. This differs from the approach taken by Rowan Williams. For

him, a diachronic reading will regard the text "in a more or less 'dramatic' way," while a synchronic reading will treat it "more like the surface of a picture than a performance of drama or music." See his "The Literal Sense of Scripture," *Modern Theology* 7:2 (January 1991): 121 f. As I indicated, I prefer to regard dramatic readings, too, as synchronic and to reserve the term diachronic for those readings that try to determine the factors underlying a text's creation.

9. Balthasar, *Love Alone*, p. 41 f. Cf. *Theo-Drama* 2, pp. 92 f., 98 ff., 114.

10. *Glory* 1, p. 31.

11 *Glory* 1, p. 174.

12. The term "excavative" is Robert Alter's, from his *The World of Biblical Literature* (New York: Basic Books, 1992), p. 34, quoted in Nicholas Wolterstorff, *Divine Discourse: Philosophical Reflections on the Claim that God Speaks* (Cambridge: Cambridge University Press, 1995), p. 16.

13. *Glory* 1, p. 31.

14. Friedrich Nietzsche, "On the Uses and Disadvantages of History for Life," in *Untimely Meditations,* trans. R. J. Hollingdale, ed. Daniel Breazeale (Cambridge: Cambridge University Press, 1997), p. 97.

15. Edgar Krentz, *The Historical-Critical Method* (Philadelphia: Fortress Press, 1975), p. 36, quoting Marc Bloch, *The Historian's Craft* (Manchester: Manchester University Press, 1967), p. 32.

16. *Glory* 7, p. 112 n. 5.

17. Ibid.

18. See *Glory* 1, pp. 31 f., 44, 75 ff., 198 f., 591 f. I highlight at the end of this section an example of Balthasar's exegesis in which dogmatic theology and historical criticism are of *mutual* benefit. For a related example, see Balthasar's "Exegese und Dogmatik."

19. *Glory* 1, p. 26.

20. Inasmuch as redaction criticism arose out of concern for the way form criticism fractured the biblical texts into virtually countless discreet units, it might be argued that it represents the sort of holistic approach Balthasar preferred. Setting aside the question whether he actually used redaction-critical techniques in his exegesis, it is important to realize that on his terms it is still a diachronic or genetic reading. To ask along with a redaction critic why the redactor(s) of John placed the cleansing of the Temple at the beginning rather than the end of Jesus' public ministry still entails an attempt to determine the conditions influencing the creation of the text.

21. We will examine several examples of Balthasar's uses of historical criticism in his exegesis later in this section. I treat the topic at length in the fifth chapter.

22. See the introduction, p. 1 for specific citations.

23. "Then, after a certain intimacy with the language of the Holy Scriptures has been achieved, we should begin to uncover and examine thoroughly those

passage which are obscure, selecting examples from clearer texts to explain such as are more obscure, and allowing some proofs of incontestable texts to remove the uncertainty from doubtful passages." St. Augustine, "Christian Instruction," bk. 2, chap. 9, in *The Fathers of the Church,* ed. Roy Joseph Defarrari, vol. 2, *Saint Augustine* (1947; Washington, D.C.: Catholic University of America Press, 1950), p. 72. In this century, the technique's most vigorous proponent was Karl Barth, who used it to considerable effect in his doctrine of predestination. For a discussion of Barth's exegesis, see Mary Kathleen Cunningham, *What Is Theological Exegesis? Interpretation and Use of Scripture in Barth's Doctrine of Election* (Valley Forge, Pa.: Trinity Press, 1995), especially pp. 19–67.

24. As we will see in the next chapter, Balthasar on several occasions granted that historical critics are able to identify the uniqueness of the fruits of Israel's transformation of the concepts and practices it borrowed from its near eastern neighbors.

25. *Glory* 1, p. 499.

26. Troeltsch's views are well known. For brief summaries, see Edgar Krentz, *The Historical-Critical Method,* p. 55 ff. and Peter Stuhlmacher, *Historical Criticism and Theological Interpretation of Scripture: Toward a Hermeneutics of Consent,* trans. Roy A. Harrisville (Philadelphia: Fortress Press, 1977) ["Historische Kritik und theologische Schriftauslegung," in *Schriftauslegung auf dem Wege zur biblischen Theologie* (Göttingen: Vandenhoeck & Ruprecht, 1975)], p. 44 ff.

27. Van Harvey, *The Historian and the Believer: The Morality of Historical Knowledge and Christian Belief* (New York: Macmillian, 1966).

28. See James M. Robinson, "Hermeneutic since Barth," in *The New Hermeneutic,* ed. James M. Robinson and John B. Cobb (New York: Harper & Row, 1964), especially p. 49 ff.

29. Norman Perrin, *Rediscovering the Teaching of Jesus* (1967; New York: Harper & Row, 1976), p. 11 f.

30. Ibid., p. 39.

31. Burton Mack, for example, maintains that the genuine Jesus sayings are to be distinguished from those reflecting the attempt of one social group to establish itself vis-à-vis another. As Marcus Borg points out, that leaves one with a Jesus who is oddly indifferent about his social world. See Marcus J. Borg, "Portraits of Jesus in Contemporary North American Scholarship," *Harvard Theological Review* 84:1 (1991): 5 ff. The inference I am drawing from this critique is that the criterion of dissimilarity is unduly restrictive. It may isolate some of the genuine words of Jesus, thus shedding light on his uniqueness. But it also rejects other, genuine expressions of his simply because they reflect an engagement with his social world. For additional criticisms of Perrin's work, see N. T. Wright, *Jesus and the Victory of God* (Minneapolis: Fortress Press, 1996), pp. 24, 85.

32. See, among others, *Glory* 1, pp. 548ff., 591.

33. See, among others, *Glory* 1, p. 75.

34. *Glory* 1, p. 550; cf. p. 554. See also *Theo-Drama* 1, p. 127.

35. "We can very properly use paraphrases as pointers and as short-hand references provided that we know what we are doing. But it is highly important that we know what we are doing and that we see plainly that the paraphrase is not the real core of meaning which constitutes the essence of the poem." Cleanth Brooks, *The Well Wrought Urn: Studies in the Structure of Poetry* (New York: Harcourt, Brace and Co., 1947), p. 180.

36. On the following, see Brevard S. Childs, *Exodus: A Commentary* (London: SCM, 1974), pp. 215–39.

37. See, among others, *Glory* 1, pp. 26f., 31, 174, 486, 495, 618. Cf. *Theo-Drama* 2, pp. 96f., 116; *Theo-Drama* 3, p. 63ff.; and *Theo-Drama* 4, p. 459ff.

38. See *Glory* 1, p. 548f. Cf. *Theo-Drama* 2, p. 114: "It is clear that the only really Christian interpretation of Scripture is a pneumatic one, that is, one which reads the (ancient) Scripture (*graphē*) with a view to the Incarnation of the entire divine Word and all subsequent Scripture in the light of the Incarnation."

39. Nicholas Wolterstorff, "Evidence, Entitled Belief, and the Gospels," *Faith and Philosophy* 6:4 (October 1989): 431.

40. See, for example, Balthasar, *The Moment of Christian Witness*, trans. Richard Beckley (San Francisco: Ignatius Press, 1994) [*Cordula oder der Ernstfall* (Basel: Johannes Verlag, 1966)], p. 97, where he accused historical critics of plying their trade in order *"to shelve or postpone the decision of faith*, at least until scientific and scholarly exegesis has produced some sufficiently clear results." In fairness, it should be noted that Balthasar was by no means unique in this sentiment. Edgar Krentz observes that "[m]any Christians feel, as did Søren Kierkegaard, that the study of the Bible with commentary, dictionary, and the other tools of scholarship often is a way 'of defending oneself against God's Word,' not hearing it." *The Historical-Critical Method*, p. 3, quoting Kierkegaard, *For Self-Examination and Judge for Yourselves and Three Discourses, 1851*, trans. Walter Lowrie (Princeton: Princeton University Press, 1944), p. 56.

41. *Glory* 1, p. 31; cf. p. 208, where he referred to the Old and New Testaments together constituting the "total form of revelation." Cf., as well, the following: "It is the final form that is normative" (*Theo-Drama* 2, p. 106).

42. For the former, see *Glory* 1, pp. 548, 551; for the latter, see *Glory* 7, p. 15.

43. *Glory* 1, p. 554.

44. Ibid.

45. *Glory* 1, p. 591.

46. *Glory* 6, p. 226; Balthasar's emphasis.

47. See, especially, *Glory* 6, pp. 227, 228, 229.

48. See *Glory* 6, pp. 246 ff., 291 ff., 306 ff.

49. *Glory* 6, p. 255.

50. *Glory* 7, p. 9, and *Glory* 6, p. 27.

51. *Glory* 6, p. 276 n. 20.

52. *Glory* 6, p. 289.

53. Brevard S. Childs, *Introduction to the Old Testament as Scripture* (Philadelphia: Fortress Press, 1979), p. 539.

54. *Glory* 7, p. 448 f.

55. *Glory* 7, p. 176.

56. The fifth chapter's analysis of his exegesis of Eph 5.23 ff. takes up this issue.

57. *Glory* 7, pp. 163, 167.

58. *Glory* 7, p. 166.

59. *Glory* 7, p. 115.

60. *Glory* 7, p. 165.

61. *Glory* 7, p. 166.

62. *Glory* 7, p. 171.

63. *Glory* 7, p. 172 f.

64. *Glory* 7, p. 168.

65. Ibid.

66. *Glory* 7, p. 166, echoing Mk 13.31 and parallels.

67. John Riches, who is in a much better position than I to render judgment, calls this passage "surely one of the most original discussions of eschatology" ("The Biblical Basis of Glory," in McGregor and Norris, eds. *The Beauty of Christ*, p. 64). Balthasar pursued the topic at even greater length in his *Theo-Drama.* See *Theo-Drama* 1, p. 27 f.; *Theo-Drama* 3, pp. 87–117, 122–24, 130–34; *Theo-Drama* 4, pp. 231–40; and *Theo-Drama: Theological Dramatic Theory,* vol. 5, *The Last Act,* trans. Graham Harrison (San Francisco: Ignatius Press, 1998) [*Theodramatik,* vol. 4 *Das Endspiel* (Einsiedeln: Johannes Verlag, 1983)], p. 19 f. Hereafter, *Theo-Drama* 5.

68. *Glory* 7, p. 165.

69. Notice that Balthasar was not making the anachronistic claim that the final redactor would have articulated this view of Jesus' God-manhood in terms of the hypostatic union of his divine and human natures, a relation not clarified until the mid-fifth century at the Council of Chalcedon.

70. *Glory* 1, pp. 32, 311, 495, 568 f.

71. *Glory* 1, p. 618.

72. See *Glory* 1, p. 31, and *Glory* 7, pp. 115 f., 252 f.

73. *Glory* 1, p. 531 f.

74. See, among others, *Glory* 1, pp. 523, 532, 566, 570, 604, and *Glory* 7, p. 102.

75. See *Glory* 6, p. 92 n. 15. See also *Theo-Drama* 2, p. 182.

76. At the risk of indulging in speculation, it may be that Barth's reluctance to read Gn 1.26 as referring to angels may reflect the lingering effects of the Arian controversy. Jaroslav Pelikan observes that Arians spoke of the Son of God as an angel, while maintaining, "to be sure, he was preeminent among them." See his discussion of patristic exegesis of Gn 1.26 in *The Christian Tradition: A History of the Development of Doctrine*, vol. 1, *The Emergence of the Catholic Tradition (100–600)* (Chicago: University of Chicago Press, 1971), p. 197 f.

77. For a telling critique of the way Raymond E. Brown has used this distinction, see Robert B. Robinson, *Roman Catholic Exegesis since "Divino Afflante Spiritu": Hermeneutical Implications* (Atlanta: Scholars Press, 1988), pp. 29–55.

78. Balthasar referred to "secondary" human authors in *Glory* 1, p. 532. On the Spirit's intended meaning outstripping the limited conceptual horizon of the biblical authors, see also *Theo-Drama* 2, p. 98.

79. *Glory* 1, p. 442.

80. *Glory* 1, p. 617.

81. F. D. E. Schleiermacher, *Hermeneutik und Kritik. Mit einem Anhang sprachphilosophischer Texte Schleiermachers,* ed. Manfred Frank (Frankfurt am Main: Suhrkamp, 1977). A partial translation is available in Kurt Mueller-Vollmer, ed. *The Hermeneutics Reader: Texts of the German Tradition from the Enlightenment to the Present* (New York: Continuum, 1988), p. 73 ff.

82. W. K. Wimsatt, Jr., *The Verbal Icon: Studies in the Meaning of Poetry* (Lexington: University of Kentucky Press, 1954), p. 5.

83. See Hans-Georg Gadamer, *Truth and Method,* trans. Joel Weinsheimer and Donald G. Marshall, 2d rev. ed. (New York: Continuum, 1993) [*Wahrheit und Methode,* 5th rev. ed. (Tübingen: J. C. B. Mohr, 1960)], p. 193.

84. Gadamer, *Truth and Method,* p. 192 ff. gives a fascinating account of how its meaning changed over the years.

85. Here, I follow Gadamer's analysis. See *Truth and Method,* pp. 188, 196.

86. *Glory* 1, p. 443.

87. *Glory* 1, p. 557.

88. T. S. Eliot, *The Sacred Wood: Essays on Poetry and Criticism* (1920; New York: Barnes & Noble, 1960), p. 53.

89. Ibid.

90. Art Berman, *From the New Criticism to Deconstruction: The Reception of Structuralism and Post-Structuralism* (Chicago: University of Illinois Press, 1988), 42.

91. *Glory* 1, p. 617.

92. Wolterstorff, *Divine Discourse,* pp. 197–99.

93. For an overview, see Anthony C. Thiselton, *The Two Horizons: New Testament Hermeneutics and Philosophical Description* (Grand Rapids, Mich.: Eerdmans, 1980), and idem, *New Horizons in Hermeneutics* (Grand Rapids, Mich.: Zondervan, 1992).

94. Balthasar, "Exegese und Dogmatik," p. 388.

95. *Glory* 7, p. 272 n. 13; cf. "The Word, Scripture, and Tradition," in *Explorations in Theology*, vol. 1, p. 21.

96. *Glory* 1, p. 465.

97. Balthasar, *Love Alone*, p. 50.

98. Wolterstorff, *Divine Discourse*, p. 79. I found George Lindbeck's summary of this distinction to be of considerable help in formulating what follows. It appears in "Postcritical Canonical Interpretation: Three Modes of Retrieval," in *Theological Exegesis: Essays in Honor of Brevard S. Childs*, ed. Christopher Seitz and Kathryn Greene-McCreight (Grand Rapids, Mich.: Eerdmans, 1999), pp. 26–51.

99. This is not the only thing we need to do to determine what some speaker or writer intended to say. We would also have to ask what was the noematic and designative content of the illocutionary act, a distinction of Wolterstorff's I will explain in the fifth chapter. One need not understand that distinction, however, in order to grasp Wolterstorff's point about the so-called intentional fallacy.

100. Wimsatt, *The Verbal Icon*, p. 12 ff.

101. Wolterstorff, *Divine Discourse*, pp. 204–6. That is not the only thing that, on Wolterstorff's view, distinguishes interpreting for God's intent from doing so for human authorial intent, but it is all that needs addressing, here. We will examine Wolterstorff's proposal in more detail in the fifth chapter.

102. De Lubac, *Medieval Exegesis*, vol. 1, p. 77.

103. In the entry entitled, "Inspiration," John Goldingay characterizes this belief as "an uncontroversial part of the church's formal beliefs." See Coggins and Houlden, eds., *A Dictionary of Biblical Interpretation*, p. 315. See also John Barton's entry, "Verbal Inspiration" (pp. 719–22), in which he says: "It can reasonably be said that verbal inspiration in some form has been the majority opinion about the nature of scripture throughout most of Christian history" (ibid., p. 720). Although de Lubac did not survey Reformation era exegesis, he certainly would have concurred with Goldingay and Barton that belief in biblical inspiration among Christian theologians was universal in Antiquity and the Middle Ages. See his *Medieval Exegesis*, vol. 1, p. 266. On the universality of belief in divine inspiration among the New Testament's authors, see *Theo-Drama* 2, p. 110 f.

104. Rowan A. Greer, "The Christian Bible and its Interpretation," p. 178 ff.

105. Jaroslav Pelikan, with characteristic caution, nuances this conventional view, noting that throughout the first and second centuries and even into

the third, most Christian discussions of inspiration "pertained to the Old Testament prophets rather than to the authors of the books of the New Testament" (*The Christian Tradition: A History of the Development of Doctrine,* vol. 1, p. 60). In response to the Montanist controversy, orthodox Christianity increasingly regarded the first century as a "golden age of the Spirit's activity" thereby altering the earlier interpretation of the Spirit's role. For example, the "promise that the Spirit would lead into all truth, which figured prominently in Montanist doctrine, now meant principally, if not exclusively, that the Spirit would lead the apostles into all truth as they composed the creed and the books of the New Testament" (ibid., p.108).

106. To many modern readers, this view of biblical inspiration threatens the freedom and integrity of the human authors. I examine Balthasar's treatment of this issue in chapter 4. In light of this and other considerations, some have come to reject the idea that the Bible is inspired. For those who take this view, Nicholas Wolterstorff provides a means by which to do so without thereby denying the Bible's divine authorship.

107. Gadamer, *Truth and Method,* p. 296. Cf. *Theo-Drama* 3, p. 148.

108. *Glory* 7, pp. 111 f., 453 f. Notice that Balthasar favored the account of the Jerusalem Council in Acts 15 over that in Gal 2.

109. *Glory* 7, pp. 449–53.

110. Balthasar, "Geist und Feuer," p. 78.

111. *Glory* 7, p. 540.

112. Ibid.

113. In *Theo-Drama* 2 (p. 100) he contended that the magisterium embodied "faith's sense of the whole . . . the '*regula fidei*' of the early Fathers . . . within the community of the Church as a whole." The next page reads: "The theologian strives toward this totality; the 'teaching office' pronounces on the basis of it." Nevertheless, that did not prevent him criticizing *Lumen Gentium* (*Theo-Drama* 3, p. 317 f.) and *Gaudium et Spes* (*Theo-Drama* 4, p. 480 ff.).

114. *Glory* 1, p. 214.

115. *Glory* 1, p. 215.

116. Walter M. Abbott, S.J., ed., *The Documents of Vatican II* (Washington, D.C.: The America Press, 1966), p. 117. Cf. Avery Dulles, S.J., *The Craft of Theology: From Symbol to System* (New York: Crossroad, 1992), p. 97.

117. *Glory* 7, pp. 15, 202; cf. p. 524 f. Typically, Balthasar believed the saints understood this absolute superiority and the correlative open-endedness of the Bible's meanings far more clearly than the rest of us. "[The saint] will not do what the ordinary man, so dominated by original sin, does almost unawares, yet with such desperate persistence: confine the meaning of God's word within human bounds, admitting its truth only to the extent that it corresponds to human forms of thought and ways of life, and content himself with the meaning he has managed to elicit at some time or other, as if it were the

final one" ("The Word, Scripture, and Tradition," in *Explorations in Theology*, vol. 1, p. 21). Balthasar also conveyed this idea clearly in the first volume of *Theo-Drama*: "It is not that different texts are given out for each role; the same text sounds differently at each point, it has perspective, speaks from different angels and in dramatic dimensions" (*Theo-Drama* 1, p. 23). See also ibid., p. 128; *Theo-Drama* 2, pp. 104 f., 108; and *Theo-Drama* 3, p. 148.

118. See *Glory* 7, pp. 253, 525.

119. *Glory* 7, p. 102.

120. *Glory* 1, p. 552.

121. Although I am not concerned systematically to compare Balthasar and Gadamer, those familiar with Gadamer's work will recognize important ways in which their hermeneutical formulations overlap. Certainly one such area of overlap (though not identity) is evident in their views regarding tradition. For a quite brief foray into this complicated area, see David Brown, *Continental Philosophy and Modern Theology: An Engagement* (Oxford: Basil Blackwell, 1987), pp. 19–26.

122. Kathryn E. Tanner, "Theology and the Plain Sense," in *Scriptural Authority and Narrative Interpretation*, ed. Garrett Green (Philadelphia: Fortress Press, 1987), pp. 59–78.

123. *Glory* 1, p. 77.

124. *Glory* 7, p. 106.

125. *Glory* 1, p. 513.

126. *Glory* 1, p. 555.

127. *Glory* 1, p. 554.

128. *Glory* 1, p. 554 f.

129. *Glory* 7, p. 108.

130. See, among others, *Glory* 1, p. 177.

131. *Glory* 7, p. 101.

132. Heiko Oberman, *Forerunners of the Reformation: The Shape of Late Medieval Thought Illustrated by Key Documents* (New York: Holt, Rinehart, and Winston, 1966), p. 54.

133. De Lubac, *Medieval Exegesis*, vol. 1, p. 25.

134. *Glory* 1, p. 422.

135. *Glory* 1, p. 571.

136. *Glory* 1, p. 421.

137. *Glory* 1, p. 485.

138. Ibid.

139. *Glory* 1, p. 486.

140. See Neil O'Donaghue, "Theology of Beauty," in Riches, ed., *The Analogy of Beauty*, p. 2 ff. To his credit, O'Donaghue is careful to acknowledge a more nearly synergistic strain of thought in the *Theological Aesthetics*.

141. *Glory* 1, p. 563.

142. *Glory* 1, p. 564.

143. Balthasar, "Action and Contemplation," in *Explorations in Theology,* vol. 1, p. 238f.

144. *Glory* 1, p. 564.

145. *Glory* 5, p. 106. Cyril O'Regan suggests that Balthasar's synergism may also be due to the influence of Maximus the Confessor. See his "Von Balthasar and Thick Retrieval: Post-Chalcedonian Symphonic Theology," *Gregorianum* 77:2 (1996): 243 n. 35. We should also note, while acknowledging intellectual debts, the long shadow Bonaventure casts over the whole discussion. This is due not simply to his construal of the relations between God and the creature in terms of expression and impression, as important as that certainly is. More significantly it lies in his emphasis on the mutual—indeed nuptial—impoverishing of God and the faithful. "[Bonaventure's] whole concern is with the movement of love in the nuptial kiss of the cross between the God who has become poor and the man who has become poor" (*Glory* 2, p. 357). And again: "The marriage between God and creature takes place on the cross," where the suffering of Christ calls forth from the faithful " 'grief and painful compassion' " through which they are " 'transformed into the image of the crucified' " (*Glory* 2, p. 276, with citations from Bonaventure's works).

146. *Glory* 5, p. 104f. [*Herrlichkeit,* vol. 3.2, pt. 2, p. 457f.]. Werner Löser's excellent essay, "The Ignatian *Exercises* in the Work of Hans Urs von Balthasar," in Schindler, ed., *Life and Work,* pp. 103–20, addresses itself to this issue in ways I found illuminating. He does not, however, pursue the hermeneutical implications I wish to highlight.

147. See, for example, *Glory* 1, pp. 76f., 535.

148. *Glory* 1, p. 481.

149. This openness to what with Augustine we might call secular disciplines is by no means a modern or post-modern concession to secularism. According to de Lubac, it was an essential feature of the exegesis of theologians as different from one another in temperament and theological outlook as Origen and Augustine. To quote the latter: "For just as iron causes gold to take on a brightness and clarity, so do the secular disciplines impart a shining brightness to Sacred Scripture" (*Medieval Exegesis,* vol. 1, p. 34, with citation in text).

150. Jean-Eric Bertholet would disagree with me. After describing Balthasar's hermeneutics, he said: "Il est évident qu'une telle méthode n'est pas très proche de la critique historique qui envahit l'exégèse et qui ne brille pas par sa disponibilité à la globalité de la figure qui se révèle!" ("L'Univers théologique de Hans Urs von Balthasar. Une approche de son œuvre," *Revue de théologie et de philosophie* 117 [1985]: 188). But I wonder if it is so clear, if it is so self-evident that historical criticism is as incapable of opening itself to the

totality of the form of revelation culminating in Jesus Christ as Bertholet contends. One thinks of the critical exegesis of Raymond Brown or Joseph Fitzmyer in this regard, or, on the Protestant side, Brevard Childs.

151. See *Glory* 1, p. 77, where he described the problem as the rise of a "new Judaism [sic] in which only the 'doctors of the law' could interpret God's Word reliably, while the 'simple man ('am ha-arez) would at best remain a dilettante in his understanding of the faith." Cf. "Revelation and the Beautiful," in *Explorations in Theology*, vol. 1, p. 116.

152. Charles M. Wood, *The Formation of Christian Understanding: An Essay in Theological Hermeneutics* (Philadelphia: Westminster Press, 1981). Nicholas Wolterstorff makes the same point in *Divine Discourse*, p. 188.

153. *Glory* 1, p. 78.

154. Ibid.

155. *Glory* 1, p. 44; cf. p. 79.

156. Balthasar, "Exegese und Dogmatik," p. 389.

157. I will discuss Balthasar's view of the relation between the biblical depictions of such experiences and the subsequent appropriation thereof in greater detail in the fourth chapter, on the authority of scripture.

158. *Glory* 1, p. 485.

159. See Balthasar, "Action and Contemplation," in *Explorations in Theology*, vol. 1, p. 233. This view of proper biblical interpretation likely prompted Balthasar's lamentations about the degree to which theology and spirituality have parted ways in the modern era.

160. *Glory* 7, p. 14f.

161. The distinction I made in this chapter's first section between seeing something and believing it to be true is not incompatible with Balthasar's point, here. It does seem possible, although Balthasar denied it, for a Hindu, say, to *see* what Christians claim to be true about Jesus Christ without believing it. A non-believer can appreciate the internal logic of Christian teachings and stories without accepting (by acting in accord with them) that they aptly describe God, the world, and our place in it. Rather than diminishing the importance of Balthasar's (and John's) insight, the distinction reinforces it, for in its light one can more readily argue that believers must do the truth that others simply see.

162. Cf. *Glory* 7, pp. 23f., 389ff. Once again, a formulation of Gadamer's bears at least a passing similarity to Balthasar's emphasis on praxis: "the gospel does not exist in order to be understood as a merely historical document, but to be taken in such a way that it exercises its saving effect. This implies that the text, whether law or gospel, if it is to be understood properly — i.e., according to the claim it makes — must be understood at every moment, in every concrete situation, in a new and different way. Understanding here is always application" (Gadamer, *Truth and Method*, p. 309).

163. De Lubac, *Medieval Exegesis,* vol. 1, p. 31 (quoting Adam Scotus).

164. See de Lubac, *Medieval Exegesis,* vol. 1, p. 75 ff.

165. Ibid., p. 19.

166. Ibid., p. 18.

167. Ibid., p. 23.

168. Henri de Lubac, "Typology and Allegorization," in *Theological Fragments,* p. 163 (quoting Gregory the Great).

169. Greer, "The Christian Bible and its Interpretation," p. 192.

CHAPTER 3. THE UNITY OF SCRIPTURE

1. See Lawrence Boadt, C.S.P., H. Croner, and L. Klenicki, eds., *Biblical Studies: Meeting Ground of Jews and Christians* (Mahwah, N.J.: Paulist Press, 1980); Roger Brooks and John J. Collins, eds. *Hebrew Bible or Old Testament? Studying the Bible in Judaism and Christianity* (Notre Dame, Ind.: University of Notre Dame Press, 1990); John T. Pawlikowski, O.S.M., "Christology, Anti-Semitism, and Christian-Jewish Bonding," in *Reconstructing Christian Theology,* ed. Rebecca S. Chopp and Mark Lewis Taylor (Minneapolis: Fortress Press, 1994), pp. 245–68; and Rosemary Radford Ruether, *Faith and Fratricide: The Theological Roots of Anti-Semitism* (New York: Seabury Press, 1974). These authors would contend that the greater challenge for Christian theologians is to affirm the continuing theological relevance of the Hebrew scriptures in their own right, rather than when read in the light of Easter, as Balthasar wished to affirm.

2. *Glory* 1, p. 620. The same point is made in the following: "It is essential today to insist as strongly as possible that Christianity cannot be understood without the old covenant; every attempt to interpret the form, message and subsequent impact of Christ in the world necessarily fails unless it is able to assess it all precisely in its closeness to and its distance from the old covenant" (*Glory* 6, p. 403). It should also be noted that David H. Kelsey distinguishes between the unity of the Bible, which he maintains can only be demonstrated exegetically, and the Bible's wholeness, which is a function of its being used to a single end. See Kelsey, *The Uses of Scripture in Recent Theology,* p. 106 f. Although I do not think Balthasar would have objected to Kelsey's distinction, he did not make it himself. I will take up this issue in the following chapter, when I address Balthasar's understanding of the authority of scripture. In the interim, I have chosen to adopt Balthasar's usage.

3. See, among others, *Glory* 1, pp. 621 f., 623 f., 634, 642 f.

4. *Glory* 1, p. 641; cf. pp. 549, 659.

5. In the section of *Glory* 1 entitled "*Figura:* The Old Testament" (pp. 618–28), the place where one would reasonably expect Balthasar to have

given a definitive description of the relation of the Testaments in terms of figure and reality, he employs a host of different concepts. There is no rigid allegiance to any: the discussion flows from one pairing to another and on to a third before looping back to the first, and so on. For this reason I would disagree with John Riches when he says that for Balthasar the issue of the relation between the Testaments "is posed in terms of form and fulfilment." See Riches, "The Biblical Basis of Glory," in McGregor and Norris, eds., *Beauty of Christ*, p. 62.

6. See *Glory* 1, p. 637 ff., and *Glory* 6, pp. 322, 404, 410.

7. *Glory* 1, p. 639; cf. *Glory* 6, pp. 402 ff., 409 f.

8. See, among others, *Glory* 1, p. 628, and *Glory* 6, p. 404. Here, as elsewhere, Balthasar is indebted to Gerhard von Rad's formulation of the issue in von Rad, *Old Testament Theology*, trans. D. M. G. Stalker, 2 vols. (New York: Harper, 1962–65) [*Theologie des Alten Testaments*, 2 vols. (Munich: Kaiser, 1957–60). See *Glory* 6, p. 156 n. 11 (p. 144 in the German), where von Rad gets credit for the notion that the Old Testament has no " 'midpoint' [*Mitte*] but points out beyond itself . . . to the fulfilled and eternal covenant." According to Rolf Rendtorff ("Recent German Old Testament Theologies," *Journal of Religion* 76:2 [April 1996]: 329), the question whether the Old Testament has a center or midpoint has been debated extensively since Walther Zimmerli's review of von Rad's *Old Testament Theology*, in *Vetus Testamentum* 13 (1963): 100–111. As early as 1952, von Rad noted "the mysterious phenomenon of the lack of a center in the Old Testament" ("Kritische Vorarbeiten zu einer Theologie des AT [sic]," in *Theologie und Liturgie*, ed. L. Hennig, [Kassel: J. Stauda 1952], p. 30, quoted in Gerhard Hasel, *Old Testament Theology: Basic Issues in the Current Debate* [1972; Grand Rapids, Mich.: Eerdmans, 1991], p. 145 n. 39.) For discussions and summaries of the debate, see Hasel, as well as Henning Graf Reventlow, *Problems of Old Testament Theology in the Twentieth Century*, trans. John Bowden (Philadelphia: Fortress Press, 1986), and, more briefly, John H. Hayes and Frederick Prussner, *Old Testament Theology: Its History and Development* (Atlanta: John Knox Press, 1985).

9. *Glory* 7, p. 34.

10. See *Glory* 7, pp. 34 ff., 39 f. It is important to bear in mind that Balthasar used the terms "old covenant" and "Old Testament" interchangeably. Moreover, he rarely distinguished between the various Old Testament covenants when using the term "old covenant." This leads to a regrettable (and clearly preventable) ambiguity, especially with respect to the question whether any one or perhaps all of the Old Testament covenants were superseded by the new covenant in Jesus Christ. In the following exposition, I have adopted his more general and ambiguous usage unless it is absolutely clear from the context which covenant Balthasar referred to.

11. For what follows, see *Glory* 6, p. 388 ff.

12. *Glory* 6, p. 394.

13. Ibid.; cf. p. 396.

14. *Glory* 6, p. 389.

15. *Glory* 6, p. 207 ff.

16. *Glory* 6, p. 208.

17. *Glory* 7, p. 391.

18. *Glory* 7, pp. 90 f., 391 f.

19. *Glory* 7, p. 81.

20. *Glory* 6, p. 220 f.; cf. *Glory* 7, p. 229.

21. *Glory* 6, p. 221, and *Glory* 7, p. 229.

22. *Glory* 7, p. 229.

23. *Glory* 6, p. 404.

24. *Glory* 1, p. 652 f.

25. See *Glory* 1, p. 651 f.; *Glory* 6, p. 389 f. (with biblical references); and *Glory* 7, p. 228.

26. *Glory* 7, p. 81.

27. *Glory* 7, p. 83; cf. p. 39.

28. *Glory* 6, p. 389 f.; the image is Balthasar's. This is one instance in which Balthasar's failure to clarify exactly which of the Old Testament covenants he was referring to could cause confusion. In the passage cited, he said that this "old covenant was made between the 'living God' and the people living on earth in time" (p. 390). Since he usually referred to Israel as "the people" and humanity as "man," that might seem to indicate that he meant the Mosaic or Sinaitic covenant was impossible. Two things indicate otherwise. First, after using the flowerpot image, he went on to say that the old covenant surpasses "the possibilities of man who lives in time." And, second, when discussing the impossibility of the "old covenant" in *Glory* 7, pp. 33–40, especially p. 39, he identified the "old covenant" as having been entered into by God and Adam (i.e., humanity). That would mean that, on his view, the failure of Israel to keep the Mosaic covenant had its roots in the "inner impossibility" of any mere mortal to be in covenantal fellowship with the eternal God.

29. *Glory* 7, p. 229; cf. p. 231.

30. *Glory* 1, p. 651. To cite two such exceptions: Isaiah 6 vividly describes YHWH's heavenly throne and his winged attendants. And 2 Kgs 2 portrays Elijah's ascension to heaven in a whirlwind on chariots of fire. Balthasar asserted that by themselves, however, such accounts were little more than flashes of light that set off the "dread darkness" of Sheol with even greater clarity (*Glory* 1, p. 653).

31. *Glory* 6, pp. 326 f., 339. From Balthasar's perspective, the apocalypticists tried simply to brush aside death's boundary. Although this bravado was particularly characteristic of the extra-canonical literature, Balthasar

maintained that in post-exilic theology generally "[t]here is indeed an awareness of the boundary of death, but this knowledge is suppressed." Only in the
cultic sacrifices is the boundary respected with appropriate seriousness. See
Glory 6, p. 391.

32. Balthasar's discussion of this topic is limited primarily to the seventh
and eighth chapters of 2 Esdras (= 4 Ezra), Syrian Apocalypse of Baruch, and
Jubilees. See *Glory* 6, pp. 339–43.

33. *Glory* 7, p. 81; see also p. 228.

34. *Glory* 1, p. 651.

35. *Glory* 1, p. 656.

36. *Glory* 1, p. 655 ff.

37. *Glory* 6, pp. 169 ff., 339; cf. p. 149.

38. *Glory* 1, p. 650; cf. p. 649.

39. *Glory* 1, p. 656.

40. Ibid.

41. *Glory* 6, pp. 339, 325.

42. *Glory* 7, p. 34 f.

43. On Balthasar's view, the proximate cause of their refusal to sit patiently in death's antechamber is likely the pressure brought by surrounding
cultures to come to terms with death. Accordingly, such hopes are to be understood as standing in formal parallel to Israel's earlier plea for a king in order
to gain the respect of its neighbors. Just as the monarchy would secure Israel a
place among the nations, "late Judaism [sic] . . . demands a last judgement in
order that it can survive alongside the other religious ethical systems of the
peoples" (*Glory* 6, p. 390).

44. *Glory* 7, p. 83. This conviction is what underlies Balthasar's provocative contention that the Old Testament "must represent judgment" and that, indeed, "the Old Testament understands that it itself is predominantly a judgment" (*Glory* 1, p. 649 f., where the two quotations appear in reverse order). It
is important to recognize that the rebellion of Second Temple Judaism against
the boundaries of death and judgment is not what led Balthasar to make this
claim. It is true that he thought that this rebellion was a sign of the decaying
faith of many Judeans after the exile and that it represented a terrible repudiation of Israel's calling to be obedient to YHWH, come what may. Nevertheless,
the old covenant itself is a judgment, "in the most comprehensive sense of the
word" (*Glory* 1, p. 649). The proviso, of course, is crucial. For Balthasar, judgment meant above all a training or a breaking in (*Abrichtung*) of the people of
God according to the measure of Christ (*Glory* 1, pp. 649, 655). They are to remain faithful to this God who, so far as they knew, had provided nothing for
them beyond the grave. They must endure, without flinching, the "unbearable
contradiction" of loving the God of life without hope of life eternal. Since no
one in Israel or Judah remained completely faithful, not even those chosen few

who were prophets, priests, or visionaries, all of God's people are judged (*Glory* 1, p. 649f.). Thus the "Israel of the millennia," that is, the whole people of God and not just the northern kingdom, "represents the side of God's salvific activity in which he rejects" (*Glory* 6, p. 219). Here, as elsewhere in the *Theological Aesthetics*, Balthasar acknowledged his indebtedness on this point to Karl Barth's formulation of the doctrine of election in *Church Dogmatics*, vol. 2, pt. 2, tr. G. W. Bromiley et al. (Edinburgh: T. & T. Clark, 1957) [*Kirchliche Dogmatik*, vol. 2, pt. 2 (Zürich: Evangelischer Verlag, 1942)].

45. *Glory* 6, p. 207.

46. *Glory* 6, p. 399.

47. *Glory* 7, p. 34. This recalls, quite intentionally I suspect, Anselm's argument in *Cur Deus Homo* to the effect that the most selfless acts do not compensate for the prior (or subsequent) failings of one's own or another's sins, for we all owe perfect obedience to God already: "When you pay what you owe to God, even if you have not sinned, you must not count this as part of the debt you owe for sin" (*Cur Deus Homo*, 1.20, in *Opera omnia*, ed. F. S. Schmidt, O.S.B., vol. 2 [Secovii, 1938–], p. 87, cited in *Glory* 2, p. 250).

48. *Glory* 7, p. 36.

49. *Glory* 6, p. 172.

50. For the following, see *Glory* 6, pp. 620–24.

51. *Glory* 6, p. 222.

52. See *Glory* 1, p. 209f.; "The Implications of the Word," in *Explorations in Theology*, vol. 1, p. 54f.; and "Revelation and the Beautiful," in ibid, p. 116f.

53. As I noted in the third section of chapter 1, this understanding of necessity Balthasar likely drew from, or at a minimum shared with, Anselm. See *Glory* 2, pp. 211, 233–36, 239f., 252.

54. Because of Balthasar's conceptual eclecticism with respect to describing the relationship of the Old and New Testaments, one could just as well say that for him the second proof depends on seeing the connection between old covenant types and new covenant antitypes, or old covenant figures and new covenant realities, etc.

55. For what follows, see *Glory* 6, p. 402ff., and *Glory* 1, pp. 207f., 641f.

56. *Glory* 1, p. 208, and *Glory* 6, p. 406; cf. *Glory* 1, p. 641f. To speak of just one patristic theologian from whom Balthasar learned a great deal, Irenaeus saw with crystal clarity in his battles with the Gnostics the importance for Christians of maintaining the unity of the scriptures, however true it may be that he often secured this unity by means of an unacceptable (and, as Balthasar noted, self-contradictory) de-historicizing of the Old Testament. See *Glory* 2, p. 41, 90ff.

57. *Glory* 6, p. 402.

58. It is important to be clear about the exact nature of Balthasar's concerns. Although it often sounds as though he thought the entire pre-critical apologetic enterprise, in all its variety, had been dismantled by historical criticism, the actual target of his (and its) attack is much more specific. He believed, quite rightly of course, that an apologetics dependent upon the literal foretelling of events in the New Testament by Old Testament prophets could no longer be sustained. But he never suggested that all the Church's typological applications of the Old Testament were similarly indefensible. In fact, by his own account, his reformulated argument from prophecy is a sweeping, but nonetheless straightforward, form of typology. From Balthasar's perspective the most satisfactory account of the Church's use of typology (in the sense of that term I specified in the introduction) is provided in de Lubac's *Medieval Exegesis,* vol. 1. At a minimum, it is safe to say that Balthasar's ideas about the historical importance and contemporary fruitfulness of typology closely parallel de Lubac's, if they are not actually indebted to him. For more on Balthasar's views of de Lubac's work, see his *Theology of Henri de Lubac,* p. 73ff.

59. See *Glory* 6, p. 51f. for a list.

60. Among many others, see *Glory* 6, p. 19.

61. *Glory* 6, p. 54f.

62. The movement is not, that is to say, from a sensual to a spiritual encounter, but from a relatively fragmented appearance to a more nearly integrated one. The Hegelian echoes in Balthasar's terminology are plain, as he acknowledged on *Glory* 6, p. 36. For a brief account of Hegel's understanding of 'abstract' and 'concrete', see *Hegel's Logic: Being Part One of the Encyclopaedia of the Philosophical Sciences,* tr. William Wallace (1830; Oxford: Clarendon Press, 1975), par. 160–69. For an example of how Hegel applied these terms in a theological context, see *Lectures on the Philosophy of Religion, One-volume Edition: The Lectures of 1827,* trans. and ed. Peter C. Hodgson (Berkeley: University of California Press, 1988), p. 425.

63. *Glory* 6, p. 42 (where the first Elohist citation confuses chaps. 19 and 20).

64. Balthasar held that the juxtaposition of these two traditions effected by the post-exilic Priestly writers and final redactors does little to harmonize them: "their interior incompatibility is still clearly retained" (*Glory* 6, p. 37).

65. *Glory* 6, p. 415; on the influence of Hosea, see pp. 59, 186 n. 12.

66. *Glory* 6, p. 47f. It should be noted that there appears to have been no firm consensus among biblical scholars at the time Balthasar wrote vol. 6 of the *Theological Aesthetics* about the authorship of the decalogue. See the *Jerome Biblical Commentary* (Englewood-Cliffs, N.J.: Prentice-Hall, 1968) and *The Interpreter's One Volume Commentary on the Bible* (Nashville, Tenn.: Abingdon, 1971). More recently, the *New Jerome Biblical Commentary* (Englewood-Cliffs, N.J.: Prentice-Hall, 1990), ascribes it without reserve to the Elohist tradition.

Josef Schreiner, *Theologie des Alten Testaments: Die Neue Echter Bibel, Ergän-
zungsband 1 zum Alten Testament* (Würzburg: Echter, 1995), p. 113, contends
that it is part of the Deuteronomistic tradition and was only later placed within
the book of the covenant (cited in Rolf Rendtorff, "Recent German Old Testament Theologies," p. 333). More cautiously, the *New Interpreter's Bible,* vol. 1,
p. 839, states: "[T]here is . . . serious critical question about the date and
provenance of the decalogue."

    67. *Glory* 6, p. 245.

    68. *Glory* 6, p. 188; cf. p. 48.

    69. Here, once again, Balthasar's understanding of the matter parallels
von Rad's rather closely. See *Glory* 6, p. 234, where Balthasar quoted von Rad
to this effect: " '[W]e may ask whether this entry of the word into a prophet's
bodily life is not meant to approximate to what the writer of the fourth Gospel
says about the word becoming flesh.' " (Von Rad, *Old Testament Theology,*
vol. 2, p. 92.) See also *Glory* 6, p. 210f., where, once again quoting von Rad,
Balthasar likened God's involvement with the prophets to a divine *kenosis.*

    70. *Glory* 6, p. 241.

    71. *Glory* 6, p. 231f.

    72. On the topic of the stairway of obedience, see *Glory* 6, pp. 215–98.

    73. *Glory* 6, p. 236.

    74. *Glory* 6, p. 245.

    75. *Glory* 7, p. 34.

    76. The discussion of the Psalms is itself subdivided into two parts. See
Glory 6, pp. 74–86 and 204–11. For his discussion of the book of Lamentations, see pp. 277–80; for the "speech event," pp. 375–89; for the "blood
event," pp. 388–401.

    77. His discussion of the suffering servant appears in *Glory* 6, pp. 291–98.
It forms the final subsection of his treatment of the obedience of the prophets
(among whom he included Abraham, Moses, Saul, and Job) which begins on
p. 225.

    78. *Glory* 6, p. 211.

    79. See *Glory* 6, p. 208f.

    80. *Glory* 6, p. 207.

    81. *Glory* 6, p. 205.

    82. *Glory* 7, p. 34f.

    83. *Glory* 6, pp. 296, 399.

    84. *Glory* 6, p. 294.

    85. *Glory* 6, p. 399.

    86. *Glory* 6, p. 297.

    87. A word about Balthasar's use of the term salvation history (*Heils-
geschichte*) is in order. Although he occasionally used the term, it was not, I
would argue, in quite the same sense as von Rad. Nor was it in the same sense

in which G. Ernest Wright spoke of the "history of the redemptive acts of God." Balthasar was far more comfortable than Wright could ever have been with the notion that the primal events of salvation history are unrecoverable by historical criticism (including archaeology). This was especially true of the Old Testament for Balthasar. Although he maintained that the Old Testament bears witness to an historical relationship between God and the chosen people that undergoes changes and development over time, the description of any given event can be called the result of a " 'dramatic inspiration' which elicits the actions themselves" (*Glory* 1, p. 626, quoting P. Benoît's "Les Analogies de l'inspiration," *Revue Biblique* 67 [1960]: 177). The contrast between Wright and Balthasar on this point should not be overstated. Balthasar, to my knowledge, asserted nowhere in the *Theological Aesthetics* that the Israelites, say, simply dreamed up the Exodus. Still, in fidelity to his aesthetics of form, he did not try to drive a wedge between fact and interpretation in the way Wright tended to do. For Balthasar, the biblical witness is much more an inspired interpretation than, as it sometimes appears in Wright, an objective report. In this respect, at least, Balthasar's use of the term is much more akin to von Rad's, for whom the Old Testament, though "a history book" as he famously declared, is above all else history interpreted theologically. (See von Rad, *Old Testament Theology*, vol. 2, p. 357ff.) Furthermore, Balthasar was much more interested than Wright in the Old Testament's witness to God's self-revelation in the prophets. Here, again, Balthasar's use parallels that of von Rad. For Balthasar, like von Rad and in contrast to Wright, salvation history was not confined principally to God's acts from the days of the patriarchs through David, but expressly included God's self-revelation in the prophets. (Wright's relative disinterest in the prophets may have been due, in part, to his conscious attempt to broaden the category of revelation beyond the "Word of God" to include God's acts; see the Preface to *God Who Acts: Biblical Theology as Recital*, Studies in Biblical Theology, vol. 8 [London: SCM, 1952]. He argued that this focus on divine acts is in keeping with both the Old and New Testaments [pp. 69–76].) Finally, despite their differences, both von Rad and Wright focused almost exclusively on revelation as mediated historically. Although this was a principal concern of Balthasar's, too, he showed greater appreciation for the theological value of the biblical Wisdom literature than did either Wright or von Rad. (Wright's references to the Wisdom literature are exiguous, while von Rad devoted to the Wisdom literature just forty-two pages out of a nearly nine hundred page work.) This is reflected both in the greater attention he devoted to it, and in his conviction that the historical, prophetic, and cosmic modes of the *kabod-YHWH*, though distinguishable, cannot be fully separated (*Glory* 6, p. 85). So while it is true that he called the Old Testament the testimony that history bears to the Christ-event (*Glory* 1, p. 618ff.), I would argue that this should be interpreted to mean not salvation history narrowly conceived (as von Rad was inclined to do), but the whole sweep of God's self-revelation in history and creation. For Balthasar, Jesus Christ is the fulfillment of both salvation history (narrowly construed) and creation (cf. *Glory* 1, p. 527 and *Glory* 7, p. 272 n. 13). Balthasar's concern to broaden the scope of the faithful's understanding of God's self-revelation beyond the strictly historical dimension is also evident in his greater interest in the apocalyptic literature of Second Temple Judaism. Whereas Wright and von Rad largely ignored the so-called inter-testamental period, Balthasar regarded its probings for God's glory as, though deeply problematic, forming "an indispensable foundation" for the fulfillment of salvation history in the New Testament (*Glory* 7, p. 26). In respect of his interest both in sapiential literature and in the inter-testamental period, Balthasar anticipated developments within Old Testament theology.

88. Salvation history will lurch forward again with John the Baptist (*Glory* 7, p. 42). In this connection, it might plausibly be argued that John the Baptist, rather than the suffering servant, best exemplifies the old covenant's glorification of YHWH. After all, the distinction of being the final step on the stairway of obedience before it touches the ground in Jesus Christ belongs to him, not the servant (*Glory* 7, p. 45; cf. p. 74). Yet on Balthasar's account, because the Baptist embodies the old covenant as it transcends itself in favor of the new, he has already crossed over the boundary separating them. This is evident, for instance, in the fact that "[h]e does not foretell what is to come, but 'points to it with his finger'" (*Glory* 7, p. 53, quoting Augustine). The notion of salvation history grinding to a halt around the time of the exile's end is also found in von Rad, *Old Testament Theology,* vol. 1, p. 91 f. Whether or not Balthasar got the idea from him I cannot say. It should be noted, though, that in contrast to von Rad, Balthasar did not explicitly link the cessation of salvation history to the purported legalism and casuistry of Second Temple Judaism.

89. In the compact form of the historical proof on which this paragraph is based, Balthasar did not distinguish between the inability of humans to fulfill the requirements of the covenant that resulted from sin and that resulted from finitude. See *Glory* 7, p. 34. Yet in a discussion of the failure of all of Israel's representatives fully to realize the covenantal requirements, the reason he gave for this was that all are guilty and oppressors. See *Glory* 6, p. 399; cf. also p. 408, where Balthasar said that Israel broke down not at the boundary of "the finitude of existence, but God."

90. *Glory* 7, p. 36.

91. Balthasar "The Implications of the Word," in *Explorations in Theology,* vol. 1, p. 55.

92. Balthasar discussed this paradoxical congruence in chap. 1, pt. 3 ("Word-Flesh") of *Glory* 7 and in the second part of chap. 2 ("Christ's Mission and Person") in *Theo-Drama* 3. I should also note the Anselmian (and, later, Thomistic) character of this act by which Balthasar discerned the coherence of

what at first blush seem to be irreconcilable elements. Describing Anselm, Balthasar said: "Such unifying vision—as *speculatio, meditatio,* and particularly *consideratio*—judges what belongs together, what unites in the correct way . . . what forms a unity in spite of the initial impression . . . and produces a *concors veritas*" (*Glory* 2, p. 226; see also p. 225).

93. *Glory* 7, p. 118.

94. As Ernst Käsemann argued in *Essays on New Testament Themes,* trans. W. J. Montague (London : SCM, 1964), 37 f., cited in cf. *Glory* 7, p. 118 n. 9.

95. *Glory* 7, p. 121.

96. Ibid.

97. *Glory* 7, p. 125.

98. *Glory* 7, p. 126.

99. *Glory* 7, p. 130.

100. *Glory* 7, p. 133.

101. *Glory* 7, p. 134 f.

102. *Glory* 7, p. 138.

103. *Glory* 7, pp. 145, 262.

104. Balthasar did not address the political factors leading to Jesus' crucifixion in the *Theological Aesthetics.*

105. *Glory* 1, p. 612.

106. See, among others, *Glory* 7, pp. 216, 230.

107. *Glory* 1, p. 613.

108. Ibid.

109. *Glory* 7, p. 229, citing Thomas in support.

110. *Glory* 7, p. 230.

111. "Where man has utterly failed, the history of the covenant of God becomes a history of God with himself. There was absolutely no way to foresee the manner in which this history ultimately turned out. God wills to construct for himself a stairway in the men whom he has chosen, a stairway that is to lead him down into the godless darkness. A stairway constructed of obedience" (*Glory* 6, p. 222 f.). As Balthasar made clear, this movement of God into the nether world, into hell itself, is something only God can do. This final synthesis of heaven and hell, of almighty, everlasting glory and utter humiliation and death is God's alone to achieve. See *Glory* 6, p. 290.

112. *Glory* 7, p. 228.

113. *Glory* 7, p. 233.

114. Ibid.

115. *Glory* 7, p. 232.

116. *Glory* 1, p. 616.

117. *Glory* 7, pp. 251, 255. See also *Glory* 1, p. 255.

118. *Glory* 7, p. 248.

119. See *Glory* 7, p. 262 f.

120. *Glory* 1, p. 540.

121. *Glory* 7, p. 93 f. Cf.: "[N]ot only *Christus Caput* but *Totus Christus Caput et Membra* belongs to the total objective image of God's revelation for the world and in the world" (*Glory* 1, p. 543).

122. *Glory* 7, p. 311.

123. *Glory* 1, pp. 351, 362.

124. Breandán Leahy, *The Marian Principle in the Church according to Hans Urs von Balthasar* (Frankfurt am Main: Peter Lang, 1996) provides a timely and comprehensive treatment. I return to the topic in the fifth chapter's analysis of Balthasar's exegesis of Eph 5.23 ff.

125. *Glory* 7, p. 62.

126. *Glory* 7, p. 61.

127. Hans Urs von Balthasar, "Who Is the Church?" in *Explorations in Theology*, vol. 2, *Spouse of the Word*, translated by A. V. Littledale with Alexander Dru et al. (San Francisco: Ignatius Press, 1991) [*Skizzen zur Theologie*, vol. 2, *Sponsa Verbi* (Einsiedeln: Johannes Verlag, 1961)], p. 161.

128. *Glory* 1, p. 538.

129. Ibid.

130. *Glory* 7, p. 64 f.

131. *Glory* 7, p. 218.

132. Ibid.

133. The following chapter addresses Balthasar's understanding of such experiences.

134. *Glory* 7, p. 33.

135. Ibid.; cf. pp. 87–89.

136. *Glory* 7, p. 215, following Karl Barth.

137. *Glory* 1, p. 550.

138. *Glory* 1, p. 554.

139. See *Glory* 1, p. 536 ff., and *Glory* 7, p. 111; cf. "Unity and Diversity in New Testament Theology," *Communio: International Catholic Review* 10:2 (summer 1983): 110.

140. *Glory* 1, p. 536 ff., and *Glory* 7, p. 103 f.; cf. Balthasar, "Unity and Diversity in New Testament Theology," p. 113.

141. *Glory* 1, p. 538.

142. *Glory* 1, p. 654. Balthasar was critical of patristic exegesis for failing to give sufficient consideration to this figural quality of Old Testament faith. See *Glory* 1, p. 624 f.

143. *Glory* 1, p. 624.

144. See, among others, *Glory* 6, pp. 185, 195 ff., 206 f., 225 ff., 240, 252, 255, 317 ff., 398 f., 409; and *Glory* 7, pp. 45 f., 50, 62 ff., 90, 135 f., 185 f., 399 ff.

145. *Glory* 7, p. 401.

146. Yet for Balthasar it remained at the core of all prophecy: "The necessity of such a willingness to hear [God's *dabar*] is presupposed in the whole history of prophecy" (*Glory* 6, p. 231).

147. This is to be distinguished from claiming (as he also did) that God uses their literary product to shape the lives of the faithful, a topic to be addressed in the following chapter.

148. *Glory* 7, p. 111; cf. Balthasar, "Unity and Diversity in New Testament Theology," p. 110.

149. This topic will be developed at some length in the following chapter's section on the inspiration of scripture.

150. *Glory* 1, p. 538.

151. *Glory* 1, p. 547; cf. pp. 546, 550, 554. Such texts confirm the judgment I made in n. 2, above, to the effect that Balthasar would likely have accepted David H. Kelsey's distinction between the unity of scripture and its wholeness.

152. *Glory* 1, p. 546.

153. *Glory* 1, p. 553 [*Herrlichkeit,* vol. 1, p. 531].

154. *Glory* 1, p. 657.

155. *Glory* 1, p. 29 [*Herrlickkeit,* vol. 1, p. 26]. As I noted above, in *Glory* 7, p. 272 n. 13, Balthasar indicated that the form of revelation is not exhausted by salvation history, but includes creation, as well.

156. *Glory* 1, p. 472 f.; cf. p. 528.

157. *Glory* 1, p. 645; cf. pp. 29, 658 f., and *Glory* 7, p. 382. I do not mean to imply that Balthasar is therefore best understood as a "narrative theologian." My point is merely that despite some remarks that might suggest otherwise, Balthasar construed the Bible in its entirety as telling a story about the interactions of the triune God with creation that climaxes in the person of Jesus Christ.

158. *Glory* 1, p. 497. For the following, see also pp. 498 ff., 625 f., 643, and *Glory* 6, p. 149 ff.

159. *Glory* 1, p. 498 f.

160. *Glory* 1, p. 498.

161. Ibid.

162. *Glory* 1, p. 626.

163. *Glory* 1, p. 648 ff.

164. *Glory* 1, p. 649, quoting von Rad.

165. *Glory* 1, p. 643.

166. *Glory* 1, p. 639.

167. *Glory* 6, p. 408.

168. *Glory* 6, p. 409.

169. *Glory* 1, p. 641; emphasis mine. Balthasar reiterates this conviction at *Theo-Drama* 4, p. 207.

170. James S. Preus, *From Shadow to Promise: Old Testament Interpretation from Augustine to Luther* (Cambridge: Harvard University Press, 1969), p. 174.

171. Ruether, *Faith and Fratricide*. She also argues that a vigorous *adversus Judaeos* tradition predates the Fathers and is, in fact, "the hermeneutical basis of the New Testament" (p. 117). Thomas A. Idinopulos and Roy Bowen Ward contest her thesis in "Is Christology Inherently Anti-Semitic? A Critical Review of Rosemary Ruether's *Faith and Fratricide,*" *Journal of the American Academy of Religion* 45:2 (1977): 193–214. For a summary of their and others' criticisms, and a response that is largely sympathetic to Ruether, see John G. Gager, *The Origins of Anti-Semitism: Attitudes toward Judaism in Pagan and Christian Antiquity* (New York and Oxford: Oxford University Press, 1983), p. 24 ff.

172. Jon D. Levenson, "Why Jews Are Not Interested in Biblical Theology," in *Judaic Perspectives on Ancient Israel*, ed. Jacob Neusner et al. (Philadelphia: Fortress Press, 1987), p. 287. See also idem, "The Hebrew Bible, the Old Testament, and Historical Criticism," in *The Future of Biblical Studies: The Hebrew Scriptures*, ed. Richard Elliot Friedman and H. G. M. Williamson (Atlanta: Scholars Press, 1987), pp. 19–59; and "Theological Consensus or Historicist Evasion? Jews and Christians in Biblical Studies," in *Hebrew Bible or Old Testament? Studying the Bible in Judaism and Christianity*, ed. Roger Brooks and John J. Collins, pp. 109–46. These three articles are reprinted in Jon D. Levenson, *The Hebrew Bible, the Old Testament, and Historical Criticism: Jews and Christians in Biblical Studies* (Louisville, Ky.: Westminster & John Knox Press, 1993). Mention should also be made, as Levenson does in "Theological Consensus," of the important and earlier work on this topic by James L. Kugel, "Biblical Studies and Jewish Studies," *Association for Jewish Studies Newsletter* 36 (fall 1986).

173. Walther Eichrodt, *Theology of the Old Testament*, vol. 1, trans. John Baker from the 6th German ed. (London: SCM, 1961), p. 209f. Wellhausen's three-stage reconstruction of the history of Israel's religion differs from Eichrodt's in as much as he posited a downward slide from the freedom from the law characteristic of the patriarchs, through the increasing legalization of the Deuteronomist period, to the compulsive, self-righteous legalism he thought evident in the priestly tradition. See Levenson, *The Hebrew Bible, the Old Testament, and Historical Criticism*, pp. 28–34. Both agree, however, that post-exilic Judaism represents a retrogression from an earlier, more pristine form of piety.

174. Eichrodt maintained that this was most readily apparent in the profound changes undergone by the cult after the exile. "In the struggle against the localization of the deity, against Nature mysticism, orgiastic practices and misunderstanding of the meaning of sacrifice, the significance of the cultus as a form in which belief in a spiritual and personal God could be both expressed

and lived was safeguarded, and the claim of religion to affect every aspect of the national life upheld. Not until the period of later Judaism [sic], when piety underwent a transformation of the greatest consequence which turned the religion of Yahweh into a religion of observances, was there a threat that the soteriological character of the cultic actions might be obscured by the attempt to comprehend them all in the one-sided classification of works of obedience. This development, however, was not something based on the essential nature of the cult; it was the result of its subjection to the alien standard of legalism." Eichrodt, *Theology of the Old Testament*, vol. 1, p. 177.

175. Levenson, "Why Jews Are Not Interested in Biblical Theology," p. 287. In addition to Wellhausen, Levenson also cites the work of Gerhard von Rad, who, on Levenson's telling, did not so much attack Second Temple Judaism and Rabbinic Judaism generally, as pretend that they did not exist.

176. *Glory* 1, p. 638.

177. At this juncture, one thing about this prophetic yardstick is especially noteworthy. Because Balthasar chose to organize his remarks about pre-exilic and exilic prophecy with the metaphor of a stairway of obedience descending, as it were, from heaven to earth (and finally, as we saw, to hell itself in Jesus Christ), it might seem that he assumed that its great variety can be fitted within a more or less unilinear developmental scheme. But that would be to take the metaphor literally. He made no effort to defend the idea that God's self-humiliation in the prophets and the prophets' transparency to God's will both increase as the centuries roll by. Although he maintained that divine humiliation and human obedience climax in the (mid-sixth-century) suffering servant, he gave no indication that (late-eighth-century) Hosea, say, is further up the stairway than (late-seventh-century) Jeremiah. In fact, it would appear that he thought just the opposite to be true, for he argued that Jeremiah's personal lamentations obscured God's glory in a way not characteristic of Hosea or, for that matter, (early-sixth-century) Ezekiel. See *Glory* 6, p. 262. On the failure of any straight-line developmental theory of prophecy to garner widespread support among historical critics, see Brevard S. Childs, *Biblical Theology of the Old and New Testaments: Theological Reflections on the Christian Bible* (Minneapolis: Fortress Press, 1993), p. 175f.

178. When applied to Second Temple Judaism, the very name "late Judaism" (*spätes Judentum*) is clearly problematic. See *Glory* 6, pp. 86, 331, 390 [*Herrlichkeit*, vol. 3, pt. 2, pt. 1, pp. 78, 307, 360]. To his credit, Balthasar did not use it very often, preferring simply "Judaism". It still appears, if infrequently, in the *Theo-Drama*. See, for example, *Theo-Drama* 3, pp. 118, 244, and *Theo-Drama* 5, p. 19f.

179. *Glory* 6, p. 366.

180. *Glory* 6, p. 365, and *Glory* 7, p. 25.

181. *Glory* 6, p. 368.

182. *Glory* 7, p. 185.

183. *Glory* 6, p. 389; for a critique of the (exilic) Priestly theology's cyclic conception of time and God's glory, see, among others, p. 371 f.

184. *Glory* 7, p. 36 f.

185. See, among others, *Glory* 1, p. 657; *Glory* 6, p. 404; and *Glory* 7, p. 35 f.

186. *Glory* 6, p. 301 f.

187. *Glory* 6, p. 370.

188. Ibid.

189. At least as that has been summarized by Levenson. Although I have no disagreement with his basic argument, I would want to qualify his criticism of von Rad's treatment of the post-exilic period. At a minimum it has to be said that von Rad was inconsistent. It is true that he said "Judaism only entered history when the Torah of Jahweh was understood as 'law' " (*Old Testament Theology,* vol. 1, p. 92; cf. p. 201 f.). But he also criticized the practice, much indebted to Bernhard Duhm's *Israels Propheten,* 2d ed. (Tübingen : J. C. B. Mohr, 1922), of exalting prophecy as an institution at the expense of the cult and the law. See Gerhard von Rad, *Old Testament Theology,* vol. 2, p. 5.

190. Levenson cites the work of John Bright as an exception to the rule and contends that such exceptions are "much more likely to be found in the Anglo-American world than in the Germanic world whence the seminal works in Old Testament theology have emanated" ("Why Jews Are Not Interested in Biblical Theology," p. 288).

191. *Glory* 6, p. 382.

192. *Glory* 6, p. 382 f. It should be noted that Balthasar was here describing what he took to be the ideas of Psalm 119. He did not argue for its post-exilic authorship, however. Indeed, he seems to have assumed an earlier date, because in the passage from which this is taken, he likened its perspective on the Law to that of the post-exilic Judeans. This dating would accord with the position Mitchell Dahood, S.J., advances in the Anchor Bible edition of the Psalms: "Numerous poetic usages that were rarely employed in the post-Exilic period have been uncovered in the poem. These strongly favor a pre-Exilic date of composition. The period of the Deuteronomic reform (late seventh century B.C.E.) provides a likely background for the spirit and legal language that pervades throughout." *Psalms III: 101–150. The Anchor Bible,* vol. 17 (Garden City, N.J.: Doubleday & Company, 1970), p. 173.

193. *Glory* 6, p. 385.

194. Ibid.

195. *Glory* 6, p. 385 n. 10.

196. *Glory* 6, p. 383. This is one instance where Balthasar's ambiguous use of the term "covenant" is especially vexing; it is impossible to tell which covenant was the "original" one. The discussion at *Glory* 7, p. 37 ff. suggests

that Balthasar could have meant either the Adamic or the Abrahamic covenant. In any event, the important point is that the Mosaic covenant, on Balthasar's reading, is situated in a larger covenantal context. It is therefore no more provisional than any of the other Old Testament covenants, which, when taken as a whole, are all transcended and fulfilled in the new and eternal covenant in Jesus Christ.

197. *Glory* 6, p. 370.

198. *Glory* 6, p. 388.

199. *Glory* 6, p. 388f.

200. *Glory* 6, p. 392.

201. *Glory* 6, p. 391.

202. *Glory* 6, p. 398.

203. Ibid. This is not, of course, the only positive function Balthasar thought they can serve for Christians. He held that, together with the Old Testament fraternizing meals, the blood sacrifices foreshadow the Church's eucharistic celebration of Christ's sacrifice on the cross and the reconciliation it effected. See *Glory* 6, p. 400. I would suggest that this positive function of the sacrifices also makes their foreshadowing more positive than it was in much of the pre-modern tradition. Balthasar also insisted that the sacrifices were the sole feature of post-exilic thought and practice that gave the absolute boundary of death its due respect. See *Glory* 6, p. 391. As such, they offer particularly moving examples of the obedience of the Jews, examples that Christians feeling abandoned by God may find instructive.

204. *Glory* 1, p. 637.

205. *Glory* 6, p. 303; cf. *Glory* 1, p. 638. In light of this, it would seem that Balthasar was, at least on occasion, aware of the unsavory irony in completely disparaging the theological vision of the very group who provided the Church (and the Synagogue) with the final redaction of the Hebrew scriptures. Curiously, though, he praised "the conscience of Israel" (rather than "Judaism") for its decision to exclude from the canon much of the apocalyptic literature he found so wanting. See *Glory* 6, p. 369.

206. *Glory* 1, p. 656.

207. *Glory* 7, p. 204.

208. *Glory* 6, p. 403.

209. See *Glory* 7, p. 204.

210. *Glory* 1, p. 620. Cf.: "[T]he old covenant is 'in the logic of revelation' the indispensable access to understanding the mystery of Christ" (*Glory* 6, p. 412).

211. *Glory* 1, p. 625. Cf.: "As the one who fulfils God's story with man, Jesus is not dependent on that story: history points to Jesus, not Jesus to history" (p. 619).

212. *Glory* 1, p. 620. Cf.: "The testimony of history—that is, of the Old Testament—is not necessary to Jesus; he does not need, it, rather, he uses it only for men's sakes" (p. 618f.).

213. See, among others, *Glory* 1, pp. 337, 623, and *Glory* 6, pp. 208, 409.

214. On the Protestant side, see the work of Brevard S. Childs and, on the Catholic side, see that of Roland E. Murphy, O.Carm.

CHAPTER 4: THE AUTHORITY OF SCRIPTURE

1. Hans Urs von Balthasar, "The Word, Scripture and Tradition," in *Explorations in Theology*, vol. 1, p. 11f. I have modified the translation, cf. "Wort, Schrift, Tradition," *Skizzen zur Theologie*, vol 1, p. 11f.

2. The relevant passages in the *Theological Aesthetics* are too numerous to cite, though the more important ones will be examined in what follows. Although the doctrine of scripture in Balthasar's *Theo-Drama* falls outside the scope of this discussion, the concept of attestation or bearing witness figured significantly there, too. See *Theo-Drama* 2, pp. 106–13. I am reluctant to claim, given the absence of a specific acknowledgment by Balthasar, that he was indebted to Barth for conceiving of the Bible as a witness to God's self-revelation, but there are considerable affinities between their views in this regard.

3. Fitzmyer, *Scripture, the Soul of Theology*, p. 91 n. 70; cf. pp. 59 n. 8, 92 n. 72.

4. Balthasar, "The Place of Theology," in *Explorations in Theology*, vol. 1, p. 149. That this "body" refers, not simply to the words of Jesus of Nazareth, but to the scriptural witness his Spirit fashioned for him in the Church is apparent from the fact that Balthasar concluded the paragraph from which this quotation is taken with a call to resolve all problems of biblical interpretation christologically. Such an approach to exegesis would only make sense within the context of a view of scripture as a mode of the incarnate Son.

5. Ibid., p. 152f.

6. *Glory* 1, p. 29.

7. *Glory* 1, p. 591.

8. *Glory* 7, p. 272. See below p. 200 on the difficulties associated with identifying divine self-disclosure or self-revelation and divine speech.

9. Balthasar, "The Word, Scripture, and Tradition," in *Explorations in Theology*, vol. 1, p. 15.

10. Ibid., p. 15; cf. p. 16f.

11. *Glory* 1, p. 530 [*Herrlichkeit*, vol. 1, p. 509].

12. Balthasar, "The Word, Scripture, and Tradition," in *Explorations in Theology*, vol. 1, pp. 15, 17.

13. Balthasar, "The Implications of the Word," in ibid., p. 49. Cf. *Glory* 1, p. 529. Not that Origen was completely blind to the differences between the scriptural and physical bodies of Christ. According to Balthasar, he saw that the latter bore the sins of the world while the former was a "testimony concerning a paschal faith in the Risen One" (*Glory* 1, p. 541).

14. Cf. *Theo-Drama* 2, p. 112.

15. *Glory* 1, p. 528.

16. The dialectical pattern to his argumentation would help to account for Balthasar's otherwise inexplicably glowing assessment of Origen's "scriptural mysticism" in the introduction to his Origen anthology. See Balthasar, ed., *Origen: Spirit and Fire*, p. 10 f.

17. Cf. *Glory* 7, p. 267.

18. *Glory* 7, p. 90.

19. Among many others, see *Glory* 7, pp. 13, 86; cf. *Glory* 1, p. 449. For additional remarks about God's ineffability and how an appropriate Christian reticence is to be distinguished from the Gnostic Σιγή, see *Glory* 7, p. 157.

20. "We must . . . make good our *excessus* to God himself with a *theologia negativa* which never detaches itself from its basis in a *theologia positiva*" (*Glory* 1, p. 124).

21. *Glory* 7, p. 86.

22. *Glory* 7, p. 272; cf. p. 491.

23. *Glory* 1, p. 528.

24. *Glory* 7, p. 268.

25. *Glory* 1, p. 532.

26. Balthasar, "The Word, Scripture and Tradition," in *Explorations in Theology*, vol. 1, p. 19. Cf. *Theo-Drama* 2, p. 12.

27. *Glory* 7, p. 459.

28. *Glory* 1, p. 420.

29. The image is Balthasar's, though of course it is not unique to him. See ibid.

30. See, among others, *Glory* 6, p. 34 f. Although God remains free to conceal and reveal Godself in such forms, at God's pleasure creation can become "a monstrance of God's real presence" (*Glory* 1, p. 420).

31. For the preceding, see *Glory* 7, pp. 152, 245, 249, 255, 262.

32. *Glory* 7, p. 249.

33. *Glory* 7, p. 255.

34. *Glory* 7, pp. 251, 255. See also *Glory* 1, p. 255.

35. *Glory* 7, pp. 255 f., 267, 389 ff., among others. The fruitfulness of the triune love transcends the boundaries of the Church, of course, though Balthasar insisted that God's love for the world (and, indeed, the cosmos) is mediated by the Church. "The Spirit . . . gives the interpretation of Christ (and, in him,

the Father) through the Church to 'the world'" (*Glory* 7, p. 253). See also his discussion of the high priestly prayer of Jn 17. 20–24 in *Glory* 7, p. 259.

36. Cf. *Glory* 7, p. 252 f.

37. *Glory* 1, p. 318.

38. Although I trust the foregoing is sufficient for my purposes, I do not want to imply that I have fully discussed Balthasar's christological and trinitarian warrants for scripture being a medium of God's ineffable presence. In particular, the trinitarian dimension of his argument has been given short shrift. Not only does it bear on Christ's glorification, the very fact that God is expressible at all (in any form whatsoever) rests on the trinitarian mystery of the Son and Spirit's processions from the Father.

39. *Glory* 1, p. 31. Cf. Balthasar's description of the creation of the sapiential writings of the Old Testament "where the revelation is transmitted directly to the pen of the inspired writer" ("The Word, Scripture, and Tradition," in *Explorations in Theology*, vol. 1, p. 12).

40. *Glory* 1, p. 540.

41. *Glory* 1, p. 533.

42. *Glory* 7, p. 103. Cf. *Glory* 7, p. 110; *Glory* 1, p. 44; "God Speaks as Man," in *Explorations in Theology*, vol. 1, p. 78; and "Revelation and the Beautiful," in ibid, p. 114 f. Here one will recall from the discussion in chapter 1 that, on Balthasar's view, this theological contemplation of the form of revelation "exactly corresponds to the aesthetic contemplation that steadily and patiently beholds those forms which either nature or art offers to its view" (*Glory* 1, p. 32).

43. *Glory* 1, p. 537; cf. p. 543.

44. *Glory* 1, p. 536 f., where the two parts of this quotation appear in reverse order.

45. *Glory* 7, p. 115.

46. *Glory* 1, p. 538.

47. Langdon B. Gilkey, "Cosmology, Ontology, and the Travail of Biblical Language," *The Journal of Religion*, 41 (1961): 194–205, especially p. 201.

48. *Glory* 7, p. 115.

49. *Glory* 7, p. 254.

50. *Glory* 1, p. 30.

51. *Glory* 1, p. 539. Cf., among others, "From the Theology of God to Theology in the Church," *Communio: International Catholic Review* 9:3 (fall 1982): 198; "God Is His Own Exegete," p. 284; and *Theo-Drama* 2, pp. 92 f., 104 f.

52. Balthasar gave an account of how he believed the evangelists reinterpreted the term 'Messiah' in *Glory* 7, p. 218 ff. See also p. 323, where he attributed at least some of this reinterpretation to Jesus himself.

53. *Glory* 7, p. 252. To be more specific, it involves the Spirit's "'leading' (ὁδηγεῖν) the [disciples'] speech and proclamation ([Jn] 16.13; 14.25), [and of the Spirit's] 'instruction' (14.26), 'bearing witness' (15.26), and, in a deep sense, [the Spirit's aiding] the 'remembering' (14.26)—remembering the words and deeds of Jesus that the disciples experienced, but which only [after the resurrection] are disclosed to them in their inner depth" (*Glory* 7, p. 252).

54. *Glory* 1, pp. 247–49, especially p. 249; cf. p. 538 f., and *Glory* 7, p. 88. In the latter, Balthasar acknowledged a certain development in the early Church's understanding of Jesus' identity as Messiah and Son of God, but insisted the first intuition to link Messiah and Son of God with Jesus was no discovery, but a gift of grace.

55. See *Glory* 7, p. 156 f.

56. For Balthasar's discussion of this, see *Glory* 7, pp. 329–41.

57. Cf. the following from *Theo-Drama* 2, p. 105: "The final redaction of Scripture does not need to coincide absolutely, in a *material* sense, with the actual spoken words of Jesus, with the actual shape of his deeds and movements."

58. *Glory* 7, p. 330. Such "depaschalization [*Entösterlichung*]" is "theologically required," not in order to strip the glorified Christ of obscuring faith accretions, but to indicate the ways in which the sovereignty of the Father is revealed in hiddenness, not only in Jesus Christ crucified, but also in his birth, youth, and public ministry (cf. *Glory* 7, p. 156 f.). An analogous literary embellishment of historical revelation took place, Balthasar argued, in the formation of the Old Testament. He cited, in particular, the accounts of the Exodus and the Joshua cycle. "[W]ithout any doubt," God's salvific acts in both were more hidden than the biblical portrayals might lead one to suppose. That does not imply, however, that these events are sheer fantasy. The Spirit, whose task, as we have seen, is to bridge the gap between the ineffable glory of God and its human expression, proleptically bathed them in the light of Easter, just as the Spirit did the life of Jesus. See also *Theo-Drama* 5, p. 21 n.2.

59. *Glory* 7, p. 330; cf. p. 331 n. 22.

60. See *Glory* 7, p. 322 ff., where Balthasar developed this point in relation to Jesus' essential hiddenness. See also *Theo-Drama* 3, pp. 124–43, for a discussion of the early Church's "transposition" of discipleship, time, and Jesus' self-consciousness in light of Easter.

61. The three are as follows: the ministry of Jesus; the preaching of the Apostles; and the writing of the Gospels. These stages were enunciated by the Pontifical Biblical Commission in a document approved by Pope Paul VI and published in 1964. For an extended commentary, see Joseph A. Fitzmyer, S.J., "The Biblical Commission's Instruction on the Historical Truth of the Gospels," *Theological Studies* 25 (1964): 386–408. Fitzmyer returned, briefly, to the topic of the three stages in his "Historical Criticism: Its Role in Biblical Interpretation and Church Life," *Theological Studies* 50 (1989): 252. See also Raymond E.

Brown, S. S., *Biblical Reflections on Crises Facing the Church* (New York: Paulist Press, 1975), pp. 111–15, and *Biblical Exegesis and Church Doctrine* (Mahwah, N.J.: Paulist Press, 1985), pp. 12–14.

62. *Glory* 7, p. 329; cf. *Glory* 1, p. 540, and *Theo-Drama* 3, p. 147. It is worth noting, at least in passing, how closely Balthasar's formulation of this issue agrees with the Pontifical Biblical Commission's statement entitled, "Bible and Christology," which was published in 1984. The writings of the New Testament, it said, "stem from disciples who were witnesses of his words and deeds (Acts 1:1) and have handed them to us under the inspiration of the Holy Spirit (2 Tm. 3:16; cf. Jn 16:13). The activity of the Spirit not only saw to it that this handing on would be done with the utmost fidelity; rather, with the passage of time and through the Spirit-inspired reflection of the sacred writers, it brought about *an ever richer and ever more developed* expression of the tradition of Jesus' words and deeds. This explains the variety and the diversity in style, ideas and vocabulary detected, for instance, between the Synoptic Gospels and the Fourth Gospel. Since, however, this recalling and understanding of Jesus's words and deeds have reached maturity in the primitive apostolic community, under the guidance of God's Spirit, Christians rightly accept with firm faith these differing representations of Jesus and his message, according to their various levels of development as the authentic word of God guaranteed by the Church's authority (2.2.1.1)." The quotation comes from Roch A. Kereszty, "The 'Bible and Christology' Document of the Biblical Commission," *Communio: International Catholic Review* 13:4 (winter 1986): 359f.

63. *Glory* 7, p. 338; cf. p. 110ff.

64. *Glory* 7, p. 338.

65. *Glory* 1, p. 32; cf. p. 541, and *Theo-Drama* 3, p. 146f.

66. Balthasar, "The Word, Scripture and Tradition," in *Explorations in Theology*, vol. 1, p. 21

67. *Glory* 1, p. 542.

68. *Glory* 1, p. 537. Cf. Balthasar, "From the Theology of God to Theology in the Church," p. 196f., and *Theo-Drama* 2, p. 103f.

69. *Glory* 6, p. 380f.

70. *Glory* 6, p. 381.

71. *Glory* 6, p. 385f. Balthasar's considerable indebtedness to this aspect of Gerhard von Rad's *Traditionsgeschichte* is especially evident in this section. For a critical appraisal of the traditio-historical approach to biblical interpretation, see Joseph W. Groves, *Actualization and Interpretation in the Old Testament*, SBL Dissertation Series, vol. 86 (Atlanta: Scholars Press, 1987), especially chap. 3, pp. 103–64. Leo G. Perdue, *The Collapse of History*, pp. 45–68, provides a more appreciative, though not uncritical, treatment.

72. As we saw in the last chapter, the reworking of earlier material serves as one means by which the New Testament authors and redactors linked their

work with the Old Testament, helping to create over time what Balthasar maintained is a unified witness.

73. *Glory* 1, p. 453 f.

74. *Glory* 7, p. 244 n. 12. The description is actually borrowed from R. Schnackenburg who, no doubt to Balthasar's great satisfaction, called the Johannine writings "the most mature witness to Christ in the Early Church" (ibid., citation in text).

75. Like all theologians, Balthasar favored certain biblical texts over others. He operated with what David H. Kelsey called a "working canon." This is to be distinguished from Ernst Käsemann's "canon within the canon" because it does not place a doctrine (e.g., in Käsemann's case, justification by faith) at the center of the Christian gospel. But like Käsemann, Balthasar's selection of texts depends on a logically prior construal of what an earlier generation would have called "the essence of Christianity." We will return to this issue in the next section. See Kelsey, *The Uses of Scripture in Recent Theology*, p. 104.

76. "[I]t is not only difficult but impossible to consider and grasp the shaping form [of Christ] purely in itself, before its act of shaping. We see what this form *is* from what it *does*" (*Glory* 1, p. 527).

77. See Wolterstorff, *Divine Discourse*, pp. 63–74.

78. Ibid., p. 283.

79. Ibid., p. 284.

80. Ibid., pp. 51–54.

81. Ibid., p. 54. This should satisfy Edward T. Oakes, S.J., who voiced concern about trying to unify the scriptures on the basis of the texts themselves, something he accuses Brevard Childs of doing: "Unless one can incorporate a sense of God's action within the process of canon formation, and thus within the formation of the institutional and hierarchical Church that was instrumental in recognizing that canon, appeals to that canon to unify the diversity of Scripture will prove unavailing" ("The Usurped Town: The Canon of Scripture in Postmodern Aesthetics," *Communio* 17 [summer 1990]: 280).

82. Wolterstorff, *Divine Discourse*, p. 73 f.

83. *Glory* 7, p. 152 [*Herrlichkeit*, vol. 3, pt. 2, pt. 2, p. 140].

84. Appeals to analogy, of course, can raise more problems than they solve. In this case, Balthasar's understanding of the Bible as analogous to the incarnate Word because it, too, bears a divine content in human forms, risks turning the Chalcedonian definition of a unique, historical person into a generalizable hermeneutical principle. He would likely respond that to do that would be to fail to appreciate the uniqueness of the biblical Word and the unique hermeneutics it requires.

85. There are other difficulties with speaking of the Bible exclusively as witness that I have not discussed. One, highlighted by John Goldingay, is that because the witness points toward God, God's grace, and God's activities, the

longing for God of the faithful, the obligations they are to bear, and the role they play in consummating God's plan for salvation tend to get relatively less attention. See his *Models for Interpretation of Scripture* (Grand Rapids, Mich.: Eerdmans, 1995), p. 56. Because of Balthasar's convictions that faith's object is the graced participation of humanity in the divine life, he did not allow the category 'witness' absolutely to control his view of scripture. This freed him to devote more attention to the human dimensions of the Bible than might otherwise have been likely.

86. Kelsey, *The Uses of Scripture in Recent Theology,* pp. 160–70.

87. Kelsey refers to the second mode of God's presence, not as agential, but as a "concrete actuality" (ibid., p. 162). This formulation has the important advantage of allowing him to account for those who view God as present, say, in a cosmic process of re-creation that, while not agential, is not ideational or ideal, either. For our purposes, however, the narrower definition is adequate.

88. See, among others, *Glory* 1, pp. 305, 307, 331, 351 ff., 417.

89. *Glory* 1, p. 307. The context of this quotation makes it clear that this principle is not limited to the New Testament situation, as the elided phrase ("within the human and historical situation of Jesus Christ") might otherwise suggest.

90. Indeed, on occasion Balthasar spoke of archetypal *experiences* of God. See *Glory* 1, pp. 336, 418, 421.

91. Regrettably, Balthasar did not attend to the rich diversity of Old Testament archetypal experiences of God with the same thoroughness that he brought to his analysis of archetypal God-experiences in the New Testament.

92. *Glory* 1, p. 322. I have changed the punctuation of the translation in order better to reflect the meaning of the German. Cf. *Herrlichkeit,* vol. 1, p. 310.

93. Cf. the following: "The christological form as such is, absolutely, the form of the encounter between God and man. This encounter bears the form of the Incarnation, already in the Old Testament and still in the Resurrection" (*Glory* 1, p. 303f.). Or this: "[T]hese great [Old Testament] archetypal experiences of God, which in their structure are an anticipated Christology, are not, for all their proleptic character, to be classified as merely a lower stage which leads on up to Christian experience" (*Glory* 1, p. 336).

94. "[Christ's] archetype is both things at once: the inimitable and what must be imitated" (*Glory* 1, p. 304; see also *Glory* 1, pp. 322, 325 f., 327).

95. *Glory* 1, p. 350.

96. See, among others, *Glory* 1, pp. 257–64, 301–65, 417–25.

97. Balthasar's criticism of psychological explanations of archetypal experiences of God (and the experiences of faith, generally) as reductive are due to his absolute insistence on divine prevenience. See, for example, *Glory* 6, p. 381 n. 6, and *Glory* 1, p. 257f.

98. *Glory* 1, p. 311.

99. *Glory* 1, pp. 311, 313.

100. For an admirably concise list of the more common subjective states through which God discloses Godself in the Bible, see *Glory* 1, p. 312.

101. *Glory* 1, p. 418.

102. *Glory* 1, p. 257.

103. In concert with both Augustine and Thomas, Balthasar expressed this conviction in terms of the priority of God's vision. God first beholds those who later come to behold God. As Thomas put it, the assent of faith derives not "*ex visione credentis, sed a visione aegis cui creditor*" (*Summa Theologia*, Ia, 12, 13.3, quoted in *Glory* 1, p. 309). In effect, then, the archetypal experience of God is like "an echo of the antecedent and foundational event of being seen by God" (*Glory* 1, p. 329; cf. *Glory* 6, pp. 68, 72 f.). Balthasar maintained that God retains the initiative, not only in the archetypal experiences of God enjoyed by the patriarchs, prophets, seers, and apostles, but also in the archetypal experience of God given to the incarnate Son. During his ministry, Jesus Christ knew God the Father as one who had already been seen by the Father, as one who had already been sent on a divine mission. See *Glory* 1, p. 327. Balthasar argued that Jesus, as distinct from the prophets and John the Baptist, is not just sent by the Father, but also comes from and returns to him. See *Glory* 1, p. 322.

104. To be sure, on different occasions different sense-experiences will predominate, while others are left out of account. See *Glory* 1, p. 332 f.

105. *Glory* 1, 332.

106. *Glory* 1, p. 314 f.

107. *Glory* 1, p. 316.

108. *Glory* 1, p. 260.

109. *Glory* 1, p. 317.

110. "Christ, 'God with us', the Incarnate Word, is the fulfilment of the unimaginable. God himself is seen, heard and touched by men; he associates with them in a human way, dies for them, and gives himself to them as their food and drink. All this is a fulfilled eschatology, and yet again it is not" (*Glory* 1, p. 318; cf. p. 336).

111. *Glory* 1, p. 318.

112. *Glory* 1, p. 254. Cf. "The Word, Scripture and Tradition," in *Explorations in Theology*, vol. 1, p. 20 f.; *Theo-Drama* 1, p. 645 f.; and *Theo-Drama* 3, p. 149 ff.

113. *Glory* 1, p. 306, among others.

114. *Glory* 1, p. 306.

115. *Glory* 1, p. 323.

116. *Glory* 1, p. 263 f.

117. *Glory* 1, p. 304.

118. *Glory* 1, p. 324.

119. *Glory* 1, p. 330 f., where Balthasar quotes Marcus Barth.

120. By this I mean that for Balthasar (as well as for von Rad, on whom he depended heavily in this regard), not only did the prophets encounter God as an other, but they experienced what God experiences. See, for example, *Glory* 1, p. 657f., where Balthasar said that in Hosea's marriage to a prostitute he experienced in his own way what God experienced in relation to faithless Israel. In the same passage Balthasar made similar remarks about Isaiah's and Jeremiah's experiences of God. See also *Glory* 6, p. 234, where Balthasar acknowledged his indebtedness to von Rad on this point.

121. On the question of God experiencing humanity in the prophets, see *Glory* 6, p. 235. Since the prophet "becomes the one who exposes the word of God to the people, God exposes him to the opposition and hate of the sinners. The unheard-of element in this process is that God himself exposes himself to sin in the suffering and dying of those who are obedient to him." On the topic of the stairway of obedience, see *Glory* 6, pp. 215–98 and the second section of chapter 3 of this book.

122. *Glory* 1, p. 468; cf. pp. 264, 305.

123. *Glory* 1, p. 305.

124. *Glory* 1, p. 330.

125. *Glory* 1, p. 421.

126. See *Glory* 1, pp. 331–65.

127. *Glory* 1, p. 351.

128. *Glory* 1, p. 304; cf. p. 330.

129. *Glory* 1, p. 350.

130. Ibid.

131. *Glory* 6, p. 142f.

132. When the shepherd is slain, "the sheep are shown for what they are, as slaying wolves" (*Glory* 1, p. 346).

133. Ibid.

134. *Glory* 1, p. 408.

135. See Balthasar, "Zeugnis und Glaubwürdigkeit," *Internationale Katholische Zeitschrift* 17 (1988): 108ff.

136. *Glory* 1, p. 348f.

137. *Glory* 1, p. 347.

138. For the apostles, see *Glory* 1, p. 343f.; for Mary, p. 340f. Since Balthasar did not claim that there is anything definitive about his characterization of the four types of archetypal God-experience, there seems no reason to suppose that he would have resisted other descriptions emphasizing different aspects of each.

139. *Glory* 1, p. 349.

140. *Glory* 1, p. 351.

141. *Glory* 1, p. 309.

142. Kelsey, *The Uses of Scripture in Recent Theology*, pp. 101–4.

143. So far as I am aware, Robert Clyde Johnson was the first person to apply the technical term *discrimen* when describing biblical authority. See his *Authority in Protestant Theology* (Philadelphia: Westminster Press, 1959), p. 15 and passim. Kelsey, of course, is careful to acknowledge Johnson's contribution (*The Uses of Scripture in Recent Theology*, p. 160), although those familiar with both works will recognize the originality of Kelsey's use of the term.

144. David H. Kelsey, "The Bible and Christian Theology," *Journal of the American Academy of Religion* 48:3 (September 1980): 398ff.

145. Ibid., p. 386.

146. *Glory* 1, p. 125.

147. Kelsey, *The Uses of Scripture in Recent Theology*, p. 2f.; cf. p. 15.

148. Ibid., p. 48.

149. In "The Word, Scripture, and Tradition" (*Explorations in Theology*, vol. 1, p. 15), Balthasar toyed with a classic schema for describing God's presence to the faithful that echoes Jn 14.6. Both scripture and the Eucharist are used by God to incorporate the faithful into the mystical, living body of Christ. Their lives are thus patterned after Jesus Christ, who, as both the alpha and omega, is the way. Scripture does this insofar as he is the truth; the Eucharist insofar as he is the life. This is as close as Balthasar would come to advocating an ideational view of how God makes Godself present to the faithful through the medium of scripture. It does not play a significant role in the argument of the essay, nor does it appear in the *Theological Aesthetics*.

150. Hans Frei contends in *Types of Christian Theology* (p. 58ff.) that in ways unique to each, Rudolf Bultmann, Paul Tillich, David Tracy, and Gordon Kaufman employ a symbolic or allegorical, rather than literal, reading of the narratives about Jesus.

151. In fairness to Balthasar, we should not forget that this criticism is directed against his uses of the *discrimens* in the *Theological Aesthetics*. In the *Theo-Drama*, by contrast, we find the formerly recessive *discrimen* assuming the dominant role. It would be a mistake to assume that this reversal is due to his having construed the Bible aesthetically in the one work and dramatically in the other. As I have already indicated, when using the ideal existence *discrimen* in the *Theological Aesthetics* he regarded the Bible both aesthetically (as a gemstone) and dramatically (as a story). The difference between the *discrimens* turns on (among other things) the function he ascribed to the narrative. Did it illustrate a graced form of life, or did it render someone's identity? In the *Theo-Drama*, it far more frequently fills the second role. The reversal of priorities in the *Theo-Drama* is due to Balthasar's relatively greater interest in "acting and the ability to act" (*Theo-Drama* 2, p. 13); his having accented the belief that one's unique identity is discovered and defined (he said both) as one "freely affirms and accepts the election, vocation, and mission which God, in

sovereign freedom, offers him" (*Theo-Drama* 3, p. 263); and his concern to highlight the uniqueness and centrality of Jesus Christ's role in the theo-drama (*Theo-Drama* 4, p. 207). For an example of the agential *discrimen* at work, see *Theo-Drama* 3, p. 150 ff., where he sought biblical warrants for his claim that Jesus is unique in his "paradoxical identity of person and mission." Significantly, when Balthasar grounded his discussions of the Christian life exegetically (a relative rarity in these volumes), he tended to employ not the ideal existence *discrimen* (as we saw was true in the *Theological Aesthetics*), but the agential one. In such passages, he focused his attention primarily on the role of Jesus Christ or Christ's Spirit in the life of the faithful. See, for example, *Theo-Drama* 3, p. 124 ff.; *Theo-Drama* 4, p. 384 ff.; and *Theo-Drama* 5, p. 332 ff.

152. *Glory* 1, p. 140.

153. See *Glory* 1, p. 540.

154. *Glory* 1, p. 140.

155. See Kelsey, "The Bible and Christian Theology," p. 395 ff. He mentions the works of James Barr, Gerald Downing, and Wolfhart Pannenberg as articulating some of the same concerns he addresses in this essay. One might also include Carl E. Braaten, *New Directions in Theology Today*, vol. 2, *History and Hermeneutics* (Philadelphia: Westminster Press, 1966); Ronald F. Thiemann, *Revelation and Theology: The Gospel as Narrated Promise* (Notre Dame, Ind.: University of Notre Dame Press, 1985); and Wolterstorff, *Divine Discourse*. For a defense of the doctrine of revelation against the criticisms of Gerald Downing, see Avery Dulles, S.J., *Models of Revelation* (Garden City, N.Y.: Doubleday, 1983).

156. Wolterstorff, *Divine Discourse*, pp. 19, 35.

157. John Locke, *An Essay concerning Human Understanding*, ed. and with an introduction by A. D. Woozley (New York: World Publishing, 1964), p. 56.

158. Cf. Braaten, *History and Hermeneutics*, p. 11 f., and Thiemann, *Revelation and Theology*, p. 9 ff.

159. *Glory* 1, p. 154; emphasis mine.

160. See *Glory* 6, pp. 14–17, especially p. 17.

161. *Glory* 1, p. 119.

162. Braaten, *History and Hermeneutics*, p. 15.

163. Kelsey, "The Bible and Christian Theology," p. 396.

164. *Glory* 1, p. 553.

165. *Glory* 1, p. 548.

166. *Glory* 1, p. 530.

167. "Scripture not only reminds us in a psychological sense that all actual Christian grace is mediated by the incarnate God and bears his permanent stamp; it also reminds us of this in a theological sense, which is to say that it

serves the Spirit as a vehicle through which it constantly actualises, with grace and as grace, this total historical form of the revelation of salvation" (Glory 1, p. 548).

168. *Glory* 1, p. 542.

169. *Glory* 1, p. 548.

170. For what follows, see Kelsey, *The Uses of Scripture in Recent Theology*, p. 208ff., and "The Bible and Christian Theology," pp. 396, 398ff.

171. Balthasar came rather close to articulating this view of inspiration, which bears a striking affinity to Barth's, in the passage from *Glory* 1, p. 548, quoted above. "[T]he canonicity of Scripture may be said to hold for the believing person who seeks Christ something like an infallible promise that he will indeed encounter Christ here in a theological remembering which through grace makes Christ present." For Barth's view, see *Church Dogmatics* vol. 1, pt. 2, pp. 514–26.

172. Kelsey, *The Uses of Scripture in Recent Theology*, p. 205.

173. See Hans W. Frei, *The Identity of Jesus Christ: The Hermeneutical Bases of Dogmatic Theology* (Philadelphia: Fortress Press, 1975), p. 66ff., for reasons why such an attempt would be misguided.

174. Balthasar continued to operate with an amalgam of functionalist and content-based accounts of scriptural authority in the *Theo-Drama*. See, for instance, *Theo-Drama* 2, p. 108, where both appear. Although he relied on a functionalist account in the *Theologik* (e.g., *Theolgik*, vol. 3, *Der Geist der Wahrheit* [Einsiedeln: Johannes Verlag, 1985], pp. 294, 298, 300), he did not indicate there that he preferred it to his content-based one. Nor did he express reservations about the central role of revelation that a content-based account presupposes.

CHAPTER 5. THEOLOGICAL EXEGESIS

1. For the ascription of indifference to Mary, see *Glory* 1, p. 362. By rejecting the notion of Marian passivity, Balthasar was following a practice made popular by many of the Fathers. Shortly after his volume appeared, the practice was endorsed by Vatican II. See *Lumen Gentium*, chap. 8, pt. 2, par. 56 (Abbot, ed., *The Documents of Vatican II*, p. 88). The accompanying notes provide references to the relevant patristic writings.

2. *Glory* 1, p. 350.

3. *Glory* 1, p. 362; cf. p. 351.

4. Hans Urs von Balthasar, "Who Is the Church?" in *Explorations in Theology*, vol. 2, p. 161.

5. *Glory* 7, p. 94.

6. As Carol Stockhausen reminds us, although understanding the Church with the image of the body of Christ is original to Paul, the way the image is used in the genuinely Pauline 1 Corinthians and in the pseudepigraphical Colossians and Ephesians is quite different, both from 1 Corinthians and from each other. In 1 Corinthians, it refers to an internal unity among believers; in Colossians to an external unity of the Church with its victorious, transcendent Lord; in Ephesians to a cosmic, universal reality encompassing all Christians everywhere, living or dead. See her *Letters in the Pauline Tradition: Ephesians, Colossians, I Timothy, II Timothy and Titus* (Wilmington, Del.: Michael Glazier, 1989), p. 85 ff.

7. *Glory* 7, p. 92.

8. Cf. ibid.

9. *Glory* 7, p. 92 f.; cf. Nm 12.7.

10. Parenthetically, it is for this reason that Balthasar faulted the Second Vatican Council's Dogmatic Constitution on the Church for having given pride of place to the characterization of the Church as the people of God. Indeed, he thinks that from the second chapter on, the term is used no longer as an image of the Church, "but as a literally real expression" (*Glory* 7, p. 93 n. 4). In adopting such usage, the Council, on his view, ignored the corrective given by the New Testament writers, on the basis of the incarnation, to the Old Testament images of people, house, or temple (*Glory* 7, p. 92 f.). This provides, then, another instance in which Balthasar criticized the magisterium in light of his reading of the relevant biblical passages.

11. *Glory* 7, p. 92.

12. Balthasar, "Who Is the Church?" in *Explorations in Theology,* vol. 2, p. 145.

13. Ibid., p. 146.

14. Ibid., p. 147.

15. *Glory* 7, p. 93.

16. Balthasar believed, in opposition to the majority of historical critics, that Paul authored Ephesians. For simplicity's sake, I do not take issue with that in the following exposition, though I do return to the topic below.

17. Balthasar, "Who Is the Church?" in *Explorations in Theology,* vol. 2, p. 147.

18. Ibid., p. 147 n. 1.

19. Ibid., p. 146 f.

20. Victor Hamilton contends that by using two words that sound alike (*ishshah* = woman; *ish* = man) "the narrator wished to emphasize the identity and equality of this primal couple" (*The Book of Genesis: Chapters 1–17* [Grand Rapids, Mich.: Eerdmans, 1990], p. 180). Walter Brueggemann argues for an original "*mutuality and equity*" between man and woman that is

subsequently perverted by mistrust, leaving "*control and distortion*" (emphasis his). See *Genesis* (Atlanta: John Knox Press, 1982), p. 50f. Claus Westermann says: "What is meant is the personal community of man and woman in the broadest sense—bodily and spiritual community, mutual help and understanding, joy and contentment in each other" (*Genesis 1–11: A Commentary*, trans. John J. Scullion, S.J., from the 2d German ed. [Minneapolis: Augsburg Publishing House, 1984], p. 232). One might also ask, if woman is subordinated to man in view of having been created from his side, is man subordinate to the earth, having been fashioned from "the dust of the ground" (NRSV)?

21. Balthasar, "Who Is the Church?" in *Explorations in Theology*, vol. 2, p. 147.

22. Ibid., p. 147f.

23. Ibid., p. 148; cf. p. 180.

24. Ibid.; cf. p. 180.

25. *Glory* 7, p. 93.

26. Ibid.

27. Bathasar "Who Is the Church?" in *Explorations in Theology*, vol. 2, p. 150.

28. *Glory* 7, p. 93.

29. Ibid.

30. *Glory* 7, p. 483; cf. p. 94.

31. *Glory* 7, p. 93.

32. *Glory* 7, p. 94; Balthasar, "Who Is the Church?" in *Explorations in Theology*, vol. 2, p. 161.

33. *Glory* 7, p. 175.

34. Cf. *Glory* 7, p. 93f.

35. Cf. Balthasar, "Who Is the Church?" in *Explorations in Theology*, vol. 2, p. 161.

36. McGlasson, *Jesus and Judas*, p. 13f.

37. Harold W. Attridge, note to Heb 1.1 in *The HarperCollins Study Bible*, ed. Wayne A. Meeks (New York: HarperCollins, 1993), p. 2252.

38. Attridge, however, mounts a persuasive case against reading Heb 13.3 as suggestive of a body ecclesiology: "The 'body' has occasionally been interpreted in terms of the Pauline image of the ecclesiastical body of Christ. On that understanding, the whole phrase would ground the recommended behavior in the fact of Christian fellowship ("*since* you are in [the] body"). The particle ως, however, no doubt functions just as it does in the preceding parallel phrase [i.e., "as if"]. The notion that spectators of suffering might empathize with the victims, as if in their bodies, is also used by Philo. Our author deploys that conceit to reinforce his call to Christian solidarity." *The Epistle to the Hebrews: A Commentary on the Epistle to the Hebrews* (Philadelphia: Fortress Press, 1989), p. 386f.

39. Barnabas Lindars agrees with Attridge that there is no evidence of a body ecclesiology in Hebrews. He goes on to contend that one ought not to suppose the author of Hebrews even had a well thought out ecclesiology: "Hebrews does not have a developed theology of the church. He thinks of it as the group of those who have been baptised into Christ, who are therefore heirs of the promises made to the fathers. As such they are the people of God, and can be referred to as the house of God." *The Theology of the Letter to the Hebrews* (Cambridge: Cambridge University Press, 1991), p. 127.

40. They seek thereby, as Edgar Krentz put it, to take the Bible "on its own terms." See his *Historical-Critical Method*, p. 41.

41. Brevard S. Childs, *The New Testament as Canon: An Introduction* (Philadelphia: Fortress Press, 1985), p. 316 ff.

42. This is the implication of his defense of the Pauline authorship of the more contemplative "letters from captivity," by which he presumably meant Philippians, Philemon, and Colossians (*Glory* 1, p. 57). Of the three, the Pauline authorship of Colossians is the only one that is widely rejected.

43. See *Glory* 1, p. 352 for 1 and 2 Peter; *Glory* 1, p. 353 and *Glory* 7, p. 185 for Hebrews; and *Glory* 1, p. 357 f., and *Glory* 7, p. 85 for the Apocalypse.

44. Louis Dupré, "The Glory of the Lord," p. 407.

45. In *Glory* 1 (p. 44) Balthasar denies it by implication but later seems to accept it (p. 353). In *Glory* 7 (p. 185), on a quick reading, he seems to accept it but elsewhere clearly denies it (p. 306).

46. *Glory* 7, pp. 19, 373, indicate he denied Petrine authorship of 1 Peter. (I found no reference in which he denied the Petrine authorship of 2 Peter, but if 1 Peter is inauthentic, so is 2 Peter.) *Glory* 1, p. 336 f., suggests that he denied Johannine authorship of the Apocalypse.

47. See Rudolf Schnackenburg, *Ephesians: A Commentary,* trans. Helen Heron (Edinburgh: T. & T. Clark, 1991) [*Der Brief an die Epheser* (Zürich, Einsiedeln, and Cologne: Benziger Verlag, n.d.)], p. 255.

48. Schnackenburg, *Ephesians,* p. 248.

49. Ibid., p. 248 f.

50. Balthasar, "Who Is the Church?" in *Explorations in Theology,* vol. 2, p. 146.

51. Leon Morris, *The Gospel according to John,* rev. ed. (Grand Rapids, Mich.: Eerdmans, 1995), p. 724 f.

52. It is not as though those who reject Balthasar's symbolic interpretation are necessarily stuck with an impoverished literalism, however. While there is little agreement on what the blood and water might refer to, most commentators are unwilling to deny a symbolic significance to the account. Raymond Brown speaks for a centrist majority when he says that the evangelist most likely meant to indicate that death had claimed Jesus, but that in this death lay his return to the Father and his glorification. To affirm this death is therefore to

affirm the beginning of a new life, and therewith a new source of life for those who imitate him who was crucified and has risen. See Raymond E. Brown, S. S., *The Gospel according to John (XIII–XXI)* (Garden City, N.Y.: Doubleday, 1970), p. 950. Brown rejects the thesis, advanced by Bultmann and others, that verse 34b is an "ecclesiastical redaction." Cf. Rudolf Bultmann, *The Gospel of John: A Commentary*, trans. G. R. Beasley-Murray et al. (Philadelphia: Westminster Press, 1971) [*Das Evangelium des Johannes* (1964; Göttingen: Vandenhoeck & Ruprecht, 1966)], p. 677 f.

53. Balthasar, "Who Is the Church?" in *Explorations in Theology*, vol. 2, p. 147 f.

54. Cf. Lewis R. Donelson, *Colossians, Ephesians, 1 and 2 Timothy, and Titus* (Louisville, Ky.: Westminster & John Knox Press, 1996); Andrew T. Lincoln and A. J. M. Wedderburn, *The Theology of the Later Pauline Letters* (Cambridge: Cambridge University Press, 1993); Ralph P. Martin, *Ephesians, Colossians, and Philemon* (Atlanta: John Knox Press, 1991); Pheme Perkins, *Ephesians* (Nashville, Tenn.: Abingdon, 1987); J. Paul Sampley, "The Letter to the Ephesians," in *The Deutero-Pauline Letters,* ed. Gerhard Krodel (Minneapolis: Augsburg Fortress Press, 1993); Schnackenburg, *Ephesians,* including a comprehensive bibliography; E. K. Simpson and F. F. Bruce, *Commentary on the Epistles to the Ephesians and the Colossians* (Grand Rapids, Mich.: Eerdmans, 1957); Carol L. Stockhausen, *Letters in the Pauline Tradition;* G. H. P. Thompson, *The Letters of Paul to the Ephesians to the Colossians and to Philemon* (Cambridge: Cambridge University Press, 1967); and Bonnie Thurston, *Reading Colossians, Ephesians & 2 Thessalonians: A Literary and Theological Commentary* (New York: Crossroad, 1995).

55. See Nicholas Lash, *Theology on the Way to Emmaus* (London: SCM, 1986), pp. 37 – 46; and John Riches, "The Biblical Basis of Glory," in McGregor and Norris, eds., *The Beauty of Christ*, pp. 56 – 72, especially p. 68 f.

56. Lash, *Theology on the Way to Emmaus*, p. 42, where the quotations appear in reverse order. A variant of the second quotation, replacing the adjective "believing" with "Christian," appears on p. 45. I mention this, not out of scrupulosity, but to confess to some puzzlement over the question of who first formulated this proposal in theological circles. Patrick R. Keifert, whose "Mind Reader and Maestro: Models for Understanding Biblical Interpreters" originally appeared six years before Lash's book, uses *exactly* the same language as Lash does to define performance interpretation. He then acknowledges that the metaphor "maestro" first occurred to him when listening to an at that time unpublished lecture by N. L. A. Nash (*sic*). See "Mind Reader and Maestro: Models for Understanding Biblical Interpreters," in *A Guide to Contemporary Hermeneutics: Major Trends in Biblical Interpretation,* ed. Donald K. McKim (Grand Rapids, Mich.: Eerdmans, 1986), p. 228 n. 35. Keifert's essay was first published in *Word & World* 1 (1980): 153 – 68.

57. Lash, *Theology on the Way to Emmaus,* p. 40f.

58. Ibid., p. 40.

59. Lash, quite rightly, leaves unspecified how one is to remain true to this story. That is a matter of grace and hope. And it can range from a rather direct imitation, which itself admits of degrees, to a much more indirect response in which one, rather than imitating, say, Jesus, tries to behave in ways that accord with what he is believed to have done and be doing on one's behalf.

60. Lash, *Theology on the Way to Emmaus,* p. 45f.

61. Nicholas Wolterstorff makes a similar distinction, though without the metaphor of coaching, in his analysis of performance interpretations. See *Divine Discourse,* p. 178.

62. Riches, "The Biblical Basis of Glory," in McGregor and Norris, eds., *The Beauty of Christ,* p. 68.

63. Ibid.

64. "For Balthasar it is clearly vital that any reading that he offers should be guided by, certainly should not conflict with the central claims made by those texts, precisely because they do refer to a central mystery, are not simply meaningful in and of themselves" (Riches, "The Biblical Basis of Glory," in McGregor and Norris, eds., *The Beauty of Christ,* p. 68f.).

65. As John Riches points out in his illuminating treatment of Balthasar's interpretation, found in his *A Century of New Testament Study,* p. 208f. Interestingly, Riches does not use the metaphor of performance in this earlier discussion (that is, earlier than "The Biblical Basis of Glory") in which he also tries to describe in general terms what Balthasar did with the biblical text. This may have much to do with Riches's relatively narrow definition of performance interpretations as thematic embellishments, since on that definition Balthasar's exegesis of the New Testament texts concerning time are not well described as performances of the text.

66. Balthasar, "Who Is the Church?" in *Explorations in Theology,* vol. 2, p. 179.

67. Ibid.

68. Wolterstorff, *Divine Discourse,* p. 54.

69. Ibid., p. 200.

70. Cf. a similar example in Wolterstorff, *Divine Discourse,* p. 138f., who himself acknowledges having adapted an example from Richard Swinburne.

71. Frei, *Eclipse of Biblical Narrative,* p. 11ff. Cf. Wolterstorff, *Divine Discourse,* pp. 229–36, 240–60.

72. Wolterstorff, *Divine Discourse,* p. 204.

73. Ibid., p. 206.

74. Another is to alter the rhetorico-conceptual structure of the human discourse in order to render that of God's discourse coherent. Wolterstorff thinks it makes no sense for God to say, by appropriating the psalmist's discourse ("Have

mercy on me, O God!"), "Why not? Well, the rhetorico-conceptual structure is all wrong. It's incoherent, it makes no sense, to suppose that God said this; it can't be true" (ibid., p. 209). When one thinks, as Balthasar did, of the Church as the bride of Christ, nuptially united with him in one body, praying through God's Spirit to the Father, the prospect of God asking God to have mercy on Godself seems less far fetched.

75. Ibid., p. 214.
76. Ibid., p. 215.
77. See, among others, *Glory* 1, p. 77.
78. Wolterstorff, *Divine Discourse,* p. 181.

BIBLIOGRAPHY

Abbott, Walter M., S.J., ed. *The Documents of Vatican II*. Washington, D.C.: The America Press, 1966.

Alter, Robert. *The World of Biblical Literature*. New York: Basic Books, 1992.

Aquinas, Thomas. *Summa Theologiae*. London: Blackfriars, 1964–76.

Attridge, Harold W. *The Epistle to the Hebrews: A Commentary on the Epistle to the Hebrews*. Philadelphia: Fortress Press, 1989.

Aubert, Roger. *La Théologie catholique au milieu du XXe siècle*. Paris: Casterman, 1954.

Auerbach, Erich. *Mimesis: The Representation of Reality in Western Literature*. Translated by Willard R. Trask. Princeton: Princeton University Press, 1953. Originally published as *Mimesis: Dargestellte Wirklichkeit in der abendländischen Literatur* (Berne: Franke, 1946).

Augustine. "Christian Instruction." In *The Fathers of the Church*. Vol. 2, *Saint Augustine*. Edited by Roy Joseph Deferrari. 1947. Washington, D.C.: Catholic University of America Press, 1950.

Balthasar, Hans Urs von. "Die Armut Christi." *Internationale Katholische Zeitschrift* 15 (1986): 385–87.

———. "Basic Christological Questions." *Word and Spirit* 5 (1983): 3–19.

————. *The Christian State of Life.* Translated by Mary Frances McCarthy. San Francisco: Ignatius Press, 1983. Originally published as *Christlicher Stand* (Einsiedeln: Johannes Verlag, 1977).

————. "On the Concept of Person." *Communio: International Catholic Review* 13:1 (spring 1986): 18–26.

————. *Convergences: To the Source of Christian Mystery.* Translated by E. A. Nelson. San Francisco: Ignatius Press, 1983. Originally published as *Einfaltungen: Auf Wegen christlicher Einigung* (Munich: Kösel Verlag, 1969).

————. "Crucifixus etiam pro nobis." *Internationale Katholische Zeitschrift* 9 (1980): 26–35.

————. "Current Trends in Catholic Theology and the Responsibility of the Christian." *Communio: International Catholic Review* 5:1 (spring 1978): 77–85.

————. *Does Jesus Know Us? Do We Know Him?* Translated by Graham Harrison. San Francisco: Ignatius Press, 1983. Originally published as *Kennt uns Jesus—Kennen wir ihn?* (Freiburg im Breisgau: Herder Verlag, 1980).

————. "Death Is Swallowed Up by Life." *Communio: International Catholic Review* 14:1 (spring 1987): 49–54.

————. "Earthly Beauty and Divine Glory." *Communio: International Catholic Review* 10:3 (fall 1983): 202–6.

————. *Elucidations.* Translated by John Riches. London: SPCK, 1975. Originally published as *Klarstellungen: Zur Prüfung der Geister* (Freiburg im Breisgau: Herder Verlag, 1971).

————. "Erhaben über alle Mächte." *Internationale Katholische Zeitschrift* 13:1 (1984): 31–34.

————. "Der Erstling der neuen Welt." *Internationale Katholische Zeitschrift* 12 (1983): 214–18.

————. "Exegese und Dogmatik." *Internationale Katholische Zeitschrift* 5 (1976): 385–92.

————. *Explorations in Theology.* Vol. 1, *The Word Made Flesh.* Translated by A.V. Littledale and Alexander Dru. San Francisco: Ignatius Press, 1989. Originally published as *Skizzen zur Theologie,* vol. 1, *Verbum Caro* (1960; Einsiedeln: Johannes Verlag, 1965).

————. *Explorations in Theology.* Vol. 2, *Spouse of the Word.* Translated by Alexander Dru et al. San Francisco: Ignatius Press, 1991. Originally published as *Skizzen zur Theologie,* vol. 2, *Sponsa Verbi* (Einsiedeln: Johannes Verlag, 1961).

————. *Explorations in Theology.* Vol. 3, *Creator Spirit.* Translated by Brian McNeil, C.R.V. San Francisco: Ignatius Press, 1993. Originally published as *Skizzen zur Theologie,* vol. 3, *Spiritus Creator* (Einsiedeln: Johannes Verlag, 1967).

————. *Explorations in Theology.* Vol. 4, *Spirit and Institution.* Translated by Edward T. Oakes, S.J. San Francisco: Ignatius Press, 1995. Originally published as *Pneuma und Institution* (Einsiedeln: Johannes Verlag, 1974).

————. "Geist und Feuer: Ein Gespräch mit Hans Urs von Balthasar." *Herder-Korrespondenz* 30 (1976): 72–82.

————. *The Glory of the Lord: A Theological Aesthetics.* Vol. 1, *Seeing the Form.* Edited by Joseph Fessio, S.J., and John Riches. Translated by Erasmo Leiva-Merikakis. San Francisco: Ignatius Press, 1982.

————. *The Glory of the Lord: A Theological Aesthetics.* Vol. 2, *Studies in Theological Style: Clerical Styles.* Edited by John Riches. Translated by Andrew Louth et al. San Francisco: Ignatius Press, 1984.

————. *The Glory of the Lord: A Theological Aesthetics.* Vol. 3, *Studies in Theological Style: Lay Styles.* Edited by John Riches. Translated by Andrew Louth et al. San Francisco: Ignatius Press, 1984.

————. *The Glory of the Lord: A Theological Aesthetics.* Vol. 4, *The Realm of Metaphysics in Antiquity.* Edited by John Riches. Translated by Brian McNeil, C.R.V., et al. San Francisco: Ignatius Press, 1989.

————. *The Glory of the Lord: A Theological Aesthetics.* Vol. 5, *The Realm of Metaphysics in the Modern Age.* Edited by John Riches. Translated by Oliver Davies et al. San Francisco: Ignatius Press, 1991.

————. *The Glory of the Lord: A Theological Aesthetics.* Vol. 6, *Theology: The Old Covenant.* Edited by John Riches. Translated by Brian McNeil, C.R.V., and Erasmo Leiva-Merikakis. San Francisco: Ignatius Press, 1991.

————. *The Glory of the Lord: A Theological Aesthetics.* Vol. 7, *Theology: The New Covenant.* Edited by John Riches. Translated by Brian McNeil, C.R.V. San Francisco: Ignatius Press, 1989.

————. "God Is His Own Exegete." *Communio: International Catholic Review* 13:4 (winter 1986): 280–87.

————. "Gottes Allmacht." *Internationale Katholische Zeitschrift* 13 (1984): 193–200.

————. "Gottes Reich und die Kirche." *Internationale Katholische Zeitschrift* 15 (1986): 124–30.

————. *Herrlichkeit: Eine theologische Ästhetik.* Vol. 1, *Schau der Gestalt.* 1961. Einsiedeln: Johannes Verlag, 1967.

————. *Herrlichkeit: Eine theologische Ästhetik.* Vol. 2, *Fächer der Stile,* pt. 1, *Klerikale Stile.* 1962. Einsiedeln: Johannes Verlag, 1969.

————. *Herrlichkeit: Eine theologische Ästhetik,* Vol. 2, *Fächer der Stile,* pt. 2, *Laikale Stile.* 1962. Einsiedeln: Johannes Verlag, 1969.

————. *Herrlichkeit: Eine theologische Ästhetik.* Vol. 3, pt. 1, *Im Raum der Metaphysik,* pt. 1, *Alterium.* Einsiedeln: Johannes Verlag, 1965.

————. *Herrlichkeit: Eine theologische Ästhetik.* Vol. 3, pt. 1, *Im Raum der Metaphysik,* pt. 2, *Neuzeit.* Einsiedeln: Johannes Verlag, 1965.

————. *Herrlichkeit: Eine theologische Ästhetik.* Vol. 3, pt. 2, *Theologie,* pt. 1, *Alter Bund.* Einsiedeln: Johannes Verlag, 1967.

————. *Herrlichkeit: Eine theologische Ästhetik.* Vol. 3, pt. 2, *Theologie,* pt. 2, *Neuer Bund.* Einsiedeln: Johannes Verlag, 1969.

————. "The Holy Church and the Eucharistic Sacrifice." *Communio: International Catholic Review* 12:2 (summer 1985): 139–45.

————. "Jesus and Forgiveness." *Communio: International Catholic Review* 11:4 (1984): 320–34.

————. "Leuchtet Jesus ein?" *Internationale Katholische Zeitschrift* 7 (1978): 319–22.

————. "Liberation Theology in the Light of Salvation History." In *Liberation Theology in Latin America,* edited by James V. Schall, S.J., 131–46. San Francisco: Ignatius Press, 1982.

————. "Life and Institution in the Church." *Communio: International Catholic Review* 12:1 (spring 1985): 25–32.

————. *Love Alone: The Way of Revelation.* Edited by Alexander Dru. London: Burns & Oates, 1968. Originally published as *Glaubhaft ist nur Liebe* (Einsiedeln: Johannes Verlag, 1963).

————. *Martin Buber and Christianity: A Dialogue between Israel and the Church.* Translated by Alexander Dru. London: Harvill Press, 1961. Originally published as *Einsame Zwiesprache: Martin Buber und das Christentum* (Cologne and Olten: Jakob Hegner, 1958).

————. "Mary—Church—Office." *Communio: International Catholic Review* 23:1 (spring 1996): 193–98.

————. *Mary for Today.* Translated by Robert Nowell. San Francisco: Ignatius Press, 1988. Originally published as *Maria für heute* (Freiburg im Breisgau: Herder Verlag, 1987).

————. *The Moment of Christian Witness.* Translated by Richard Beckley. San Francisco: Ignatius Press, 1994. Originally published as *Cordula oder der Ernstfall* (Einsiedeln: Johannes Verlag, 1966).

————. *My Work: In Retrospect.* Translated by Brian McNeil, C.R.V., et al. San Francisco: Ignatius Press, 1993. Originally published as *Mein Werk— Durchblicke* (Einsiedeln: Johannes Verlag, 1990).

————. *Mysterium Paschale: The Mystery of Easter.* Translated by Aidan Nichols, O.P. Grand Rapids, Mich.: Eerdmans, 1990. Originally published as *Theologie der drei Tage* (Einsiedeln: Benziger Verlag, 1983).

————. *New Elucidations.* Translated by Mary Theresilde Skerry. San Francisco: Ignatius Press, 1986. Originally published as *Neue Klarstellungen* (Einsiedeln: Johannes Verlag, 1979).

————. "Ein Opfer, das nichts kostet?" *Internationale Katholische Zeitschrift* 14:3 (1985): 236–41.

————. "Peace in Theology." *Communio: International Catholic Review* 12:4 (winter 1985): 398–407.

————. *Prayer.* Translated by Graham Harrison. San Francisco: Ignatius Press, 1986. Originally published as *Das betrachtende Gebet* (Einsiedeln: Johannes Verlag, 1955).

————. *Razing the Bastions.* Translated by Brian McNeil, C.R.V. San Francisco: Ignatius Press, 1993. Originally published as *Schleifung der Bastionen: Von der Kirche in dieser Zeit.* (Einsiedeln: Johannes Verlag, 1952).

————. "Response to My Critics." *Communio: International Catholic Review* 5:1 (spring 1978): 69–76.

————. "A Résumé of My Thought." *Communio: International Catholic Review* 15:4 (winter 1988): 468–73.

————. "Das Selbstbewußtsein Jesu." *Internationale Katholische Zeitschrift* 8 (1979): 30–39.

————. *A Short Primer for Unsettled Laymen.* Translated by Michael Waldstein. San Francisco: Ignatius Press, 1985. Originally published as *Kleine Fibel für verunsicherte Laien* (Einsiedeln: Johannes Verlag, 1980).

————. "Should Faith or Theology Be the Basis of Catechesis? *Communio: International Catholic Review* 10:1 (spring 1983): 10–16.

————. "On the Tasks of Catholic Philosophy in Our Time." *Communio: International Catholic Review* 20:1 (spring 1993): 147–87.

————. *Theo-Drama: Theological Dramatic Theory.* Vol. 1, *Prolegomena.* Translated by Graham Harrison. San Francisco: Ignatius Press, 1988.

————. *Theo-Drama: Theological Dramatic Theory.* Vol. 2, *The Dramatis Personae: Man in God.* Translated by Graham Harrison. San Francisco: Ignatius Press, 1990.

————. *Theo-Drama: Theological Dramatic Theory.* Vol. 3, *The Dramatis Personae: Persons in Christ.* Translated by Graham Harrison. San Francisco: Ignatius Press, 1992.

————. *Theo-Drama: Theological Dramatic Theory.* Vol. 4, *The Action.* Translated by Graham Harrison. San Francisco: Ignatius Press, 1994.

————. *Theo-Drama: Theological Dramatic Theory.* Vol. 5, *The Last Act.* Translated by Graham Harrison. San Francisco: Ignatius Press, 1998.

————. *Theodramatik.* Vol. 1, *Prolegomena.* Einsiedeln: Johannes Verlag, 1983.

————. *Theodramatik.* Vol. 2, *Die Personen des Spiels,* pt. 1, *Der Mensch in Gott.* Einsiedeln: Johannes Verlag, 1976.

————. *Theodramatik.* Vol. 2, *Die Personen des Spiels,* pt. 2, *Die Personen in Christus.* Einsiedeln: Johannes Verlag, 1978.

————. *Theodramatik.* Vol. 3, *Die Handlung.* Einsiedeln: Johannes Verlag, 1980.

———. *Theodramatik*. Vol. 4, *Das Endspiel*. Einsiedeln: Johannes Verlag, 1983.

———. *Theo-Logic: Theological Logical Theory*. Vol. 1, *Truth of the World*. Translated by Adrian J. Walker. San Francisco: Ignatius Press, 2000.

———. *Theologik*. Vol. 1, *Wahrheit der Welt*. Einsiedeln: Johannes Verlag, 1985.

———. *Theologik*. Vol. 2, *Wahrheit Gottes*. Einsiedeln: Johannes Verlag, 1985.

———. *Theologik*. Vol. 3, *Der Geist der Wahrheit*. Einsiedeln: Johannes Verlag, 1985.

———. "Theology and Aesthetic." *Communio: International Review* 8 (spring 1981): 62–71.

———. *The Theology of Karl Barth: Exposition and Interpretation*. Translated by Edward T. Oakes, S.J. San Francisco: Ignatius Press, 1992. Originally published as *Karl Barth: Darstellung und Deutung seiner Theologie* (Cologne: Jakob Hegner Verlag, 1951).

———. "From the Theology of God to Theology in the Church." *Communio: International Catholic Review* 9:3 (fall 1982): 195–223.

———. "Theology and Holiness." *Communio: International Catholic Review* 14:4 (winter 1987): 341–50.

———. *A Theology of History*. 1963. New York and San Francisco: Sheed & Ward and Ignatius Press, 1994. Originally published as *Theologie der Geschichte* (Einsiedeln: Johannes Verlag, 1959).

———. *The Theology of Henri de Lubac: An Overview*. Translated by Joseph Fessio, S.J., Michael Waldstein, and Susan Clements. San Francisco: Ignatius Press, 1991. Originally published as *Henri de Lubac: Sein organisches Lebenswerk* (Einsiedeln: Johannes Verlag, 1976); and, with George Chantraine, S.J., as *Le Cardinal de Lubac: L'Homme et son oeuvre* (Paris: Éditions Lethielleux, 1983).

———. "Der Tod vom Leben verschlungen." *Internationale Katholische Zeitschrift* 11 (1982): 1–5.

———. *Truth Is Symphonic: Aspects of Christian Pluralism*. Translated by Graham Harrison. San Francisco: Ignatius Press, 1987. Originally published as *Die Wahrheit ist symphonisch: Aspekte des christlichen Pluralismus* (Einsiedeln: Johannes Verlag, 1972).

———. "Unity and Diversity in New Testament Theology." *Communio: International Catholic Review* 10:2 (summer 1983): 106–16.

———. "Was bedeutet das Wort Christi: 'Ich bin die Wahrheit'?" *Internationale Katholische Zeitschrift* 16 (1987): 351–56.

———. "Was heißt aggiornamento wirklich?" *Herder-Korrespondenz* 21 (January 1967): 1–30.

———. "Why I Am Still a Christian." In *Two Say Why: Why I Am Still a Christian by Hans Urs von Balthasar and Why I Am Still in the Church by Joseph Ratzinger*. Translated by John Griffiths. Chicago: Franciscan Herald Press, 1971. Originally published as "Warum ich noch ein Christ bin," in Balthasar and Joseph Ratzinger, *Zwei Plädoyers* (Munich: Kösel Verlag, 1971).

———. "A Word on *Humanae Vitae.*" *Communio: International Catholic Review* 20:2 (summer 1993): 437–50.

———. "The Work and Suffering of Jesus: Discontinuity and Continuity." In *Faith in Christ and the Worship of Christ: New Approaches to Devotion to Christ,* edited by Leo Scheffczyk, 13–21. San Francisco: Ignatius Press, 1986.

———. "Das Wort verdichtet sich." *Internationale Katholische Zeitschrift* 6 (1977): 397–400.

———. "Zeugnis und Glaubwürdigkeit." *Internationale Katholische Zeitschrift* 17 (1988): 104–10.

———. "Zugänge zu Jesus Christus. In *Wer ist Jesus Christus?* edited by Joseph Sauer, 9–25. Freiburg im Breisgau: Herder Verlag, 1977.

———, ed. *Origen: Spirit and Fire.* Translated by Robert J. Daly, S.J. Washington, D.C.: Catholic University of America Press, 1984. Originally published as *Origenes: Geist und Feuer: Ein Aufbau aus seinen Schriften,* translated with an introduction by Hans Urs von Balthasar (Salzburg: Otto Müller Verlag, 1938).

Barr, James. *The Bible in the Modern World.* New York: Harper & Row, 1973.

———. "Revelation Through History in the Old Testament and in Modern Theology." *Interpretation* 17 (1963): 193–205.

———. *The Semantics of Biblical Language.* London: Oxford University Press, 1961.

———. "Trends and Prospects in Biblical Theology." *Journal of Theological Studies NS* 25, pt. 2 (October 1974).

Barth, Karl. *Church Dogmatics.* Vol. 2, pt. 2. Translated by G. W. Bromiley et al. Edinburgh: T. & T. Clark, 1957. Originally published as *Die Kirchliche Dogmatik,* vol. 2, pt. 2 (Zürich: Evangelischer Verlag, 1942).

Berman, Art. *From the New Criticism to Deconstruction: The Reception of Structuralism and Post-Structuralism.* Chicago: University of Illinois Press, 1988.

Bertholet, Jean-Eric. "L'Univers théologique de Hans Urs von Balthasar. Une approche de son œuvre." *Revue de théologie et de philosophie* 117 (1985): 185–95.

Boadt, Lawrence, C.S.P., H. Croner, and L. Klenicki, eds. *Biblical Studies: Meeting Ground of Jews and Christians.* Mahwah, N.J.: Paulist Press, 1980.

Borg, Marcus J. *Jesus: A New Vision.* San Francisco: Harper & Row, 1987.

———. "Portraits of Jesus in Contemporary North American Scholarship." *Harvard Theological Review* 84:1 (1991): 1–22.

Braaten, Carl E. *New Directions in Theology Today.* Vol. 2, *History and Hermeneutics.* Philadelphia: Westminster Press, 1966.

————, ed. *Reclaiming the Bible for the Church*. Grand Rapids, Mich.: Eerdmans, 1995.

Braham, Randolph L., ed. *The Origins of the Holocaust: Christian Anti-Semitism*. New York: Columbia University Press, 1986.

Brett, Mark G. *Biblical Criticism in Crisis?* Cambridge: Cambridge University Press, 1991.

Brooks, Cleanth. *The Well Wrought Urn: Studies in the Structure of Poetry*. New York: Harcourt, Brace and Co., 1947.

Brooks, Roger, and John J. Collins, eds. *Hebrew Bible or Old Testament? Studying the Bible in Judaism and Christianity*. Notre Dame, Ind.: University of Notre Dame Press, 1990.

Brown, David. *Continental Philosophy and Modern Theology: An Engagement*. Oxford: Basil Blackwell, 1987.

Brown, Raymond E., S.S. *Biblical Exegesis and Church Doctrine*. New York: Paulist Press, 1985.

————. *Biblical Reflections on Crises Facing the Church*. New York: Paulist Press, 1975.

————. *The Death of the Messiah: From Gethsemane to the Grave. A Commentary on the Passion Narratives in the Four Gospels*. Vol. 2. London: Geoffrey Chapman, 1994.

————. *The Gospel according to John (XIII–XXI)*. Garden City, N.Y.: Doubleday, 1970.

Brown, Raymond E., S. S., Joseph P. Fitzmyer, S.J., and Roland O. Murphy, O.Carm., eds. *The Jerome Biblical Commentary*. Englewood Cliffs, N.J.: Prentice-Hall, 1968.

————. *The New Jerome Biblical Commentary*. Englewood Cliffs, N.J.: Prentice-Hall, 1990.

Brueggemann, Walter. *Genesis*. Atlanta: John Knox Press, 1982.

Bultmann, Rudolf. *The Gospel of John: A Commentary*. Translated by G. R. Beasley-Murray et al. Philadelphia: Westminster Press, 1971. Orignally published as *Das Evangelium des Johannes* (1964; Göttingen: Vandenhoeck & Ruprecht, 1966).

Burnham, Frederic B., ed. *Postmodern Theology: Christian Faith in a Pluralist World*. San Francisco: HarperCollins, 1989.

Casarella, Peter. "Experience as a Theological Category: Hans Urs von Balthasar on the Christian Encounter with God's Image." *Communio: International Catholic Review* 20:1 (spring 1993): 118–28.

Childs, Brevard S. *Biblical Theology in Crisis*. Philadelphia: Westminster Press, 1970.

————. *Biblical Theology of the Old and New Testaments: Theological Reflections on the Christian Bible*. Minneapolis: Fortress Press, 1993.

————. "Critical Reflections on James Barr's Understanding of the Literal and the Allegorical." *Journal for the Study of the Old Testament* 46 (1990): 3–9.

————. *Exodus: A Commentary*. London: SCM, 1974.

————. *Introduction to the Old Testament as Scripture*. Philadelphia: Fortress Press, 1979.

————. Review of James Barr, *Holy Scripture: Canon, Authority, Criticism* (Philadelphia: Westminster Press, 1983). *Interpretation* 38 (1984): 66–70.

————. "Some Reflections on the Search for a Biblical Theology." *Horizons in Biblical Theology* 4 (June 1982): 1–12.

————. *The New Testament as Canon: An Introduction*. Philadelphia: Fortress Press, 1985.

————. "The Old Testament as Scripture of the Church." *Concordia Theological Monthly* 43 (1972): 709–22.

————. "The Sensus Literalis of Scripture: An Ancient and Modern Problem." In *Beiträge zur Alttestamentlichen Theologie: Festschrift für Walther Zimmerli zum 70. Geburtstag,* edited by Herbert Donner, 80–93. Göttingen: Vandenhoeck & Ruprecht, 1976.

Chopp, Rebecca S., and Mark Lewis Taylor, eds. *Reconstructing Christian Theology*. Minneapolis: Fortress Press, 1994.

Coggins, R. J., and J. L. Houlden, eds. *A Dictionary of Biblical Interpretation*. London: SCM; Philadelphia: Trinity Press International, 1990.

Collins, Raymond F. *Introduction to the New Testament*. London: SCM, 1983.

————. *Letters That Paul Did Not Write: The Epistle to the Hebrews and the Pauline Pseudepigrapha*. Wilmington, Del.: Michael Glazier, 1988.

Conway, Eamonn. *The Anonymous Christian — A Relativised Christianity? An Evaluation of Hans Urs von Balthasar's Criticisms of Karl Rahner's Theory of the Anonymous Christian*. European University Studies Series 23, vol. 485. Frankfurt am Main: Peter Lang, 1993.

Crossan, J. D. *The Historical Jesus: The Life of a Mediterranean Jewish Peasant*. San Francisco: HarperSanFrancisco, 1991.

Cunningham, Mary Kathleen. *What Is Theological Exegesis? Interpretation and Use of Scripture in Barth's Doctrine of Election*. Valley Forge, Pa.: Trinity Press, 1995.

Dahood, Mitchell, S.J. *Psalms III: 101–150. The Anchor Bible*. Vol. 17. Garden City, N.J.: Doubleday, 1970.

D'Ambrosio, Marcellino. "Henri de Lubac and the Critique of Scientific Exegesis." *Communio: International Catholic Review* 19:3 (fall 1992): 365–88.

Donelson, Lewis R. *Colossians, Ephesians, 1 and 2 Timothy, and Titus*. Louisville, Ky.: Westminster & John Knox Press, 1996.

Dulles, Avery, S.J. *The Craft of Theology: From Symbol to System*. New York: Crossroad, 1992.

———. "Hermeneutical Theology." *Communio: International Catholic Review* 6:1 (spring 1979): 16–37.

———. *Models of Revelation.* Garden City, N.Y.: Doubleday, 1983.

Dupré, Louis. "The Glory of the Lord: Hans Urs von Balthasar's Theological Aesthetic." *Communio: International Catholic Review* 16:3 (fall 1989): 384–412.

———. "Hans Urs von Balthasar's Theology of Aesthetic Form." *Theological Studies* 49 (1988): 299–318.

Eichrodt, Walther. *Theology of the Old Testament.* 2 vols. Translated by John Baker from the 6th German ed. London: SCM, 1961. Originally published as *Theologie des Alten Testaments* (1959; Stuttgart: n.p., 1964).

Eliot, T. S. "Tradition and the Individual Talent." In *The Sacred Wood: Essays on Poetry and Criticism,* 47–59. 1920. New York: Barnes & Noble, 1960.

Fackre, Gabriel. "Narrative Theology: An Overview." *Interpretation* 37:4 (October 1983): 340–52.

Farkasfalvy, Denis. "The Case for Spiritual Exegesis." *Communio: International Catholic Review* 10:4 (winter 1983): 332–50.

———. "A Heritage in Search of Heirs: The Future of Ancient Christian Exegesis." *Communio: International Catholic Review* 25:3 (fall 1998): 505–19.

———. "In Search of a 'Post-critical' Method of Biblical Interpretation for Catholic Theology." *Communio: International Catholic Review* 13:4 (winter 1986): 288–307.

Fischer, Rainer. *Die Kunst des Bibellesens: Theologische Ästhetik am Beispiel des Schriftverständnisses.* Beiträge zur Theologischen Urteilsbildung, vol. 1. New York: Peter Lang, 1996.

Fitzmyer, Joseph A., S.J. "The Biblical Commission's Instruction on the Historical Truth of the Gospels." *Theological Studies* 25 (1964): 386–408.

———. "Historical Criticism: Its Role in Biblical Interpretation and Church Life." *Theological Studies* 50 (1989): 244–59.

———. *Scripture, the Soul of Theology.* New York and Mahwah, N.J.: Paulist Press, 1994.

Ford, David F. *Barth and God's Story. Biblical Narrative and the Theological Method of Karl Barth in the Church Dogmatics.* Frankfurt: Peter Lang, 1981, 1985.

Frei, Hans W. *The Eclipse of Biblical Narrative: A Study in Eighteenth and Nineteenth Century Hermeneutics.* New Haven: Yale University Press, 1974.

———. *The Identity of Jesus Christ: The Hermeneutical Bases of Dogmatic Theology.* Philadelphia: Fortress Press, 1975.

———. "The 'Literal Reading' of Biblical Narrative in the Christian Tradition: Does It Stretch or Will It Break?" In *The Bible and the Narrative Tradition,* edited by Frank McConnell, 36–77. New York: Oxford University Press, 1986.

————. "Theological Reflections on the Accounts of Jesus' Death and Resurrection." *The Christian Scholar* 49 (1966): 263–306.

————. *Theology and Narrative: Selected Essays*. Edited by George Hunsinger and William C. Placher. New York: Oxford University Press, 1993.

————. *Types of Christian Theology*. Edited by George Hunsinger and William C. Placher. New Haven: Yale University Press, 1992.

Froehlich, Karlfried. "Biblical Hermeneutics on the Move." In *A Guide to Contemporary Hermeneutics: Major Trends in Biblical Interpretation*, edited by Donald K. McKim, 175–91. Grand Rapids, Mich.: Eerdmans, 1986. Originally published in *Word and World* 1 (1981): 140–52.

Frymer-Kensky, Tikva, et al., eds. *Christianity in Jewish Terms*. Boulder, Colo.: Westview Press, 2000.

Gadamer, Hans-Georg. *Truth and Method*. 2d rev. ed. Translated by Joel Weinsheimer and Donald G. Marshall. New York: Continuum, 1993. Originally published as *Wahrheit und Methode*, 5th rev. ed. (Tübingen: J. C. B. Mohr, 1960).

Gager, John G. *The Origins of Anti-Semitism: Attitudes toward Judaism in Pagan and Christian Antiquity*. New York: Oxford University Press, 1983.

Gilkey, Langdon B. "Cosmology, Ontology, and the Travail of Biblical Theology." *Journal of Religion* 41 (1961): 194–205.

Gnuse, Robert. *The Authority of the Bible: Theories of Inspiration, Revelation and the Canon of Scripture*. New York: Paulist Press, 1985.

Goldingay, John. *Models for Interpretation of Scripture*. Grand Rapids, Mich.: Eerdmans, 1995.

Green, Garrett, ed. *Scriptural Authority and Narrative Interpretation*. Philadelphia: Fortress Press, 1987.

————. *Theology, Hermeneutics, and Imagination: The Crisis of Interpretation at the End of Modernity*. New York: Cambridge University Press, 2000.

Greer, Rowan A. "The Christian Bible and Its Interpretation." Pt. 2 of James L. Kugel and Rowan A. Greer, *Early Biblical Interpretation*. Edited by Wayne A. Meeks. Philadelphia: Westminster Press, 1986.

Groves, Joseph W. *Actualization and Interpretation in the Old Testament*. SBL Dissertation Series, vol. 86. Atlanta: Scholars Press, 1987.

Hamilton, Victor. *The Book of Genesis: Chapters 1–17*. Grand Rapids, Mich.: Eerdmans, 1990.

Happel, Stephen. Review of *The von Balthasar Reader*. *Religious Studies Review* 10:4 (October 1984): 354–56.

Hartley, Thomas J. A. *Thomistic Revival and the Modernist Era*. St. Michael's in Toronto Studies in Religion and Theology Dissertation Series, vol. 1. Toronto: Institute of Christian Thought, University of St. Michael's College, 1971.

Harvey, Van. *The Historian and the Believer: The Morality of Historical Knowledge and Christian Belief.* New York: Macmillan, 1966.

Hasel, Gerhard. *Old Testament Theology: Basic Issues in the Current Debate.* 1972. Grand Rapids, Mich.: Eerdmans, 1991.

Hastings, Adrian, ed. *Modern Catholicism: Vatican II and After.* New York: Oxford University Press, 1991.

Hayes, John H., and Frederick Prussner. *Old Testament Theology: Its History and Development.* Atlanta: John Knox Press, 1985.

Hays, Richard. "Response to Robert Wilken, 'In Dominico Eloquio.'" *Communio: International Catholic Review* 25:3 (fall 1998): 520–28.

Heft, James. "Marian Themes in the Writings of Hans Urs von Balthasar." *Communio: International Catholic Review* 7:2 (summer 1980): 127–39.

Hegel, G. W. F. *Hegel's Logic: Being Part One of the Encyclopedia of the Philosophical Sciences.* 1830. Translated by William Wallace. Oxford: Clarendon Press, 1975.

———. *Lectures on the Philosophy of Religion, One-volume Edition: The Lectures of 1827.* Translated and edited by Peter C. Hodgson. Berkeley: University of California Press, 1988.

Idinopulos, Thomas A., and Roy Bowen Ward. "Is Christology Inherently Anti-Semitic? A Critical Review of Rosemary Ruether's *Faith and Fratricide.*" *Journal of the American Academy of Religion* 45:2 (1977): 193–214.

Johnson, Robert Clyde. *Authority in Protestant Theology.* Philadelphia: Westminster Press, 1959.

Kay, Jeffrey Ames. "Aesthetics and a posteriori Evidence in Balthasar's Theological Method." *Communio: International Catholic Review* 2:3 (fall 1975): 289–99.

———. "Hans Urs von Balthasar, a Post-critical Theologian?" In *Neo-Conservatism: Social and Religious Phenomenon,* edited by Gregory Baum 84–89. *Concilium* 141 (January 1981): Sociology of Religion. New York: Seabury Press, 1981.

———. *Theological Aesthetics: The Role of Aesthetics in the Theological Method of Hans Urs von Balthasar.* European University Papers Series 23, vol. 60. Bern: Herbert Lang; Frankfurt am Main: Peter Lang, 1975.

Keefe, Donald J. "A Methodological Critique of von Balthasar's Theological Aesthetics." *Communio: International Catholic Review* 5:1 (spring 1978): 23–43.

Kelsey, David H. "The Bible and Christian Theology." *Journal of the American Academy of Religion* 48:3 (September 1980): 385–402.

———. *The Uses of Scripture in Recent Theology.* Philadelphia: Fortress Press, 1975.

Kereszty, Roch A. "The 'Bible and Christology' Document of the Biblical Commission." *Communio: International Catholic Review* 13:4 (winter 1986): 342–67.

Kevern, John R. "Form in Tragedy: Balthasar as Correlational Theologian." *Communio: International Catholic Review* 21:2 (summer 1994): 311–30.

Kierkegaard, Søren. *Either/Or.* Vol. 1. Translated by David F. Swenson and Lillian Marvin Swenson. 1944. Princeton: Princeton University Press, 1972.

———. *Either/Or.* Vol. 2. Translated by Walter Lowrie. 1944. Princeton: Princeton University Press, 1972.

Klaghofer-Treitler, Wolfgang. *Gotteswort im Menschenwort: Inhalt und Form von Theologie nach Hans Urs von Balthasar.* Innsbruck: Tyrolia, 1992.

Knight, Douglas A., and Gene M. Tucker. *The Hebrew Bible and Its Interpreters.* Philadelphia: Fortress Press; Chico, Calif.: Scholars Press, 1988.

Konda, Jutta. "Das Verhältnis von Theologie und Heiligkeit im Werk Hans Urs von Balthasars." Diss., Rheinische Friedrich-Wilhelms-Universität Bonn, 1990.

Kort, Wesley A. *"Take, Read": Scripture, Textuality, and Cultural Practice.* University Park, Pa.: Pennsylvania State University Press, 1996.

Krentz, Edgar. *The Historical-Critical Method.* Philadelphia: Fortress Press, 1975.

Kugel, James L. "Biblical Studies and Jewish Studies." *Association for Jewish Studies Newsletter* 36 (fall 1986).

Lacoste, Jean-Yves. "The Unfailing Witness: Notes on the Canon of Scripture." *Communio: International Catholic Review* 10:2 (summer 1983): 167–84.

Lash, Nicholas. *Theology on the Way to Emmaus.* London: SCM, 1986.

Leahy, Breandán. *The Marian Principle in the Church according to Hans Urs von Balthasar.* Frankfurt am Main: Peter Lang, 1996.

Lehmann, Karl, and Walter Kasper, eds. *Hans Urs von Balthasar: Gestalt und Werk.* Cologne: Communio, 1989.

Levenson, Jon D. "The Hebrew Bible, the Old Testament, and Historical Criticism." In *The Future of Biblical Studies: The Hebrew Scriptures,* edited by Richard Elliot Friedman and H. G. M. Williamson, 19–59. Atlanta: Scholars Press, 1987. Reprinted in Jon D. Levenson, *The Hebrew Bible, the Old Testament, and Historical Criticism: Jews and Christians in Biblical Studies* (Louisville, Ky.: Westminster & John Knox Press, 1993), 1–32.

———. "Theological Consensus or Historicist Evasion? Jews and Christians in Biblical Studies." In *Hebrew Bible or Old Testament? Studying the Bible in Judaism and Christianity,* edited by Roger Brooks and John J. Collins, 109–45. Notre Dame, Ind.: University of Notre Dame Press, 1990. Reprinted in Jon D. Levenson, *The Hebrew Bible, the Old Testament, and Historical Criticism* (Louisville, Ky.: Westminster & John Knox Press, 1993), 82–105.

———. "Why Jews Are Not Interested in Biblical Theology." In *Judaic Perspectives on Ancient Israel,* edited by Jacob Neusner et al., 281–307. Philadelphia: Fortress Press, 1987. Reprinted in Jon D. Levenson, *The Hebrew Bible, the Old Testament, and Historical Criticism: Jews and Christians in Biblical Studies* (Louisville, Ky.: Westminster & John Knox Press, 1993), 33–61.

Lincoln, Andrew T., and A. J. M. Wedderburn. *The Theology of the Later Pauline Letters.* Cambridge: Cambridge University Press, 1993.

Lindars, Barnabas. *The Theology of the Letter to the Hebrews.* Cambridge: Cambridge University Press, 1991.

Lindbeck, George A. "Barth and Textuality." *Theology Today* 43:3 (October 1986): 361–82.

———. "The Bible as Realistic Narrative." *Journal of Ecumenical Studies* 17 (winter 1980): 81–85.

———. "Confession and Community: An Israel-like View of the Church." *The Christian Century* (May 9, 1990): 492–96.

———. "Ebeling: Climax of a Great Tradition." Review of Gerhard Ebeling, *Dogmatik des christlichen Glaubens.* Vol. 1. *The Journal of Religion* 61 (1981): 309–14.

———. "Post-critical Canonical Interpretation: Three Modes of Retrieval." In *Theological Exegesis: Essays in Honor of Brevard S. Childs,* edited by Christopher Seitz and Kathryn Greene-McCreight, 26–51. Grand Rapids, Mich.: Eerdmans, 1999.

———. "Scripture, Consensus, and Community." *This World* 23 (fall 1988): 5–24. Reprinted in Richard John Neuhaus, ed., *Biblical Interpretation in Crisis: The Ratzinger Conference on Bible and Church* (Grand Rapids, Mich.: Eerdmans, 1989), 74–101.

Locke, John. *An Essay concerning Human Understanding.* Edited and with an introduction by A. D. Woozley. New York: World Publishing, 1964.

Longenecker, Richard N. *Biblical Exegesis in the Apostolic Period,* 2d ed. Grand Rapids: Eerdmans, 1999.

Louth, Andrew, *Discerning the Mystery.* Oxford: Oxford University Press, 1983.

Lubac, Henri de. *Medieval Exegesis.* Vol. 1, *The Four Senses of Scripture.* Translated by Mark Sebanc. Grand Rapids, Mich.: Eerdmans; Edinburgh: T. & T. Clark, 1998. Originally published as *Exégèse médiévale,* vol. 1, *Les Quatre sens de l'Écriture.* (Paris: Éditions Montaigne, 1959).

———. *Theological Fragments.* Translated by Rebecca Howell Balinski. San Francisco: Ignatius Press, 1989. Originally published as *Théologies d'occasion* (Paris: Desclée de Brouwer, 1984).

———. "A Witness of Christ in the Church: Hans Urs von Balthasar." *Communio: International Catholic Review* 2:3 (fall 1975): 228–49.

Mack, Burton L. *A Myth of Innocence: Mark and Christian Origins.* Philadelphia: Fortress Press, 1988.

Martin, Ralph P. *Ephesians, Colossians, and Philemon.* Atlanta: John Knox Press, 1991.

McCool, Gerald A., S.J. *From Unity to Pluralism: The Internal Evolution of Thomism.* 1989. New York: Fordham University Press, 1992.

———. *Nineteenth-Century Scholasticism: The Search for a Unitary Method.* New York: Fordham University Press, 1989. This is a reissue, with identical pagination, of *Catholic Theology in the Nineteenth Century: The Quest for a Unitary Model.* New York: Seabury Press, 1977.

McGlasson, Paul. *Jesus and Judas: Biblical Exegesis in Barth.* AAR Academy Series, vol. 72. Atlanta: Scholars Press, 1991.

McGregor, Bede, O.P., and Thomas Norris, eds. *The Beauty of Christ: An Introduction to the Theology of Hans Urs von Balthasar.* Edinburgh: T. & T. Clark, 1994.

McKim, Donald K., ed. *The Authoritative Word: Essays on the Nature of Scripture.* Grand Rapids, Mich.: Eerdmans, 1983.

———. *The Bible in Theology and Preaching.* Nashville, Tenn.: Abingdon Press, 1994. This is a revised edition of *What Christians Believe about the Bible* (New York: Thomas Nelson Publishers, 1985).

———, ed. *A Guide to Contemporary Hermeneutics: Major Trends in Biblical Interpretation.* Grand Rapids, Mich.: Eerdmans, 1986.

Meeks, Wayne A., ed. *The HarperCollins Study Bible.* New York: HarperCollins Publishers, 1993.

Megivern, James J., ed. *Official Catholic Teachings: Bible Interpretation.* Wilmington, N.C.: McGrath, 1978.

Meyer, Ben F. *Reality and Illusion in New Testament Scholarship: A Primer in Critical Realist Hermeneutics.* Collegeville, Minn.: Liturgical Press, 1994.

Morris, Leon. *The Gospel according to John.* Rev. ed. Grand Rapids, Mich.: Eerdmans, 1995.

Mueller-Vollmer, Kurt, ed. *The Hermeneutics Reader: Texts of the German Tradition from the Enlightenment to the Present.* New York: Continuum, 1988.

Nassif, Bradley. "The 'Spiritual Exegesis' of Scripture: The School of Antioch Revisted." *Anglican Theological Review* 70:4 (1993): 437–70.

Nichols, Aidan, O.P. *No Bloodless Myth: A Guide through Balthasar's Dramatics.* Washington, D.C.: Catholic University of America Press, 2000.

———. *Say It Is Pentecost: A Guide through Balthasar's Logic.* Washington, D.C.: Catholic University of America Press, 2001.

———. *The Word Has Been Abroad: A Guide through Balthasar's Aesthetics.* Washington, D.C.: Catholic University of America Press, 1998.

Nietzsche, Friedrich. *Untimely Meditations.* Translated R. J. Hollingdale. Edited by Daniel Breazeale. Cambridge: Cambridge University Press, 1997.

Novak, David. *Jewish-Christian Dialogue: A Jewish Justification.* Oxford: Oxford University Press, 1989.

Oakes, Edward T., S.J. *Pattern of Redemption: The Theology of Hans Urs von Balthasar.* New York: Continuum, 1994.

———. "The Usurped Town: The Canon of Scripture in Postmodern Aesthetics." *Communio: International Catholic Review* 17:2 (summer 1990): 261–80.

Oberman, Heiko A. *Forerunners of the Reformation: The Shape of Late Medieval Thought Illustrated by Key Documents.* New York: Holt, Rinehart, and Winston, 1966.

O'Donnell, John, S.J. "Hans Urs von Balthasar: The Form of His Theology." *Communio: International Catholic Review* 16:3 (fall 1989): 458–74.

———. *Hans Urs von Balthasar.* Outstanding Christian Thinkers Series. Collegeville, Minn.: Liturgical Press, 1992.

———. "Truth as Love: The Understanding of Truth according to Hans Urs von Balthasar." *Pacifica* 1 (1988): 189–211.

Ogden, Shubert. "The Authority of Scripture for Theology." *Interpretation* 30 (1976).

O'Meara, Thomas F., O.P. "Of Art and Theology: Hans Urs von Balthasar's Systems." *Theological Studies* 42:2 (June 1981): 272–76.

O'Regan, Cyril. "Von Balthasar and Thick Retrieval: Post-Chalcedonian Symphonic Theology." *Gregorianum* 77:2 (1996): 227–60.

———. "Newman and von Balthasar: The Christological Contexting of the Numinous." *Église et Théologie* 26 (1995): 165–202.

Ouellet, Marc. "Hans Urs von Balthasar: Witness to the Integration of Faith and Culture." *Communio: International Catholic Review* 18:1 (spring 1991): 111–26.

———. "The Message of Balthasar's Theology to Modern Theology. *Communio: International Catholic Review* 23:2 (summer 1996): 270–99.

Palmer, Richard E. *Hermeneutics: Interpretation Theory in Schleiermacher, Dilthey, Heidegger, and Gadamer.* Evanston: Northwestern University Press, 1969.

Pelikan, Jaroslav. *The Christian Tradition: A History of the Development of Doctrine.* Vol. 1, *The Emergence of the Catholic Tradition (100–600).* Chicago: University of Chicago Press, 1971.

———. *Jesus through the Centuries: His Place in the History of Culture.* New Haven: Yale University Press, 1985.

Perdue, Leo G. *The Collapse of History: Reconstructing Old Testament Theology.* Minneapolis: Fortress Press, 1994.

Perkins, Pheme. *Ephesians.* Nashville, Tenn.: Abingdon, 1987.

Perrin, Norman. *Rediscovering the Teaching of Jesus.* 1967. New York: Harper & Row, 1976.

Petit, Pierrette, S.S.A. *Hans Urs von Balthasar: un grand théologien spirituel.* Montréal: Les Éditions du Méridien, 1985.

Placher, William C. *Unapologetic Theology: A Christian Voice in a Pluralistic Conversation.* Louisville, Ky.: Westminster & John Knox, 1989.

Potterie, Ignace de la. "Reading Holy Scripture 'in the Spirit': Is the Patristic Way of Reading the Bible Still Possible Today?" *Communio: International Catholic Review* 13:4 (winter 1986): 308–25.

———. "The Spiritual Sense of Scripture." *Communio: International Catholic Review* 23:4 (winter 1996): 738–56.

Potworowski, Christophe. "Christian Experience in Hans Urs von Balthasar." *Communio: International Catholic Review* 20:1 (spring 1993): 107–17.

Powell, Mark Allan. *What Is Narrative Criticism?* Philadelphia: Fortress Press, 1990.

Preus, James S. *From Shadow to Promise: Old Testament Interpretation from Augustine to Luther.* Cambridge: Harvard University Press, 1969.

Proterra, Michael. "Hans Urs von Balthasar: Theologian." *Communio: International Catholic Review* 2:3 (fall 1975): 270–88.

Quinn, Arthur. "Rhetoric and the Integrity of the Scripture." *Communio: International Catholic Review* 13:4 (winter 1986): 326–41.

Rad, Gerhard von. *Old Testament Theology.* 2 vols. Translated by D. M. G. Stalker. New York: Harper & Row Publishers, 1962–65. Originally published as *Theologie des Alten Testaments,* 2 vols. (Munich: Kaiser, 1957–60).

Rendtorff, Rolf. "Recent German Old Testament Theologies." *Journal of Religion* 76:2 (April 1996): 328–37.

Reumann, John. *The Promise and Practice of Biblical Theology.* Minneapolis: Fortress Press, 1991.

Reventlow, Henning Graf. *Problems of Biblical Theology in the Twentieth Century.* Translated by John Bowden. Philadelphia: Fortress Press, 1986. Originally published as *Hauptprobleme der biblischen Theologie im 20. Jahrhundert* (Darmstadt: Wissenschaftliche Buchgesellschaft, 1983).

Riches, John K. *A Century of New Testament Study.* Valley Forge, Pa.: Trinity Press International, 1993.

———. "The Theology of Hans Urs von Balthasar: 1 and 2." *Theology* 75 (November-December 1972): 562–70 and 647–55.

———, ed. *The Analogy of Beauty: The Theology of Hans Urs von Balthasar.* Edinburgh: T. & T. Clark, 1986.

Roberts, Louis. *The Theological Aesthetics of Hans Urs von Balthasar.* Washington, D.C.: Catholic University of America Press, 1987.

Robinson, James. "Scripture and Theological Method: A Protestant Study in *Sensus Plenior.*" *Catholic Biblical Quarterly* 27 (1965): 6–27.

Robinson, James M., and John B. Cobb, Jr., eds. *The Later Heidegger and Theology.* New York: Harper & Row, 1963.

———, eds. *The New Hermeneutic*. New York: Harper & Row, 1964.

Robinson, Robert B. *Roman Catholic Exegesis since Divino Afflante Spiritu: Hermeneutical Implications*. Atlanta, Scholars Press, 1988.

Ross, Susan A. Review of *The von Balthasar Reader. Religious Studies Review* 10:4 (October 1984): 358–60.

Roten, Johann G. "Hans Urs von Balthasar's Anthropology in Light of His Marian Thinking." *Communio: International Review* 20:2 (summer 1993): 306–33.

Ruether, Rosemary Radford. *Faith and Fratricide: The Theological Roots of Anti-Semitism*. New York: Seabury Press, 1974.

Ryle, Gilbert. *The Concept of Mind*. Chicago: University of Chicago Press, 1949.

Sampley, J. Paul. "The Letter to the Ephesians." In *The Deutero-Pauline Letters*, edited by Gerhard Krodel. Minneapolis: Augsburg Fortress Press, 1993.

Sanders, E. P. *Jesus and Judaism*. Philadelphia: Fortress Press, 1985.

Schindler, David L., ed. *Hans Urs von Balthasar: His Life and Work*. San Francisco: Ignatius Press, 1991.

Schleiermacher, F. D. E. *Hermeneutik und Kritik. Mit einem Anhang sprachphilosophischer Texte Schleiermachers*. Edited by Manfred Frank. Frankfurt am Main: Suhrkamp, 1977.

Schmid, Johannes. *Im Ausstrahl der Schönheit Gottes: Die Bedeutung der Analogie im "Herrlichkeit" bei Hans Urs von Balthasar*. Münsterschwarzach: Vier-Türme-Verlag, 1982.

Schnackenburg, Rudolf. *Ephesians: A Commentary*. Translated by Helen Heron. Edinburgh: T. & T. Clark, 1991. Originally published *Der Brief an die Epheser* (Zürich, Einsiedeln, and Cologne: Benziger Verlag, n.d.).

Schneiders, Sandra. "The Literal Sense of Scripture." *Theological Studies* 39 (1978): 719–36.

Scola, Angelo. *Hans Urs von Balthasar: A Theological Style*. Grand Rapids, Mich.: Eerdmans, 1995. Originally published as *Hans Urs von Balthasar: Uno stile teologico* (Milan, Editoriale Jaca Book SpA, 1991).

Sicari, Antonio, O.C.D. "Hans Urs von Balthasar: Theology and Holiness." *Communio: International Catholic Review* 16:3 (fall 1989): 351–65.

Simpson, E. K., and F. F. Bruce. *Commentary on the Epistles to the Ephesians and the Colossians*. Grand Rapids, Mich.: Eerdmans, 1957.

Smalley, Beryl. *The Study of the Bible in the Middle Ages*. 1952. Notre Dame, Ind.: University of Notre Dame Press, 1964.

Smart, James D. *The Strange Silence of the Bible in the Church: A Study in Hermeneutics*. Philadelphia: Westminster Press, 1970.

Smith, Charles. "Mary in the Theology of Hans Urs von Balthasar." *One in Christ* 22 (1986): 387–93.

Spangenberg, Volker. *Herrlichkeit des Neuen Bundes: Die Bestimmung des biblischen Begriffs der "Herrlichkeit" bei Hans Urs von Balthasar.* Tübingen: J. C. B. Mohr (Paul Siebeck), 1993.

Speyr, Adrienne von. *The Letter to the Ephesians.* Translated by Adrian Walker. San Francisco: Ignatius Press, 1996. Originally published as *Der Epheserbrief,* 2d rev. ed. (Einsiedeln: Johannes Verlag, 1983).

Steinmetz, D. C. "The Superiority of Pre-critical Exegesis." *Theology Today* 37 (1980): 27–38.

Stephenson, Keith D. "Roman Catholic Biblical Interpretation: Its Ecclesiastical Context in the Past Hundred Years." *Encounter* 34 (1972): 303–28.

Stockhausen, Carol L. *Letters in the Pauline Tradition: Ephesians, Colossians, I Timothy, II Timothy and Titus.* Wilmington, Del.: Michael Glazier, 1989.

Strawson, P. F. *Individuals: An Essay in Descriptive Metaphysics.* London: Methuen, 1959.

Stuhlmacher, Peter. *Historical Criticism and Theological Interpretation of Scripture: Toward a Hermeneutics of Consent.* Translated and edited by Roy A Harrisville. Philadelphia: Fortress Press, 1977. Originally published as "Historische Kritik und theologische Schriftauslegung," in *Schriftauslegung auf dem Wege zur biblischen Theologie* (Göttingen: Vandenhoeck & Ruprecht, 1975).

Tanner, Kathryn E. "Theology and the Plain Sense." In *Scriptural Authority and Narrative Interpretation,* edited by Garrett Green, 59–78. Philadelphia: Fortress Press, 1987.

Taylor, Walter F., Jr., and John H. P. Reumann. *Augsburg Commentary on the New Testament: Ephesians, Colossians.* Minneapolis: Augsburg Publishing House, 1985.

Thiemann, Ronald F. *Revelation and Theology: The Gospel as Narrated Promise.* Notre Dame, Ind.: University of Notre Dame Press, 1985.

Thiselton, Anthony C. *New Horizons in Hermeneutics.* Grand Rapids, Mich.: Zondervan Publishing House, 1992.

———. *The Two Horizons. New Testament Hermeneutics and Philosophical Description with Special Reference to Heidegger, Bultmann, Gadamer, and Wittgenstein.* Grand Rapids, Mich.: Eerdmans, 1980.

Thompson, G. H. P. *The Letters of Paul to the Ephesians to the Colossians and to Philemon.* Cambridge: Cambridge University Press, 1967.

Thurston, Bonnie. *Reading Colossians, Ephesians, and 2 Thessalonians: A Literary and Theological Commentary.* New York: Crossroad, 1995.

Turner, Denys. *The Darkness of God: Negativity in Christian Mysticism.* Cambridge: Cambridge University Press, 1995.

Van Beeck, Franz Joseph, S.J. "Tradition and Interpretation." *Bijdragen, tijdschrift voor filosofie en theologie* 51 (1990): 257–71.

Voccaro, Jody L. "Digging for Buried Treasure: Origen's Spiritual Interpretation of Scripture." *Communio: International Catholic Review* 25:4 (winter 1998): 757–75.

Waldstein, Michael. "Hans Urs von Balthasar's Theological Aesthetics." *Communio: International Catholic Review* 11 (1984): 13–27.

———. "An Introduction to von Balthasar's *The Glory of the Lord*." *Communio: International Catholic Review* 14:1 (spring 1987): 12–33.

Westermann, Claus. *Genesis 1–11: A Commentary*. Translated by John J. Scullion, S.J., from the 2d German ed. (1976). Minneapolis: Augsburg Publishing House, 1984.

Wilken, Robert Louis. "*In Dominico Eloquio*: Learning the Lord's Style of Language." *Communio: International Catholic Review* 24:4 (winter 1997): 846–66.

———. "Wilken's Response to Hays." *Communio: International Catholic Review* 25:3 (fall 1998): 529–31.

Williams, Rowan. "The Literal Sense of Scripture." *Modern Theology* 7:2 (January 1991): 121–34.

Wimsatt, W. K., Jr. *The Verbal Icon: Studies in the Meaning of Poetry*. Lexington: University of Kentucky Press, 1954.

Wolterstorff, Nicholas, *Divine Discourse: Philosophical Reflections on the Claim that God Speaks*. Cambridge: Cambridge University Press, 1995.

———. "Evidence, Entitled Belief, and the Gospels." *Faith and Philosophy* 6:4 (October 1989): 429–59.

Wood, Charles M. *The Formation of Christian Understanding: An Essay in Theological Hermeneutics*. Philadelphia: Westminster Press, 1981.

Wright, N. T. *Jesus and the Victory of God*. Minneapolis: Fortress Press, 1996.

Wright, G. Ernest. *God Who Acts: Biblical Theology as Recital*. Studies in Biblical Theology, vol. 8. London: SCM, 1952.

INDEX

W. T. DICKENS is visiting assistant professor at Cornell University.